CIRCLE
OF
SERVICE

CIRCLE
OF
SERVICE

SECRETARY OF THE AIR FORCE
MICHAEL W. WYNNE
& THE FAMILY BUSINESS

RICHARD P. BESSETTE

RTN PRESS
ORLAND PARK, ILLINOIS

20.00

Circle of Service – Secretary of the Air Force Michael W. Wynne and the Family Business. © 2011 by Richard P. Bessette

Printed and Bound in the United States of America

Published by
RTN Press LLC
P.O. Box 2333
Orland Park, Illinois 60462
Web site: www.rtnpress.com
E-mail: rtnpress@comcast.net

Cover Design by
Jeremy Clouse

FIRST EDITION

First Printing, Winter, 2011
Library of Congress Control Number: 2011914711
ISBN: 978-0-9747970-4-5

Cover Photo: Secretary of the Air Force Michael W. Wynne is interviewed at the Pentagon on September 18, 2006. Source: United States Air Force photo by Tech. Sgt. Cohen A. Young released at www.af.mil/shared/media/photodb/photos/060918 -F-3798Y-045.jpg **Back Cover Photographs**: top to bottom, courtesy of Wynne Family, United States Military Academy photo courtesy of Wynne Family, and United States Air Force photo courtesy of Wynne Family.

main

We use words like honor, code, loyalty.
We use these words as the backbone of a life spent defending
something.

Colonel Nathan R. Jessep in *A Few Good Men*.
Play and screenplay by Aaron Sorkin.

Contents

Preface

In his farewell address in January 1961 that was broadcast on radio and television, President Eisenhower coined the phrase "military-industrial complex." His speech dealt with the symbiotic relationship between the armed forces of the United States and the defense industry contractors that supplied the military; Washington, D.C. and the political machine could either facilitate or encumber that process. The president's speech was half warning and half informative. Fifty years later, little has changed and we still must wrestle with issues raised by the military-industrial-political complex. The subject of this biography worked in each phase of that complex.

With the exit of the Bush Administration from Washington, a swell of new books by and about those that had been in power was expected. This has occurred. Some of those volumes try to reshape the events that took place. This one does not. This biography illustrates difficult issues being confronted directly, hard decisions being made with courage, and consequences being faced without sacrificing integrity.

Mike Wynne was a major figure with national impact on Washington affairs that could be a model for American and Leadership studies—how America develops individuals such as Wynne and how they come from every corner of the nation. Having devoted more than 40 years of his life in the service of his country, this is a broad chronicle. Mike Wynne's father, brothers, and brothers-in-law served their nation in one fashion or another, making service much like the family business.

Where else but in the United States of America can a second-generation Irishman, or any other nationality for that matter, work hard and reach the highest levels of business and government? In business his efforts touched many weapon systems, including the F-16 lightweight fighter, *Los Angeles*–class fast attack submarines, the M-1A1/A2 advanced main battle tank, and the Atlas ballistic missile with dozens of rocket launches off Cape Canaveral. In government, as secretary of the Air Force, Wynne helped lead a military department with almost 700,000 personnel. He worked directly for the secretary of defense who is sixth in the presidential line of succession. So "highest levels" is not braggadocio.

He would refer to his upbringing as one of adventuring. This is what it was called in a day when free time was spent playing outside rather than sitting in front of a computer screen. He grew up to be a charming and self-effacing leader, a man who listened and sought others' opinions. He was also far from perfect.

He gained somewhat of a reputation for his short and to-the-point responses. His brevity bordered on the terse. Often one gained more insight from what Wynne didn't say than what he did. He also had a backbone, which some interpreted as a stubborn streak. In any discussion of length, one noticed his imperious habit of ending most statements with an inquiring "Eh?." It was similar to the Canadians but with an "Eh?" instead of a "Hey!," seeking confirmation that one heard and understood the comment just made. It was his shorthand way of turning a statement into a question.

This biography does not travel to London and Paris and Moscow but from Wright-Patterson and Patrick Air Force Bases to the Hudson River and the Front Range of the Colorado Rockies to Air Force Plant 4 in Fort Worth and Plant 19 in San Diego to the Pentagon and halls of Congress in Washington, following Wynne's progression from private life to the military to the defense establishment. Mike Wynne did not rant and rave his way through the years and not at either side of Congress. But he did make sweeping changes and he did leave a wake.

This is, at once, a family story of Edward, Patrick, and Michael. Pieces and parts of this account have been written from time to time, but the grand narrative placing everything in perspective was missing. This biography shapes the memories into that narrative, an inspirational story of one family's service to the nation.

Chapter One

The Different Shades of Service

□——————————————————————————□

THE WARNING SIGNALS INSIDE the McDonnell F-4 Phantom II aircraft screamed at his senses. His mind struggled to focus on quick action, sorting through the threatening cockpit alarms and the stark fire caution light. Even emergencies followed a sequence. Pat Wynne reached above his helmet and grabbed the yellow and black handles and jerked them forcefully, initiating the ejection sequence and pulling the face curtain close over his head. His legs were snapped tight against the seat pan. It became visceral. His body tensed and his muscles tightened as his diaphragm cut off his air and he held his breath, waiting for it.

Some eight thousand miles away, his brother, Second Lieutenant Michael W. Wynne signed in at his first active duty assignment at Hanscom Field outside Boston, Massachusetts. Two arcs in the same circle of service.

❧

IT HAD BEEN A WHIRLWIND 60-day leave for Mike since graduation from the United States Military Academy on June 8, 1966. He had married his sweetheart, Barb Hill, back home in Florida. They honeymooned for a week in Jamaica, stopping at Half-Moon Bay, the Playboy Club, and Kingston. As with most newlyweds, they would have stories for their children. For Mike and Barb, it was a brown recluse spider.

Half way through their honeymoon, Mike was bitten on the left arm by a brown recluse, rendering his arm useless as it blew up triple the normal size. He couldn't shift their manual rent-a-car and Barb had to learn on-the-go how to drive stick-shift. Her right arm caught quite a workout as Mike drove while Barb shifted for the whole ride to Kingston in their right-hand drive car. Somewhere along the way they called an on-staff doctor and, after getting a shot in the posterior with a syringe whose bore grows with every telling, the swelling began to go down. They had their start and their story for the next generation.

Once back home in Florida, the couple said their goodbyes to family and headed straight up the coast for New England. September and December babies respectively, Mike was 21 years old and his wife but 19. Mike, who couldn't know about his brother's troubles in Vietnam, was excited on his first assignment for the Air Force. He graduated on June 8 and signed in on August 8.

Soon after signing in, the first sergeant at Hanscom came looking for Mike and informed him that the story had come out of his brother being shot down in Vietnam. Not much other intelligence was available. Reports did not indicate whether it was over North Vietnam or South Vietnam, and no one could report definitively whether his brother was killed in action, a prisoner of war or something in between. All Mike knew was that, given the time change, he had signed in at Hanscom on the same day his brother Patrick had been shot down.

Mike's family burned up the telephone lines for days afterward, but no details were forthcoming. It would take time. Besides Mike and his two parents, two sisters and two other brothers were involved. Days would stretch into weeks and then months. Particulars were few because no recovery had been possible due to the location. This early in the war, the Vietnamese were not likely to inform the invaders when they captured a downed American pilot. Everyone would have to wait. Pat was eventually listed as missing in action, but the not knowing would be the hardest part. Mike had to direct his attention to his new duty.

WHEN MIKE ARRIVED at his first duty station, Hanscom was home of the Air Force's Electronic Systems Division, a joint effort with Massachusetts Institute of Technology in developing early warning systems to counter nuclear threats whether delivered by long-range bomber or intercontinental missile. Even with the war in Vietnam consuming so much effort, the primary Air Force mission continued to be that of defending against a nuclear attack.

Hanscom Air Force Base was built on 500 acres in the picturesque countryside tucked neatly between historic Concord and Lexington, the same ground Paul Revere traversed at the start of the American Revolutionary War. Hanscom and the Air Force dated back to the 1940s, when it was founded under the auspices of the Army Air Forces at the start of World War II. The electronics mission in those early days centered on radar applications and development. The work at Hanscom matured into ballistic missile early warning systems, and ground-based radar arrangements evolved into airborne radar systems. When Michael pulled in to Hanscom Field the mission had grown to encompass intelligence gathering, and Michael's first assignment was as an engineer for the National Security Agency.

Mike was assigned to a program office in the Electronic Systems Division. He was responsible for a project that entailed highly-classified digital communications systems, remarkable for the time, bought by the Defense Communication Agency. Mike had gained a functional understanding of digital computing back at the Academy, and was assigned at Hanscom to monitor the purchase of this advanced digital switch.

The contractor was ITT Federal Systems out of New Jersey, and for months Mike flew back and forth among Hanscom, Newark, and Washington acting as the middle-man between the contractor and the purchaser. With small per diems from the Air Force, when in Newark or Washington, Mike would opt for lodging and dining at places he would never take his young bride. In Newark, this was the run-down city center; in Washington, it bordered the red-light district at 14th and H streets. At either, six dollars gained him a chicken dinner and a beer. The following year, in July 1967, these neighborhoods would explode in the news with 26 dead in the Newark riots and his old Washington hotel in flames.

Home at Hanscom was a trailer, one in which Mike could not stand up straight in the shower. Mike could humbly admit to the Hills that he had married their lovely, hazel-eyed daughter and promptly moved her into a trailer park. He worked out of the Waltham Federal Center, about 15 miles southeast of Hanscom and essentially a suburb of Boston, while Barb had a retail position in town. Then, quarters became available at Fort Devens, an Army base about 20 miles west of Hanscom and flanked by the Nashua River.

As part of the buildup for Vietnam in 1965, the 196th Light Infantry Brigade, dormant since 1946, had been reactivated at Fort Devens. The brigade was deployed to Vietnam in 1966 and began operations in Tay Ninh Province. When the brigade moved out of Fort Devens, housing became available because most of the women decamped when the men left. Mike and Barb moved out to lodging at Fort Devens, a bit distant from work but a grand leap above a trailer park.

From Fort Devens, one was still close enough to hitchhike to Boston. Nearby towns of Leominster and Fitchburg provided some diversion on the weekends. The young couple could hike the trails and canoe the rivers. During the winter, they could ice skate on Robbins Pond after it froze over. They set up a car pool back to Hanscom and Waltham with others in the same situation. Life was good, especially so for a low-level second lieutenant. Mike played on the softball team, and he and Barb had an ever-growing circle of friends. One was an Air Force Academy graduate, Ron Schillereff.

BORN AND RAISED IN PENNSYLVANIA, Ron had worked out his life plan at an early age. When Schillereff was in high school, he decided he wanted to go to one of the major academies, West Point or Annapolis. An excellent athlete and a very good student, he considered himself signed and sealed for one of the military academies. But, with a medical problem, Schillereff found out that the major academies, which had no trouble filling out their ranks and were pretty staid in their ways, didn't want him. The Air Force Academy, on the other hand, was more adventurous and working to build its status and size. It was willing to take a marginally deficient prospect who had everything else in the package. A waiver for pilot training at some later point was a possibility.

The military conundrum was that Mike Wynne probably would have gone to the Air Force Academy had it not been for his lousy eyesight. Ron Schillereff, on the other hand, wanted to go to the U.S. Military Academy but was prevented from doing so because of color blindness. So Wynne ended up at West Point while Schillereff attended the Air Force Academy. In a day and age when the academies graduated on the same date, Mike and Ron had both graduated on June 8, 1966, one on the Colorado Front Range and the other on the Hudson River. They both had the academy experience, possibly neither at their first choice.

Ron's waiver did not materialize, neither did his dream of earning wings and becoming a pilot.[1] Having majored in political science and international affairs, Ron became an acquisitions expert. His first duty assignment, after the normal 60 days off and appropriate travel time, was to Hanscom Air Force Base. Ron Schillereff and Mike Wynne both signed in on the same date, and worked out of the Waltham Federal Center. They promptly ran into each other in the cafeteria and began a relationship that would lead to intersecting careers across decades.

As they took to each other, Ron made the connections and figured out he had met Mike's brother years before. Ron had met Pat Wynne at the Air Force Academy but only in passing. Pat was in his final year at the academy when Ron started his program. That was the summer of 1962 and, as usual, the first classmen ruled the grounds and gave the fourth classmen their first taste of academy life. So Pat may have played a part in Ron's initial training, but the two were not in the same cadet squadron with much contact. Circumstances now put Ron with a different Wynne, Michael.

BACK AT HANSCOM, the constant changeovers of military life played out. Colonel Henry Dittman, a friend of Mike's father and the former base commander from the Air Force Missile Test Center at Cape Kennedy, was assigned as the new base commander at Hanscom. The new first sergeant had also come over from Patrick Air Force Base in Florida. Mike's sister Maureen had been best friends with the first sergeant's daughter so, for Mike, things were looking up. It was as if moving into a neighborhood of friends and acquaintances.

Colonel Dittman knew Mike was a swimmer. The academy required each cadet to participate in athletics each year, whether varsity or intramural level. While Mike spent some time on the soccer team, his sport was swimming. Having spent years in Florida, Mike had sharpened his swimming talent. His lanky frame lent itself to water sports and he ended up swimming competitively at West Point. Colonel Dittman asked Mike to take responsibility for coaching the base swim team, populated by the children of the service people and civilians employed on base, and Mike readily agreed. With age-group swim coach duties, the commute soon became an inconvenience.

Mike dropped out of the car pool between Fort Devens and Hanscom because with the swim team work his agenda no longer fit the schedule. So he and Barb bought a run-down little beater and matched their arrangements to the new timetable. Colonel Dittman by and by figured out the commute was becoming a burden for the young couple. He worked in the background to arrange quarters on base at Hanscom instead of at the Army base.

Most everyone working at Hanscom but quartered at Fort Devens wanted back on to the Air Force base, and this is where one's vaunted rank came into play. With the right rank, officers could force their way back to Hanscom housing as it became available. In turn, captains would be able to relocate and first lieutenants would apply for any remaining slots. Mid-level second lieutenants were not offered much hope. Colonel Dittman did Mike and Barb proud though, getting them an end unit on the Cape Cod row house section, one step above the townhouse subdivision. This would prove to be a lesson on reflected glory.

After moving back to Hanscom while Mike was away one

day, Barb received a visit from a neighbor, the wife of another, presumably senior, officer. On appearing at her door, the visitor jumped right to the point and asked Barb what rank her husband held. Nonplussed but quick enough for a 20-year-old officer's wife, Barb simply said, "Lieutenant." Missing the subtlety, the visitor left mumbling about how she was going to look into the matter. When Barb shared her day with Mike that evening, he explained that she had just experienced an age-old tradition related to rank and privilege. Some wives would conform to their husbands' rank and work to make sure they achieved what was their due. Someone was not happy with the Wynne's end unit on the Cape Cod row. Life went on and the seasons changed.

One quiet winter Sunday morning on the base, Mike was working his rotation as the officer of the day. It snowed the previous night, and the plows hadn't yet attacked the drifts, so getting around was tricky. As he rotated off shift and handed off duties, Mike thought it might be nice to pick up Barb and the kids and attend Sunday Mass. Having been on duty, he hadn't had a chance to dig his car out and, with the snow, his car wasn't going anywhere. The base staff car, with deep-treaded tires and winter chains, would make the perfect vehicle to get to church and back in no time. Mike executed his plan, and the staff car was back within the hour. A few days later, Mike was called to the colonel's office.

Imagine the conversation. Mike reports to the base commander's office, door open, and begins.

"You wanted to see me, Colonel Dittman?"

"Yes Mike. It has been reported that you misappropriated the base staff car last Sunday," responded the colonel with just a hint of formality to make sure each remembered their place.

"Yes sir," answered Mike, taken aback for a moment.

"Did you in fact take the staff car for purposes related to a civilian service, not related to your job?"

"Yes sir."

"And did you in fact use the car to pick up your family and attend Mass over at the chapel?"

"Yes sir."

"About how long did you have the base staff car out?"

"With the snow and everything, the chaplain kept it pretty short, about 40 minutes sir."

"And it was just a regular Mass service, nothing else out of the ordinary?"

"Yes sir," replied Mike. He understood and respected the chain-of-command and willingly submitted to its vagaries. But for the moment, he wasn't quite sure where this was headed and he bristled imperceptibly as the Q & A remained officious.

"So you had the staff car for personal purposes for about an hour?"

"Yes sir, no more than an hour."

"You know, your neighbors are watching you," the colonel offered.

Mike finally *got it*. "Apparently so, sir" and he went on to share the episode of the officer's wife pounding on his door.

"Hmm. Let me ask you, how's that swim team coming along," the colonel inquired with an effortless jump-shift and not a segue in sight?

"Fine, sir. We've increased membership, and I feel we should look for ways to extend the time we use the pool. We might even consider trying to acquire an air dome over the pool, so the kids can have access to it all year."

"Not a bad idea Mike. Now regarding the staff car, I have to write up a reprimand."

"Sir?"

"Someone has made an official complaint, so I have to write it up. I am going to write it up as a reprimand for your file, but I wouldn't worry about it at all."

"Sir," Mike hesitated? A reprimand on one's OER—officer efficiency report—was a speed-bump in promotions.

"I'll write it up, and put it here in my desk. If someone comes to inquire about it, I'll have it available for review. But I wouldn't give it much thought, if I were you. It'll sit here in my desk for awhile and then go away."

"Sir?"

"Yes, it will just go away. In fact, it will probably retire with me, so don't give it another thought."

Looking at the first sergeant outside his door, the colonel asked, "Did you get that, sergeant?"

"Yes sir," responded the sergeant.

"And by the way," the colonel continued with the sergeant, referring to Mike, "look out for this guy because apparently some of his neighbors don't like him."

"I'll handle it, sir."

In time, Mike did arrange to acquire that air dome for the base swimming pool. It cost some $20,000 but he was able to fund it entirely from donations. No government money went into the project. And the security police, who routinely patrolled the base, made an extra trip or two by the Wynnes' quarters every once in awhile, just to make sure everything was a-okay. If an occasional traffic stop happened in the area, base security could quietly inquire about the Wynnes in the end unit of the Cape Cod row to determine if anyone might have a problem with them.

MIKE AND HIS FRIEND RON, young-at-heart officers with great futures, were still able to act similar to kids from time to time and relive childhood experiences. Ron and Mike played together on one of the 12-inch fast pitch softball teams at Hanscom, Ron as shortstop and Mike as center fielder. The term fast pitch was used a bit loosely on the Hanscom teams, as not everyone had an underhand pitcher with speed. Underhand it might be, fast maybe not so much. Ron and Mike were on the ESD squad, one of eight teams, and usually finished second in the league to the engineers' lineup.

The ESD team would send out its members to some interesting careers. Two players ended up as generals, and another as secretary of a military department. Team catcher Bill Simpson was from Pat Wynne's 1963 graduating class at the Air Force Academy; graduating with an Order of Merit of 29, Bill came to Hanscom via Harvard Law School. Chuck Williams from the academy class of 1965 also played.

THE MILITARY BEING WHAT IT WAS, once everyone settled into a routine, it was time for change. Mike's time and grade caught up.

His time-in earned him a promotion to the grade of first lieutenant in the United States Air Force, and the juncture for a new duty assignment. It was 1968, and the demands of the ever-escalating war in Southeast Asia caused a great deal of personnel movement in the service branches. Vietnam had become the touchstone of a generation, and it had an impact on everyone, military and civilian. It had touched the Wynne family in 1966.

❧

OF COURSE, VIETNAM was a country with more than its share of history. Geographically more than 1,000 miles long, from north to south, the country was but 30 miles wide at parts. Its climate encompassed cold, rainy monsoons in the north and hot, steamy tropics in the south. With flat marshland and mountains interspersed on the west, and the Gulf of Tonkin and South China Sea flanking the east, it had an arresting landscape.

Vietnam was comparable to Korea, divided in both geography and society. Vietnam had a more unassuming, rudimentary and rural way of life in the north, with its heart in Hanoi, and a more affluent, sophisticated and fast-paced economy in the south, centered around Saigon. Old Highway 1 connected the two city hubs, passing through Hué and Da Nang in the middle section of the country. The 1966 population of 38 million was nearly split between north and south.

The countryside was fully invested with an agricultural economy, a patchwork of rice paddies, fruit orchards, and sugar cane fields to accompany the rubber plantations. The coastal regions sustained a vibrant fishing market. Vietnam had beautiful deltas serving as bookends, the Red River on the north and the Mekong on the south. It was this fertile land and vast food source that attracted the colonial French a hundred years earlier. Countries had fought over and in Vietnam for hundreds of years.

Even in recent times, within little more than a century, Vietnam had struggled with one power after another for independence. French colonists had taken control in 1885, signing treaties to end the Sino-French War. They were only temporarily unseated by the Japanese during World War II. After the war, a new faction would vie with the tricolor for the country's heart, the Viet Minh headed by Ho Chi Minh. Still, the French would not cede their colony without a fight. The decisive battle took place in 1954 at Dien Bien Phu.

The United States became involved in the 1950s, supplying the French with money and materials. But America, with its own war festering in Korea, was hesitant to commit ground forces in Vietnam. Thus, the French were left with just an airlift of supplies at the crucial time. With the French defeat, Vietnam was divided into north and south at the 17th Parallel. The struggle for control continued, the south striving for independence and Ho Chi Minh straining for unification.

Vietnam was destined to resist easy answers. Four American presidents, two Republican and two Democratic, would seek a solution. The change from one president to another reflected the deep divisions within the United States. President Eisenhower took up the vocation for South Vietnam and decided to send advisors. This would expand to U.S. trainers, then aircraft, and then mechanical and technical assistance. In 1961 Khrushchev resolved to nourish the north, and Kennedy determined to sustain the south. Operation Ranch Hand, the first use of chemical defoliants in South Vietnam, began in 1962 under President Kennedy's watch. Then Lyndon Johnson inherited the presidency and the problems.

In time President Johnson would settle on a policy of military operations in South Vietnam and a plan for bombing in the north, if provoked. Provocation would arrive in the guise of the Gulf of Tonkin incident in mid-1964 when North Vietnamese Navy vessels attacked the American destroyer USS *Maddox* (DD-731), allegedly twice. In response, Congress passed the Tonkin Gulf Resolution on August 7 giving the president the legal basis for entangling the United States in Vietnam.[2] Always mindful of bargaining position, the military plan became one of reprisal airstrikes. In the ensuing months, a series of guerrilla actions in the south demonstrated that the insurgency and the issues were far from decided. Combat in Pleiku in early 1965 helped propel the American response, with the U.S. Air Force on the wing in Operation Flaming Dart in February 1965, bombing targets in the north.

The blueprint of the war changed with ground troops. Committing ground forces in Vietnam began with the Marines landing at Da Nang in South Vietnam on March 8, 1965 to defend the American air base. These were front-line troops, not advisors and trainers. Thus, President Johnson made the ground war in South Vietnam the first priority and the air war in North Vietnam second.[3] A number of people maintain it was at that moment in 1965 and with that decision on priorities that the United States lost the war in Vietnam.[4] The air war would continue and even escalate to a much larger affair, starting with Operation Rolling Thunder in March 1965. On the ground, the Ia Drang Valley would follow in the fall of 1965, but it was just prologue.

At home the United States was unsettled with the overarching fear that Vietnam would blossom into World War III. Student demonstrations against the war began back in 1964, primarily in New York's Times Square and in San Francisco. The year 1965 saw organized protests in Washington, focused on the White House and Pentagon. The U.S. Congress created legislation to stop protestors from destroying their draft cards, and a group promptly burned their draft cards in public to test the country's resolve. By 1966, antiwar protests and sit-ins reached college campuses throughout the nation. Muhammad Ali turned into a lightning rod when he declared himself a conscientious objector, and Pat Wynne became one of a number of young Americans shot down in Vietnam.

Such was the decade of the 1960s, spanning the incredible and the inspirational. Two Kennedys and a King were assassinated, and the space race put a man on the moon. Surrounding it all—the women's movement, the civil rights movement and the antiwar movement with the growing concern for prisoners of war—coalesced into a rage of dissatisfaction.

In the end, the generation that matured in the 1960s became inextricably entwined with Vietnam, a country that had barely registered as a footnote in their grade school history books. It was in this atmosphere that Pat and Mike Wynne came of age.

Pat and Mike Wynne were remarkably well-adjusted kids. Other than the constant movement among a procession of army bases and air fields during their youth, their childhood was normal. The term military brats just didn't quite fit the two boys, which is probably due to their mom and dad being pretty grounded people. Pat was born in Alaska, at his father's first duty assignment after leaving West Point and marrying. Second-born Mike's birthplace was a bit harder to nail down.

After Alaska, Mike's father was on the move with a number of short assignments, some at temporary military facilities. To be exact, Mike was born in a firehouse on Drew Field outside Tampa, in Hillsborough County, Florida. Drew Field, founded in 1928, was a municipal airport owned by Tampa. The city had leased Drew Field to the U.S. government in 1940 to be used as a training facility for the Army Air Forces during the war. With the cessation of hostilities in 1945, Drew Army Airfield was transferred back to Tampa control. Mike was born on September 4, 1944, right in the short period when Drew Field was a military installation. Today, Drew Field is essentially one of the runways at Tampa International Airport. Mike's birth certificate shows he was nine pounds 14 ounces and lists Hillsborough County as his birthplace, but for ease of explanation he'll usually mention the closest city across the bay, Clearwater, as his hometown.

Mike spent his adolescence, at least the memorable years from grade school, in Maryland. His dad was assigned to Air Weapons Development at the Air Research and Development Command Headquarters in the Baltimore area. The family stayed in Baltimore until Mike graduated from eighth grade, at which time a new Air Force assignment required their move to Florida. So, Mike's early childhood experiences were fashioned in Baltimore.

Mike and his childhood friends, Basil Tydings and Ricky O'Cassock, did the normal, innocent but goofy, things most kids do growing up in the city. During the snowy winters Basil and Mike would throw snowballs at passing trucks on Loch Raven Boulevard. The goal was to launch them on top of the trailer for a more-satisfying boom. One landed on a windshield and resulted in a race through the neighborhood, cutting down alleys and across yards, until Basil's sister Mary Ellen came to their rescue by pointing the pursuer in the wrong direction. After hiding in the Tydings' basement for what seemed like hours, they had stories to crow about for a week.

Baltimore was home to Memorial Stadium, famed for the Colts in football and the Orioles in baseball. Built in 1954, the stadium was one of the big draws in the city. Johnny Unitas started with the Colts in 1956 and Brooks Robinson began his career with the Orioles in 1955, so Mike was present at the start of the halcyon days of Baltimore sports in the 1950s.[5] Mike and Ricky O'Cassock used to hitch hike rides to Memorial Stadium in the summer and buy cheap tickets to the Orioles games. They would spend the rest of the day, as people left the game, working their way down the aisle until they reached the box seats. Their sport was betting nickels and dimes on balls and strikes. Oftentimes, they would give the winnings to the panhandlers at the exit gates.

Mike and older brother Pat both caddied at the Country Club of Maryland. They did not carry bags together though, as the club generally paired a young caddy with an older one to make sure the golfers were taken care of properly. Mike, just a youngster of 13, was barely able to carry two bags for the 18-hole course. Pat worked hard at being a caddy and was good enough to be chosen to carry a bag at the 1957 Eastern Open Invitational, held at nearby Mt. Pleasant Municipal Golf Course.

In between tee times, Mike and Pat ran errands for the older caddies and hunted for lost balls. This is probably where the brothers smoked their first cigarettes and tasted their first beer, undoubtedly Baltimore's own National Bohemian. From throwing snowballs at cars and trucks to smoking cigarettes when no one was looking, their neighborhood's level of disorder and conflict fit the 1950s to a tee.

The two boys attended Catholic schools in Baltimore, Pat at Loyola High and Mike at Immaculate Heart of Mary elementary. Mike can still remember Sister Winnifred, an archetypical nun of the 1950s, from his days in sixth grade. Mike was an altar server and often assigned to the early Mass, the one the nuns attended. On one occasion, wearing a cassock much too long, Mike had a hitch transferring the Mass book from the epistle side to the gospel side of the altar.

In precise military maneuver, the job was to genuflect, move up the stairs and retrieve the book on the epistle side of the altar, work your way down the steps to a center position, genuflect again, work back up the stairs to the gospel side of the altar for presentation, and then exit. The exercise went in cadence until the rise from genuflection number two, at which time his heel caught the bottom of the cassock. The resulting face-first fall made it a fiasco as the good book took off on a trajectory of its own across the marble platform. All this took place with Sister Winnifred watching.

Seventh grade was looking at girls in a different light for the first time, a brief kiss while escorting a blonde girl on the way to school once. Eighth grade was judo classes in the old Sun Building on Charles Street in downtown Baltimore, and basketball games against the public schools in the city. Mike played basketball with the Catholic Youth Organization team representing Immaculate Heart of Mary grade school. He also tried his hand at baseball, but basketball seemed more in line with his lanky build.

Mike was more into adventuring than organized activities. These years saw the neighborhood kids having fun in the corn fields behind their row houses, and playing tag and jumping in the hay stacks in a barn out back. One time Mike had to set one of the other kids straight after he started picking on Mike's sister, Maureen. It seems the other kid wanted seven year old Maureen to jump off a rise into the dirt to earn her way into the club; "Let her be, she's in," was all it took from Michael to settle the matter. Another time, Mike jumped off a hay stack and right onto a nail. Driven through his foot, the nail ended play for that day and resulted in a trip to Fort Meade Hospital. To pick up a few dollars, he even tried his hand at selling the *TV Guide*, often with his little sister, Maureen, in tow.

Pat did well at Loyola High and played tennis but after three years of high school in Baltimore, the family was on the move

Clockwise from upper left: Mike and Pat Wynne at Wright-Patterson Air Force Base in Dayton around 1949, the brothers in Baltimore at Easter 1953, and Mike in his IHM/CYO baseball jacket in Baltimore. *Source:* Wynne Family.

again. He would complete his senior year of high school in Florida, where he went out for football and made the varsity team. Pat's real desire though was to be a debater, and he joined the high school debate team in Florida. Being on the football team guaranteed he could be on the debate team with little or no hassle from others. In the end, he won awards at the state debate tournament. Pat also played the piano by ear. His high school sweetheart in Florida was Betty Creech.

When Mike lived in Florida, he swam and worked when out of school. He was the guy who checked identification cards of base children coming into the Officers' Club. Mike also worked at the Officers' Club pool, the beginnings of a love for the water. He liked science fiction novels, the pap of the fifties and the substance of the sixties. Many of these came packaged as two books in one, the second printed upside down on the flip side. On the military base in Florida, the kids were not allowed to solicit in the neighborhood, so it was out with the *TV Guide* business. What money he made, he banked. Unlike others his age, he did not sink his savings in a car as a teenager. He just didn't need wheels to maneuver around on base. Money was different in the 1950s.

Florida would bring the family three different homesteads in the first four years. The first base housing would be North Wherry on Riverside Drive. This was opposite the Banana River, an offshoot of the Indian River Lagoon, and within walking distance of the Officers' Club and beach. The second home was Capehart housing, now called Pelican Landing, where Mike spent most of his high school years.[6] Their last place, right at the end of Mike's high school years, would be off the base at 305 Glenwood in a newer community called Satellite Beach, just down the road from Patrick Air Force Base. This last home also was within a block of Mike's future wife, but neither of them knew that at the time. Raised in the middle of rocket country, Mike benefited from the intellectual atmosphere.

THE ARRIVAL OF THE ROCKET PROGRAM in Florida was just the latest in a series of moves, each connected in one way or another to Wernher von Braun. When the expatriates of the German science community came to the United States, they set up shop at the Army's Fort Bliss near El Paso, Texas, where the von Braun team of engineers and scientists was organized. After launching dozens of reassembled V-2 missiles into the sand dunes and scrub land of the Tularosa Basin at nearby White Sands Proving Ground, the team was transferred to the Army's newly opened Ordnance Rocket Center at Redstone Arsenal in Huntsville, Alabama. The year was 1949, and the Army really didn't trust the Germans, the definitive bad guys of the 20th century. Huntsville was a place where the Army could keep their eye on the émigrés.

Redstone Arsenal had been built on roughly 30,000 acres of mostly cotton fields, at the southwestern edge of Huntsville in northern Alabama. It was bordered on the south by the Tennessee River and flanked on the east by the Ridge-and-Valley belt of the Appalachian Mountains. The site had been chosen in the early 1940s partly because of the protection provided by its inland location, but that was when it was intended for chemical manufacturing. When it came to launching rockets, with deference to its neighbors in Mississippi, Tennessee, and Georgia, the facility did not provide adequate room. As rockets became Redstone's *raison d'être* in the 1950s, attention turned to a little spit of land on the coast of Florida, shaped like a parrot's beak and jutting into the Atlantic.

For launching rockets, the von Braun team traveled to Cape Canaveral, von Braun on temporary duty to oversee the National Aeronautics and Space Administration facilities but many others permanently. They established an operations base in the area, and many members of the team set up residence in Florida. Little Brevard County would become a sister city of Huntsville but as the launch site for rockets rather than the development site.

Along with the scientists came their families, who needed the amenities of everyday life. With the homesteading came stores and shops and schools. The Wynne family move to the locale coincided with major changes in the region, including the education system, to the Wynne's good fortune.

With the flood of rocket science, much of the best of both American and German intellectual capital was constellating in this largely undeveloped area of coastal Florida. The German scientists brought with them an interest in and appreciation for the arts and sciences, and the requirement for a first-class public education was part of that. Just as they had in Huntsville, the German colony changed the culture of the area, in this case, from average high schools in the orange groves to places of advanced learning.

The German scientists pushed their employer, the United States Army, until a college professor was brought in to lead the area's main secondary school, Melbourne High. This leader, Dr. B. Frank Brown, was principal at Mel High when Mike Wynne attended. Dr. Brown, a Rhodes Scholar in his youth, brought innovation in education to Mel High, including such ideas as independent study and mentoring. He published extensively and wrote a treatise suggesting the value of non-graded school curriculums.[7] He also brought in higher-level educators and pushed the lower level schools, the feeder system, to make changes to keep pace with what would be required when their students graduated into the secondary school system. While some factions fought the changes, when a junior at Mel High won an award in the National Science Fair one year, it was game over. Everyone bought into the program.

Dr. Brown went on to leave quite a legacy in Florida. After Mel High he became the Brevard County school commissioner and later the state commissioner of education. His early work in secondary education set an example for even the higher education schools in the area, including the establishment in 1958 of the Brevard Engineering College, now the Florida Institute of Technology, in Melbourne. Academically structured to mimic Rensselaer Polytechnic Institute in Troy, New York, Florida Institute of Technology still exists today and has a satellite facility in, of all places, Huntsville, Alabama. Each of the Wynne family children profited from this educational movement in Florida.

TRACKING THEIR FATHER'S AIR FORCE CAREER, the family spent time in Alaska, Ohio, Michigan, New York, the Washington, D.C./ Maryland/Virginia area and, finally, Florida. None of this seemed to hurt the children who, in not having the advantage of long-term friends, relied on each other and became that much closer. Mom Wynne had the strong nature to do what it took to raise a family, while dad was the perfect partner. She represented the discipline and he the veiled threat, and dad shouldered his mantle mildly. The boys respected their father, who set quite an example, in the sense of both achievement and desire. Mike's dad was one of that "greatest generation" that was steeled in the Great Depression. Ed Wynne was a self-made man, and he did much with the gifts he had been given.

Chapter Two

Ed Wynne's Army Air Corps

Michael's father, Edward Patrick Wynne, born August 23, 1918, grew up in a rough and tough Irish neighborhood just inside Hell's Kitchen in New York City. The family address during those early years was 412 West 54th Street, between 9th and 10th avenues. Today it's called midtown Manhattan. He was one of three children of Patrick and Mary (Cunningham) Wynne. For much of his youth, Ed's father was a bus driver, and his mom was a department store clerk.[8]

One way or another, Patrick and Mary made a living for their two boys, Edward and William, and only girl, first-born Margaret. Similar to millions before them, Ed's paternal grandparents had come from Ireland, working their way through Castle Garden or Ellis Island in the 1890s. They didn't stray far from either, crossing over to New York's lower harbors on Manhattan Island.

As the scion of what would become a family with deep roots in the military, Ed's father, first generation Irish-American Patrick Edward Wynne, signed up for both world wars. He registered with the draft board for World War I in June 1917 when he was 23 years old. He re-registered, this time for World War II, on April 26, 1942, when he was 48 years old.[9] Even though he was not called to serve, he set a pattern.

The middle child, Ed, was a quick study and determined to work his way to better things, especially since his impressionable years spanned the Roaring Twenties and the Great Depression. After a grammar school track through a couple of the public schools in the neighborhood, his academic achievement was high enough to earn him a place in one of the city's elite public high schools that specialized in mathematics and science instruction.[10] Privilege, whether race, religion, or riches, didn't count. The only way in was merit. Ed began his studies at Stuyvesant High School, located at 345 East 15th Street in lower Manhattan, at the start of the 1932–33 school year.

The two inner-city high schools for the academically gifted when Ed was coming of age were Stuyvesant High and Brooklyn Technical, which unabashedly focused their teaching effort into mathematics and the sciences. This usually meant the humanities, and English and composition received short shrift. The rigorous course content and heavy workload would serve him well in the future. In the same fashion as many of his contemporaries in these "science schools," Ed took an accelerated course load and finished high school in three years.

Ed graduated in 1935 at 16 years of age, the same year as future jazz great Thelonious Monk.[11] Ed parlayed early graduation into early entrance at the partner college, City College of New York in September 1935. He stayed on one year at City College in the Department of Military Science and Tactics, earning the rank of corporal on April 16, 1936.

In those days, a city boy such as Ed undoubtedly maneuvered around town using public transportation, especially since his dad was a streetcar conductor and later a bus driver. The same year Ed started high school at Stuyvesant, the new Eighth Avenue subway line opened up, linking the far ends of Manhattan. Within months this line spanned Brooklyn Heights to the south and Inwood to the north.[12] Ed could ride this line downtown to 14th Street and transfer over to the BMT-Canarsie line for a short hop east, and be within walking distance of Stuyvesant High School on 15th Street. The Eighth Avenue line also could drop Ed off close to City College, reached through stations at 135th and 145th Streets.

This subway burrowed under Eighth Avenue, hard by the

overcrowded Irish projects and the eastern boundary of Hell's Kitchen. The line traced north northeast up to 207th Street in Inwood, opening that uptown neighborhood for settlement by any Irish families moving up and out of the midtown tenements. The subway bridged the Irish neighborhoods by tunneling underneath the Upper West Side and Harlem. Ed's parents followed suit and became part of the exodus relocating uptown.

The family moved to Post Avenue in the Inwood neighborhood around 1935. They lived at 39 Post and 66 Post in the ensuing years. Their home was equidistant from the last subway stops. This was three blocks southeast of the station at Dyckman and Broadway and three blocks southwest of 207th and Broadway at the end of the line, and the 207th Street yards.

After one year at City College, Ed's chronological age caught up and he was old enough to accept an appointment to the United States Military Academy, effective July 1, 1936. He had received the nomination to West Point from John J. Boylan who represented New York's Fifteenth Congressional District covering their new neighborhood in upper Manhattan.[13]

Family history recalls that Ed's name had been passed to Congressman Boylan by a newspaper man known to the family, which carried just enough weight to obtain Ed a nomination as the second alternate. Since nomination to a service academy didn't mean admittance, the entrance exam had been one more hurdle to jump on the way to meeting the requirements for appointment. When the original nominee failed the physical and the first alternate lost interest and committed to another university, the appointment opened for Ed Wynne. As Ed left for adventure in upstate New York, he could look back on achieving his dreams. And he wasn't done yet.

For two hundred years, the training of our country's military leadership had been centered in a few military academies, three of which were more than 160 years old. The U.S. Naval Academy was founded in 1845 in Annapolis, Maryland. Virginia Military Institute was founded in 1839 in Lexington, Virginia. West Point predated both of them. The United States Military Academy, West Point for short, was a scenic campus situated at a bend in the Hudson River some 50 miles north of New York City. A fine academic institution in its own right, West Point's mission was military leadership. This was Ed Wynne's next stop.

Similar to thousands of prospective cadets before him, life at West Point began with "Beast Barracks"—Cadet Basic Training. At the Military Academy, the school years were filled with academics and athletics, but the summers were also overflowing with activities, keeping the cadets on the grounds for long periods. For Ed Wynne, it began in the summer of 1936. As their class history would later remark, "South Gate was closed and hermetically sealed behind us" on entering that summer.[14]

A jumbled group of city kids and farm boys, fired in the depths of the Depression, they were helped along in their first days by the prior year's freshmen, now on Yearling Beast Detail. Only later would they ascertain that the upperclassmen were even worse. They would learn about reception, first inspection, acceptance, "plebe" (freshman) hike, parade, and on and on. Everything was a learning experience. Take cadet mess where, for their entire plebe year, their backs were not allowed to touch the seatback of the chair. With a year of athletics, academics and army training, it wasn't until Saturday, June 12, 1937, that they were finally recognized as human on leaving their plebe year.

Yearling summer in 1937, the months between freshman and sophomore years, had Ed moving forward and learning the rudiments of infantry weapons, the Browning 30-caliber machine gun, the 155 mm howitzer and other armaments. Yearling picnic and afternoons at Delafield Pond on the grounds of West Point broke the monotony of instruction. Then it was a school year of education and training including calculus, French, public-speaking, history, drawing, and physics.

During Ed's yearling experience, Hollywood came to campus, filming a movie that was set in the era of top-hats and tails. *Rosalie* starred Nelson Eddy and Eleanor Powell, both of whom would earn their star on the Walk of Fame, the former on Hollywood Boulevard and the latter on Vine Street. William Demarest played the Army football coach. The movie was a musical drama with compositions by Cole Porter. The story line was about a West Point cadet (Eddy) who fell in love with a foreign princess (Powell). The film was released in 1937.

After 76 days of furlough during the summer of 1938, Ed and his mates returned to campus on August 28 for their third year of instruction. They were now upperclassmen. Descriptive geometry, chemistry and mechanics made a seamless transition into aerodynamics and field artillery. June 12, 1939, marked the

Company L of the Third Battalion during the 1939–40 academic year at the academy. Ed Wynne sports the wry smile in the second row from the top, second from the left. *Source:* United States Military Academy photo published in Paulick et al., *1940 Howitzer*, p. 92.

end of third year and the start of Ed's first class year. Ed spent his fourth year at West Point in L Company of the Third Battalion.

Ed's final year at West Point began with a busy summer, being exposed to the specialties of the Army. From instruction in signal communication held on the academy grounds to artillery practice at the Tobyhanna Military Reservation, it also encompassed cavalry training, both horsed and mechanized, and experience with coast artillery at Fort Hancock in Sandy Hook, New Jersey. At Fort Hancock the men saw one of the Army's newest weapons, a light gun built to counteract the ever-growing threat from the air, 37 mm antiaircraft artillery. They also had time for a tour of nearby Fort Monmouth, where the Army worked on early versions of radar.

As the 1939 version of an American air force was still firmly a part of the Army, in the form of the Army Air Corps, Ed and the other first classmen were also exposed to what could be accomplished in the air. In bombing and observation flights at Mitchel Field on the Hempstead Plains of Long Island, Ed had the opportunity to fly on Douglas B-18 Bolo light bombers and North American O-47 observation aircraft. He also viewed some leading-edge vehicles, such as the experimental long-range Boeing B-15 bomber, and its progeny, the state-of-the-art Boeing B-17 Flying Fortress. In 1940 West Point provided Air Corps training trips to Langley Field in Virginia and Patterson Field in Ohio. These encounters were also a part of the academics, including instruction in aeronautics.

In concert with the academy's dictum for its cadets to be athletes, Ed's sport of choice was lacrosse, although he also had tried football in his plebe year. As complementary sports, many athletes took up football in the fall and lacrosse in the spring to stay in shape, but for Ed it would be lacrosse for four years. Army lacrosse was a major team sport and on a par with football, basketball, and baseball. The sport was beginning its 20th season on the Hudson River when Ed joined during the 1936-37 school year. Ed earned his numerals during his first year and his varsity Army "A" in his last year. The team had a record of 31 and 9 during his four years, under F. Morris Touchstone, who would coach for 29 years at West Point.

Ed accomplished something else in his four years at West Point,

With the uniform number one, Ed is easy to pick out on the lacrosse field. Here he just wears hand protection. *Source:* United States Military Academy photo published in Paulick et al., *1940 Howitzer*, p. 338.

he became an academic coach. Born with talent, he also was blessed with the capacity to help others. As Ed's 1940 *Howitzer* yearbook biography noted, he missed earning his stars, the uniform designation of the top 5 percent in the class, because of the "cultural" studies. Ed was a whiz at mathematics and sciences but not so much in the humanities. Even with that social handicap, he devoted himself to helping those with academic troubles, often called the goats. In fact, that bio noted "Ed was an 'engineer' with the attitude of a 'goat'".

Graduation at West Point was called "June Week." Ed graduated from the United States Military Academy in 1940, ranked 80th out of the 449 graduates that year. The Class of 1940 paraded into the new armory field house on Tuesday, June 11 and the address was given by Lieutenant General Hugh A. Drum, commander of the First Army and the senior line officer. President Franklin D. Roosevelt, nearing the end of only his second term in office,

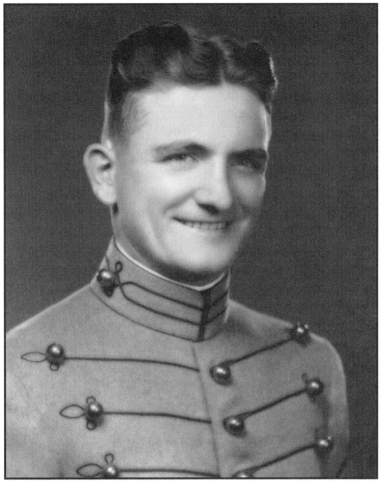

Edward Patrick Wynne in a view taken for his official graduation photo from the United States Military Academy in 1940. *Source:* United States Military Academy photo courtesy of Wynne Family.

made the presentations and congratulated each of the new second lieutenants.

Ed's cadet class was the second largest to graduate from West Point up to that time. Harold Clifton Brown, from Concord, New Hampshire, was the top academic student; Alan Edward Gee, from Golden, Colorado, placed second. The first captain, the cadet regimental commander, was John Finzer Presnell, from Portland,

Maine. The yearbook biographies of each showed stars for four years.

During graduation week, talk of the gathering storm in world events varied among groups, but it was impossible to completely ignore the fact that Germany was invading France and the low countries. June Week included military services and baccalaureate sermons in the Cadet Chapel, Cadet Gymnasium, and Catholic Chapel, the last being given by Bishop John Francis O'Hara, former president of Notre Dame and future cardinal in the Catholic Church.[15]

TWO MEN WHO WOULD PROVE IMPORTANT in the history of the Air Force had been distinguished visitors to West Point during the 1939-40 school year: Chief of Staff General George C. Marshall, on November 3, 1939, and Chief of the Air Corps Major General Henry "Hap" Arnold, on February 2, 1940. But the Air Force of Second Lieutenant Ed Wynne's day had a different look. In fact, for a long time no one knew whether an Air Force would be a fad or the future.

❧

DATING THE START OF THE AIR FORCE is a matter of choice.[16] In one sense, an American air force dates back to before the Civil War when intrepid souls started using balloons for aerial reconnaissance. But the future of air power was destined to be more than balloons and blimps, reporting troop movements and directing artillery fire. Observation would evolve into offense.

Soon after someone thought of using balloons to view the battlefield, others began working on ideas to drop ordnance from that platform. As early as 1863 the U.S. Patent Office issued letters on an "improvement in discharging explosive shells from balloons."[17] But the balloon service during the Civil War remained largely a civilian operation in support of a skeptical military. By 1863 the balloon corps was under the guidance of the Army Corps of Engineers. There it languished and fell into disuse even before the war ended. The use of balloons would be reprised under the auspices of the Army Signal Corps for the Spanish American War in 1898, but the intervening years had witnessed considerable experimentation in air machines—a shift from lighter-than-air to heavier-than-air. The need to hover was being supplanted by the desire to maneuver, and airships were being mechanized.

The year 1907 was a touchstone, albeit a tardy one, as an aeronautical division was established in the Army's Signal Corps. It was a bit overdue, given that it was four years after the Wright Brothers proved there was more to aeronautics than surveillance over hillsides. Dayton, Ohio's own Wright brothers supplied the aeronautical division with its first airplane on August 2, 1909— Signal Corps Airplane No.1. Not counting balloons and dirigibles, this single aircraft represented the sum total of America's aerial fleet for the first few years. The Army at this time had only three pilots, Lieutenants Frank Lahm, Fred Humphreys, and Ben Foulois, all largely self-taught.[18] Thus began America's military adventure in the air.

This early edition of the Air Force bounced around the Army Signal Corps for more than a decade, until just months before the 1918 cease fire in World War I. The value of air power was still viewed primarily as one of forward observation and reconnaissance, despite the appearance of French Spads, British Sopwith Camels, German Fokkers and American JN-4 "Jenny" aircraft, and pilots of the likes of Captain Eddie Rickenbacker and the Red Baron, Manfred von Richthofen.

During the 23 years of peacetime between the great wars, whether called a service or a corps, the nascent American Air Force acted as an organizational division of the Army. Even though it was not viewed as a combat arm, such as artillery or armor or infantry, the Army kept experimenting. In 1924 the Army Air Service attempted the first circumnavigation of the world by air. Douglas Aircraft modified four of its torpedo bomber models, confidently dubbed Douglas World Cruisers or DWCs, for the effort. Departing Seattle in April, two of the aircraft, those christened Chicago and New Orleans, completed the challenge with a homecoming in Seattle 175 days later. This was emblematic of the state of the art as the development of aircraft surged ahead far and wide during these years in a panoply of military and nonmilitary applications.

Aeronautics expanded to intercity air mail service with DeHavilland DH-4s and war-surplus Curtiss Jenny biplanes. It spread to interstate transportation of passengers, flown in single-engine, single-wing Douglas DC-2s. It encompassed international air travel with Pan American Airways and its Boeing-built China Clipper fleet leapfrogging islands to cross the Pacific. In time, the consequence of air force applied in combat situations was recognized and the Army Air Corps became the Army Air Forces in 1941 on the cusp of another World War.

The development of aviation followed that of the other weapon programs. This was especially true in taking to the air because, absent government funding, private industry would not have achieved so much so fast. Flying, as an industry during its fledging years, rested solely on the shoulders of a number of grand and fearless entrepreneurs and their machines. History would prove the leap to a larger stage could only be accomplished through government support.

The Army Air Force showed its mettle and proved its merit during World War II. American fighters and bombers sacrificed much to rule the skies and sweep the Luftwaffe from the landscape in the European theater. The delivery of the atom bomb proved to be the capstone event in the Pacific theater. World War II ended with two winners, one on the western front and one on the eastern. Emboldened by their victories, the United States and the Soviet Union were thus poised as the first superpowers. In the meantime, their industrial infrastructures were teetering.

In the United States, the rapid demobilization of the services left chaos—thousands of tons of surplus equipment with no organized effort to harness the resources. The new superpowers would soon settle in to familiar postures—the Soviets threatening a massive offensive and the United States pledging a catastrophic response. The atom bomb had changed everything.

During the 20 years leading up to VE-Day and VJ-Day, a number of men had worked to prepare for a time when the Air Force would vie for independence. General William "Billy" Mitchell was one of the early and most vociferous proponents of an independent Air Force, dating back to the 1920s. But it was the triad of senior staff officers Frank M. Andrews, Henry Harley Arnold, and George C. Marshall that made it happen. Andrews and Arnold did the work, and Marshall had the influence.

Frank Andrews gained the trust of Marshall through the years and rose to major general and command of the General Headquarters in the Air Corps. He laid much of the groundwork behind the scenes for an independent service. His unfortunate death in a 1943 crash in a Consolidated B-24 Liberator cut short his legacy. Henry "Hap" Arnold, who had been working toward the same ends and who would one day rise to become the only permanent five-star General of the Air Force, continued the quest for independence. Many feel that Arnold's agreement to not press for an independent Air Force during World War II is what facilitated its independence in 1947 with Army support.[19]

The enabling legislation was the National Security Act of 1947, creating an independent Air Force service branch of equal stature with the Army and Navy. This act essentially made permanent a prior Army Air Force arrangement that had set up the Strategic Air Command, Tactical Air Command and Air Defense Command, along with a number of support groups. The act also established the Department of Defense and Joint Chiefs of Staff. Stuart Symington was sworn in as the first secretary of the Air Force and General Carl Spaatz the first Air Force chief of staff.

The Navy did not believe an independent Air Force was needed. They felt carrier-based planes could reach most destinations and wanted their own fleet of bomber aircraft. The Army, on the other hand, was all for partition, since it was their service being promoted. To appease the Navy regarding separation, when the National Security Act of 1947 established the Defense Department and an independent Air Force, Navy Secretary James V. Forrestal was appointed the first secretary of defense.

But détente with the Navy would be short-lived. Eighteen months after creating the Office of the Secretary of Defense, President Truman removed Forrestal and replaced him with Louis A. Johnson.

With the need for post-war cuts in defense, Johnson promptly canceled the Navy's USS *United States* (CVA-58) aircraft carrier program. The Navy thought the Air Force, in building its strategic bombardment force, was cornering funds from Navy programs. Acting in spite, Navy insiders claimed the Air Force B-36 program had purchasing irregularities, which beget an inquiry.[20] The newly created Air Force service was already in a "he said, she said" contest with the Navy, setting the stage for future relations. While few were happy, an independent Air Force still needed to be assembled.

Men and material had to be extricated from the Army and transferred into the Air Force. The newly independent service had to vie with its sister services for missions and money. Each military service had to agree on individual responsibilities and had to coordinate operations. This would take time, years in some instances. This first United States Air Force was given the task of deterring a Soviet offensive, considered the next great threat to world peace. Delivery of nuclear weapons, early on under the Strategic Air Command, was a primary function. This was the temper, sometimes fractious and sometimes toxic, of the Air Force to which Ed Wynne would cross over in 1947.

❖

AT WEST POINT, Ed Wynne befriended a number of people. Upon graduation from the U.S. Military Academy in 1940, his circle of friends and acquaintances began to broaden. It started immediately. Although cadets were forbidden to be married while at West Point, a number of weddings occurred right after graduation.

That same week in June 1940 that Ed graduated, in fact on the day after, he stood up in New York City as best man for one of his friends from the Class of 1940. Lieutenant Henry H. Arnold Jr., son of Major General Henry "Hap" Arnold, chief of the Army Air Corps, was married to Beatrice Hickey at the Belmont Plaza Hotel on June 12. Along with Ed as best man, Second Lieutenants Frank Shawn, Marchant Woodward, Larry Klar, William Coleman, and William Clook attended as ushers.[21] These kinds of contacts would follow his career through the Air Force.

ONCE HE WRAPPED UP STUDIES at West Point, Second Lieutenant Wynne departed for 60 days to visit friends and family. Right in the middle of leave, on July 5, 1940, he received word of his first assignment, which happened to be temporary duty. He was ordered to report after leave to Governors Island, an Army garrison situated on a small land mass in upper New York bay just south of Manhattan and adjacent to South Brooklyn.

Dorothy and Ed Wynne leaving the church after their August 24, 1940, wedding ceremony. *Source:* Wynne Family.

Governors Island, with a history dating back to the American Revolutionary War, had become headquarters of the U.S. First Army in 1939. Ed's orders called for him to be stationed at that location until August 28, when a boat was scheduled to convey him to San Francisco on the way to final destination at Fort Lewis in Washington. But Ed had other, unfinished business.

With his brother Bill as best man, Ed married his East Bronx sweetheart, Dorothy Turbush, in New York City. Ed and Dot had met on February 11, 1939, a Friday, probably on a blind date when Dot came up from New York City to West Point with a friend. Ed was in his third year at the Military Academy. Ed and Dot were engaged the following year on March 30, 1940, and married on August 24. Ed's orders for boat passage to the west coast had included an alternative—the option of proceeding to Fort Lewis by privately owned vehicle. Awarded 21 days of detached service for travel, this would be their honeymoon.

The couple set off on a cross-country road trip via Niagara Falls to Ed's first active duty assignment. Ed had been commissioned

Once relocated to Washington state, the newlyweds settled into everyday life. Dorothy and Ed on November 3, 1940, leave home to go skating at nearby Lakewood Ice Arena on the shores of Lake Steilacoom. *Source:* Wynne Family.

a second lieutenant in the United States Signal Corps, U.S. Army, in June 1940, right on the edge of a changing world dynamic. Winston Churchill's storm was gathering in Europe, and everyone expected war to transform the military, as the balance shifted from a peacetime condition to a wartime footing. Civilian life would follow the change, with rationing and war bonds and women taking over the manufacturing work.

Fort Lewis was located on Pacific Coast Highway, halfway between Olympia and Tacoma in the state of Washington, roughly 2,900 miles from Governors Island. Grooming for hostilities, the garrison was in transition. Fort Lewis was home to the Army's Third Infantry Division, with the Forty-first Infantry soon to join. Tacoma Airfield, 10 miles north of Fort Lewis, had been transferred to the Army Air Corps in 1938 and subsequently renamed McChord Field. The Northwest Air District, charged with the responsibility for air defense of northwestern United States, was established in October 1940 at McChord Airfield. Ed Wynne arrived the following month.

Dorothy and Ed Wynne while stationed in the West. Note the Signal Corps branch insignia on Ed's collar.
Source: Wynne Family.

At Fort Lewis Ed completed Signal Corps training, much of the communications work revolving around the latest developments in radios and radars. His timing was perfect. He was a young, up-and-coming officer with a military specialty that would come of age during the war. He proudly sported the Signal Corps branch insignia of crossed signal flags. Ed's address during his stay at Fort Lewis was on American Lake, which bordered the original property of the fort and would become North Fort Lewis.

Ed went through advanced training and was organized into a detachment headed for Alaska—the edge of America. On February 19, 1941, Ed received orders making him the supply and transportation officer for the Signal Company, Aircraft Warning, Alaska-Fort Lewis Washington. Ed left for Alaska on March 10, just a week after the Third Infantry Division's Lieutenant Colonel Dwight Eisenhower made the grade to full colonel. Thus when Pearl Harbor exploded in the newspapers across America at the end of the year, Ed was on duty in Alaska.

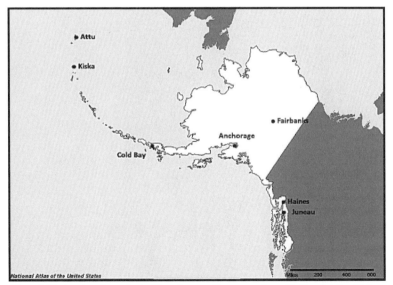

Map of Alaska showing select cities. *Source:* Base map from National Atlas Web site of the United States Department of the Interior. Reference cities added by author. www.nationalatlas.gov/mapmaker.

ALASKA, ON THE EVE OF WORLD WAR II, was still the frontier of the United States. At the end of the 1930s, the only real military presence in Alaska had been a barracks with a small detachment of men at Haines, about 50 miles north of Juneau.[22] Second Lieutenant Ed Wynne had been assigned to Alaska to help establish and operate radar stations. For a time, the young couple was stationed in Fairbanks, while Ed would travel where necessary on military assignments. First born son Patrick, all nine pounds eight ounces of him, took his first breath on October 8, 1941 in Anchorage, probably at the Fort Richardson base hospital, roughly 350 miles south of their quarters in Fairbanks.

AS HOSTILE FORCES from the land of the rising sun riveted world attention, the Wynne family would be on the move constantly during this period. Ed's wife, Dot, and their not quite four-month-old son, Pat, were evacuated out of Alaska; they traveled back to New York, arriving in February 1942. Meanwhile, Ed spent time working in radars in Cold Bay, Alaska, at the eastern end of the Aleutians, hundreds of miles southwest of Anchorage. A few months after Dot and Pat were evacuated, the Japanese began an operation in the western reaches of the 1,600-mile long Aleutian Island chain.

Whether a diversion related to their attack at Midway Island or a flanking maneuver to protect their homeland, the Japanese initiated the Aleutian campaign. Essentially undefended, it took but a small force of Japanese in June 1942 to overrun two little islands in the Aleutians. It would take thousands of American troops and more than a year to drive them out. At the height of this activity, Ed rotated out of Alaska in August and through a signal staff officers course at the Fighter Command School in Orlando, Florida. He was headed back to Alaska by the end of September.

Cold Bay was home to Fort Randall Army Air Base, built in 1941–42 with a 10,000-foot runway, the largest in Alaska at the time. That first year after Pearl Harbor, the war was in the balance and Alaska had a bit part to play in the overall scheme. Cold Bay would serve as a transportation hub and distribution center for many operations during World War II, and it supported the American effort in the Aleutians. While the temporary population at Cold Bay surged to 20,000 during the war, the 2000 U.S. Census tallied but 100 residents. The 10,000-foot runway remains today as an anchor for the surrounding area.

The Army did not have the officer uniform tradition shown by the Navy. Army colors evolved from the light blue trousers and dark blue coats of the Civil War to the light taupe trousers and dark yellow-green coats of World War II, familiarly called "pinks and greens," on the way to a standard dark gray-green uniform in 1954. Ed Wynne, still a part of the Army Air Forces, is shown in his "pinks and greens" circa 1944 at Selfridge Field in Michigan. *Source:* Wynne Family.

BESIDES WORKING IN AIR DEFENSE in Alaska, Ed also was assigned to a number of training centers and in the northeast during these early years. While posted to a training center in Florida, Drew Army Airfield, his second son, Michael, was born in Hillsborough County, Florida. Ed remained in the Signal Corps and by 1945 had reached the rank of major. His assignment was assistant chief of staff for the First Air Force for communications and electronics. He was stationed during this period up at Mitchel Field on Long Island. At the end of his duty assignment in the northeast, Ed was chosen a candidate for graduate school.

The mid-1940s was still an age when a college degree made someone stick out from the crowd. A graduate degree in those years really was something special. Major Wynne began his graduate studies in 1946 at the University of Michigan in Ann Arbor. In 1947 he received credits equivalent to completion of Advanced Signal Corps School and continued on at the Rackham School of Graduate Studies in the Department of Aeronautical Engineering. In 1948 he was awarded a master's degree in aeronautical engineering, having studied aerodynamics, electronics, design, and propulsion. His time in Ann Arbor spanned the spinoff of the Air Force from the Army. It also included the birth of his third child and first daughter, Maureen, on July 27, 1947.

Fresh out of his master's program at the University of Michigan in 1948 and slated to teach at West Point in the fall of 1949, Ed Wynne had a period of about 15 months when he was ineligible for any long-term duty assignment. As such, he served a number of short-term assignments during those months. The newly independent Air Force involved him in several teams, such as the evaluation of the Firebird air-to-air missile system and some of the research behind the site plan for the eastern range of the proposed missile test center in Florida. During this period, he worked out of the program offices at the old Sun Building in downtown Baltimore. This would be just his first tour through Baltimore.

COMBINING KNOWLEDGE IN ELECTRONICS AND PROPULSION, 30-year old Major Ed Wynne was thus on the leading edge of missile development. U.S. involvement in missiles, having essentially ignored most of the early work of Robert H. Goddard in the 1920s, only started in earnest with the acquisition of German expertise at the end of World War II. A number of small missile programs were then undertaken, with the Army and Navy competing to best each other. When the Air Force became an independent service in 1947, missile programs thought to be in their sphere of influence were transferred over, such as the Firebird air-to-air missile program. Ed became project engineer on the Firebird air launched system, part of the team mediating retention of the program.

Propulsion on the Firebird system had largely been figured out, as exemplified by the successful launch of a prototype in October 1947, before Ed joined the team. The real challenge was solving guidance, whether radio command or radar, and this played to Ed's strengths in radar and aerodynamics. Testing continued through 1949, but the program was eventually canceled, undoubtedly because it was a subsonic contender with a supersonic challenger on the horizon. While the Firebird could claim to be the first viable air-to-air system, credit for being the first operational one would fall to a missile eventually dubbed the Falcon.

THE QUEST TO ESTABLISH the first long-range missile test center was pressed as soon as World War II ended, in order to capitalize on the technology collected in the German V-1 and V-2 programs. A number of missile test centers existed in the 1940s, but each had its shortfalls. For example, the Army Air Force's White Sands Proving Ground in New Mexico was land-locked, and the U.S. Naval Air Missile Test Center at Point Mugu on the California coast was just 50 miles from Los Angeles.

In 1946 a development board under the Joint Chiefs of Staff had established a Committee on the Long-Range Proving Ground to evaluate potential sites for the desired missile test range. Three sites were selected in 1947: one in the state of Washington, with a range along the Aleutians; one in southern California, with a range along the Baja coastline; and one in Florida, with a range along the Atlantic Ocean.[23] When problems arose in 1948 with the first choice of California, the second choice of Florida rose to the fore.

Research into the appropriateness of utilizing the United States Navy's Banana River Naval Station and nearby Cape Canaveral was fleshed out. One surmises this is where Ed played a part in justifying location. Research showed that the cape protruded into the ocean a bit for safety, thousands of acres were available, the site was not close to highly populated areas, and the weather was generally favorable, especially since few hurricanes had been experienced in recent history. Many factors pointed to Cape Canaveral's suitability, and in May 1949 President Truman signed legislation that fixed the missile test center at the Cape in Florida.[24] By late 1949 Ed had been drawn back to New York to teach at his alma mater—the United States Military Academy.

THE YEARS 1949–52 saw Major Wynne teaching at West Point, helping develop the next generation of rocketeers and missileers. Some of his time was spent teaching ballistic trajectories, where classical physics ruled on the missile frontier. In this context, he rewrote West Point's instructional materials for *Ordnance*, a two-volume, loose-leaf textbook. Updated through the years, it would be in use well into the 1960s. The text itemized firing tables for the various Army artillery pieces, showing trajectory and distance for equipment all the way up to the larger 155 mm howitzers. Major Wynne also taught engineering materials and weapon systems engineering. His work influenced hundreds of cadets. During his years on the faculty, a number of cadets passed through the academy on their way to starring roles in space. Frank Borman '50, Buzz Aldrin '51, Ed White '52, and Michael Collins '52 all went on to serve as astronauts, after flying fighters for the United States Air Force.

While back on the Hudson River, Ed's second daughter and fourth child, Cathleen, was born on November 21, 1949. Ed also found time to help out his old lacrosse coach, F. Morris Touchstone, then in his 22nd year at Army. The lacrosse squads would have a record of 24 and 8 during the three years Ed helped with coaching, beating Navy all three years, and the 1951 squad rang up Army's fourth national championship in lacrosse, one shared with Princeton. Ed was the officer representative of the 1952 squad. The years passed quickly, and Ed readied to move on to his next slot. He ended his teaching assignment as instructor and assistant professor for armament engineering in the Department of Ordnance.

THE NEXT APPOINTMENT, spanning 1952–58, was at the Air Research and Development Command Headquarters, beginning in Baltimore and later moving to Andrews Air Force Base. Air Force Chief of Staff General Hoyt Vandenberg had just established the Air Research and Development Command two years earlier. World War II clearly illustrated that even though the Allies were victorious, the enemy had been working on weapons, such as guided missiles and jet propulsion, far in advance of Allied research capabilities. The new and separate research command was tasked with narrowing that gap, and research was to be consolidated under its aegis in 1951. Ed Wynne's appointment in 1952 showed how near the forefront he was in the youthful stages of the Air Force.

Early in this career move, Ed worked in the program offices concerned with helicopters and other light aircraft, such as target drones. With helicopters, the first useful single-rotor version didn't take to the air until 1939. Numerous improvements were rolled out in the ensuing years, such as Piasecki's H-21 Flying Banana which the Air Force first ordered in 1952. With remote-controlled target drones, it was a variation on the theme of guided missiles. Technology development in this area undoubtedly played a part in the advance to the smart cruise missiles seen today.

Ed's assignment progressed into administering much of the Air Force research and development program in nonnuclear aircraft weapons, warheads and fuzes for guided missiles. His titles reflected his work: deputy director for air weapons development and deputy chief, Air Weapons Division. During this period, Ed traded in his seven-pointed, gold-colored oak leaf for a silver one, that of a lieutenant colonel in the United States Air Force.

With his growing knowledge of weapons, Lieutenant Colonel Wynne was asked back to the Military Academy as a guest lecturer on Air Force ordnance activities. Ed put on a special lecture, limited to the top third of the first classmen, on May 21, 1957. He was accompanied by Colonel Norair Lulejian, who would later play a significant role in early planning of lunar landing craft.[25] Toward the end of Ed's assignment in Air Weapons, he was promoted to the pay grade of O-6, the senior field grade of colonel with a matching mirrored pair of silver eagles for his uniform.

IN WHAT WOULD BE THE CAPSTONE ASSIGNMENT of a 22-year military career, Colonel Ed Wynne was appointed director of range development at the Air Force Missile Test Center headquartered at Patrick Air Force Base. The Air Force intended the range to facilitate testing and development of strategic missiles, including versions of the intercontinental ballistic missile (ICBM), the nuclear deterrent. In the same year, President Eisenhower authorized the creation of the National Aeronautics and Space Administration (NASA). The goal of NASA was human space flight. This was the time when the possibilities in space were beginning to be understood by the public and to be funded by the government.

This period also marked the height of the rivalry between the Army and the Air Force over ballistic missiles and space. The Army had organized its research around the von Braun group. The Air Force, on the other hand, did most of its development work through various subcontractors in a program headed up by General Bernard Schriever. This was an active period in ballistic missile research for each of the service branches.

The Army had its Redstone, Jupiter-C, and Saturn; the Air Force had its Atlas, Thor/Delta, and Titan; the Navy even chipped in with its Viking, Vanguard, and Polaris. Both the Air Force and the new civilian agency NASA vied to acquire the Army's rocket capability. The Air Force thought the Army should stay out of space and focused on ground combat. NASA wanted the Army's expertise because it had no rocket development center of its own, and it needed to make human space flight a reality. In the end, the Army transferred its ballistic missile capability to NASA, in large part to avoid giving it to the Air Force.[26] The Air Force helped move the Army out of the space program but missed getting the von

Braun group for itself. This was the competitive climate in which Colonel Wynne began working in range development.

Whether used for military ordnance or human exploration, the missile test range needed a system to track performance. Tracking stations were essential along the flight path to facilitate guidance and navigation from launch command. Having room for error also was necessary since America's first satellite launch exploded seconds after lift-off. On the cusp of a space race, testing and development of missiles required monitors along the range.

Both the Russian launch of Sputnik in October 1957 and the failed American effort with Vanguard that December, predate the establishment of a complete network of tracking stations along the Air Force missile range. When the U.S. launched a Jupiter-C rocket with the satellite Explorer I aboard in January 1958, scientists could not know it was successful until it completed an orbit, circling the Earth and coming back into view. Not enough tracking stations were in place to confirm orbit, engine shutdown, and separation of stages.[27] The network was incomplete.

Besides a central tracking station at Cape Canaveral, a second had been built down the Florida coast at Jupiter, to aid in guiding early missile launches. The first island-based tracking station, at Grand Bahama Island, was operational in 1954. With the original goal of seven tracking locations, resembling pearls strung along a necklace, stations had been constructed on the islands of Eleuthera, San Salvador, Mayaguana, and Grand Turk. By 1955 missiles could be followed as far as the existing technology, roughly 700 miles. It would take a larger network of sites to cover the whole length of the 5,000 mile range and eventually to circle the earth.

Ed Wynne arrived at Patrick Air Force Base and Cape Canaveral in 1958.[28] He encountered competing demands for tracking and data acquisition, civilian pressure through NASA, and military emphasis through the Department of Defense in the form of the Air Force. Ed was in the advance guard of expanding and completing the network of military tracking stations, locating and managing the sequence to suit the military goals of the country. With much of the missile range work contracted to a division of Pan American

Airways, subcontractor RCA Services operated and maintained the actual tracking and telemetry equipment. Colonel Wynne oversaw the engineering and planning aspects of the range contractor. What resulted was a progression of islands and ships across an expanse of 5,000 miles, cobbled together as a series of reporting stations.[29]

In due course, a perfect alliance of wants and wishes emerged. With much overlap and parallel work between the civilian and military organizations, NASA and the Air Force eventually forged interagency cooperation for their launch and tracking work. The Air Force test center and the NASA launch operations coalesced at Cape Canaveral in 1962, although not without a suitable amount of interagency squabbling in the ensuing years. Right about the time that NASA fixed its launch operations at Cape Canaveral, 44-year-old Colonel Wynne retired from the Air Force but not from missiles and the space program. His career continued with General Electric as manager of the Apollo Support Program.

THE CONTEST TO LAND the first man on the moon was of great consequence to an entire generation, a challenge led by President Kennedy and followed by his successor President Johnson. By 1962 Project Mercury was shaping up as a resounding success, and Project Gemini was coming together on the drawing boards, although it would be plagued by cost overruns and technical difficulties. The year 1962 also saw the second group of astronauts selected. Since the envisioned Apollo Project was the linchpin, NASA began making changes.

In late 1961 NASA announced its first director of manned space flight, Brainerd Holmes. Shortly thereafter General Electric was contracted to perform reliability and quality assurance studies on the Apollo Program spacecraft and booster. This marked the beginning of an assessment role by General Electric in the Apollo Program, which would evolve into the hiring of scores of people. Bringing particular knowledge and experience to the work, Ed was offered a position. He began with General Electric's support engineering area and progressed into its advanced engineering in support of the Manned Lunar Landing Program.

Ed stayed with the Apollo Support Program long enough to see the first man land on the moon—Neil Armstrong in 1969. Through his work with tracking stations for the Air Force and Apollo support at General Electric, Ed had a hand in the first three programs to launch humans into space: Project Mercury from 1959–63 with six manned flights, Project Gemini from 1963–66 with 10 manned flights, and Project Apollo from 1961–72 with 11 manned flights.[30]

Ed's retirement from active business coincided with the end of the Apollo Program. It was time to turn over the reins to a younger, even better-educated generation of engineers and scientists. Those who followed would advance moon shots to space stations, such as the Air Force effort with a manned orbital laboratory and the NASA effort with Skylab. After space stations, it would be space shuttles which were reusable orbital spacecraft. Although not a pilot himself, Ed certainly was one of the pioneers in the Air Force with a career spanning the creation of an independent Air Force and the landing of the first man on the moon. As he left the field, the spotlight focused on a new generation, one that included his sons.

CHAPTER THREE

Pat Wynne's Air Force

THE BOYS DID NOT FEEL PRESSURE from their father to go into the military but just the same it was something they knew from childhood. Their choices paralleled many other teenagers who followed their fathers into business or the sciences. Some become doctors because their dads are doctors. Some become businessmen or lawyers because that is what they watched their father do for a living. For the Wynnes, their dad was a career military man, an Air Force officer. Following his footsteps wasn't encouraged or discouraged nor would it be easy, but it did seem to be a natural progression.

First-born Patrick was always a good student. From an early age, he wanted to track his father in the Air Force. By the time Pat was ready to begin his quest, an alternative existed to the United States Military Academy. The building of an Air Force Academy while Pat was in high school did nothing but fan his desire to fly. He saw the opportunity to join the Air Force and be in one of the early classes to graduate from the new academy. Thus, the die was set for Pat and the Air Force Academy.

❦

THE ENABLING LEGISLATION to create the United States Air Force Academy was passed on April 1, 1954. The academy opened in temporary quarters the following year at Lowry Air Force Base outside Denver, Colorado. The Class of 1959 was the inaugural group of students. The academy achieved formal accreditation as an educational institution before this founding class graduated. Operations at the academy's newly constructed permanent facilities began in 1959, as instruction to the Class of 1963 commenced. All of this was some 50 years in the making.

For a long time, it was questionable whether a separate Air Force Academy was needed. In the past, a portion of the officer requirements for the air service had been fulfilled by West Point and Annapolis, the Army and Navy academies respectively. As the demand for aviation officers intensified and the technology of the air specialty matured, the means for becoming a flying officer evolved with the times and the need for a separate academy became more understandable.

In the beginning, flying instruction had been informal. In fact, many civilians trained by local aero clubs became military pilots. The buildup for World War I and aviation expenditures by Russia, France, and Germany spurred growth in this new dimension for warfare. Early ground schools were established at major American universities such as Massachusetts Institute of Technology and the Universities of Illinois and Texas in 1917. Flying instruction was carried on at fields such as those built at Dayton, Ohio, and Rantoul, Illinois. While interest in an Air Service was building, World War I ended before air power could prove its value. Thus, little support existed for an independent service and even less for a separate training school.

Demobilization after World War I did not favor the Air Service. Responsibility for the Air Service remained in the Army but transitioned from being under the Signal Corps into a separate combatant section of the Army. The Army Reorganization Act of 1920 set the postwar Army at 280,000. Of that total, Section 13a of the act called for the Air Service to have only 1,516 officers and 16,000 enlisted men, of which 2,500 could be flying cadets. Even though these numbers grew during the next two decades, it took another world war to reframe the needs and wants.[31]

Between the great wars, the development of aviation came in

fits and starts. While the names of the experimenters and tinkerers who gave birth to the industry faded, such as Curtiss and Langley and the Wrights, the follow-on generation of William Boeing, Donald Douglas, Leroy Grumman, Allan and Malcolm Lockheed, Glenn Martin, James McDonnell, Jack Northrop, and others rose to take their place. Through mergers, acquisitions, bankruptcies and breakups, these individuals would define and redefine aviation.

The importance of air power was proved during World War II as Army Air Force operations rose to a larger stage. The air dimension played a defining role in winning the war, and this field experienced substantial growth in doing so. But growth in air operations was brought about through temporary war powers, rather than legislation. It needed permanence to avoid being weakened in the next round of demobilization. In the end, establishing a separate school for aviation training had to wait for the independence of the Air Service itself, which occurred in 1947. Activity to establish an aviation academy continued to grind away in the background.

Aviation training had evolved from the flying cadet program of World War I to the aviation cadet program of World War II. Neither means of aviation instruction required a college degree. Most of the college-degreed officers came from the military academies or the Air Force Reserve Officer Training Corps program, initiated in the 1920s. The ever-increasing role of technology in flying, not the least of which was the advent of jet propulsion, caused Air Force leadership in the early 1950s to make a college degree a prerequisite for future officers. Supplying officers to this much larger, post–World War II Air Force became a problem. West Point and Annapolis could not supply enough and still provide for their own services. The final puzzle pieces fell into place.

The Korean War ran its course, and Dwight Eisenhower replaced Harry Truman as president. Aircraft evolved from propeller-driven to jet-powered. Strategic bombardment rose to the fore of deterrence. The technological challenges and possibilities of aviation were clear. These factors favored defense expenditures. In the final analysis, a separate aviation academy was needed if the new Air Force was to be controlled by aviation officers. The need rose to center stage, and site selection efforts were put in motion.

From a prospect list exceeding 500 locations, 67 were inspected by a site committee. Site selection eventually narrowed to three: Alton, Illinois; Lake Geneva, Wisconsin; and Colorado Springs, Colorado. Politics, price, and public support would each weigh heavily in the final choice. Illinois Senator Everett Dirksen and Missouri Senator Stuart Symington favored Alton while Wisconsin Senator Joseph McCarthy was expected to lean toward Lake Geneva. Colorado Springs did not have a staunch political patron. The expense of land acquisition favored Colorado Springs, where an estimated cost of $2.15 million easily trumped quotes of $12.28 million for Lake Geneva and $18.75 million for Alton.[32] Because the Alton and Lake Geneva sites were closer to heavily populated areas, public opinion rallied against locating the proposed academy in those areas. Thus, Colorado Springs became the site of the new Air Force Academy.

In 1955 aviation instruction began with a nucleus of 306 cadet airmen. This formalized the training of aviation science that was differentiated from the military science of the Army and the naval science of the Navy. The new academy was patterned after the West Point approach to discipline and honor, including a similar congressional nomination and appointment system. The Air Force vision was a four-year college blending a broad offering of challenging academics with specialized training in military art and science, grounded in a focus on leadership and character development. As members of the service academy for the Air Force, cadets were exposed to facets of airmanship—soaring, parachuting, and powered flight. Pat Wynne started in 1959 and graduated as part of the Class of 1963. His class was the fifth to graduate and the first to have gone through all four years of instruction in the permanent facilities in Colorado Springs. The 1963 graduates proudly considered themselves the true first class of the Air Force Academy.

❧

WHILE FIRST YEARS were called plebes at West Point, at the Air

Force Academy they were "doolies." Pat's first three years on the ramparts in Colorado Springs changed the boy into a man. His nickname was "Pew," based simply on his initials. Gregarious and charming, Pat's circle of acquaintances grew each year. He ended up the editor of the school magazine and became well known within the cadet wing.

In January 1962, half way through his third year at the academy, Pat was fixed up on a blind date by his classmate, Jim Martin. It was with a young lady named Nancy, who attended Loretto Heights College, a Catholic women's college in nearby Denver. Their first date was to one of the coffee shops in Denver, probably the Exodus Cafe where many couples started relationships. It was a coffee house that served nothing stronger than beer but was a wonderful place to hear some of the emerging stars on the 1960s folk music scene, such as 21-year-old Joan Baez who had released her first album just 18 months earlier.

Pat was sometimes called "Happy," because of his spirit and his way of meeting everything with a smile. He could charm anyone, and most everyone loved him. Pat liked nothing better than the opportunity to show off a bit and had many occasions to do just that, displaying his piano-playing skills. He was the outgoing type, which fed into his debate skills and piano playing. He also had an Elvis impersonation he worked at perfecting. All in all, Patrick was a thoroughly charming individual.

Five months after their blind date, Pat and Nancy were still an item. One of the highlights of the social activities during the June Week 1962 graduation at the academy was the formal ball for second classmen, the Ring Dance. This was where the cadets, who would be rising to first classmen the following year, danced their way through a replica of the class ring with their partners. Pat and Nancy did just that. The two were falling in love.

Pat spent weeks of the summer before his senior year receiving pilot indoctrination. The students would pair up with rated pilots and have the opportunity to fly the back seat of jet aircraft. This was a thrill for those that wanted to become pilots but also necessary for the academy men who had to catch up to their Air Force Reserve

Officer Training Corps mates who were a bit ahead of them in this respect.

Arguably Pat's best friend at the academy was a fellow cadet who was catching up on a path of a different kind. Locked in the moment deep in the middle of the African American civil rights movement, the early Air Force Academy was making a push to be more inclusive with its student body. Enter Charles Bush. In

The *Rocky Mountain News* made Air Force Academy business part of its social beat. The newspaper attended the 1962 Ring Dance at the end of Pat Wynne's third year, where outgoing juniors had the opportunity to give a replica of their senior class rings to their girlfriends. Pat and his friend, Nancy Opalinski, proceed through the giant mockup of the class ring during June Week of 1962. The photo appeared in the newspaper the following day. *Source: Rocky Mountain News* photograph by Bob Talkin, courtesy of Denver Public Library, Western History Collection. Reprinted with permission.

1954 at age 14, Chuck Bush had been selected the first African American page on Capitol Hill by recently appointed Chief Justice Earl Warren.[33] The Warren court was active in civil rights matters and had passed the *Brown v. Board of Education* case that same year. Chuck Bush went on to be among the first African American cadets at the Air Force Academy. Chuck and Pat made a formidable team in speech contests and developed a grand friendship working together in a variety of venues.

The 1962–63 school year would be Pat's last and filled with events. The first classmen gave the orders, and the doolies did what they were told. The academy dedicated its new stadium, and General Jimmy Stewart was there to emcee. Louis "Satchmo" Armstrong and Carlos "Fingers" Montoya performed on the academy stage. On field trips and football games, the academy traveled to Dallas,

Patrick Edward Wynne in his official graduation photo from the United States Air Force Academy in 1963.
Source: United States Air Force Academy photo published in Fullerton, *1963 Polaris*, p. 259.

Texas, for a victorious match against Southern Methodist University. Back in Colorado Springs, the winter sports played on for months. Visitors to the academy included stand-up comedian Bob Newhart, Secretary of State Dean Rusk, and the cadets from the Royal Air Force College at Cranwel. In due course June Week 1963 arrived.

Graduation from the United States Air Force Academy was a week-long project. On Friday, May 31st, it was the Athletic Awards Banquet. Saturday, June 1st, brought the Organizational Awards Parade Review, followed by the Cadet Dance in Arnold Hall. Sunday, June 2nd, was Baccalaureate Services in the chapel. Monday encompassed the Individual Awards Ceremony and the Ring Dance for seniors-to-be. Tuesday brought the Tapping Ceremony, Open House, and Graduation Parade. Wednesday, June 5th, capped the entire week with the official graduation exercises in Falcon Stadium. Through all, Patrick proved to have excelled in his four years at the academy.

At the Individual Awards Ceremony, the academy gave out 40 awards to 30-some individual students for their particular

Pictured at the individual awards ceremony held in Arnold Hall are (left to right) John Elfers, Kent Harbaugh, Sam Westbrook, Patrick Wynne, and Glen Rowell. *Source:* United States Air Force Academy photo published in Fullerton, *1963 Polaris,* p. 81.

excellence. Pat was one of five students who were multiple-award winners. Patrick received the Major General James E. Fechet Award for intercollegiate speech and the Captain Earl N. Findley Award as editor-in-chief of the *Talon*, the academy's monthly. The other four multiple-award winners were Sam Westbrook III and Kent Harbaugh, with three each, and John Elfers and Glen Rowell, with two each. Of the five, four became pilots and one a navigator. Four of the five would serve in Vietnam.

ONCE OUT OF THE AIR FORCE ACADEMY in June 1963, Pat married his sweetheart, Nancy Opalinski. Pat's best man was his brother, Mike, who was just finishing up his first year of college, a skinny plebe at the Military Academy. The family memory of the wedding was Mike passing out in the chapel during the ceremony, partially due to not eating enough at West Point and partially due to the fact that the small Spanish mission-style church was not air conditioned. But it remained an auspicious start for Pat and Nancy.

The Wynne family gathers for a picture outside Pauline Chapel in Colorado Springs on Pat's wedding day on June 6, 1963. Left to right, Cathy, Maureen, Michael, Patrick, Mom, and Dad, with little brothers, Steve and Peter, in front. *Source:* Wynne Family.

Pat and Nancy had been a couple ever since their blind date, and they seemed to be following the pattern set by others. Nancy started college with about 350 girls in her class. Nancy dropped out to marry Pat and begin a life together. It seems many others did also, as only about 60 of the 350 young women would remain all four years and graduate with a degree. Many ended up marrying cadets down the road at the Air Force Academy. For several such as Nancy, this was their first exposure to a military life.

Nancy had been born and raised in northern Minnesota, in Crosby to be exact. If one conjured up the movie *Fargo*, one would instantly recognize Crosby, all the way down to the "you betcha." Crosby was a small city of but 2,000 residents situated in the middle of the Cuyuna Range, a series of underground iron ore mines, southwest of the larger Mesabi Iron Range. It was about 100 miles from either Duluth or Minneapolis, both to the east. Nancy's mom and dad were the old-fashioned, midwestern housewife and businessman. None of her family had background in the military service.

Pat and Nancy were married in Pauline Chapel and welcomed to married life with a reception at the nearby Broadmoor Hotel in Colorado Springs. They began their journey together with tons of friends and ounces of money. Their honeymoon essentially was driving around the Great Plains in their old Chevrolet Corvair. But if anything would substitute as a honeymoon, soon after getting married Pat and Nancy drove up to her parent's home in Crosby. Her parents threw a second wedding reception, with approximately 300 people showing up for the event. Then with little to no time for themselves, they packed up an assortment of used furniture from Nancy's parents and headed out for Georgetown University in Washington, D.C., still driving the high-mileage Chevy Corvair.

NEWLY COMMISSIONED, GRADUATED AND MARRIED, and all of 21 years old, these were days of discovery for Pat, untroubled and full of exploration. Their honeymoon driving around the prairies and grasslands of America, which had fit their budget to a tee, was over, and Pat was off to his first duty assignment. Following the custom of the service academies, ranking in a high enough percentile of the class earned one the privilege of being able to attend graduate school as the first active duty assignment. So it was for Pat, who graduated with the Order of Merit of 60 out of a class of 499.

Pat's standing at the Air Force Academy was high enough that he earned entrance into the Air Force's one-year wonder program, and the young couple headed for Washington and Georgetown University. With but a fortnight of free time, the students came directly from the Air Force Academy and started right in on two consecutive summer sessions. An additional quarter of classroom studies followed, yielding enough credits for a degree, once a master's thesis was submitted and accepted. A number of academy graduates chose graduate school as their initial assignment.

Fifteen second lieutenants came from the Air Force Academy to Georgetown University in the summer of 1963, including Pat's debate partner, Chuck Bush. The others were Pete Hammerton, Kent Harbaugh, Doug Hardgrave, Bob Heavner, Bob Kennedy, Owen Lentz, John Nehring, Bill Olson, Bob Parra, Ed Pickens, Dan Taylor, Harry Wilson, and Al Wolf, representing at least 11 different states and the District of Columbia.[34]

Pat and Nancy settled in an apartment just across the street from the Marine Corps' Iwo Jima memorial. This was on the west side of the Potomac River in Arlington, Virginia. A richly historic area, Arlington National Cemetery was located just to their south. Since no buildings obstructed the view, on a clear day looking straight east from the Marine Corps remembrance, the Wynnes could see the Lincoln Memorial across the Potomac, the Washington Monument on the other side of West Potomac Park, and down the National Mall to the Capitol building in the distance. Washington during the 1963–64 school year was a time of relative peace and calm in world affairs but full of sadness for the country.

President John F. Kennedy was assassinated in the fall of 1963, and the entire nation mourned the loss. Pat and Nancy were in Washington as Kennedy's successor, Lyndon B. Johnson, rose to power. It would be some time before President Johnson began the escalation of hostilities in Southeast Asia that would envelop so many of the nation's young adults. It would be a few more years before antiwar sentiments and civil rights demonstrations would rock the area. Pat's time in the nation's capital made for a nice graduate college experience, even though it entailed working through an accelerated course load at Georgetown. For Nancy's part, she kept busy and out of their small apartment with a job selling gloves at the Hecht's department store.

Pat had always been interested in a wide variety of subjects and activities that one might call eclectic. In high school he played both athletics and music, and excelled inside the classroom with his slide rule and outside school on the state champion debate team. His days at the Air Force Academy saw his interests swing from the sciences and mathematics to politics and law, but he also made time to display his intercollegiate speech prowess. At Georgetown Pat studied international affairs and by spring 1964, not yet one year out of the academy, he was almost ready to graduate. One hurdle remained.

The academic rigor at Georgetown was high. The students were pushed along a faster track and still had to complete an acceptable master's paper. For Pat, an excellent student in his own right, this would prove to be a stumbling block. He had expected to hand in the thesis at the end of the winter quarter, leave Georgetown, and head for a March start at Williams Air Force Base for pilot training. It didn't work out that way as his paper was not accepted when first submitted. So Pat had a slight delay as he applied a bit more of his time and talent to the tension of the master's thesis. His second go at acceptance flew through. His 150-page thesis, *The Republic of the Congo: nationbuilding before and after United Nations intervention*, was accepted for publication.

Pat graduated with a master's degree in international relations. With his first duty assignment now history, it was time for his next—fulfilling his dream of becoming a pilot. Only the best ever had the chance, and Pat's next challenge was earning his wings. Having slipped only a few weeks off schedule with the thesis glitch, Pat was able to join the following class at Williams. While two classmates from the academy, one following Georgetown and one following

Purdue, made Class 65-F, Pat was right behind them in Class 65-G. Pat and Nancy drove the 2,300 miles from Washington to Mesa, Arizona, in their oil-burning, butt-ugly brown Chevrolet Corvair.

PAT'S MOVE FROM ACADEMICS TO AVIATION occurred shortly after the Air Force revamped its pilot training. In prior years, aviation instruction had been split among 13 facilities, six equipped with primary aircraft and seven with the more-advanced basic trainers. To accommodate the influx of pilot cadets and the all-jet future, the Air Force changed over to eight single bases, each of which covered both phases of training.[35] From 1962 on the primary and basic training occurred at the same facility, so the students simply changed aircraft. This was the aviation education scenario Pat joined.

Leaving Georgetown, Pat and Nancy headed cross country to Williams Air Force Base, located south and east of the Phoenix-Scottsdale area in Arizona. "Willie" had been the site of Air Training Command since the formation of an independent Air Force service and routinely supplied one-quarter of the Air Force's requirement for pilots. Willie's role was general, undergraduate pilot training. With the Vietnam conflict on the horizon, pilot training had been split into general and specialized phases. All students received the same standard instruction using trainer aircraft. Once completed, newly minted pilots would move to other bases to gain specialized training in the operational aircraft to which they were to be assigned. Pat arrived in Arizona in April 1964.

Williams Air Force Base was home to the 3525th Pilot Training Wing, which had begun operations on the first of October in 1960. The 3525th Wing was organized into two squadrons for training, the 3525th and 3526th Pilot Training Squadrons. Pat was assigned to the 3525th Squadron. His undergraduate pilot training class expected to complete the one-year of training in May 1965.[36]

The group started right in on the 55-week course, seeing who would make it and who would drop by the wayside. It began with ground school, three weeks in the classroom and unremitting physical training. The first hurdles were the altitude chamber, simulating the high-altitude effects of low oxygen and low pressure, followed by the boom bucket, famous for its instant acceleration. The students had yet to leave the ground but were starting to feel as if they had. They began learning the academics of the aircraft. Emergency procedures were covered as were local area restrictions, what areas to avoid. The relentless physical training claimed the first wash out of 65-G.

Class 65-G had started on April 23, 1964, with 43 students, 34 Americans and 9 Germans. Having German students exhibited how far America had come in 20 short years, from a world at war to training former enemies. The German student pilots were a split delegation, some from the Luftwaffe and some from the Federal German Navy. In the typical class, the washout rate ranged between 20 and 30 percent. But then, washout rates differed among the routes taken to undergraduate pilot training.

One study showed that less than 7 percent of the Air Force Academy graduates washed out of pilot training. For those students that had been commissioned into the Air Force through Officer Candidate School, the attrition rate in pilot training was more than 50 percent. Those who arrived through the Aviation Cadet Program washed out at a 42 percent rate. For Air Force Reserve Officer Training Corps program cadets, if they received some flight indoctrination before moving on to pilot training, the washout rate was less than 16 percent; if not, the rate was almost 38 percent.[37] Preparation was comprehensive and competitive.

The starting class of 43 was divided up, 22 students assigned to the 3525th Pilot Training Squadron and 21 to the 3526th Squadron. Student pilots could wash out during any part of the training, starting with physical training and working through all the advanced stages. Once through the maze of preliminaries, the students actually had the opportunity to have a few flying lessons, in between briefings and training sessions in the Link simulator. The students were itching to fly, and in time would operate two different jet trainers.[38]

The primary trainer was the small, twin-jet Cessna T-37 Tweety Bird or Tweet, for short. The T-37 had a two-seat, side-by-side cockpit arrangement which facilitated training. The aircraft had a service ceiling of 25,000 feet and a maximum speed of 425 miles per hour. Students racked up 125 hours in the T-37 over the first six months learning their way. Most of the washouts occurred during the primary phase of training. During this time, the students' day was usually split among physical training, classroom work, and actual seat time in the trainer.

In the classroom the focus was the study of visual flight rules, in the air they began piling up the hours in the T-37. The classroom emphasis shifted to weather phenomena for a few weeks, accompanied by more lessons in the T-37. Within 45 days of initial training, the students had soloed in the Tweet. Then it was back in the classroom for instrument flight rules and the beginning of navigation. As the hot summer days eased into the cooler mornings of fall, flying time in the T-37 became more pleasant with the moderating temperatures. The students finished primary training on October 26, 1964, and segued right into basic training, in the T-38.

The basic trainer was the Northrop T-38 Talon. The T-38 was the first supersonic jet trainer, full afterburners and more difficult to control. With one-behind-the-other seating, the twin-jet T-38 had a service ceiling of 50,000 feet and flew faster than the speed of sound, twice the speed of the T-37. This performance made the area and altitude restrictions even more important. The students didn't know it when they first checked out their new g-suit gear, which helped them sustain the higher rates of acceleration force, but they were starting to stampede up the learning curve. They began in the basic trainer with their "dollar ride," a tradition where the student pilots' first hop was not graded in exchange for handing the instructor a single dollar bill. But to give the trainees time to learn, the priority during this early phase of instruction was flying the gauges from the back-seat. They would solo out of the T-38 before Christmas.

Back from Christmas break, students finished up learning instruments, which were harder than they expected. Then it was formation flying, with the added twist of low-level missions. Solo operations back and forth to San Diego started to build confidence, right when the wrinkle of night flying was introduced. After 125 hours training in the T-38, student pilots were ready for any type of aircraft. All told, undergraduate training encompassed roughly 250 hours in two types of jet aircraft during a 13-month period in the hot sun of the Sonoran Desert.[39] Pat loved his life.

PAT AND NANCY lived in an apartment west of the base in downtown Chandler, Arizona. They had welcoming hearts and often invited some of the other student-pilots to their place when the social scene moved out of the Officers' Club. Of Pat's squadron class of 22, only three men were bachelors, and Pat and Nancy went out of their way to share a meal with them, especially during the holidays.

The three bachelors spent Thanksgiving 1964 with the Wynnes, and the five of them did their part to add to the lore of Willie. The three flying solo arrived for Thanksgiving with the beverage du jour. Not to be caught short, they showed up with a garbage can full of ice and champagne for the celebration. Among the five of them, one or the other remembered to check in on the turkey coming along in the oven every now and then. Forty-five years later the memory of that Thanksgiving and other home-cooked meals with the Wynnes still bring a smile to the faces of Second Lieutenants John NePage, Mac Armstrong, and Bill Koelm.

AS AN INDEPENDENT COMMUNITY, members of the pilot training class also had their fun and fears. For leisure, the students often played soccer, in spite of the Arizona heat. They were sure to always split up the German students in these soccer games, even amounts to each side to keep things fair. Soccer was much bigger in Germany than the States in the 1960s. As to anxiety, some were concerned that they would not make it, that they would wash out even as they neared the final stages.

One of the bachelors, Bill Koelm, was tall and always worried about his seating height. If a student had a seating height in excess of 36 inches or so, they could not fly fighters. Even though Bill had not flown in an airplane until he arrived at Williams, he was hooked and wanted to become a pilot. It was rumored Bill always scrunched down when he was measured.

When it came to pilot training, Pat was as enthusiastic as anyone and wanted to secure the most out of the experience. He was competitive with his classmates but unfalteringly courteous and friendly. One of his friends in training at Williams Air Force Base was a comparably personable African American, First Lieutenant Don Stewart. Pat and Don were serious about their profession and both became pilots, but if a prank was going on somewhere, one or both of them was probably involved.

OF COURSE, AS OFTEN HAPPENS, some of the most interesting events were not documented, but that was advantageous for then no one had to come up with explanations. For Pat, it was on an exercise during primary training. The assignment in question was to take a lengthy trip in the T-37, along with the instructor pilot, to another air base. The task was to fly to the determined destination, lay over the night, and then fly back the next morning. All the details were to be worked out by the student pilot, picking any base they wanted to visit and determining the flight plan. The essence of the exercise was for the student pilot to find his way there and find his way back. Pat chose Buckley Air Force Base, then called Buckley Air National Guard Base.

Buckley was located just east of Aurora, Colorado, and about 10 miles outside of Denver. This area anchors the Colorado Front Range, just off the foothills of the Rocky Mountains. To the north was Fort Collins and Greeley, while to the south was Colorado Springs and Pueblo. The climate in the region was mild and dry, for the most part. With an elevation of 5,471 feet above sea level and some 300 days of sunshine a year, the locale promoted itself as the Gateway to the Rockies. Buckley Field had gone through a number of iterations since its construction by the U.S. Army Air Forces in 1943.

After the Army Air Forces in 1943, Buckley was designated an auxiliary field of nearby Lowry Air Field as World War II came to an end. It subsequently was turned over to the Colorado Air National Guard and within a year transferred to the U.S. Navy and labeled the Denver Naval Air Station. In 1959 control was handed over to the U.S. Air Force. Buckley quickly became the home of the Colorado Air National Guard once again. The Air National Guard would stay 40-some years. It was during the Air National Guard's tenure that Pat decided he would fly his out-and-back exercise to its field. He undoubtedly wanted to fly in that direction because the route would take him over his Air Force Academy in Colorado Springs on the way to Buckley.

No one quite remembers the particulars, but on takeoff or landing at Buckley, Pat and his instructor had somewhat of an adventure. Maybe mishap was a fairer description. Nothing serious, as far as anything while airborne can be considered trifling. It was comparable to a mid-air fender bender. No personnel hurt and no reportable damage to the aircraft, but one way or another Pat's T-37 and someone else's T-38 clipped each other in-flight. Part of the problem was the T-37 was such a small plane. It was often hard to see. The T-37 and T-38 came too close, and by the time the pilots did see each other, their emergency maneuvers prevented a serious collision and kept it to a bump in the air.

The event was alluded to in the class book for 65-G, where each new pilot had an official graduation picture with a quip about his time at Williams. Pat's write-up couldn't help but hint at the Buckley tale.

> Hard working classbook staffer, shoe shine boy, and would be golfer from Florida. Made most enemies by assigning flight duties. "A funny thing happened to me on the way to Denver." Given Diner's Club Award for cleanest snack bar east of Norton's Corner.

In the end, Pat and the bachelors made it through pilot training, mastering the rudiments of pitch, bank, and power. They pinned on their silver wings in a ceremony on May 13, 1965. Pat's military occupational specialty was now 1111R, one of the codes designating a pilot. The graduation highlight was a spectacular air show put on by the famous World War II combat pilot and prisoner of war Bob Hoover, flying his mustard-yellow North American P-51 Mustang.

The three bachelors were promoted to first lieutenant shortly after graduation. Pat, already a first lieutenant because of his time at graduate school, was on to advanced training.

Pat appears in front of a T-38 trainer in his yearbook photo when he graduated from pilot training at Williams Air Force Base. *Sources:* United States Air Force photo published in Young et al., *Class Book 65-G*; Wynne Family.

At this point, Pat and the others knew where they were headed. For Pat, it was to the 40th Tactical Fighter Squadron of the 33rd Tactical Fighter Wing stationed at Eglin Air Force Base. But two matters had to be handled first, one personal and one military. With pilot's pay pushing their income, Pat and Nancy treated themselves after he earned his wings. The couple stayed with Chevrolet but traded in their beat-up, brown Corvair for a shiny-new, flaming-red convertible Corvette, priced at a bit more than $4,000.

The 1964 model year represented the second generation Corvette, and was the first to sport the Sting Ray insignia. The only engine option was the 327 cubic inch V-8. Now Pat had the sport's car style to match his pilot's wings panache. If he wanted, Pat could drive down the street with a scarf trailing in the wind reminiscent of Snoopy the fighter pilot who debuted that year in the "Peanuts" comic strip. As to the military matter, Pat and Nancy had an intermediate stop en route to the operational unit at Eglin.

PAT'S NEXT ASSIGNMENT was temporary duty at Davis-Monthan Air Force Base, a Strategic Air Command base just down the road from Williams in Tucson, Arizona. During the summer of 1965, Pat was assigned to the 4453rd Combat Crew Training Wing, outfitted with the U.S. Air Force's most advanced fighter—the McDonnell F-4C Phantom IIs. Designed by the Navy for fleet defense, the F-4 was adapted by the Air Force as a fighter-bomber. At Davis-Monthan, the F-4Cs were painted for peacetime, Air Force high-gloss gray with standard markings, including the red, white, and blue stars and bars insignia.

Destined to become the principal air-superiority fighter of its day, the F-4C had a two-pilot tandem cockpit and was rated at twice the speed of sound, thanks to its twin General Electric J79 turbojet configuration. The F-4 was big with a maximum takeoff weight approaching 30 tons and fast with a top speed in excess of 1,400 miles per hour. Because of its size, the F-4 utilized its speed to make up for its lack of agility. In time, it would affectionately be referred to as a "flying brick." Flying Mach 2 and on top of the world, 23-year old First Lieutenant Pat Wynne was one happy Air Force pilot. After a few months academics, training, and getting acclimated in the F-4C, he was ready for duty by the end of the summer.

In changing air force bases, Pat and Nancy drove the 1,600 miles from Davis-Monthan to Eglin. When they arrived, they began to notice subtle differences. The F-4Cs were being repainted in the no-gloss green, tan and brown irregular patterns that would become common throughout the service. The stars and bars changed to flat-black markings. During the fall of 1965, the United States was moving to a wartime footing. The camouflage scheme would make the aircraft harder to pick out when parked on the ground.

Pat sequenced into one of the four squadrons (4th, 16th, 25th, and 40th Tactical Fighter Squadrons) of the 33rd Tactical Fighter

Wing based out of Eglin Air Force Base at the western end of the
Florida Panhandle. The 33rd had been activated in February 1965
and organized two months later. Pat's assignment to the 33rd was
early on, as it outfitted F-4C aircraft and aircrews for deployment
to Vietnam. His mission was not training anymore. The 33rd was
a brand new wing that was being built up to combat readiness. It
moved closer to that goal as new pilots such as Pat were absorbed
into the wing.

The 33rd Tactical Fighter Wing passed its operational readiness
inspection in the fall of 1965. It was declared combat ready, another
way of saying ready for deployment, in November or December.
The Air Force then started peeling off pilots from the squadrons
of the 33rd Wing for reassignment, many to the combat theater in
Southeast Asia. The process of peeling off pilots for reassignment
took months, and not everyone went to the same operational units.
It was spring 1966 by the time Pat knew he was going from the 40th
Tactical Fighter Squadron of the 33rd Tactical Fighter Wing to the
555th Tactical Fighter Squadron of the 8th Tactical Fighter Wing. He
was going to be a pilot with the soon-to-be-dubbed "Wolf Pack."[40]

EVEN WITH VIETNAM the proverbial elephant in the room, everyone
tried to live as normally as possible while they waited for the next
assignment. While at Eglin, Pat stood up as best man for his friend
Mac Armstrong, one of the bachelors from Williams Air Force
Base. Nancy stood up as matron of honor for Mac's bride, Margaret.
So the three bachelors were down to two. But as it came time to
deploy, any semblance of normal would change. The squadrons of
the 33rd Tactical Fighter Wing were broken up and Pat was headed
for Thailand.

What became of the three amigos, Pat's bachelor friends from
pilot training at Williams Air Force Base? The three had come
to Williams through Air Force Reserve Officer Training Corps
programs. John NePage worked his way from Central Washington
State University, Mac Armstrong through Louisiana State University
and Bill Koelm out of the University of Illinois Champaign-Urbana.
John went on to fly KC-135 Stratotankers in Vietnam and then

During winter 1965–66 on leave between assignments Pat visits
with family in Florida. Above: Pat and Mike sporting their academy
rings. Mike still had the last half of his senior year to complete
before graduation. Below: the Wynne family congregate in front
of Pat's Chevy Corvette, with Peter and Steve anchoring the front,
Mike, Pat, Dad, Maureen, Mom, and Cathy filling out the back.
Source: Wynne Family.

had a career with Northwest Airlines, retiring off the Boeing 747 airliner. Mac flew F-4 Phantom IIs and F-111 Aardvarks in Vietnam and made a career out of the Air Force. He retired as a three-star lieutenant general and commander of the Twenty-first Air Force. Bill also served in Vietnam, his first tour flying F-105 Thunderchiefs and his second flying OV-10 Broncos as a forward air controller. He retired as a group commander after 26 years of service.

For Pat, the past yawned behind him and a limitless future stretched before him. He was a pilot, but a career in the Air Force might be a near run thing. Pat also was an excellent student and had a streak of the scholar in him that surfaced. Only time would tell what he did after his commitment to the service of his nation, whether he ended up as a scientist or an educator or with a career in the Air Force. For the time being, Pat's imminent future was in a combat zone.

ONE OF THE PROBLEMS in Southeast Asia in early 1966 was the lack of sufficient air crews. They had plenty of aircraft but not enough pilots to fly them. Pilots were reaching their 100 mission marks earlier than personnel people had expected. This rotated pilots back to the United States faster and earlier than projected, causing the shortage. Thus, Combat Crew Training Squadrons (CCTSs) evolved into Replacement Training Units (RTUs). The amount of turnover was significant.

With Southeast Asia as Pat's next duty assignment, he and Nancy had 30 days off before reporting to the Military Airlift Command in California, which was the airlift hub for transfer to Vietnam. This was time to visit family and friends, and the trip would put the Corvette to good use. The young couple packed up their belongings at Eglin Air Force Base on the Florida Panhandle and headed for Pat's parents near Patrick Air Force Base, 475 miles east. After a number of days catching up on news, with plenty of time for swim and sun, it was on to the next leg of the trip.

Pat and Nancy packed up once again, and drove more than 1,700 miles straight north northwest to Crosby, Minnesota to visit her parents, Rosella and Emmett. Pat loved to play cards and had ample opportunity to do that with Nancy's family members. Still much the big kid, he even played monopoly for hours, always clad in his ratty bathrobe in the morning, with Nancy's younger brother David. The ratty robe was a holdover from the Air Force Academy, something of a tradition as they sewed on patches and all sorts of mementos. Over time, the robe took on a patina that one couldn't shake, or one could just call it ratty.

Then it was time to head west with a 1,900 mile ride to the coast, ready to serve. Pat and Nancy drove the Corvette together and treasured the time crossing the expanse of the country, through the Great Plains and traversing the Rocky Mountains until finally dropping out of the Sierra Nevada range and passing through Sacramento on the way to the Bay Area. They spent a few days in San Francisco, but a hitch developed when it was time to report.

When inexperienced pilots arrived in Vietnam, their initial duty was as a back-seat weapons specialist. The Air Force had not yet trained Pat in some small but significant part of his specialty, and the Air Force wanted him fully outfitted. So Pat and Nancy shed their tears and said their goodbyes at the San Francisco airport. Pat was headed back to Eglin Air Force Base for additional training and Nancy back to Crosby. Even though the change in plans was on short notice, Nancy's mom flew to San Francisco, missing Pat's departure by but an hour, and the two women drove the Corvette back to Minnesota together, just in time for another wrinkle.

Pat flew back to Eglin and completed the instruction he needed in short order. He then hopped another plane and flew to Brainerd, Minnesota, about 15 miles from Crosby. Pat almost beat Nancy and her mom back to Minnesota. He surprised Nancy's family when he called from Brainerd and was able to spend a few last days with his wife. Nancy had been home just a day or two, but this was one of those good surprises. Pat and Nancy shared the week in Crosby, until he was driven to the Minneapolis airport where he caught a flight to San Francisco, this time ready for Vietnam. Maybe.

AFTER HIS TIME OFF before shipping out, Pat reported to Travis Air Force Base, 40 miles outside San Francisco for transfer to Thailand.

It was April 1966. While waiting for transport, the Air Force figured out that, in its hurry to ready pilots, it also had neglected to put some of the crews through basic survival school. So Pat was redirected to Stead Air Force Base located near Reno, Nevada, for three weeks of survival training. Then it was back to Travis in May, and this time he soon boarded a piston-powered, propeller-driven commercial airliner for transfer out of the States.

Pat's flight took him through Hickam Air Force Base in Hawaii, followed by Wake Island in the Pacific and then Clark Air Base in the Philippines. At Clark, the airmen had to lay over a week waiting for the next jungle survival class, so they used the time to visit Manila. They took the opportunity to ride a hydrofoil across Manila Bay to the Bataan Peninsula and the island of Corregidor. A few days later they were back at Clark and participated in jungle

Six first lieutenants from the 33rd Tactical Fighter Wing at Eglin Air Force Base headed for the 8th Tactical Fighter Wing in Thailand. At Travis Air Force Base awaiting airlift to the Vietnam War. All six were slated to be GIBs (guys in back) until gaining enough experience to move to the front seat.[41] As fighter pilots, they were in a tough business as four of the six men would be shot down in Vietnam.[42] No one recalls why Pat was in his Air Force blues, while the others were in their summer uniforms. Left to right: Pat Wynne, Bunny Talley, Tom Fryer, Joe Merrick, Bob Clements, and unknown. Photo dates to late May or early June 1966. *Source:* Tom Fryer survival school. They were inching their way closer to the combat theater.

After jungle class, they loaded on to a C-130 Hercules for the 1,400 mile flight to Udorn Royal Thailand Air Force Base (RTAFB). Their intermediate stop was Bangkok, where they changed C-130s to the local that ferried Americans to the Thai bases. This added a few hundred miles on to the direct route. They arrived in-country in late May or early June of 1966. After a period getting acclimated and processed, Pat would fly his first missions with the 555th Tactical Fighter Squadron in late June out of Udorn RTAFB.

CHAPTER FOUR

Mike Wynne's Winding Way

PAT'S LAST YEAR at the Air Force Academy, the 1962–63 academic year, turned out to be Mike's first year at the Military Academy. Mike didn't have the perfect eyesight needed for entrance into the Air Force Academy, so it was off to West Point, New York, to obtain the academy experience. After passing the Presidential Qualifying Test and physical, probably at MacDill Air Force Base outside Tampa, Mike followed the path his father had journeyed more than 25 years earlier to upstate New York.

THE UNITED STATES MILITARY ACADEMY was established by President Thomas Jefferson and the Congress in 1802. In the 200 years since, the academy graduated tens of thousands of second lieutenants. West Point graduates ran the gamut of American history including Presidents Grant and Eisenhower, Senators and Congressmen, generals, and more than a dozen astronauts. Seventy-four of its graduates have been awarded the Medal of Honor.

Each summer a new class of cadets began training at West Point. They learned the language of the establishment: the main entrance of Thayer Gate, the parade field called The Plain, and meals in Washington Hall. New cadets were stripped down to nothing, and then built back up as officers and gentlemen. They were taught the West Point way. While each cadet brought a different background and experience, they were taught duty, honor, and country the exact same way. But it was a process, and it took four years.

Each cadet was assigned a sequence number upon graduating indicating what academic position they held at the end of their studies. This was the General Order of Merit or class ranking. These sequence numbers were called cullum numbers, after Colonel George W. Cullum who invented the process to keep track of graduates. Mike's father, Ed Wynne, graduated with the cullum number 11,870 in the "long gray line," which has since extended past 65,000.[43]

❦

Similar to brother Pat's entrance at the Air Force Academy, Mike had received an at-large presidential nomination to West Point, generally reserved for sons of former graduates or active duty commissioned military officers. Arriving at West Point Military Academy in July 1962, Mike figured he was prepared for what was coming—hazing, harassment, and hell weeks. After all, his father had graduated in 1940 and Mike had heard the stories around the dinner table as he was growing up. But enduring six weeks of cadet basic training—Beast Barracks—brought a different flavor to the words. Just as they had for decades, "Firsties" and "Cows" (seniors and juniors) jumped on the potential cadet plebes from the very beginning, R-Day.

Mike had come up from Florida a few days before and stayed with his Aunt Shirle and Grandma Tebbie in New York City. His aunt gave him a ride up to West Point on the appointed day of July 2, 1962. Mike arrived for Beast Barracks fortified with the spartan advice of his father, "Don't carry a big bag." As a result, he hopped out of his aunt's car carrying nothing more than a shaving kit. With this miniscule gear, Mike provided little fodder for the upperclassmen who enjoyed stopping the new recruits at every opportunity, which required them to drop and pick up their baggage countless times. Thus armed, Mike cleared most of the first day's din in relative peace.

The prospective cadets numbered 828 on reception day, and the winnowing process started immediately. Mike remembered one arrival never made it through the first day, essentially walking in through the sally port on to the central field and, later that day, walking right out the other side. Mike started basic training in first new cadet company, garrisoned in Old South. Before R-Day concluded, he met his new roommates, Sam Champi and Pete Donnell.

Sam Champi was a stocky sportster from Seton Hall Prep in South Orange, New Jersey. Gifted in athletics and academics, Sam had finished at the top of his class. Pete Donnell, who had followed his father's military career around the world, arrived at West Point with requisite skills. He would teach his roommates how to polish shoes, shine brass, and pass inspections. Through Donnell, Mike met another prep school graduate, Frank Hartline, who would be a Beast Squad buddy.

The six weeks were hard as the prospects were pushed right past the point of exhaustion. It was physically challenging, pressing each young man to new levels of achievement. One had to make it through cadet basic training to be accepted into the corps of cadets.

The purpose of cadet basic training, wholly under the guise of instilling a measure of actual training, was discipline and punishment to weed out the weaker souls. It could border on savage at times. Only one way to do things existed, and the way to which one was accustomed was not it. Instantaneous and exact response to any and all orders was mandatory. And even when one responded correctly, it might not be right. The rigor would find your bottom and then build you back up. It was a focused transition from civilian to military life.

THE VARIOUS AND SUNDRY INFRACTIONS Mike perpetrated in his first weeks of Beast Barracks at West Point were often parried by the withholding of food. Not all the upperclassmen reveled in this form of punishment but a number did. The result for Mike was that he sheared off weight at a remarkable rate. He arrived at West Point tipping the scales around 170. Within weeks he was down to 135. At roughly six foot three inches, 135 pounds were spread pretty thin across such a frame. While few would expect zealous upperclassmen to understand the chemical function of salt in the body's ability to perform, withholding food was certainly a way to see its result. As it was, a salt deficit accompanied losing such a high percentage of body weight so quickly.

One day during cadet basic training, Mike was running across the field when he dropped to the ground as if he'd been shot. His legs cramped up in spasms as a result of the sodium imbalance. Joe Palone, a faculty member, saw Mike go down and went over to see if he could help. Besides being on staff, Joe Palone was the coach of the soccer team. Once the coach determined the problem, he took it upon himself to bring about the solution and put a stop to it. He put Mike on the soccer team.

Meeting with the team later, Coach Palone told the guys that Mike was now on the squad and he assigned a special duty to the other players. Their job was to put weight on the new recruit, and coach wanted to see 10 pounds put on in quick order. Being on a varsity team, Mike was consigned to eat at his corps squad athletes table in the mess hall, which effectively isolated him from his cadet company mess table and the problems of the past. Their leverage thwarted, the upperclassmen made sure Mike experienced payback when not under the patronage of the soccer team, but the medical difficulties subsided.

Mike made it through, from R-Day to A-Day, from reception to acceptance. As the cadet plebes were organized and distributed into formal units, Mike was placed in I-2, I-Company of the Second Regiment. I-2 had its quarters over in the north area, back by the gymnasium and below the cadet chapel. As it would turn out, Mike's class was on the vanguard of changes at the academy.

THE CLASS OF 1966 would be the last one with only two regiments, as the academy expanded under President Johnson's orders. The plan was for West Point to grow from roughly 2,400 cadets, two regiments of eight companies each, to more than 4,400 cadets, in four regiments. The growth was in part a response to the heightening conflict in Vietnam but also an effort to position the academies on the same footing regarding size, such as the Naval Academy which had always been at about 4,000 students.

While the prospective Class of 1966 would be celebrated throughout the world one day, with its share of war heroes, generals, presidential candidates, and captains of the business world, all that was on the horizon.[44] Once accepted into the corps of cadets, the next step was making it through plebe year. If one thought Beast Barracks was a wake-up call, plebe year was an intervention.

WHETHER CALLED SLUGS OR DEMERITS OR CONFINEMENTS, the principle was the same: punishment. Discipline was instituted with a strictness found in few other places. Cadets could earn penalties for not having their quarters in perfect order, for uniform brass not shiny enough, or for hundreds of other transgressions both terrible and trifling. That was just the point, as it was simply an excuse to channel discipline to the cadets. It was a yoke, submit by bending or break. Mike learned.

So it went for the first two years, the upperclassmen pretty much having their way with the underclassmen, much the same way it had been for more than a century. All the upperclassmen participated to some extent in the festivities because it was part of the conditioning and tradition of the academy. Only a few took it over the top. Mike endured his share of the unfriendly ones. Besides the reprisal ramification of being sheltered on the soccer team, Mike saddled some trial just because he was one of 53 cadets who were sons of prior graduates.[45] That distinction didn't bring one a "get out of jail free" card but rather an extra tribulation every now and then.

Mike earned a measure of notoriety at West Point, undoubtedly due to all the infractions he was seen marching off on one-hour tours of the area. Part of his group of plebes in I-2, where Mike spent the first two years, was thought of by the upperclassmen to be somewhat lacking in military discipline. In fact, I-2, K-2, L-2, and M-2 were four companies branded as exhibiting that pattern of behavior and were disparagingly referred to as the "greeks" of the Second Regiment. Some in the First Regiment didn't think these companies of the Second even had the real cadet experience. While they would develop the same pride and strength and camaraderie as the rest, they were viewed for a time as the slackers of the class. It would take awhile.

Of course, most plebes being but 18 years old, they managed to find holes in the system and time for extracurricular exploits. In the vernacular, they "had their moments" and found ways to inscribe their names in the pantheon of cadets. The Class of 1966 would establish its own distinctive lore, as every class did. Mike would participate in his share of memorable events and meet his share of memorable people. One was a character named Thomas J. Hayes, or just TJ. Most everyone had a good story about TJ, and absolutely everyone had fond memories.

IN THE ACADEMY CURRICULUM, foreign language was one of the core requirements. Even though Mike had taken three years of Spanish in high school, he couldn't pass the advanced placement test for the language. He wasn't eligible for the basic course, so he had to choose another. On advice from brother Pat, he took Russian, the language du jour during those days of the great red menace. Mike immediately fell behind. Eventually, his classmate TJ came to the rescue and told him, "You're not going to fail Russian." TJ would come up after taps and work with Mike for an hour or so on memorizing what he needed to know. So Mike didn't learn Russian—he memorized it, getting the guttural sounds down just right so he could repeat them. The professor was flabbergasted when Mike spurted back to him understandable Russian words.

Classroom seating in each course was arranged from the smartest cadet in front to the polar opposite in back, and one's position was adjusted after every test. Mike, who had slowly but inexorably drifted to the back of the class in Russian, now started advancing. Across the row he went and around the corner, comparable to a Kentucky Derby, Mike charged toward the front. He owed it to TJ who, when not teaching Russian to Mike, was teaching someone else math, physics, or chemistry. TJ, a hero for many of his classmates, was the epitome of duty, honor, and country.

THEN THERE WERE THE UNIFORM CHANGES, a drill that everyone suffered at one time or another, which became a distinct challenge for one of Mike's classmates. This drill began when an upperclassman would tell the cadet to appear at a certain place and time dressed in a particular uniform, such as dress whites. Pressure mounted as the cadet was then directed to return to his room and change into a different uniform, such as raincoat, dress grays, or under arms, and return on the double. This form of punishing discipline could go on indefinitely. One of Mike's classmates, Frank Pratt, suffered this turmoil one time and the occasion became memorable.

After a number of times back and forth changing uniforms, Frank returned as ordered and under arms as requested. He had been at it for an hour, and he was approaching his limit. As required, Frank knocked on the door of the upperclassman administering the event.

The reply came blunt and brash, "I cannot hear you."

Frank knocked again, a bit louder, and waited for reaction.

Once again but with even more reproach, "I cannot hear you."

A time or two more and it bubbled over.

Frank was on the swim team, his specialty the butterfly stroke, and he had the considerable shoulders to prove it. He used them. On the last "I cannot hear you," Frank took the butt of his rifle and caved in the right side of the upperclassman's door. Now in a quandary, the upperclassman told Frank he could return to his quarters, but Frank wasn't quite done.

Frank shifted his hold, reversing his hands on the rifle, and caved in the left side of the door with the rebuke, "You asked me to come."

Now with two holes in his door from the butt of Frank's rifle, the upperclassman realizing he had perhaps taken Frank all the way, came the *coup de grâce*. Frank caved in the middle of the door.

Of course, repercussions followed. Frank was finally spent, but it would take some time to settle up. It was a big deal, maintenance had to be called, the tactical officer had to make a report, as did the company and regimental commanders. The principal problem was that the upperclassmen were in danger of squandering one of their perquisites. From that time on, they watched the one who pushed the cadet over the edge to make sure he didn't ruin it for everyone.

ANOTHER INDIVIDUAL, this one a partner in crime, was J.T. Unger, with whom Mike roomed as a yearling. Showcasing their electrical engineering prowess, Mike and JT wired a radio through their quarter's light switch, trying to control operation with the door. The goal was to have the radio automatically shut off anytime someone opened the door, rendering their quarters in compliance, and turn back on when the door was closed. When they went to engage the light, they shorted the circuit blowing the fuse out and sending JT, who happened to be holding a screwdriver near the light switch, across the room. Even though the electrical experiment darkened most of the north area, it was a commotion with no consequence, as the two hurried and were able to rewire the switch before the officer of the day reset the fuse.

MIKE'S SECOND YEAR AT WEST POINT would prove as momentous and as ordinary as the first, a sign of the times. His yearling year began in July 1963 with the class spending seven weeks at Camp Buckner training under the auspices of the 101st Airborne. They were getting a taste of the real Army. Sophomore year would include a bit of fun. In the fall of 1963, most of the student body boarded trains that clickety-clacked the 850 some miles to Chicago, Illinois, in a 22-hour trip to Soldier Field to watch the Army versus Air Force football game. This rivalry hadn't been in existence very long and was far from a classic, but the cadets enjoyed the diversion and left Chicago in pretty much the same shape they found it. The Military Academy beat the Air Force Academy 14–10. The following month, President Kennedy took his fateful trip to Dallas.

MIKE'S SPORT OF CHOICE at the Military Academy was swimming. He had been a competitive swimmer back home, where he swam for the Melbourne High School Bulldogs, and served as a lifeguard at the Officers' Club at Patrick Air Force Base. At West Point, once past Beast Barracks, he latched on to the swim team. Soccer coach Joe Palone passed Mike off to swim coach Jack Ryan. Long and lanky, Mike was a natural in the water; his specialty was freestyle, especially the sprint distances. But after competing in swimming during his plebe year, he dropped off the team in his second year.

Plebe year had been pretty hard with the hazing, and as a yearling he cared a great deal less. Nonchalance was his problem. A 19-year-old man-child, he just didn't give a damn as a sophomore. He was hit pretty hard by the demerit system, nothing big but scores of little stuff. This is where he earned a reputation marching off infractions, 97 to be precise, just shy of the infamous Century Club. He was, in the parlance of adults, a bit of a discipline problem—at a school steeped in discipline.

The 1966 varsity swim team includes (front row, left to right) Dennis Hergenrether, Bob Cresci, Lewis Robertson, Mike Havey, Alan Aker, Sam Freas, John Dodson, (second row) Joe Guignon, Geoffrey Burke, Jack Gatesy, Charles Gantner, Captain Frank Pratt, John Landgraf, Phil Krueger, Kerry O'Hara, Ken Cummings, (back row) Coach Jack Ryan, Jim McCallum, Dick Kline, Warren Trainor, Mike Wynne, John Williams, Lynn Hunt, Tom Guignon, and Assistant Coach John Lovstedt. *Source:* United States Military Academy photo published in Booth et al., *1966 Howitzer*, p. 104.

As a yearling, his classmates ranked him low in military order of merit, so much so that in the spring of his sophomore year he had to appear before a review board of officers regarding retention. At the board, two men stepped forward to speak on his behalf: senior Bill Landgraf who was captain of the swim team and the head of the computer center where Mike had shown a good deal of aptitude. The board's ruling reflected the significance of his sins.

The board concluded that since Mike had the talent, the cure for nonchalance was not to give up on him but rather to involve him in things in which he had an interest and watch him develop wings. In the end, Mike applied to the swim coach to rejoin the team in his third year, eventually earning his way back. This is why Mike's entry in the *Howitzer* yearbook shows "Swimming 4,2,1," missing only his third class, sophomore year.

MIKE SERVED HIS THIRD LIEUTENANT DUTY, an army orientation internship, during the summer before junior year at an Army base in Hanau, Germany. Out in the field, he learned how things actually were accomplished in the Army in general, and particulars such as scrounging materials to build storage buildings. As his time came to an end at Hanau, he partnered up with one of his classmates, Noble Hart, and arranged to stay an extra two weeks touring Europe. Mike's dad had given him a few hundred dollars to extend his visit. Mike spent Bastille Day in Paris, roomed on the left bank of the Seine, took the train to Barcelona, went to a bull fight, and flew to Majorca on a C-47, which was an adventure in itself.

When the Spanish commercial airline canceled their flight to Majorca, Noble and Mike exploited alternatives. With a little effort they found a charter airline, contract pilot who owned a World War II vintage-Douglas C-47 Dakota. After some negotiating, Noble and Mike were able to charter the pilot and the plane for the passage at a cost of 163,000 pesetas, roughly $2,300. While a couple thousand dollars was a good-sized sum of money, when divided by 40 some passengers, it even beat the commercial airline's fare. Mike and Noble approached the other passengers who had been stranded by the commercial airline and sold the remaining seats to them, defraying substantially all of the cost. This would be the start of Mike's international negotiating prowess. At the start of the new school year, the cadets of the Class of 1966 were scrambled on rising to second class and becoming cows.

ONE TRADITION WITHIN THE ACADEMY was to reassign cadets going into their third year across companies to familiarize them with more of their classmates. Having completed two years in I-2, Mike relocated across the plaza, transferring from I-2 to H-2 for his third year. This would be Mike's introduction to cadet Wilson "Wil" Kone, who would have a strong influence on Wynne's attitude and aptitude for the next two years. The fact that Wynne was an avid Catholic and Kone was an ardent Mormon broadened it into a learning exchange.

About the time Mike switched roommates, a new world's fair opened. The 1964–65 New York World's Fair was under way in Flushing Meadows in the borough of Queens, less than 60 miles from West Point. It was scheduled to be opened for 360 days, spread across two elongated summers. The two cadets had a chance to visit the fair and initiate wide-ranging discussions about each other's religious cultures. Mike took Wil to the Vatican Pavilion, explained some of the Catholic traditions, and they viewed Michelangelo's *Pietà* on its first display outside Rome. Wil returned the favor and toured Mike through the Mormon Pavilion, sharing some of the art and culture of the Church of Jesus Christ of Latter-day Saints.

They would enjoy many carefree weekends in the New York area, finding entertainment in a number of venues, oftentimes in conjunction with swim meets. As time passed, Wil met a young woman named Barbara from Ithaca, New York, a strong enclave of the Mormon community up in the Finger Lakes region. On a swim meet at Cornell University one day, Mike was shown around the city by Wil's Barbara. Such was their friendship and such was their time at West Point, Wil keeping Mike firmly grounded in the basics of life.

THE FOLLOWING SCHOOL YEAR brought the firstie trip. During the summer between junior and senior years, Mike was a platoon sergeant assisting with new cadet barracks, Beast Barracks for the new class of plebes. Right before Beast Barracks though, the entire senior class of 20-somethings from West Point spent three weeks traipsing around the country visiting Army installations. This was both an orientation trip and a propaganda pitch. The purpose was to showcase the Army branches to the West Point seniors in the hopes they would choose that particular military occupational specialty when commissioned.

Approximately 500 seniors piled on a series of charter jets and flew around the country. They visited a number of installations including Fort Bliss near El Paso, Texas; Fort Sill outside Oklahoma City, Oklahoma; and Fort Benning on the Alabama-Georgia border, to name just three. The specialty at Fort Bliss was antiaircraft artillery and guided missiles, at Fort Sill field artillery, and at Fort Benning infantry. But at each fort, the class also had time to partake of some of the local amusements. Civic fathers in most cities threw dances and had escorts for the cadets, so they would have a memorable time. The firsties even had the opportunity to slip across the border into Juarez City, south of El Paso. While the journey sometimes dissembled into something more reminiscent of a frat party, with the participants drunk and disorderly and trying to date the stewardesses, it was a once in a lifetime experience.

As a FIRST CLASS CADET, Mike was put in B-4 as the structure of the academy changed into a four regiment organization, and West Point began to build the student body numbers back up. From the ranks of B-4 came the first captain, first corporal and the class valedictorian. First captain was the highest graduating rank a senior cadet could achieve and earned the position of brigade commander; First Captain Norm Fretwell had his name etched on a plaque outside a room in Eisenhower barracks. The first corporal was the senior underclassman. Wes Clark was the valedictorian and the top scorer academically in the Class of 1966. It was quite an honor to have all three in the same company.

The 24 first classmen of B-4 were housed in the Eisenhower rooms. An advantage of being a firstie was that one didn't have to walk tours of the area anymore as punishment. Now it was confinements, roughly the equivalent of an adult time out and basically a three-hour study hall. Mike served his share of confinements, but even that wasn't as straightforward as it sounded.

MIKE'S LAST YEAR AT THE ACADEMY featured running into his

father's old friends. Mike had three superintendents during his time at West Point, William Westmoreland and James Lampert, both from the Class of 1936, and Donald Bennett, from Mike's father's Class of 1940. Bennett took the reins in January 1966, Mike's last year. In addition, Richard Scott, Class of 1941 and his father's lacrosse team chum, became the commandant of cadets in 1965. Mike's family was close to the Scotts. Ed Wynne and Richard Scott had both returned to teach at the academy in 1949. During the 1951–52 academic year, the sesquicentennial for the Military Academy, both men were lieutenant colonels on the faculty, Wynne in Ordnance and Scott in English.

First classmen from Company B of the Fourth Regiment or simply B-4 include (front row, left to right) Crocker, Parker, Clark, McKnight, (second row) Wright, Anderson, Mulligan, (third row) Alexander, Robbins, Lingle, (fourth row) Wynne, Gunderson, Kone, Murphy, (fifth row) Tarpley, Albright, Thornbloom, and Kirk. Not Pictured: Berry, Deponal, Fretwell, Hart, Lawrence, and Meccia.
Source: United States Military Academy photo published in Booth et al., *1966 Howitzer,* p. 190.

While stationed at West Point, the two oldest Wynnes, Pat and Mike, and the three Scott girls, Barbara, Peggy, and Sandy, were childhood pals. Years later, when Ed Wynne was stationed at Andrews Air Force Base in Baltimore and Richard Scott was assigned to the Department of the Army in Washington, the whole Wynne family took the train for the 40-mile hop to the capital to attend the coming out party for one of the Scott girls held at the Army Navy Country Club. At that time Mike was in junior high and his brother Pat in high school. The Wynnes and Scotts stayed close, so when the Scotts transferred back to the academy into the commandant's quarters, Mike was easily reacquainted with them.

OVER TIME, Mike and Mrs. Scott progressed into the habit of making and trading puzzles. Mike would work on a puzzle in his room, to pass the time working off a confinement, and then present the finished product to Mrs. Scott on one of his visits. She frequently would reciprocate. One time Mike had a particularly difficult, circular puzzle that he just couldn't finish. When the tactical officer arrived in Mike's quarters for Saturday morning inspection, the puzzle was out on a little table, making Mike's room unprepared for inspection and Mike due for a confinement. Then it happened the next week and again the following week. Finally, the tactical officer put in a piece or two and, looking at Mike, said "concentrate and finish this." In the long run, the shared passion for puzzles gave Mike occasion to be at the commandant's house.

During Christmas break of his third year at the Military Academy, Mike met and began dating a young woman from back home in Florida, Barbara Hill. Mike's family lived in three different places in Florida, the last of which was just a few blocks from Barb's house. By the time Mike neared the end of his academy training, Barb and he had developed a wonderful relationship, which had quickened to the point where they discussed marriage. In Mike's senior year, Barb asked her dad if she could go up to West Point. The answer was yes, as long as she had a job. As it worked out, Mrs. Scott would help Barb fulfill that condition.

Because of the close relationship with the Wynnes, the commandant's wife had invited Barb to come up to West Point and stay with them. She told Barb she should check in at the post exchange and find employment because they were always looking for help. One day Barb drove up to West Point and went to find a job at the post exchange. Since no one there had been clued in, Barb was told no jobs were available. So Barb headed back up the hill, jobless for the moment. She ran into Mrs. Scott who was throwing her golf clubs in the back of the cart. She determined the problem and had Barb march back down the hill to the post exchange where this time staff members were falling over themselves to employ her.

"Oh, you're that Barb Hill," they said with newfound insight.

Barb lived with the Scotts for three months in Mike's firstie year.

MIKE'S TIME OVER AT THE COMMANDANT'S HOUSE began to escalate. When Barb was visiting, General Scott would call Mike's tactical officer and ask if Mike could be relieved from his confinement to come over to the commandant's for dinner. This took place a couple of days a week. Eventually Mike began to spend so much time at the commandant's that Mike's regimental leader was forced to start counting the interval at that location as a confinement, for there were not enough other hours in the day for the confinements to be worked off. As Mike neared the end of his time overlooking the Hudson River, he had another ritual to fulfill.

True to academy traditions, Mike bought a new car as he approached graduation from West Point. While his brother Pat had lived up to a pilot's panache with a flaming-red Corvette, Mike was a bit more grounded and saddled up a 1966 Oldsmobile Cutlass, burgundy with black interior. It was a two-door sports coupe with a two-speed automatic transmission, but it satisfied Barb's minimal requirement of at least having a backseat. While Mike was far from being a gearhead of the 1960s muscle-cars, he still had an engineer's eye for detail. He knew the Cutlass came with the four-barrel Quadrajet carburetor, introduced the previous year. It was a spread-bore carburetor with two little ports on the primary side, for fuel economy and normal driving requirements, and two huge ones in the secondary, so gasoline could pour into the engine cylinders and hustle on demand. This typed the car with a cast-iron, small-block Jetfire Rocket 330-cubic inch engine equipped with a Rochester carburetor, rating the engine at 320 horsepower. He was a product of the Sixties.

DURING MIKE'S FIRST CLASS YEAR numerous guests came to the Academy. Distinguished visitors included Army Vice Chief of Staff General Creighton Abrams; Academy graduate and former superintendent, General Maxwell Taylor; retired five-star General Omar Bradley, one of only nine men to achieve that rank; Gemini and Apollo program astronauts Ed White and Frank Borman, both academy graduates commissioned into the Air Force; and the Shah of Iran. Eventually June Week 1966 arrived.

ALL THINGS COME TO AN END. Militarily and politically, it had been an interesting four years. In the fall of Mike's plebe year, the nation worried through the Cuban missile crisis in October 1962. In November of his second year, President Kennedy was assassinated. During the latter-half of his third year, while civil rights issues boiled over, Congress authorized war against North Vietnam. As a capstone, during the fall of his last year at West Point, Vietnam rose to a larger stage with the battle in the Ia Drang Valley and thousands of war protestors marching on Washington. Mike couldn't wait to see what the future held.

On June 8, 1966, Mike's family came up to West Point to watch him graduate. The keynote address was delivered by Vice President Hubert H. Humphrey. Ed Wynne had the honor of swearing in his son, commissioning him directly into the U.S. Air Force. Due to Ed's connections, this took place in the superintendent's backyard. Mike received the class gift of a silver tray directly from Superintendent Bennett. The tray was engraved with congratulations on his commission in the Army, which ended up being the only memento Mike received with "United States Army" on it. Thus ended Mike's four years at the United States Military Academy in West Point, New York.

Another choice point was passed. Mike's career diverged from that of most of his fellow second lieutenants. Mike graduated with the Order of Merit of 362 out of the graduating class of 579, what Mike would euphemistically refer to as "among the great unwashed." Out of his graduating class, 17 seniors were commissioned directly into the Air Force and one into the Navy.[46] Much of Mike's future

Pictured above: Ed Wynne swears in his son, Michael, into the United States Air Force on June 8, 1966. *Source:* United States Military Academy photo by Mr. Murphy, USMA Archives (reference 66-2101 R), courtesy of Wynne Family. Below: Major General Donald V. Bennett congratulates Mike and hands him the class gift of a silver tray. *Source:* United States Military Academy photo courtesy of Wynne Family.

shared learning would not be with the cadets with whom he had spent the last four years. They were off on an experience in the Army, while Mike was off to horizons in the Air Force. Unlike Mike, most of the 17 commissioned into the Air Force were headed to be pilots. For Mike, it was weapons development.

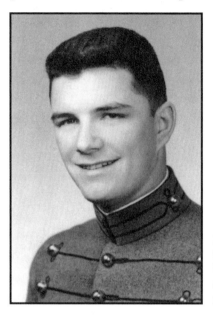

Michael Walter Wynne in a view taken for his official graduation photo from the United States Military Academy in 1966. *Source:* United States Military Academy photo courtesy of Wynne Family.

In May 1962 General Douglas MacArthur had visited West Point and spoken his famous words about "duty, honor, country." Two months later, Mike Wynne showed up at the Military Academy with 827 others beginning a journey as new cadets. Eight hundred and twenty-eight started in 1962, and 579 finished in 1966. It has been noted with more than a little pride that the Class of 1966 was the last of the Eisenhower classes, a nod to the men, the times, and the institution. The graduates from the Class of 1966 have gone on to live admirable lives, some in quiet peace and some in a more celebrated way, but all marked by their experience at the academy.

The Class of 1966 marched out of Michie Stadium right into the buildup of the Vietnam War and sustained more casualties in that conflict than any other class. Two hundred and seventy-three West Point graduates lost their lives in Vietnam, 30 from the Class of 1966 alone.[47] As for Company B-4, upon graduation, 20 of the 24 young men would serve in Vietnam, most in front-line combat units and a handful as advisors in the Military Assistance Command, Vietnam (MACV). Two of Company B-4 were lost in Vietnam. David Crocker lost his life on May 17, 1969, in combat in the Tay Ninh Province of South Vietnam. Art Parker was killed in a helicopter accident on May 29, 1968, in the Thua Thien Province in South Vietnam.

As a group, the length of time these men remained in the service was average for the times. Some made it a career, and some resigned soon after meeting their commitment. Half of the men in B-4 would stay in the service long enough to retire: one four-star general, two colonels, and nine lieutenant colonels. Ten men from B-4 resigned their commissions in the 1970s, all but one having reached the rank of captain. The remaining two were Vietnam casualties.

One of the stars of B-4 was Wesley Clark. Clark went on to a distinguished career in the Army, achieving four-star rank and serving as supreme allied commander of the North Atlantic Treaty Organization (NATO) during the war in Kosovo. General Clark was one of ten individuals who ran for the presidential nomination of the Democratic Party in 2004, losing to Senator John Kerry.

What of those first contacts Wynne made on R-Day? Plebe year roommate Sam Champi flourished in football for four years, often playing both ways. Ranked in the top 5 percent of the class, he netted stars on his uniform collar and was regimental commander of the Third in his firstie year. After service in Vietnam, he earned a master's degree in engineering from Princeton University. Pete Donnell qualified for Airborne, served in Vietnam with the Second Battalion of the 501st Infantry of the 101st Airborne Division and was killed in action by small arms fire on April 26, 1968, at the age of 25. He rests in Arlington National Cemetery. Beast Squad companion Frank Hartline stayed in the Army for 25 years, retiring as a full colonel. He later worked with Texas Instruments, moved to Arizona and pursued his passion for singing.

What became of Mike's memorable characters from the class? T.J.

Hayes, the selfless tutor, graduated ninth in the class and was killed in action in Vietnam in 1968. The son and grandson of West Point graduates, he had served with honor and valor in the First Infantry Division, The Big Red One. Frank Pratt, of uniform change fame, ended up as a two-time All-American in swimming and captain of the team in his final year, which was an undefeated season. He went on to serve in Vietnam and later became a doctor. J.T. Unger, who is credited with writing Mike's mini-bio for the 1966 *Howitzer*, also served in Vietnam, where he was awarded the Silver and Bronze Stars. Deciding he wanted to be a pilot, he crossed over the "blue line" to the Air Force in the early 1970s, serving in Guam and with the Strategic Air Command, receiving the Distinguished Flying Cross. JT ended up operating a string of movie houses in California. Nobel Hart, Mike's internship partner in Majorca, resigned as a captain in 1970 and then spent years as a teacher in Indiana.

Wil Kone, Mike's roommate during the last two years, was all Army. He served in Vietnam, leading daunting long-range reconnaissance patrols and commanding a company in the 229th Assault Helicopter Battalion. Wil remained in the Army for 20 years, retiring as a lieutenant colonel with a final assignment in the Pentagon. He struggled with bouts of the newly distinguished posttraumatic stress disorder in the ensuing years. Wil returned to Ithaca and his Barbara, raised a large family, dabbled in politics and Cornell, and found recovery by devoting himself to others by assisting the Red Cross.

Joe Palone, who placed Mike on the team so he could regain his health, completed 29 years coaching soccer at West Point between the years 1947 and 1978. He retired with a record of 226 wins, 80 losses, 37 ties, and fond memories from hundreds of students. Swim captain Bill Landgraf from the Class of 1964 served with the 101st Airborne in Vietnam and retired as a colonel in 1984. Coach Jack Ryan directed the swim program at the Military Academy for 29 years, retiring in 1988 with a combined record of 308 wins, 145 losses, and one tie. During the 1965–66 school term when Mike Wynne was a firstie, Mike Krzyzewski was a plebe and a very young Bobby Knight was coach of the basketball team. While the number of West Point alumni now exceeds 65,000, not another Wynne has graduated since Mike, Cullum # 26444.

✦

SO IT WAS FOR MIKE WYNNE'S FIRST TWO YEARS as an officer and a gentleman—a transition from West Point right into work with his first duty assignment at Hanscom Air Force Base and the Electronic Systems Division. While poor eyesight kept him out of the Air Force Academy, he just took a more circuitous route and ended up in the Air Force service. By 1968 Mike had completed the bubble over the pool at Hanscom and had passed 24 months on his first duty assignment. He now proudly wore the silver bars of a first lieutenant in the United States Air Force. It was time for a new adventure.

The 1960s was a period of great opportunity for young officers rising through the ranks. As men moved through jobs, openings were created in many areas, providing just the opportunity for someone ready to grab at the chances. On top of that, the technical aspects of the Air Force were ever increasing. Much akin to his peers in civilian life, Mike moved to bolster his educational background.

The next adventure in Mike's career was being chosen for graduate training in engineering. His superiors thought enough of his ability that he was selected to attend graduate engineering school at the Air Force Institute of Technology. The institute was located in Ohio so similar to thousands of other military families, it was time for a change in quarters. Mike and a very pregnant Barb, along with their first daughter, packed up and moved. Their destination was Wright-Patterson Air Force Base in Dayton.

CHAPTER FIVE

Teach, Taught, Teaching

WRIGHT-PATTERSON AIR FORCE BASE had been a work in progress in the Dayton area for fifty years. Often referred to as the "cradle of aviation," Dayton was home to two families who shared a part in the development of flight, the namesake Wrights and Pattersons. The Wrights earned their spot by being the first with controlled flight of a heavier-than-air machine. The Pattersons, probably better known for founding the National Cash Register Company, secured their place in aviation history when one of their family members died testing aircraft in the service of his nation.

After the Wrights flew on Kill Devil Hill in North Carolina in 1903, they returned home to the Dayton area and set up an experimental flying field and workshop on less than 100 acres of grassland, a place named Huffman Prairie. This was just minutes outside Dayton at a stop on the interurban train called Simms Station. This is where Signal Corps Second Lieutenant Henry "Hap" Arnold earned his wings in 1911. By the end of World War I, the Army Signal Corps had purchased the property and established Fairfield Air Depot, and within a decade the facilities were combined to form Wright Field and headquarters of the Army Air Corps' Material Division.

On the north side of Dayton, the Army Air Corps had another facility, McCook Field, where they performed aeronautical engineering work. Because of size constraints, the Army's Airplane Engineering Division from McCook was relocated to Wright in the 1920s. In 1931 a portion of Wright Field was sectioned off and renamed in honor of the Patterson family. With the end of World War II, the ever-expanding Wright and Patterson fields were merged and shortly after the establishment of an independent Air Force, it was renamed Wright-Patterson Air Force Base.[48] Functionally, Wright Field was the research and development arm of the installation and Patterson Field was the logistics and procurement effort.

THE ARMY AIR SERVICE's first efforts at teaching its own the aeronautical science can be traced back to 1919 when the Air School of Application was established at McCook Field. This subsequently became the Air Service Engineering School and then the Air Corps Engineering School at Wright-Patterson. In its first 20 years, the school graduated less than 300 officers, but some of these formed the intellectual core of the next air generation. Generals such as Jimmy Doolittle and Bernard Schriever were two early graduates.

The Army's engineering school grew into the Air Force Institute of Technology by 1947.[49] In the ensuing years, the institute would broaden its offerings to include three schools of advanced education: the School of Engineering and Management, School of Systems and Logistics, and Civil Engineer and Services School. Each provided continuing professional education tailored to Air Force service personnel. The Air Force Institute of Technology began conferring bachelor's degrees in 1956 and was accredited at the master's level in 1960 and the Ph.D. level in 1965.

As the youngest of the service branches, the U.S. Air Force was at the leading edge of technology, from aeronautics and flying machines to space launches and spy satellites. The Air Force needed career people more than the other services because the required special skills could not be simply filled in with drafted personnel. These specialized individuals came only after much training, and good deal of that training was at the institute. The Wynnes pulled in to Dayton right at the height of the engineering school's expansion. The graduate school facilities were located in Area B of Wright-Patterson, which comprised the original Wright Field areas.

M<small>IKE ARRIVED AT THE</small> A<small>IR</small> F<small>ORCE</small> I<small>NSTITUTE OF</small> T<small>ECHNOLOGY</small> in the summer of 1968. Yet, graduate school would start on an off-note as he was enrolled in some dubious courses. Mike had a chance to look at the schedule of courses in which he was enrolled for the fall term and immediately saw one or two that were problematic. The administration had registered him in a couple of courses that he had already taken at the Military Academy, just two years ago. One of them was a "weeder" course, set up with the specific purpose of driving out the underperformers in the class. This would not do. Mike went to the department offices with his West Point grade sheet in hand. After a bit of explanation, Mike was excused from the weeder class and placed in a different subject. So the stars were beginning to align, out of calculus and into statistics.

That summer before classes started was busy as Mike and Barb welcomed their second daughter into the family and moved into base housing, which was a melting pot of the community from all over Wright-Patterson and not just those attending the Institute of Technology. Through base housing and associations that traced back to Patrick Air Force Base, Mike made immediate acquaintances at Wright-Patterson. One such connection was Russell "Rusty" Hale.

Rusty Hale was a Naval Academy graduate from the Class of 1966 who decided to join his father's service and was commissioned directly into the Air Force upon graduation. His initial assignment was into the foreign technology division at Wright-Patterson. Mike met Rusty soon after arriving at his new station. Rusty introduced Mike and Barbara to his co-workers and the business of foreign technology, which discerned how weapons were developed and employed by competitive nations. This presented Mike with an introduction in the community of the base and the shop talk of an elite intelligence organization. When Mike's classes started his connections expanded to include his classmates, a mixed group of civilian and Air Force people. This crowd would turn out to be a bit kinky.

P<small>AGE</small> M<small>ANOR</small>, a 1950s-era Wherry housing project, served as quarters at Wright-Patterson. Adjacent to Area B, Page Manor was more or less stacked row housing, essentially military ghetto accommodations. Mike and Barb moved in with their two children into a corner unit and learned that many of the young marrieds such as themselves didn't seem to quite fit in on the social scene. This period was at the height of the free-sex, open-marriage era, as exemplified by the theatrical release of *Bob & Carol & Ted & Alice*.

While the Wynnes were generally invited to the parties in the neighborhood, years later they found out that most of the fun, exchanging keys and the like, really didn't start until the more family-oriented retired for the night. This was the Guidance Navigation & Control Class of 1970 (GNC-70), roughly 40 to 50 students in size. For Mike and Barb with two young daughters, it was natural for them to spend most of their leisure time with neighbors. They thought nothing of it. When on duty but in between classes, Mike, being raised in the service, was more involved with the base personnel at Wright-Patterson than his classmates in GNC-70. From a professional development standpoint, he probably should have been more involved with his classmates, because GNC-70 had more than swinging couples going for it.

A NUMBER OF REALLY BRIGHT PEOPLE were studying guidance and control theory. One such classmate was Walt Murch, with whom Mike was unofficially competing in some of their math courses. Walt would acquire an A on a particular test, and Mike would answer with his own A. On the next examination Walt would merit another A and Mike would match up with a B. The next would obtain an added A to Walt's file but only a C to Mike's. Eventually, the unspoken contest ended as Walt simply leveled the competition, whether the subject was theories of plasticity or how surfaces merge under heat or most any other topic. Walt's master's thesis, *Open Loop Optimal Feedback Control for Continuous Linear Stochastic Processes*, consumed 69 pages, the core of which was but a spare 18 pages. This was a tribute to Walt's intellect and accomplishment.

Mike's thesis partner was Rich Holdeman, a bright guy in his own right who spent the occasional night on the Wynne's couch. Rich came from Holloman Air Force Base, outside Alamogordo, New

Mexico, where he was a civilian employee at the Central Inertial Guidance Test Facility. Mike and Rich's thesis on the guidance of multiple re-entry vehicles was a computer-based analysis and covered 200-some pages.[50] Rich, who wrote out the equations by hand, would return to Holloman after GNC-70 and continue on with his work. For 1970 technology, their thesis touched on an interesting field and was cited in later research. Their study covered unpowered control of vehicles re-entering the atmosphere, something needed on a multiple independently targetable re-entry vehicles (MIRV) platform, a missile warhead.

Another character was Tom Rand, Mike and Barb's neighbor a few doors away. Tom came to the Air Force as a major, being that he was already an accomplished orthopedic surgeon when he joined the service. But starting at that rank didn't mean he had the grounding in pomp and circumstance. He would occasionally arrive at the Wynnes' front door, half way to a sweat, to request help in squaring away his uniform and arranging his medals of service and rank. But everyone has strong points. When Tom came to the Institute of Technology, he brought with him the singular ability to make a remarkable daiquiri and he wasn't afraid to prove it. On many evenings the neighbors would share stories of the day with great eye-hand coordination: an eye on the kids and a daiquiri in hand.

MIKE SPENT TWO YEARS at the Air Force Institute of Technology earning his master's degree in electrical engineering. A few months before graduating from the institute, time and grade working as they did, Mike exchanged the silver bars of a first lieutenant for two pair of silver bars and moved up to pay grade O-3, becoming a captain in the United States Air Force. The obvious question: What adventure would be next?

The old saying about not burning one's bridges still held weight. Here was Mike in 1970, four years out of West Point. He could not pass the physical for entry into the Air Force Academy because of his eyesight, but upon graduating from the Air Force Institute of Technology, the academy immediately asked him to consider teaching cadets. It appeared he might achieve admittance to the

Air Force Academy anyway, just in a round-about fashion and as faculty rather than student.

❖

TOWARD THE END OF MIKE'S TIME at the Air Force Institute of Technology, one of his instructors inquired as to whether he might be interested in teaching at the Air Force Academy. This particular instructor had taught at the academy once himself. With an emphatic yes, Mike started the process of applying for a position on the academy faculty. First up would be an interview, and his professor let him know when a staff-member from the academy was coming to the base. On the appointed day, Mike waited for arrival of the interviewer from Colorado Springs, Captain Jack Henry.

As the situation developed, Captain Henry was massively delayed, due to weather or some other problem. Mike was stationed at Wright-Patterson, and Captain Henry was due to fly in at Vandalia-Dayton Municipal Airport, roughly 10 miles to the northwest. Published schedules went out the window, and personnel at the ticket counter could only guess when the flight might land. Captain Wynne called the Vandalia-Dayton air traffic control tower and tried to obtain a fix on the plane's arrival. The traffic controllers were not used to receiving calls from Air Force officers regarding estimated time of arrival of commercial flights, so they were a bit mystified by his call. Still, they soon produced the ETA.

When Captain Henry landed, he was incredulous that Captain Wynne was waiting to greet him. The captain wasn't used to that kind of attention, and over and above the respect he could not figure out how Captain Wynne had managed to meet a plane so far off schedule. Mike probably locked up the job right then. In short order, he was formally invited to come to Colorado and join the academy faculty.

Mike graduated from the Air Force Institute of Technology in June 1970 with a specialization in control theory. After 30 days leave, which he and his growing family spent in Florida with relatives, they were off to Colorado Springs. Mike arrived in the summer of 1970 and quickly set about preparing for the coming fall term.

SHORTLY AFTER ARRIVING at the academy, Mike met Major Ed Bauman, a professor who wanted to take a sabbatical from his teaching duties. Besides his teaching load, Professor Bauman was helping with issues related to the AC-130 gunship development. He wanted leave to help work on an electrical problem, but he needed someone to take charge of his classes. In steps Mike Wynne, soon equipped with Bauman's class notes and all the confidence that 25 years of age could buy. Only later did Mike find out that the class was a senior honors class in engineering, and these soon-to-be graduates were headed for the Purdue engineering master's program after they finished at the academy. This was going to be a challenge.

On Mike's first day with Bauman's class, he found out the students didn't even have books. Luckily, Mike had a friend in procurement, Ron Schillereff, from his Hanscom days. Ron had spent two years at Hanscom, beginning an MBA program at Boston University. He finished at the University of Colorado in Colorado Springs when transferred to the Air Force Academy. Mike's path had taken him from Massachusetts to Ohio to Colorado. So while the two young officers started at Hanscom together, their careers diverged for a year or two and then converged back at the Air Force Academy. And none too soon as Mike still needed textbooks.

Ron saved the situation and had books air expressed within 48 hours, so Mike at least had something by the end of that first week of class. Not all academy students entered right from high school. A number of them had gone to college and as such some were in their early twenties. So Mike was barely a couple of years older than a number of cadets. But they were a good bunch of young men, and they helped Mike out with his first teaching duties.

On one occasion, Mike came back from working on a research project at Wright-Patterson and had not had time to prepare for a particular class. He walked in and found the department head in attendance, ready to proctor the class. It was evaluation time. The department head wanted to see the makings of this rookie teacher and whether he might have a future in education. Mike was completely unprepared but fast with a fallback format, he announced to the class that they were going to have a review. He had to do something. The cadets picked up on it immediately and piled on for the ride. They virtually ran the class and showed such enthusiasm that the department head mentioned as much to Mike upon leaving. When Mike exited after the proctor left, a number of the cadets were outside waiting for him.

Mike smiled and observed, "Boy, are you guys in for it now? You'll be stuck with me."

The cadets chirped back, "No sir. We love ya and want to keep ya."

❖

ON MOVING TO THE ACADEMY, Mike and Barb's first billet for their family of four had been an apartment in town, a location that immediately began to squeeze their finances. As with most service destinations, getting suitable quarters always took some doing. Mike, at 25 years old and a captain for all of seven months, ranked pretty low on the list for on-base lodging. Barb worked at J.C. Penney in town, which helped some, but they were still slowly losing altitude. Toward the end of the first academic year at the academy, about the normal rotation time, Mike worked with housing and came up with one option. It turned out this was the only residence the housing agent couldn't pawn off on someone else. But with the arrival of the Wynne's third daughter, they had to try something.

It was an old 1870s-era farmhouse, indigenous housing that had been closed in on academy grounds when the boundaries were fixed and turned into military housing. This dilapidated farmhouse had a well in the center of the living room and was located behind a maintenance area down in a little valley. Even though it was on the base, the house was off in the middle of nowhere among the 16,000 acres of campus property. So Mike put on his best negotiating shoes and struck a deal. Mike offered that they'd take the house off of the real estate agent's hands on one condition. After a year, if they really hated the place, they would have priority to move into other base accommodations. And so it was, they spent a year in the farmhouse and moved "uptown" the following school year.

In a twist of fate, Professor Bauman, newly promoted to lieutenant colonel in the intervening year, pictured the house as a pastoral

The astronautics faculty in 1972 includes (front row, left to right) Major Rabe, Major Gerson, Major Trimble, Colonel Callero, Department Head Colonel Wittry, Lieutenant Colonel Preyss, Major Brandt, Major Jordan, (second row) Captain Johnson, Captain Bredvik, Captain Nolan, Mr. Whitesell, Captain Fretwell, Captain Wynne, Captain Fosha, Captain Hicks, Captain Mauger, Captain Burns, Major Krupinski, Major Anderson, Major White, Captain Swanson, (third row) Captain Roeder, Captain Gyauch, Captain Henry, Captain Kruczynski, Captain Cox, Captain Edwards, Captain Neeland, Captain Jones, Captain McMaster, and Captain Raymer. *Source:* United States Air Force Academy.

sanctuary and grabbed it when the Wynnes left. Where the Wynnes saw raccoons trying to burrow in the eaves of the roof and scaring the babysitter, Bauman envisioned a serene setting in nature and a refuge from his active campus life. Where the Wynnes found the location devoid of other children for the kids to play with, Bauman viewed it as the perfect venue for his born-again Christian bible study meetings with cadets. Everyone was happy with the change.

BESIDES TEACHING AT THE AIR FORCE ACADEMY, Mike had the opportunity to work on a variety of research projects. In one case, he had a small role in the development of something called the snap-shoot gun sight. This gun sight was both an evolutionary and a revolutionary means of improving the accuracy of weapons fired in air combat.

The current state of the art was the lead-computing optical sight, which was a complex way of describing a gun sight that acted much as a duck hunter. The pilot would sight the target and the optical device would predict the flight path and how much lead had to be provided so the projectile would hit the target. The snap-shoot gun sight took into consideration other dynamics, such as distance and wind variation. With approximately every fifth projectile being a tracer, the snap-shoot gun sight took a number of measurements or snapshots along the flight path of the projectile out through the atmosphere and automatically adjusted the next rounds. Thus, in aerial combat at most any distance, the pilot simply had to sweep his tube through the target and fire. The improved accuracy also saved ammunition, allowing the aircraft to stay on duty longer.

Rick Willes and Al Preyss, aeronautics and astronautics professors at the academy, were the two leads on the project, something they had been working on since the late 1960s. Mike and his friend, Ron Schillereff, came on the team in the early 1970s and acted as principal investigator and contracting official, respectively. The occasion arrived when the project required the acquisition of an actual, current-model gun sight for assessment and evaluation in relation to the prototype. Mike and Ron were on a mission.

The two men traveled to Kelly Field in San Antonio, Texas, to pick up a surplus optical gun sight, one that had been stripped out of a Convair F-106 Delta Dart. Kelly Field, a center of American military aviation dating back to World War I, was situated adjacent to Lackland Air Force Base. Theirs was a straightforward job, hustle the gun sight back to the academy research labs in Colorado Springs. Travel-wise, it was a pretty straight shot, roughly 875 miles north-northwest from San Antonio. They were booked on Texas International Airlines and after hauling the appliance through the airport soon faced the first of many choice points: checked or carry-on.

The steadfast custodians intuitively knew that checked baggage would be problematic, especially since the gun sight contained restricted components and was fragile. The instrument was about two feet long, and took up two or three cubic feet of space. Wynne and Schillereff, smartly attired in their Air Force dress blues with the double-bars of captains on the shoulders, made a command decision and brought the device on board as carry-on luggage. The second choice point was where to stuff it. It didn't quite fit in the overhead compartment, so it was smashed on the floor between their row and the row in front of them, centered in their three-across seats. There they were wedged, legs akimbo and feet jacked up over the mechanism jammed on the floor, but with their seatbelts on. Mike was splayed on the window side and Ron was awkwardly positioned half in and half out on the aisle.

To make sure they weren't questioned too much, Ron had taken the liberty of bringing along a pad of labels with the word "SECRET" stamped in red letters and had pasted a few of them to the container housing the gun sight. Then the stewardess came along. "You can't fly like this."

Quite, confidant, nonchalant, and acting as if this was an every-day occurrence, Ron dismissed the problem out of hand, "It'll be okay." Silenced but not convinced, she retreated for the moment.

Having recharged her argument, the stewardess returned with an oblique approach. "Gentlemen, you just can't fly like this. If we have an accident, he (gesturing at Wynne on the window) won't be able to get out."

Pointing at the container covered with tags marked SECRET and always with a fresh answer, Ron countered, "He's more expendable than this is."

She looked down among their high-gloss lace-up style military oxfords, saw the labels clearly identifying the piece of equipment as SECRET and surrendered, "Okay." She didn't want to know any more and simply walked off.

Mike and Ron eventually brought the gun sight back to the Air Force Academy. With it, the team was able to begin attaching the mechanical and electrical interfaces to convert the apparatus into a snap-shoot gun sight for installation on the F-106. While Mike was not on the project early enough to be one of the creators, he did have the opportunity to help bring it to realization. The snap-shoot gun sight subsequently became the exemplar for future generations of fighter aircraft. One of the projects in which Mike had a more direct impact involved the AC-130 gunship, a focus of the Astronautics faculty as the sabbatical of Professor Bauman revealed.[51]

As a weapon for close air support of ground troops, a number of Lockheed C-130 Hercules transport aircraft were converted into AC-130 Spectre side-firing gunships, building upon the concept demonstrated in Vietnam with the Douglas C-47 Dakota. The four-engine AC-130 was initially armed with multiple 7.62 mm Miniguns and 20 mm M61 Vulcan six-barreled cannons. AC-130 tactics generally involved night operations flying low and slow in a circular banking turn around a fixed land target, a maneuver called a pylon turn. This allowed the aircraft to saturate a small area with a tremendous amount of firepower with almost surgical precision. Mike worked on a team of researchers, led by Air Force Lieutenant Colonel Brad Parkinson, developing improvements to the gunship concept.

Team leader Brad Parkinson was a 1957 Naval Academy graduate who like Mike upon graduation chose instead to be commissioned into the U.S. Air Force. He followed up with a master's degree in aeronautics and astronautics from Massachusetts Institute of Technology and a doctorate in guidance, control and navigation from Stanford University. In 1969 Parkinson was named chair of the astronautics department at the Air Force Academy, shortly before Mike arrived in Colorado Springs. It was Brad Parkinson and his development teams that refined much of the technology in the new AC-130 gunship.[52] Mike worked on these improvement teams, which included academy cadets and developers from Honeywell.

One of the distinctive characteristics of the AC-130 in action was the tendency for the aircraft to slowly spiral lower. The pilot had his hands full trying both to stay on target and at a proscribed altitude without disrupting the aiming of the weapons. While the AC-130 could direct its firepower in a relatively accurate manner, the biggest variable remained the pilot. Researchers knew that precision could be enhanced by improving the ability to accurately point the aircraft. The research project on which Wynne played a major part resulted in an autopilot that would automatically control the altitude of the gunship along the correct sight line and make real-time adjustments to keep it on line. Thus, the excellent gunship became an outstanding gunship with the addition of the sight line autopilot.

The AC-130A initially came to Vietnam in 1967 at Nha Trang with the 14th Commando Wing. By the time improved models that resulted from research projects such as those at the Air Force Academy appeared, the AC-130s were allocated to the 16th Special Operations Squadron stationed at Ubon Royal Thailand Air Force Base and assigned to the 8th Tactical Fighter Wing. The AC-130 Spectre gunships would be credited with knocking out thousands of trucks in Vietnam. The team of designers who worked on the sight line autopilot was awarded the military citation of Unit Excellence for its AC-130 gunship development. Wynne's other effort with the AC-130 included working out the firing tables for a 105 mm cannon upgrade, which eventually appeared as the AC-130H model in 1972.

Most of Mike's research during his military years—one paper at the Air Force Institute of Technology and two papers at the Air Force Academy, in addition to other projects where he was not involved with writing the report—revolved around closed-loop systems and feedback control. These were driving concepts for Mike, brought home by the fact that battlefield casualties occurred due to a lack of these capabilities. The ability to direct fire, for ground troops to be able to inform close air support what was needed and where, was critical and saved lives. This was one reason Mike took a special interest in feedback loop creativity.

WHILE WORKING ON THE SIGHT LINE AUTOPILOT, Mike had occasion to view other high-tech projects. One in which he was not involved since it had started before he was out of the Military Academy was the Lockheed SR-71 Blackbird. A superior reconnaissance aircraft that began operations in the mid-1960s, it could fly at Mach 3.2, approaching 2,200 miles per hour. Shielded under tight security and secrecy, less than three dozen of the aircraft were built and they were rarely seen in action. On one of Mike's outings with the autopilot team, they happened to be running experiments at Eglin Air Force Base in Florida when they had a chance sighting.

Mike had earlier proved he was physically up to the routine of autopilot experiments, confirmed by his flight worthiness certificate earned at Lowry Field near the academy. Flying at an altitude of 13,500 feet while hanging weapons out the side of the AC-130 required some stamina, and the Air Force wanted to make sure Mike's heart didn't fail from the physical exertion. In testing the autopilot, the team performed daily trials using the night range, so as to avoid disrupting daylight operations at the base. Each day's tests wrapped up around four in the morning, at which time the team would stop for breakfast at a 24-hour pancake house nearby.

As their eating ritual became habit, they heard the SR-71 returning from its overflight one morning as they exited breakfast. The first time, they wondered, "What was that?" The second time confirmed what they were viewing. The third time, they knew they were observing a regular operation rather than a test, so they began to watch for the Blackbird returning to Eglin. Same time, same station.

Eventually the breakfast buddies had a front-row seat to one landing back at Eglin. The aircraft came waffling down through the thick, heavy air of Florida. Built for speed, the aircraft labored with the challenge to slow down yet stay aloft for landing. As the

SR-71 approached the runway, one could see all the way down the airstrip to a hangar, whose doors started to open as the Blackbird approached. The aircraft touched down and kept right on motoring down the landing strip toward the hanger. By the time it reached the doors, they were fully open. Without pause, the Blackbird eased right in the hangar and the doors immediately closed behind it. The window of opportunity to view the SR-71 was but a minute or so. It shimmered into view as a mirage, preceding the dawnlight. It arrived and disappeared with the sun not yet above the horizon, just the promise of light and day.

WHILE LIFE HAS A CERTAIN EBB AND FLOW TO IT, one learns to expect that most days have a routine. Still, every once in a while life intervened on its own timetable. As the pages of the calendar turned semester after semester during his teaching career at the Air Force Academy, Mike settled into that scheduled life. A typical day began with arrival at the academy, coffee in one hand and briefcase in the other, as he worked his way to Fairchild Hall, the main academic building. It was after hopping on the elevator one day for the short ride to his classroom that his day slammed to a stop.

As chance determined, only two of them were on the elevator that morning. The other man was a uniformed Air Force officer. This was certainly not an unusual sight on the campus of the Air Force Academy, but then he began to lose his composure. It was only a brief interlude, but Mike asked the man if he could do anything for him.

The stranger looked at Mike and released his sentiment, "Your brother took my flight."

Catching himself, Mike exited the elevator with the man, and they talked for a few minutes. Mike had run into Doug Hardgrave, who had been the assigned back-seater for pilot Larry Golberg flying F-4 Phantom IIs in Vietnam. It was Doug's seat that Mike's brother, Patrick, had taken that August 8 in 1966, when he was shot down over North Vietnam. Hardgrave was at the academy to teach.

What Mike did for the man was tell him to put that bag of responsibility down on the floor right then and there. He told him he shouldn't carry it with him because it was over, in the past, and neither of them could change the past. It was a burden Doug Hardgrave did not have to carry. While Hardgrave said he immediately knew who Mike was, because the brothers looked much alike, Mike repeated that Doug had to stop going there with his thoughts. In any event, no final resolution had been determined on Pat's shoot-down, and the family still hoped he would turn up a prisoner of war.

❧

A NICE BENEFIT ABOUT TEACHING AND ACADEMICS was the opportunity to watch bright young minds go off and reshape the world. Mike Wynne was a professor in astronautics at the Air Force Academy for three years and had the opportunity to make the acquaintance of many of the students, the last of which were those in the Class of 1973, the 15th to graduate from the academy. Some of these students went on to remarkable careers in the service of their country.

The current Air Force chief of staff, the 19th in line, replaced General T. Michael Moseley in the 2008 shake-up of Air Force leadership. Four-star General Norton A. Schwartz graduated from the academy in 1973, having been a cadet lieutenant colonel as wing operations and training officer and in the 34th Squadron in his final year. He immediately went into pilot training at Laughlin Air Force Base and followed that with C-130 training at Little Rock Air Force Base. His next active duty assignment found him with the tactical airlift squadrons working out of Clark Air Base in the Philippines and participating in the airlift evacuation of personnel during the fall of Saigon in 1975. His career never looked back.

One 1973 graduate who did not make the military a career, ended up with a significant amount of press. Chesley "Sully" Sullenberger, a member of Cadet Squadron 18, flew F-4 Phantom IIs for the Air Force in the 1970s. Moving over to the airline industry, he was captain of U.S. Airways flight #1549 on January 15, 2009. After the loss of power in all engines, he landed the Airbus A-320 in the Hudson River with no casualties. Another 1973 graduate, capping a long and illustrious career in the Air Force, returned as superintendent of the academy. Lieutenant General John F. Regni retired as superintendent in June, 2009.

Two students from the Class of 1973 became astronauts, each having two missions in space. Sidney M. Gutierrez was the pilot of the space shuttle *Columbia* on STS-40, a nine-day mission beginning on June 5, 1991. His second flight was as spacecraft commander on STS-59, an 11-day mission aboard the space shuttle *Endeavour* that began on April 9, 1994. Gutierrez racked up more than 480 hours in space. L. Blaine Hammond, with 460-plus hours in space, piloted STS-39, an eight-day mission aboard the space shuttle *Discovery* that began on April 28, 1991. Hammond's second journey was his second as pilot of *Discovery*. Hammond flew with STS-64, an almost 11-day expedition that began on September 9, 1994. These four space shuttle flights rocketed into space from Cape Canaveral in Florida.[53]

As THE 1972–73 SCHOOL YEAR neared completion and the Vietnam War made an exodus from the front pages of every newspaper in the United States, Mike was completing his third year on the faculty of the Air Force Academy. One way or another, Mike had spent pretty much an entire decade in the service of his country, starting at West Point back in 1962. As it worked out, much of Mike's extended family would also spend time in the service as many were drawn into the military during the Vietnam era.

CHAPTER SIX

The Family Circle

IN ED AND DOROTHY WYNNE'S NUCLEAR FAMILY, four siblings followed Pat and Mike, two girls and two additional boys. While all were raised at a number of military installations, the girls Maureen and Cathy have lasting impressions of their time in Florida. This was due to their age at the time and the number of years the family spent in the sunshine state. Their upbringing fashioned them into young women, with much of the charm and grace of the old South. They shared the same room growing up and experienced the joy and angst of childhood together. While different in personality and temperament, Maureen and Cathy would grow close, as intimate as echoes.

The girls' mother, Dorothy, had experienced a relatively exacting Dutch-uncle upbringing in New York during the Roaring Twenties and Great Depression years. Dot passed on her strict childhood to her daughters and was a compelling influence. Part of the reason was simple coincidence. During those impressionable years, the first two in birth order, Pat and Mike, were off at their respective military academies for a large part of the time and the last two, Stephen and Peter, were just youngsters who were oblivious to most commotion. It was the two in the middle, Maureen and Cathy, who were most affected by and molded by mom. The two girls had only each other, to assimilate and absorb mom's tutelage. Dad, of course, was at work.

The girls revered their father, Ed, and that respect and admiration extended to their older brothers in the military academies. Pat and Mike were the center of the military family, and the girls had a special affinity for their older brothers. Besides Pat, Mike, and their dad in the U.S. Air Force, in time other close family members also served the nation, each in their own way.

Mike's two brothers-in law and his own two brothers were a part of the military-industrial complex. Among the four, three served in the military, two of those in the Air Force. The lone member without military experience served his time with a major defense contractor. Three of the four are still engaged in supporting the military.

❧

THE GIRLS IN THE FAMILY were raised much according to military custom, if not the manual itself. Such was the tradition and fashion of the day—much stricture in their structure. Cathy was the rebellious one, perhaps because she was the second of the girls. But Maureen, maybe not so much.

When it came time for college, Maureen started at the University of Florida. Following her heart and utilizing her full quota of kismet, she met and fell in love with someone who also had ties to the Air Force—Al Guarino. They met at the Officers' Club at Patrick Air Force Base. Love won out, and Maureen and Al soon married. Maureen dropped out of the University of Florida to be a homemaker, but a few years later when the couple was attached to Moody Air Force Base in Valdosta, Georgia, she would commute to Gainesville and complete her studies at the University of Florida. Twenty-year-old Maureen's move out of the homestead in Satellite Beach proved to be but a short hop. She kept it in the family and married her Air Force man in June 1968.

Al's lineage complemented that of his new bride and predestined him for the Air Force. Al's father, Air Force Major Larry Guarino, was a downed pilot who spent years in the Hanoi Hilton during the Vietnam War.[54] Al had spent his childhood traipsing around the world following his father's career. He attended Wagner High

School at Clark Air Base above Manila Bay in the Philippines and finished high school at Itazuki Air Base at Fukuoka, Japan in 1963. With his father destined for Vietnam, the family transferred back to the States.

Showing just how many ways exist to garner a position in the Air Force, Al went through the Air Force Reserve Officer Training Corps program while in college at the University of Florida. He earned his wings through pilot training at Williams Air Force Base outside Phoenix, Arizona, and completed combat crew training at Hurlburt Field in Florida. Second Lieutenant Guarino graduated from both in late 1969. As things worked out, Al went through reserve officer training, earned his wings, and served a tour in Vietnam while his father was a prisoner of war. But getting there himself entailed a number of hurdles, beginning with his mother.

With one prisoner of war in the family, Evelyn Guarino did whatever she could to keep her son from going to Vietnam. But Al stubbornly wanted to do his share and quietly hoped whatever role he played might help gain his father's return that much faster. At that point, Al was in Air-Ground Operations School training for duty in the Cessna O-1E Bird Dog with a heading for Southeast Asia. He had already passed through two Air Force review boards of successively higher ranking officer panels, gaining permission to serve a tour in Vietnam. And then his father's sister entered the fray.

Al's aunt turned out to be the biggest obstacle as she grumbled to her Congressman and forced the Air Force to reassign him. He was yanked out of O-1 training and switched into the North American F-100 Super Sabre on a course for Spangdahlem Air Base in Germany. But Al was not to be put off so easily.

Al camped out in the commander's office until he received assistance. In the end, the deputy commander placed a call to one of his contacts in Washington, D.C., one of President Nixon's aides. Al was successful. His instruction in the F-100 with probable assignment to Germany was changed back to schooling in the O-1 as a forward air controller with a bearing set for Vietnam. He finished training and checked out in the O-1 at Holley Field in Florida.

He arrived in-country at Tan Son Nhut Air Base, a few miles

northwest of Saigon, in November 1969. He received his in-country checkout in the O-1 at Bien Hoa. Assigned to the 19th and then 22nd Tactical Air Support Squadrons, he was stationed primarily at an airfield in An Loc—Detachment B-33 team camp—in support of the U.S. Army Special Forces. The Special Forces effort, pacification and rural security, was one of training, advising, and assisting Vietnamese special forces, Montagnard irregulars, and paramilitary regional and popular forces. The forward air controllers job was visual reconnaissance and close air support, helping direct air strikes and marking targets for Special Forces actions.

Al flew his O-1E/G over scores of obscure little villages, chiefly in the III Corps area of operations. He flew over places with names such as Bu Dop, Loc Ninh, Minh Thanh, and Tong Le Chon, and even flew missions in the north of Cambodia, north and east of Snoul. Al flew 322 missions during his tour in Vietnam.

Al was quick to state that getting shot at in the O-1 was no big deal. Flying low and slow while looking for the enemy makes it more of a certainty, so one went in half expecting it. Lending credence to the comment, Al often brought along a small tape recorder or movie camera on his flights, narrating what he did and saw. On one of his forced landings, he recalled hearing a great deal of rifle and small arms fire as he descended. Looking for a place to set down, he soon found the gunfire source as a squad of Special Forces troops appeared, lighting up the whole area and snatching him up. Forward air controllers were important, and the Special Forces made sure no one silenced their "eyes and ears."

Al was promoted to first lieutenant while in Vietnam. During his tour that spanned from November 1969 through the following November, he flew in support of U.S. Army Special Forces, the 11th Armored Cavalry Regiment, and Army of the Republic of Vietnam Rangers. He flew out of a number of small fields, such as Lam Som with its 2,000-foot temporary runway. Besides flying, he also had time to stand shoulder to shoulder with Montagnard guerrillas, a Vietnamese ethnic minority sympathetic to the Americans, in defending the perimeter of the airfield. Just like his father, who was off flying in China during World War II when Alan was born in 1945, Al was flying missions in Vietnam in July 1970 when his first child was born back home in Florida.

Al returned from Vietnam and made a career out of the Air Force. He would tally more than 5,200 hours of flying time, almost 900 of those in combat theaters. During that time, he also served in the Persian Gulf, flying Desert Storm sorties and enforcing the no-fly zone. He served in various senior capacities at Air Force bases across the United States and overseas in Iceland, the Netherlands, and twice in Saudi Arabia, where he was quartered in the soon-to-be infamous Khobar Towers complex. He served in the Air Force in a number of command positions including instructor pilot, weapons officer, flight commander, operations officer, squadron commander, operations group commander, and composite wing vice commander.

Besides the O-1 Bird Dog, Al marked hours in the North American T/AT-28 Trojan, Northrop T-38 Talon, McDonnell Douglas F-4 Phantom II, General Dynamics F-16 Fighting Falcon, and McDonnell Douglas F-15 Eagle. A highly decorated command pilot, he has been awarded the Legion of Merit (twice) and Distinguished Flying Cross, among other awards. His terminal military assignment was chief of operations, First Air Force at Tyndall Air Force Base. This was the same First Air Force to which his father-in-law had been assigned in the 1940s. Al would retire a colonel, the same as his father, after 30 years and two months of service in the Air Force.

Still actively involved in the military-industrial complex, Al crossed over to industry after retirement, teaching F-15 academics and simulators. He was lead F-15 instructor for Lockheed Martin at Tyndall Air Force Base in Florida. Al now has essentially the same role, but is back on the government payroll as a GS-14. So much for retirement.

As brothers-in-law, it was especially nice for Mike and Al to have common interests and shared experiences. In 1971 Al Guarino and Mike Wynne were both young, 20-something captains in the Air Force. Mike was teaching at the Air Force Academy. Al was back from Vietnam, serving as instructor pilot at Keesler Air Force Base outside Biloxi, Mississippi. Al was assigned to the 3389th Pilot Training Squadron, which provided training to pilots and mechanics of foreign countries, especially those of South Vietnam. The 3389th was activated in 1967 to provide training in the North American T/AT-28 Trojan, a single-engine, propeller-driven aircraft. During the next six years the 3389th graduated more than 900 pilots. This reflected Captain Guarino's expertise, as only the best became instructor pilots.[55]

Mike was in Florida visiting family and friends, and made the short journey over to Biloxi to see his sister, Maureen, and brother-in-law Al, who lived in base housing. On his visit to Keesler, one thing led to another. Since Mike was not a pilot, Al offered him a ride in the T/AT-28. Mike jumped at the chance and suited up to be Alan's rear-seater for a flight.

Takeoff was uneventful as they lifted off the end of the runway on a bearing out over the Back Bay of Biloxi. Shortly thereafter, the engine started to run rough. Al immediately came around in a left climbing turn to accomplish two things, head back toward the airfield and reach high key. They were on a return course but barely at high key when the engine seized. Al and Mike were in for a brief adventure. After all, given this flight was somewhat of an unscheduled jaunt, two Air Force captains parachuting out over the airfield would not look very professional.

As an instructor pilot, Al knew exactly what to do, especially since he regularly taught pilots how to recover from an engine failure. Al executed a perfect flameout landing from high key. High key described the altitude position of the aircraft over the airfield, high enough to allow the pilot to make a spiraling descent with a certain angle of attack and glide slope, and land the aircraft with the engine out. Landing gear up and flaps up to maximize speed as long as possible, it was a matter of managing the aircraft's energy state. As the T/AT-28 spiraled earthward, Al deployed as little flaps as possible to carry speed through low key and base key and then turned base leg. He let the gear down when he had the runway made, flared out, and landed safely on the concrete landing strip.

This was surely a bonding experience. One wonders what was going through the back-seater's mind while Al executed? Consider the consequences had these two Air Force captains shared more than a brief adventure.

❖

NEXT IN LINE in the Wynne family was Mike's sibling, Cathy. She exited the Florida nest in a different fashion, eventually heading north. When it was time for college, she eschewed the in-state schools and set her sights on Alabama. She started at Springhill College in Mobile, Alabama. After two years at that Jesuit institution, she and a girlfriend left for the Midwest where they relocated to Miami University Ohio. Cathy completed her studies, graduating with a degree in sociology. Raised in a military family replete with officers, some thought that she might one day marry into the military. Probably no one expected her to end up with someone from the ranks. But life unfolds on its own terms.

Of course, many ways can be found to be part of the circle. Not every Wynne relation passed through the Air Force. Philip Bessette, who married Mike's sister, Cathy, served a tour of duty in Vietnam. His story was undoubtedly more typical for many of his generation.

With the growing discontent about the war in Vietnam, enlistments were not high enough to support the massive deployments in Southeast Asia. Unlike World War II, tours during the Vietnam War were limited to a single year in a combat zone. This placed huge demands for constantly rotating fresh troops through the theater. To remedy the situation, the Selective Service instituted a draft lottery to determine the order in which men would be called for induction into the military. No draft lottery had been held since 1942, so men were grouped for a series of lotteries. The first grouping of citizen-soldiers included a million young men, those born between 1944 and 1950. The first lottery occurred on December 1, 1969, with live television and radio coverage.

For the lottery, each of the 366 birthdates of the year was placed in a blue-plastic capsule and hand drawn, one at a time. September 14 was the first number pulled, relegating those between 19 and 25 born on that day first in line for induction. Philip and his two older brothers were in that age group and fell into that first lottery pool. Phil's two older brothers drew numbers 250 and 362, while Phil drew 145. In the end, numbers through 195, depending on one's draft classification, were called to report for possible induction. Numbers through 174 were actually inducted.[56]

Inducted in July 1970, Phil had his basic training at Fort Lewis in Tacoma, Washington, and was assigned a military occupation specialty (MOS) of 11 Bravo—rifle infantryman. He finished advanced infantry training at the same Fort Lewis and shipped out for Vietnam on December 3. He left the States from the processing facility in Oakland, California. His flight routed him through one of the commercial airports in Alaska and then a United States staging area in Yokohama, finally arriving in Saigon through Tan Son Nhut airport.

Phil was a member of the Army's First Team—the First Cavalry Division (Airmobile).[57] The First Cavalry was one of two divisions to bring the new helicopter-driven airmobile tactic to the Vietnam theater. Phil served in two units—D27 and C25. D27 was Delta Company of the Second Battalion of the Seventh Calvary Regiment, made famous by George Armstrong Custer at Little Big Horn. C25 was Charlie Company of the Second Battalion of the Fifth Calvary Regiment, the "Black Knights" of the First Calvary Division, later reorganized into the Third Brigade (Separate).

Phil first experienced the hot and humid climate of Vietnam when he arrived in-country in December 1970, just one month after his future brother-in-law, Alan Guarino, returned to the States. This time period coincided with a transition phase in the war. It was shortly after the war had expanded with the incursion into Cambodia, by which Americans tried to curtail the enemy's ability to use the country as a sanctuary. It was just before the real push for "Vietnamization" of the war occurred, when the American policy shifted to turn the fighting over to the Army Republic of Vietnam. Thus, Phil entered the conflict during a counteroffensive and left during a consolidation.

Phil spent the first part of his tour with D27, training regional and popular forces in the countryside around Saigon. Similar to a territorial militia, these counterinsurgency groups were under provincial and local authority, respectively, and nicknamed "Ruff-Puffs." Their training was a necessary prelude to the people of Vietnam taking over the war. Training encompassed civilian defense and national police units, composed chiefly of local villagers. The goal was to put them in a position to patrol and defend their own borders.

During this time, D27 worked around Tay Ninh, roughly 70 miles northwest of Saigon and within 20 miles of the Cambodian border. D27 then moved east to the Tri Tam area in March 1971. Tri Tam anchored the southern tip of a large Michelin rubber plantation. Both Tay Ninh and Tri Tam were within sight of a 3,200-foot-high mountain, the only geographic blip found on maps of the surrounding flatland. The mountain, called Nui Ba Den or Black Virgin Mountain, was used for communications as a radio relay station by the Americans. About this time, Phil transferred units and duties.

Prior to most of the First Calvary Division standing down and leaving Vietnam as part of the United States troop withdrawal in April of 1971, Phil transferred with other men who had not served their full year in-country. He was assigned to C25, which was headquartered out at Bien Hoa. C25 spent the ensuing months on field operations, trudging through the jungle and flying the First Cavalry helicopters in and out of the countryside looking for enemy camps. The objective was to block Viet Cong infiltration and supply routes. C25 marked time in the Xuan Loc region and at the battalion's main fire support base, Firebase Mace. Both areas entailed search and clear missions at forward operating areas in free fire zones.

Xuan Loc, in Long Khanh province, was roughly 35 miles northeast of Saigon, essentially a suburb. Control of Xuan Loc was key for it anchored a main route into the South Vietnamese capital, and it acted to guard the U.S. air base at Bien Hoa. In 1975 Xuan Loc would be the site of the last major battle of the Vietnam War for the Army of the Republic of Vietnam.

Firebase Mace, part of the outer defense of the Bien Hoa area, was at the foot of Hill 837, Nui Chua Chan, a hilltop radio relay station located about 45 miles northeast of Saigon. This was a hot area for field operations, and Phil experienced everything from firefights with Viet Cong AK-47s to friendly fire from Army of the Republic of Vietnam artillery. He also witnessed a tragic accident east of Firebase Mace, while working out of fire support base Sandra. His own squad leader, walking point with the squad on a short reconnaissance patrol, misidentified an ambush and fatally shot an American soldier from a different squad of the company.[58] Phil can still distinguish the helicopter hovering overhead that night, dropping a cable to pull the body bag–lined stretcher up and away, while artillery flares eerily lit up the zone and Blue Max Cobra gunships flew close cover.

Phil reached the grade of specialist fourth class. He had progressed from point man on day one to point radio for a time, walking fourth in line with the platoon. Working his way up the responsibility chain, he spent time as the company radio telephone operator (RTO) and ended up battalion RTO. In time his tour came to an end, and he rotated back home, exactly one year after arriving in-country.

❖

THE PENULTIMATE WYNNE, Stephen, was born on November 11, 1952, in the Portsmouth Naval Hospital, just across the river from Norfolk, Virginia. That date was the next-to-last time November 11 was called Armistice Day before being memorialized as Veterans Day. A few years later, the family moved to Florida where the kids spent most of their childhood. After elementary and secondary school, Steve had the same opportunity for college as his siblings, but that didn't draw his interest. Steve followed up with a year at Springhill College in Mobile and with a few jobs here and there, but none you would call a career. The pull of the Air Force was strong in Steve, and he enlisted in 1977 in his 20s. Steve began what would be a 17-year career in the Air Force with basic training at Lackland Air Force Base outside San Antonio, Texas.

As the sole entry station for basic military training for Air Force enlisted recruits, every enlisted person's career begins at Lackland Air Force Base. After basic training, Steve moved to Lowry Air Force Base outside Denver for technical school. Lowry had long been a center for Air Force training. One of Lowry's specialties was ground and armament training, and munitions handling. This would be Steve's calling as an armament systems specialist.

After technical school, newly minted Airman First Class Steve Wynne reported for his first duty assignment at Keflavick, Iceland. With roots back to World War II, Keflavick became host to a NATO command before the Korean War and the U.S. Air Force's 1400th Air Base Group in 1951. After a decade in occupancy as a U.S. Air Force installation, operations at Keflavick were transferred to the Navy in 1961, rendering Keflavick a naval air station. The U.S. Air Force remained as a tenant. Thus Steve's first active duty assignment was with the 57th Fighter-Interceptor Squadron, under the Aerospace Defense Command, with its complement of McDonnell Douglas F-4C Phantom IIs. The next stop was Germany.

Remaining in the NATO family, Steve's next assignment was to Hahn Air Base in Germany, long a frontline NATO facility. Hahn became host to the U.S. Air Force in 1952, when American units took over from French occupation forces. Hahn, which would become the second largest U.S. Air Force installation in Germany, would evolve into Frankfurt-Hahn airport years later. Steve was assigned to the 50th Tactical Fighter Wing and kept the F-4E Phantom IIs armed and flying while they were being phased out at Hahn Air Base in favor of the newer F-16s. Steve's time at Hahn overlapped that of Major Terryl Schwalier, who was an instructor and commander in the 10th Tactical Fighter Squadron, a unit of the 50th Tactical Fighter Wing. Schwalier would rise to brigadier general. As the F-4Es rotated out of Germany, so did Steve.

Wurtsmith Air Force Base, in the north of Michigan's lower peninsula, was his next station. Wurtsmith began as an aerial gunnery range in the 1920s. It had worked training exercises for years in concert with Selfridge Air Force Base, where Steve's father had been stationed. Wurtsmith had developed into a Strategic Air

Command base, from a time when the Air Force was spreading its strategic bombers throughout the States. Steve was assigned to the 379th Bombardment Wing, constantly on nuclear alert, with its complement of Boeing B-52G Stratofortresses. The next 12 years were split between California and Germany.

Steve spent three years at George Air Force Base, part of the Tactical Air Command, and nine years at Spangdahlem Air Base, a NATO host command. Each assignment entailed two separate tours. On his first assignment at George, Steve was attached to the 35th Tactical Fighter Wing, whose mission was training F-4E flight crews and F-4G "Wild Weasel" operations air crews. Transferring to Germany, Steve was attached to the 52nd Tactical Fighter Wing in support of its F-4E/G Phantom IIs. Then he repeated the rotation.

Back to George Air Force Base in California, Steve was assigned to the new 37th Tactical Fighter Wing, which used the F-4Gs of its 561st and 562nd Tactical Fighter Squadrons in enemy air defense suppression missions. His last duty in Germany was again with the 52nd Tactical Fighter Wing. He was there during the period the 52nd swapped out its F-4 Phantom IIs for the newer F-16 Fighting Falcon. Through a mix of field training detachment classes and on-the-job training, Steve became a weapons load specialist on the F-16C/D Block 30.

Staff Sergeant Steve Wynne retired from active duty in 1994 and promptly put his technical background to use. He hired on with Lockheed Martin Space Systems Company at Cape Canaveral. Steve was with the space division for the next 10 years working on the Atlas, Atlas-Centaur, and Titan-Centaur missiles, and solid rocket motors. Quality control had become his specialty, and he was at the Cape during a busy time. NASA had 58 launches of expendable vehicles, 29 of which were from the eastern range at Cape Canaveral.[59] Still with Lockheed Martin, Steve presently works at Tyndall Air Force Base in Florida.

❧

THE LAST WYNNE was Peter, who arrived on June 30, 1956, at Fort Meade in Maryland but soon ended up in Florida when the family moved in the late 1950s. He rounded out Colonel Wynne's family to a perfect half-dozen children. He followed the predictable path of a series of schools, attending Surfside Elementary, Holy Name, Melbourne Central Catholic, and then Satellite High. Surfing and soccer accompanied academics at the University of South Florida in Tampa. Eventually, it was time to begin a career and the influence of the Air Force was telling.

Since college, Pete has worked his entire career in the industrial sector of the military-industrial complex. In fact, he has worked just about as close as one can to the U.S. Air Force without being on active duty. Upon graduation, Pete interviewed at and landed a position with General Dynamics in Fort Worth, Texas, in the summer of 1979. His timing was spot on to allow him to be deeply involved with the General Dynamics F-16 Fighting Falcon program.

Experience gained in the Korea and Vietnam conflicts called for a new type of aircraft in the U.S. inventory. In Korea, the United States utilized light and lean fighters, primarily the North American F-86 Sabre. In Vietnam, attack aircraft had evolved into the much heavier and more complex McDonnell F-4 Phantom II fighter bomber that relied on missiles and electronics. The F-4 could fly farther and faster but had given up a measure of agility.

Post-Vietnam, the design that resulted was a lightweight, single-engine, supersonic aircraft that was smaller and lighter than most competitors. This yielded a fighter that could exceed Mach 2 and had a ceiling above 50,000 feet. It was relatively inexpensive to build and simple to maintain, but those accomplishments didn't hamper its performance as a weapons system. Even at low speed and low altitude, it was highly maneuverable.

The F-16 fighter was reminiscent of the Chevrolet Corvette sports car, where the product was affordable but the technology remained decidedly high performance. The F-16 was one of the first fighters with a thrust-to-weight ratio greater than one, meaning it could accelerate in a vertical climb. After testing in 1974 at Edwards Air Force Base, production began the following year at General Dynamics Fort Worth facility, with the first production aircraft rolling out in August 1978. The first operational delivery took place in January 1979 to Hill Air Force Base in Utah, the same year Pete arrived in Fort Worth.

Pete has spent most of his 30-year career at General Dynamics and its successor Lockheed Martin in program finance and business sector management. Starting with military electronics, Pete became the business manager for electronics manufacturing of F-16 components. Shadowing his father's basic work with radar in the early 1940s, Pete progressed to director of military electronics, where General Dynamics built radars and other radar equipment for the Air Force to utilize on the Nellis Air Force Base training range. This was Red Flag territory.

Red Flag was the Air Force combat training exercise established in 1975 for the purpose of schooling aircrews by simulating realistic aerial warfare. Before Red Flag, Air Force pilots would train against each other, usually in similar aircraft. As enemy aircraft characteristics such as climb, turn, roll, and speed diverged from those of American fighter equipment, the old training methods became ineffectual. The American success rate in the skies over Korea was not repeated in Vietnam, and outdated training was part of the reason. General Dynamics radar developments helped close the gap.

The linchpin to imitating realistic aerial combat, besides varying the types of aircraft one practiced against, was to simulate missile and gun radars used by the enemy. General Dynamics developed the Multiple Threat Emitter System (MUTES). As pilots flew their combat missions over the Air Force range, the MUTES equipment locked on to the aircraft and transmitted radio frequencies that simulated the tracking systems of various threats, such as air-to-air and surface-to-air missiles, and antiaircraft artillery. The aircrews had the opportunity to practice identifying and countering threats, without becoming more than an electronic casualty. After radars, Pete repositioned to direct the business management for the F-16 fighter aircraft.

Facilitating and financing aircraft sales entailed more than a simple charge per copy and generally involved a package price. This included the cost of the aircraft, any mission equipment and a support package. Pete's expertise was in estimating and negotiating financial performance for foreign and domestic F-16 programs. Originally a General Dynamics product, the F-16 gained a new patron when General Dynamics sold its aircraft business to Lockheed in 1993. Pete's employer, still in Fort Worth, eventually was renamed Lockheed Martin Aeronautics. Success of the F-16 program was exemplified by the fact that more than 4,400 units have been produced and 25 nations have selected this aircraft for their air force.[60]

The burgeoning growth of computers in the early 1980s established a new paradigm for managing and hosting data and information. Pete's work during this period involved automating F-16 Line Replaceable Unit estimates utilizing learning curve techniques. The outcome facilitated pricing and negotiating exercises for multiyear estimates. In the 1990s Pete worked on the automation of the Fort Worth plant's business system for budgeting, updating, and forecasting contract costs and schedules. The resulting approach to managing program costs also was applied to the Lockheed Martin C-130 Hercules, C-5 Galaxy, and Palmdale Skunk Works programs.

Most recently, Pete Wynne was promoted to the corporate program management ranks. He oversees Lockheed Martin's program performance process, which touches a majority of the business units managing U.S. government contracts across the country. Pete established a consolidated process for the management of contract costs and schedule performance. He now works with the various business areas to ensure consistency in the execution of contracts and open communication for continuous process improvement.

❧

As it developed through the years, members of Mike Wynne's extended family found their own way to serve the country—some directly in the military, some in those areas of industry that work closely with the military, and some in both arenas. It was now 1973 and the war in Vietnam, which had pulled at the fabric of the nation for so long, was at end. Mike's active duty assignment at the Air Force Academy continued, but unbeknownst to him other courses of action were brewing. He remained a captain in the United States Air Force, the highest company grade he could attain. The next step was the field grade of major, but simple time and grade did not earn everyone that promotion. It was a time for decisions.

CHAPTER SEVEN

Transition to Entrepreneur

MIKE RECEIVED A LETTER ONE DAY from the Air Force reviewing his career. He had graduated from the Air Force Institute of Technology in 1970, leaving with a master's degree in electrical engineering and a commitment to remain in the Air Force for six more years. Three years had elapsed since then and the Vietnam War had ground to a halt. As happens when the United States departs a war time footing, the services were purging their ranks to return to a peacetime force level. The letter stated that the Air Force had a surplus of his specialty code (guidance and control) and inquired about Mike's intentions. Thus, he had arrived at a choice point.

Still not 30 years old, Mike was a captain in the U.S. Air Force, with the attending respect, position, and future. He was an officer and a gentleman. He was happily married, with a young and growing family of three daughters. Mike was in a comfortable place in his life and career, and he loved the academy. He was the officer representative for the swim team, helped coach and traveled with the water polo team, and ran the Fal-Fins age-group swim team on base.

Professionally, he was a researcher in the astronautics and astrophysics departments and on occasion had the opportunity to work on advanced projects in the Flight Dynamics Lab. He also was involved with weapons development of some note—publishing research on the sight line autopilot for the AC-130 Spectre gunship and working on the snap-shoot gun sight, the leading technology in aircraft weapons aiming devices. He was teaching three, sometimes four courses at a time at the academy and even at the point of establishing new course offerings. The Air Force letter announced that he could leave the service, forgiving the last three years of his commitment, and he had 30 days to decide.

One of the considerations that would work through Mike's thought process was the promotion list. Generally speaking, making captain was simply a matter of time and Mike had achieved that rank. Reaching major, with the grade of O-4 was another matter. It was not a foregone conclusion and it was not for all officers. The end of hostilities in Vietnam translated into less movement on the promotion list and also meant less chance of an early, below-the-zone promotion. Mike had most of the tickets needed to be considered for a below-the-zone jump but not all.

Below-the-zone promotions were a little tougher for Air Force officers who were not pilots. Not having the panache associated with being a pilot was only one strike though. Anything but a perfect officer efficiency report would be another. One factor to be considered in any decision to leave his beloved Air Force was indirectly tied to his time in graduate school at the Air Force Institute of Technology. The only flawed officer efficiency report Mike ever received was from his time at the institute.

Mike's period there saw him spending more time with the base personnel from Wright-Patterson rather than his classmates from Guidance Navigation & Control 70. Conservative by nature and nurture, he and Barb had eschewed the behavior of his classmates, who engaged in the swinging sixties lifestyle. This earned him a small blip on his officer efficiency report, possibly enough to prevent him from getting a below-the-zone promotion to major even though he was held in very high regard at the Air Force Academy. This was also a mark he could not remove from his personnel jacket—it was a permanent smudge, more or less a "doesn't play well with others." It played a part in Mike's choice between making the Air Force his future or going on with the rest of his life in a different field of endeavor.

He talked with his leadership at the academy. Even though Mike's position was very nice, academy leadership hurried to arrange an even better situation, making every effort to encourage him to make the academy his future. The tentative arrangement was to send Mike to the University of Texas at Austin for his doctorate in engineering. This was intended to position him for return to the Air Force Academy, slotted for a department head. As Mike well knew, this opened up the possibilities of a star on his shoulder. Retiring as a department head from the Air Force Academy was usually a graveyard promotion to one star brigadier general. He was walking over much the same ground his father had covered.

Years before it involved two men, Ed Wynne and Robert McDermott, who had taught together at West Point, their alma mater, in the 1950s. After teaching at the Military Academy, their careers went in different directions. Bob McDermott became brigadier general and dean of the faculty at the U.S. Air Force Academy. He modernized the curriculum at the academy and developed the astronautics course in support of the United States' missile program. Ed Wynne became Colonel Wynne and head of range development at the Cape Canaveral missile facility.

In 1962 Ed Wynne was approached by the Electronic Systems Command to become vice commander at Hanscom Field in Massachusetts, a groove to a one-star slot. Hearing about the possible move, General McDermott offered an alternative to Ed, a department head position back at the Air Force Academy. Colonel Wynne was at a comfortable place in his life and career. But the grind of moving had taken its toll through the years and with his wife having just returned to some semblance of good health, he didn't want to uproot the family again. So, with a grateful heart, he turned down both offers. Fast forward to 1973, with the Army issuing "pink slips" and the other services offering early outs on commitments, it was Mike's turn to crystallize his thoughts.

Mike talked with his leadership on the home front, Barb. He had made a point of including his wife in his activities and decisions from the start, and this situation was no different. She was his sounding board and life partner. As a youngster, Mike's experiences were centered on the military. He never owned a draft card, but he always had an ID card, trading in his dependent ID for a West Point ID and then an active duty Air Force ID. For Barb, it was the opposite.

Barb's father had been a lieutenant colonel in the Air Force during the Korean War, stationed in Nova Scotia working on radars. After the war years he worked in business for RCA. She was familiar with careers in business. While going into business might be an adventure for Mike, quite possibly the opportunity to stay in the Air Force was the adventure for Barb. As a couple, the Air Force had provided a wonderful journey, admittedly a great state of affairs but a narrow circumstance. As many young couples, they wondered about the alternatives.

Just a few years earlier, on a weekend in New York City's Times Square when they were talking about getting married, they had made "Cast Your Fate to the Wind," the jazz tune by the Sounds Orchestral, their favorite.[61] In the end, this is precisely what they did. They wanted to explore their options. The predictable path, marvelous as it was, just wasn't an adventure anymore. Mike waited until the 30-day period was at hand and sent in the papers to resign his commission in the Air Force. Only then did he call his parents.

As one could predict, Mike's dad was heartbroken. Ed Wynne was many things but a shrinking violet wasn't one of them, and he let Mike know his opinion. Blowback. But after grumbling about Mike's decision, Ed tried to let it go. He knew he had to let his children make their own way, no matter how much trouble he had sitting on the sidelines. Ed did not mention it again, but a small unseen cloud remained between them. Ed wished that his son had trusted him enough to take the chance dad would come down on his side of the decision. Mike, for his part, didn't want to argue about his life in the Air Force when his dad had had his own life in the Air Force. So, in the end, Mike struck off on a new path in his life and career.

MIKE LEFT THE AIR FORCE ACADEMY for a number of reasons. One was the opportunities presented at a small research outfit in the Colorado Springs area. Research Analysis & Development Incorporated was a firm founded and run by a group of ex–Air Force guys. Rick Willes, a Naval Academy graduate with a background in aeronautics, and Albert Beerman, with experience in accounting and finance, were the principals at the company, along with Jack Brush, Chuck Fosha, and Ron Schillereff. The firm had been in existence for a short time when 1973 rolled around and Mike Wynne received his notice from the Air Force indicating the downsizing of the service. The principals at Research Analysis & Development asked Mike to join them, indicating they had a position and an office ready to go. So the stage was set.

Mike's resignation from the Air Force represented the third West Point graduate in three years to resign teaching duties in the astronautics department at the academy. This made the academy a bit gun-shy of taking graduates from the Military Academy, even though it was the Air Force that started the ball rolling. So Mike set his course and had a party—his last big military blowout. At midnight the party-goers found one of their own with suitable rank that could stand up and swear Mike into the Air Force Reserves, officially terminating his active duty service. Thus he joined the reserves and became a civilian at the same time. The next day he joined Research Analysis & Development, his first foray outside the military. He also immediately signed up at the University of Colorado, Colorado Springs, in the two-year MBA degree night-school program.

Research Analysis & Development had two distinct business areas, both concerned with modeling and control theory. The first was working with the Office of the Secretary of Defense in program analysis, designing scalar models to evaluate the effectiveness of weapon systems. The other side of the business was modeling for the financial markets—stocks, bonds and interest rates, information that could be sold to banks, brokerage firms, and similar financial institutions.

In modeling for weapon systems, Mike was involved with Lanchester equations; game-on-game and force-on-force structures;

air, ground and naval warfare simulations; and the like. To differing extents, these models were aimed at piecing together a prediction of the cause and effect of warfare or the outcome of a conflict. Rick Willes and Chuck Fosha took the lead in preparing the models attendant to weapons fire control. This era marked Mike's first work for the Pentagon as a civilian.

In financial modeling, Mike worked with stock market prediction models that were based on an interest rate forecaster. The forecaster was grounded in Nobel laureate William Sharpe's work from the 1960s on the capital asset pricing model, a key parameter of which was the beta coefficient. Jack Brush and Al Beerman directed the effort preparing models attendant to financial markets. In helping develop financial market models and money management tools, Mike also had the responsibility for customer sales, working with firms such as Harris Bank & Trust and Mesirow Company, both in Chicago, and California Bank & Trust in the Los Angeles area.

The essence of Research Analysis & Development's business was the implementation of research started at military laboratories, such as the Air Force Academy's Frank J. Seiler Research Laboratory or Massachusetts Institute of Technology's Charles Stark Draper Laboratory. The labs performed much of the initial research and development while private sector companies such as Research Analysis & Development were engaged under government contracts to implement the research, bringing it to market. At the early stages of Research Analysis & Development, much of its work in weapons fire control centered on the snap-shoot gun sight design from the Air Force Academy, conceived by then Lieutenant Colonel Rick Willes.

In the final analysis, it was the gun sight work that brought together these scientists as only a small group of people knew this research material, and most were either Air Force Academy graduates or instructors. Unburdened by the task of instruction but still well-known within the weapons development community, it was easy for these men to transition from the academy to the private sector, working on the same projects. In fact, Mike's last

major paper for the Air Force Academy was completed while he
was at Research Analysis & Development, under contract with the
academy's Frank J. Seiler Research Lab.[62]

This final report supported work on inertial guidance systems,
specifically advanced gyroscopes that are very sensitive to vibration.
A key requirement in the enhancement of gyroscopes was the
availability of a "quiet" facility that would permit testing of more
sophisticated components for precision, accuracy, and reliability.
Dino Lorenzini and Mike Wynne teamed up to perform an
analysis of the micro-flat table installed in the Seiler Laboratory's
Seismic Isolation Gyro Test Facility. Their analysis, which involved
instrumenting and mapping the table, proved the facility's micro-
flat table was suitable for cutting-edge engineering work. So Mike
was active, interested, and employed. His career marched forward.

CHAPTER EIGHT

Final Flight - 21°33′N, 106°46′E

FIRST LIEUTENANT PATRICK WYNNE came to the Vietnam War through Thailand, reporting for duty with the 555th "Triple Nickel" Tactical Fighter Squadron at Udorn RTAFB. At the time, the 555th was a split-squadron of the 8th Tactical Fighter Wing. Half the assets were stationed at Ubon RTAFB and the other half at Udorn.[63] In June the 555th consolidated its operations at Ubon, about 75 miles south of Udorn. Ubon was a World War II era British-built airfield, surrounded by rice paddies and bordered on one side by the Mun River, a tributary of the Mekong River. The 555th, identified by the tail code FY, was the third squadron to be attached to the 8th Tactical Fighter Wing at Ubon and brought with it the latest equipment, the C-model McDonnell F-4 Phantom IIs.[64] The 8th Wing was commanded by Colonel Joe Wilson.

While the Republic Aviation F-105 Thunderchief fighter-bomber would fly a majority of the missions in the mid-1960s, F-4s would grow to be the workhorse fighter aircraft for the U.S. Air Force in Vietnam. Their numbers grew steadily after initial deployments, from less than two dozen in 1965 to more than 180 in 1966. The number of F-4s would exceed 350 by 1972, the majority stationed at air bases in Thailand.[65]

Of the approximately 180 F-4s in Thailand and South Vietnam by the end of 1966, the three squadrons of the 8th Tactical Fighter Wing at Ubon RTAFB accounted for 76 aircraft. While the 8th

Wing's F-4Cs were the first in Thailand, they were not the first in the theater. The U.S. Air Force 12th Tactical Fighter Wing earned that distinction with F-4Cs at Cam Ranh Bay in November 1965.

During the course of the war, most of the air sorties and the greater percentage of bomb tonnage would be seen in South Vietnam, but the mid-1960s was a period of major air operations in the north—Rolling Thunder. What began as psychological persuasion soon evolved into armed interdiction. These missions were an attempt to stem the flow of men, machines, and material from the North to South Vietnam. Pat was not alone. Of the 385,278 American military members in South Vietnam in 1966, 52,913 were Air Force personnel. Another 26,113 assigned duty in Thailand.[66]

Operation Rolling Thunder started in March 1965 and lasted for three and one-half years. President Lyndon Johnson, who already oversaw an air war in the south, began the bombing in North Vietnam as a way to pressure the Communists into capitulating. But the President's bombing plan wasn't committed. It did not allow attacks near the cities, nor did it allow strikes against the dams and dikes that permitted controlled irrigation and prevented flooding in the agricultural land. Rolling Thunder started with restrictions that neutered its effectiveness. The President wanted only measured and limited sorties, gradual escalation to demonstrate American determination.

At the beginning of Rolling Thunder, the Joint Chiefs of Staff had proffered a list of 94 targets to accomplish the goals of President Johnson. But the target list was eventually rejected by both the President and Secretary of Defense Robert McNamara, thus setting up an operation to be directed by the White House. McNamara, who would try to redact most of his service as secretary of defense in retrospect, was the force to be reckoned with in 1965. McNamara and the Joint Chiefs of Staff directed the bombing program in Vietnam from Washington during this early period, leaving the on-site warriors little say in the matter.

The policy control from Washington would continue as Rolling Thunder missions were not allowed within miles of the Chinese border or the city centers of Hanoi and Haiphong. It would be the decade of the 1970s before some of those restrictions became targets, under Operation Linebacker I and II during the Nixon administration. In the gradual escalation during the 1960s, target packages were slowly widened to include more than just trains, planes, and automobiles. Targets were expanded to include oil and gas storage facilities, and ammunition dumps. Limited as it was, an air war took place throughout Vietnam, in the south and north.

One of the reasons for the no-fly zone for U.S. aircraft around the border between North Vietnam and China was because it was a land border, as opposed to one based on a river or another natural barrier. It was often difficult to determine the border that spanned hundreds of miles. Overarching those concerns was the risk of a confrontation. The Vietnam-era border with China was the same one that had been hammered out by French colonials in 1885, after France gained control of northern Vietnam. During Rolling Thunder operations in North Vietnam, the opportunity for mistakes was high and for political reasons no one wanted to risk incursions over Chinese airspace.

The services could not agree on a plan for integrating their air operations over North Vietnam to keep Air Force and Navy fighters from treading in each other's surrounding area, so the U.S. Pacific Command carved up the airspace into sections in September 1965. Each service was assigned responsibility for specific subdivisions. Whether puckish or providential, the Americans labeled the sections packs or packages since six existed at the beginning. The first package, Route Pack I, was that segment closest to the border between North and South Vietnam and included the demilitarized zone (DMZ). Route Pack VI was that sector at the far north and northeast, close to the border of China. In time, Route Pack VI was split into A and B, to further delineate accountability.

A line drawn from Hanoi northeast to the Chinese border at a 45° angle bisected Lang Son and Ha Bac provinces, forming the division between Route Pack VI-A and VI-B. Route Pack VI-A was west of that line, and Route Pack VI-B was to the east. Route Pack VI-A included the restricted area around Hanoi and was tasked to the U.S. Air Force, which flew out of Royal Thailand air bases.

Route Pack VI-B included the similarly restricted Haiphong Harbor and was the assigned duty of U.S. Navy carrier-based aircraft.[67] At least that's how it worked most of the time. Pat Wynne was flying an armed reconnaissance mission in Route Pack VI-B on the day he was shot down by enemy antiaircraft artillery fire.

Rolling Thunder missions were crafted to be tactical strikes rather than strategic bombing runs because of the restricted areas and the meager industrial base found in the north. The operations were a sequential chain of air strikes, and the sortie for August 8 was in series 51. Rolling Thunder 51 had as its focus the strangulation of North Vietnam's petroleum, oil, and lubricant supply. Series 51 was approved by the Joint Chiefs of Staff on July 6, 1966, and went into effect three days later. Scheduled attack sorties were increased from 8,100 to 10,100 per month.[68]

As Pat relocated from Udorn to Ubon, the 555th Tactical Fighter Squadron continued to experience unbalancing transfers in and out of the group. The 555th had been in the Southeast Asia theater since February 1966, and pilots were reaching the mission level where they could rotate home. The general policy was that an aircrew could rotate back home after completing 100 missions or 12 months in-country. One of these interchanges affected Pat. The pilot in charge of the paperwork for awards and decorations for the section, Robert S. Hopkins, was offered the opportunity to rotate back home. The offer was made on less than 24 hour notice, so it undoubtedly had to do with filling a quota for the month. With 107 missions, Bob happened to be high man and he had first chance at this rotation out of the squadron. Having a new baby at home, Bob jumped at the prospect but had to transfer responsibility for the awards and decorations paperwork to someone else.

A 1962 graduate of the Air Force Academy, Bob knew Pat had been editor of the *Talon* back in Colorado Springs as well as an author of the 65-G class yearbook from pilot training back at Williams Air Force Base. With Pat's writing prowess in mind, Bob prevailed upon him to take over sponsorship of the awards and decorations formalities. Since he knew taking responsibility for

Map of Vietnam and surrounding countries with route packs shown. *Sources:* Blank map by Uwe Dedering at http:// en.wikipedia.org/wiki/File:Vietnam_location_map.svg. Route packs redrawn from map in Thompson, *To Hanoi and Back*, p. 296–7. Cities and other landmarks added by author.

the work would facilitate Bob's transfer back to the States, Pat was pretty good about the situation, knowing full well Bob would turn over a pile of unfinished business. For the files that were already typed up, Bob passed them up the chain of command for approval as he left. Other files and hand-written notes had to be typed up and run through the whole approval process. One such case was that of Don Dodgen.

Don was a pilot in the Triple Nickel nearing the end of his tour as he approached 100 missions. On the request of senior officers, Bob had scribbled the notes recommending Don for the Distinguished Flying Cross for extraordinary performance on a recent mission. The honor of the Distinguished Flying Cross was such that it customarily took more than just completing 100 combat missions to be so decorated. Bob had been working on the notes for Don's decoration when he rotated back to the States. Pat inherited the files, but the timing was off.

Bob was notified after his morning mission on July 30, 1966, that he could rotate back home but had to decide and be ready to leave by 10:00 a.m. the next day. Bob worked overnight to finalize what papers he could and turned over the remaining awards and decorations records to Pat.[69] Always a great writer, Pat was now pressed with additional work for the squadron. But this was wartime, and Pat was busy in the flow of performing his own combat missions.

PAT'S FLIGHT PROBABLY UNFOLDED in much the same way as his other missions. Daily air strike orders came down the day before the mission, and a flurry of activity began with the operations duty officer. Aircraft and pilots were selected, generally rotating duty cycles, since competition was keen among the air crews for combat sorties. Pat's aircraft on August 8—McDonnell Aircraft serial number 63-7560, an F-4C Block 19 Phantom II model—was itself a recent acquisition of the 8th Tactical Fighter Wing. It was a replacement unit that had arrived on July 5 from the 366th Tactical Fighter Wing, either from the wing's assets at Holloman Air Force Base in New Mexico or Phan Rang Air Base on the coast of Vietnam below Cam Ranh Bay.[70]

Captain Larry Golberg, who had worked his way through the Air Force Reserve Officer Training Corps program at the University of Minnesota en route to earning pilot's wings, was designated the aircraft commander. Lieutenant Pat Wynne, a pilot himself but in-country only a few months, was anxious to catch flight time. Since Larry's usual rear, Doug Hardgrave (a classmate of Pat's from the Air Force Academy) was out, Pat snatched the back seat for this mission as the pilot systems officer.[71] Preparations continued.

Armaments were gauged to match the target package assigned, ordnance weight to fuel weight optimized. Cluster bombs and missiles were scheduled for August 8. Mission data cards and maps were reviewed to familiarize crews with the target areas, but they quickly became easily recognizable as missions and targets were regularly repeated. In fact, aircrews often attacked the same targets on the following mission, flying the same ingress routes and arriving at the same time of day.

Early morning of mission day, it was business as usual, with briefings an hour or two before takeoff, from both the intelligence officer and flight leader. This included last minute study of targets and available photo reconnaissance, with weather forecasts and the latest news of defensive measures in the area, chiefly antiaircraft artillery. Briefings also included discussion of weapons delivery and emergency airfields. Then it was suiting up with helmet, flight suit, parachute harness with underarm life preservers, .38 caliber Smith & Wesson Model 15 sidearm, a pair of two-way radios, and a lightweight vest containing survival, and escape and evasion kits.

Air crews left their personal items, such as pictures and wallets and expensive watches, in the locker. They flew with just their military identification and Geneva Convention cards. Pat stuffed his good luck charm, his academy ring, in his pocket. Then it was shuttling out to the flight line. After a quick walk around inspecting the exterior, they wedged into the cockpit of F-4 Phantom II serial 63-7560, already bristling with ordnance hung by crew members.

The typical armament package was a variety of missiles and bombs, although the F-4C Phantom IIs could also carry a 20 mm Gatling gun, rockets, and external fuel tanks. The F-4 had nine armament stations on the underside, four of which were always taken up by Raytheon AIM-7 Sparrow radar-guided missiles that were partially recessed into the fuselage body of the aircraft. That left five mounts or hardpoints, an inboard and outboard pylon on each wing and one centered directly under the fuselage. On August 8 the two outboard pylons were equipped with 370-gallon auxiliary fuel tanks. The inboard pylons each held a pair of Raytheon AIM-9 Sidewinder heat-seeking missiles. On the center-line hardpoint, four pods of CBU-2 cluster bombs were mounted on a multiple-ejector rack. It was time to begin the mission.

The crew chief helped buckle in the pilots, threading the shoulder straps on the men's parachute harness vest through the connectors on the parachute built into the ejection seat, and finished the preflight check lists. Even though equipped with a cartridge turbine starter system, which allowed the F-4Cs to operate from air fields with little ground support, an auxiliary power unit was generally used at Ubon RTAFB to bring the F-4C to life. The flight was strapped and started.

Golberg and Wynne's ride, part of a flight of four F-4s, with call sign "Ozark," taxied to the end of Ubon's runway to the arming area.[72] Just before takeoff, the arming crew pulled the safety wires and devices off the missiles and bombs, rendering them the proverbial armed and dangerous. The CBU-2 cluster bombs were submunition dispensers loaded with hundreds of fragmentation bomblets that became active only when ejected rearwards from the dispenser.

A few minutes later, at approximately six in the morning on the flight tower operations clock, Ozark Flight went wheels up. The flight traveled east across the southern edge of Laos and over the central provinces of South Vietnam straddling the demilitarized zone, skirting some of the Truong Son mountains, headed for the South China Sea. Somewhere between Ubon and the sea, Ozark Flight was handed off to Panama Control, the air traffic control center at Da Nang.

Passing over sandy beaches with the South China Sea lapping at the shoreline, Golberg and Wynne had reached "feet wet" with the sea now beneath them and headed north toward the Gulf of Tonkin. The August 8 mission was scheduled in to the Red River Delta on an approach route from the east side, rather than the more typical west approach over the higher mountains and Thud Ridge usually tracked by the Air Force. Ozark Flight's line of attack was through the Navy's Route Pack VI-B area. But no conflict arose on August 8. No Navy strikes were scheduled from Task Force 77 cruising at Yankee Station off Da Nang. Ozark Flight flew north headed for a rendezvous with the KC-135 aerial refueling tankers at 21,000 feet.

The refueling tankers, developed along the lines of the Boeing 707 airframe with internal tanks and fuel cells holding roughly 30,000 gallons of aviation fuel, were the life source of the fighters. When loaded with the maximum fuel allocation, a typical F-4 Phantom II held 3,313 gallons. Ozark Flight's armament package precluded the 600-gallon centerline tank, so it flew with a 2,713 gallon fuel allotment. With this set up, a KC-135 tanker could refuel a dozen or more F-4s, before having to return and reload.

Refueling allowed fighters to reach far off objectives and remain at the front once there, increasing time on target. Refueling tracks were located over Thailand for aircraft approaching the Red River Delta from the west and in the Gulf of Tonkin for those approaching from the east. Ozark Flight refueled at the anchor over the Gulf of Tonkin, before entering North Vietnam airspace. Since the "flying boom" receptacle used for in-flight refueling on the F-4C was located on top of the aircraft fuselage right behind the back seat cockpit, Pat had a perfect view of the process as the boom locked in right over his head. Ozark Flight was less than an hour from the mission target.

Ozark Flight had started the armed reconnaissance mission with four F-4C Phantom IIs. Golberg and Wynne were flying in the Ozark 3 position. Ozark 1, the lead aircraft, was crewed by Captain Chris Wright and First Lieutenant Charles Smyth Jr. Ozark 2 was manned by two first lieutenants, Ray Salzarulo and John Nasmyth. Ozark 4, with Major John Hallgren and First Lieutenant Charles Clifton, protected the rear.[73] In refueling over the Gulf of Tonkin, Ozark 2 had to abort the mission as their aircraft could not take on fuel. Ozark 4 moved into Ozark 2's position in a streamlined diagonal formation. Thus Ozark Flight entered enemy territory with a flight of three aircraft.

In mid-1966 surface-to-air missiles were not yet the foremost concern of flight crews. Antiaircraft artillery was the threat. As each month passed, the district around Hanoi and Haiphong presented an ever growing concentration of 37 mm and 57 mm antiaircraft artillery fire. North Vietnam ground fire, which began in the hundreds, would grow into the thousands. After refueling over the Gulf of Tonkin, Ozark Flight pressed forward and moved to a lower elevation, flying less than 100 feet above the water to avoid enemy radars. Ozark Flight returned to "feet dry" roughly 40 miles north of the port city of Haiphong and climbed to around 1,000 feet above ground level to begin their search. The plan was set up for a low-altitude attack run, fast and low.

Sightseeing was over, and the focus was on the target package; approach routes, altitude, air speed, and adrenalin all mattered. For Golberg and Wynne, this was business. This is what they had been trained to do. No matter how many times they did it, they did not take the routine for granted. They knew they represented their nation and the United States Air Force. They heard any last minute orders and received any last minute intelligence. In they flew. Mission reports stated the weather was 200 feet of fog, scattered to broken. Visibility was 10 miles or better. Terrain was low mountains and cultivated areas in the valleys.[74] Ozark Flight approached the target area at low altitude, sweeping the area.

The mission crews found "no joy" on the scheduled targets on the inbound segment but saw targets of opportunity on the looping return. Dropping ordnance on a truck convoy, the flight soon crossed a valley where, flying at a speed of just under 500 knots per hour, it ran a gauntlet of ground fire. Ozark Flight, flying between 400 and 600 feet above ground level at that point, tried to pick its way through flak blanketing the space between 200 and 1,000 feet above ground level. They varied altitude, airspeed, and direction, jinking the aircraft from side to side to avoid the artillery fire, but it was heavy and accurate.

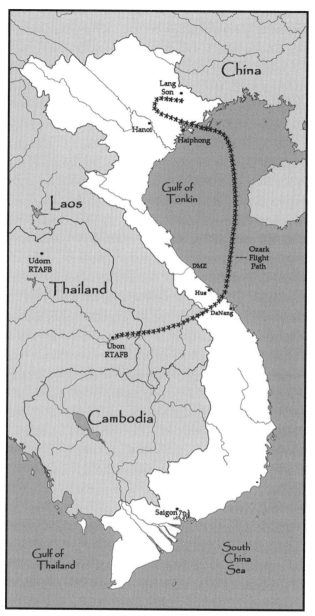

Map of Vietnam and surrounding countries with Ozark Flight path shown. *Source:* Blank map by Uwe Dedering at http://en.wikipedia.org/wiki/File:Vietnam_location_map.svg. Cities and other landmarks added by author.

Ozark 1 made it through but in maneuvering to avoid the antiaircraft fire lost visual contact with the other aircraft. Ozark 4 reported being hit and was quickly followed by Ozark 3, reporting it also had taken fire. Ozark 4 had a utility hydraulic system failure, and Ozark 3 was losing flight controls. Flying last in the right echelon formation, the crew of Ozark 3 wrestled with the aircraft to gain altitude but dropped back, out of sight.

In after-action reports, Ozark 1 was able to recollect the hurried radio transmissions. Ozark 1 asked most of the questions, and Ozark 3 tried to answer. Severely damaged Ozark 4 maintained radio silence and headed for the Gulf of Tonkin, since Ozark lead was in contact.

Ozark 1 tried to assess the situation, "How are you doing 3?"

"I have control difficulties; I can't move the stick; I have my RAM air turbine out," responded Ozark 3.

"Try your autopilot?"

"I'm steering with rudders only."

"Where are you?"

"I'm three miles behind you and high."

"Are you going to make the water?"

"My radio is going out, how do you read," Ozark 3 asked?

Ozark 1 again checked status, "I am turning back to pick you up visually if I can; are you going to make it?"

"I think I'm going to make it."

"How are you reading me now, I don't have you in sight?"

"I can only get one afterburner to work."

"Rodger, how far have you got to go to the coast?"

"About 30 miles."

"How do you read?"

Then came a short period of silence. Ozark 1 continued to try and re-establish communication with Ozark 3, but no response was heard. Then, after several attempts, Ozark 3's pilot systems operator, Pat Wynne, made the final transmission.

"Ozark 3's position is 21 degrees 33'N, 106 degrees 46'E."

Then silence.

GOLBERG AND WYNNE in Ozark 3 were west of Haiphong and north of Hanoi when hit, somewhere over Lang Son or Ha Bac province. It was approximately 8:35 in the morning when they reported to Ozark lead that they were about 30 miles from the coast. Unable to reach the safer ditching areas in the Gulf of Tonkin, they veered north so as not to double back over Hanoi and Haiphong. Struggling to control the crippled fighter, they flew north to a point near the village of Lang Son, where they were last heard from, close to the Chinese buffer border. Since radio contact had been maintained for several minutes after Ozark 3 took antiaircraft fire, it was possible the pilots had time to eject.

Golberg and Wynne were the only casualties from Ozark Flight. No other aircraft observed serial number 63-7560 vanish into the countryside. No one was sure where or if they were able to eject from the aircraft. "No chutes, no beepers," was the chatter. Given the terrain and location, rescue was difficult and doubtful. But a search mission began immediately, and one of the participants was Pat's friend and roommate, Tom Fryer.

TOM AND PAT had arrived together at Udorn RTAFB and, subsequently, Ubon RTAFB. Both had been peeled off the 33rd Tactical Fighter Wing at Eglin Air Force Base and assigned to the 555th Tactical Fighter Squadron. Tom came from the 25th Squadron of the 33rd Wing and Pat from the 40th Squadron. They went through basic and jungle survival schools together and were roommates in Thailand. But these two had had a shared history that predated arrival in the combat theater.

Pat and Tom were both from the Class of 1963 at the Air Force Academy. They separated for awhile as they attended different graduate schools, Pat at Georgetown University while Tom specialized in engineering at Purdue University. They moved a little bit closer a year later at Williams Air Force Base for pilot training, Tom being in the class ahead of Pat, 65-F for Tom and 65-G for Pat. They stayed nearby through their time at Eglin Air Force Base, assigned to next-door squadrons of the 33rd Tactical Fighter Wing. These two squadrons were in the same building at Eglin, the old Strategic Air Command alert facility genially referred to as the "mole hole," because of its partially recessed design. By the time they arrived in Thailand, Pat and Tom were fast friends.

While they had not had the opportunity to fly together, by the first week of August 1966 Pat and Tom had each flown about two dozen missions in North Vietnam. Roughly half of these flights were escort missions to acclimate the new pilots to the business at hand. On relatively quick notice, the opportunity to leave Ubon RTAFB and grab a bit of rest and relaxation came up.

R&R time was not always on a schedule, and one had to seize it when the opportunity presented itself. They set out initially for Okinawa, which was a key staging point for American military operations in North Vietnam. The pair then flew to the British colony of Hong Kong, where they could let down a bit and do some sightseeing in the port city. They spent a couple of nights in Hong Kong, but the days passed quickly and it was soon time to return. Pat and Tom returned to Ubon, reversing their original flight path, via Okinawa. They were back to the air war in Vietnam.

On the morning of August 8 two flights had been launched on armed reconnaissance missions into Route Pack VI-B in North Vietnam. Pat and his pilot, Larry Golberg, were in the lead flight, and Tom Fryer and his pilot, Captain McLelland, were in the flight right behind, trailing by about 15 minutes. As Tom's flight approached the area, they heard the emergency calls from Pat's flight. When they heard about Pat's aircraft being shot down, Tom's mission was diverted on the spot from armed reconnaissance to search and rescue. His flight was sent to find Pat and Larry.

No parachutes had been seen, and they were deep in-country. The chance for a helicopter rescue was slim, but the trailing flight carried out a search mission. Tom's flight combed the area until low on fuel and then found the KC-135 tankers and refueled. They were not allowed to return to the area, as other search and rescue efforts were under way. They were ordered back to base. Golberg and Wynne were declared missing in action shortly thereafter. That August 8 mission was number 27 for Tom Fryer, just about what it would have been for Pat Wynne as well.

What of the others in the August 8 flight? Ozark 1 refueled over the Gulf of Tonkin and made it back to Ubon RTAFB. Ozark 2, unable to take on fuel inbound, had turned around and made it back to base, ready to take up arms another day. Ozark 4, having lost normal hydraulics, on the return could not open its door to the boom receptacle to take on extra fuel and could not operate its brakes easily. Thus handicapped, Ozark 4 headed for the closest air base, Da Nang, South Vietnam. Ozark 4 reached Da Nang, where it dropped its tail hook and made an arrestor-assisted landing.

The hard stuff followed. The duty always fell to someone, and in Pat's case it fell to his buddy, Tom Fryer. When Pat was declared missing in action, Tom was the airman who packed up Pat's personal belongings and had them shipped back to the States to Pat's wife, Nancy. Pat had been out of the United States less than 90 days. Now it would just take time to see if he was a prisoner of war or a casualty of war.

BACK HOME IN FLORIDA, Pat's mom, Dorothy, was probably at her kitchen sink, doing dishes as moms have done since plates and silverware became the social custom. In their L-shaped house, the kitchen was situated at the inside angle formed where the two wings of the building joined. Her sink faced a window that looked out on to the driveway, and that is where she most likely stood when the official military vehicle pulled up and two uniformed officers stepped out and approached the door. No one had to tell her why they were there.

❖

PAT'S FLIGHT OVER NORTH VIETNAM the day he was shot down was above much the same ground French soldiers marched 80 years earlier in their quest for colonial control. The site where his F-4C was brought to ground was near a battlefield from the past. In 1885 the French and Chinese battled for control of the village of Lang Son, a centerpiece in the traditional land bridge between China and Vietnam on the way to Hanoi.

Lang Son village, the largest and only recognized town in a province of the same name, was situated on a small plain bisected by the Ky Cung River. Lang Son province was mostly rolling hills of tall grass and cultivated land, such as rice fields, and scattered areas of karst. The area was better known for its bauxite mines. The province adjacent to Lang Son to its south was Ha Bac, another area of rolling plains and grasslands but also one with forested areas. The annual rainfall in this part of Vietnam was 20 inches less than that of Saigon.[75] One could crash land in this topography and still have a chance to come out alive.

Once again, Pat was not alone. In the third quarter of 1966, 104 American aircraft were shot down, 80 of those were U.S. Air Force combat losses.[76] The U.S. Air Force lost 638 aircraft over North Vietnam during the war, and 195 of those losses were standard F-4s, with an additional 39 in the RF-4 reconnaissance configuration.[77]

Similar to Pat's F-4 being brought down, numerous crews suffered comparable fates. These included U.S. Navy Lieutenant Junior Grade Everett Alvarez Jr., the first POW, captured on August 5, 1964; U.S. Air Force Major Larry Guarino, captured June 14, 1965, and imprisoned for the next 2,801 days; and U.S. Air Force Major James Kasler, downed on his 91st mission, on August 8, 1966, the same day that Pat's aircraft disappeared. The family of a downed pilot saw their hopes change in a heartbeat, from "We hope our son is safe" to "We pray our son is alive."

After Pat Wynne was downed in North Vietnam in August 1966, a great deal more fighting remained on the horizon. It would occur on the ground in places such as Khe Sanh and the A Shau Valley and during holidays such as the Tet Nguyen Dan, celebrating the lunar New Year. It also continued in the air, through two more years of Rolling Thunder and even later in Operation Linebacker missions. The 8th Tactical Fighter Wing would be credited with destroying 38.5 enemy aircraft in Vietnam. Nineteen of those downed aircraft would be attributed to the attached 555th Tactical Fighter Squadron. Two officers from the Triple Nickel would earn the status of "ACE," two of only three from the Air Force in the war.[78] For the most part, victory could only be claimed in body count. The end of 1965 saw 200,000 Americans in Vietnam. The count grew to 400,000 in 1966 and 500,000 in 1967.

Chapter Nine

The Business of Weapons Development

As OFTEN HAPPENS in small start-up companies, Mike had varied duties and was able to see the business from numerous perspectives, beginning at ground level and working his way up to the financial reporting aspects. Research Analysis & Development was no different. On one project in modeling for the financial markets, Mike even enlisted Barb at home on the weekends for help. They sought out and recorded weekly closing prices on a few hundred stocks from the *Wall Street Journal*. The aim was to supply data to

Mike and Barb Wynne with their three daughters in the early 1970s.
Source: Wynne Family.

test converting the interest rate forecaster into a stock forecasting model. This tedious work was done manually one by one.

Mike's old friend from Hanscom and the academy, Ron Schillereff, was the secretary-treasurer of the firm. Ron and Mike were across-the-street neighbors who shared the ups and downs of working in a start-up, high-tech business. They also had the pleasure of young families. Ron started his family with a girl, not quite matching the Wynne's three daughters. The financier and the engineer experienced the ubiquitous Christmas tradition of putting together a number of plastic pre-fab children's kitchen sets, working past midnight to unravel the complexities as they eschewed the feckless instructions.

After a year as secretary-treasurer of Research Analysis & Development, Ron left and moved on to other opportunities, primarily filling out his credentials by finishing up work on a terminal degree in finance from the University of Colorado. Ron and Mike had both left the Air Force about the same time to work for Research Analysis & Development. Ron was now the first to bail out. He would finish his degree and embark on a teaching career. This evolved into a career in the private sector that included banking, consulting, and executive management for such firms as Ross Perot's Electronic Data Systems. For the time being, Mike remained at Research Analysis & Development.

Mike took over the vacated position of treasurer and soon experienced the competing pressures to show results. One particular contract that came through posed a few challenging accounting issues for Mike. When he was encouraged to perform a little financial legerdemain with the company's books, Mike was slammed into his principles. He wasn't comfortable with the suggested accounting treatment and refused to record the contract in a particular way. On another occasion, Mike felt compelled to do the opposite of what had been asked.

Small company dynamics being what they were, Research Analysis & Development had taken out a few loans from relatives of employees. One such small advance was owed to a family member of a worker who was situated on one of the lower rungs of the corporate ladder. With tight financials, one principal of the firm wanted to just default and write off the loan. Instead, Mike made provisions in the financials and paid the loan. This soon led to a disagreeable work relationship, and the end of Mike's commitment and tenure at the company. Mike's moral code pointed him in only one direction, and that is the pointer he followed. This would not be the last time Mike would be accused of "doing his own thing."

While one cannot say Mike left in the good graces of all concerned, given that one of the principals threatened to sue him personally, he did escape with his integrity unruffled. The threatened lawsuit ended up being just bluster. Thus, Mike went from being an officer and a gentleman to a businessman to an unemployed graduate student, in less than 24 months. While it had been an eye-opening lesson in business, he needed to make other arrangements and he still had to finish school. Once again, Mike and Barb were poor.

MIKE AND BARB were doing famously in their marriage, knowing they kept it that way by working on it. In spring 1975, the couple decided to take a marriage encounter course, rather like a retreat for married couples to help strengthen relationships. Mike was busy with work and graduate school, so Barb was happy to have his undivided attention for a few days. Her only requirement was that Mike leave the school work at home and devote his attention to the encounter. With the three girls staying with friends, Mike and Barb were off to the marriage conference that ran Friday through Sunday.

Mike was taking upwards of 20 hours at the university night school so he could finish his master's program as soon as possible. As the timing worked out, he had a major test on the Monday following the encounter. But Mike knew what was important, and he left his study materials back home. They returned from the encounter having had a wonderful time. Next day, Mike took his examination.

Mike graduated from the University of Colorado with a master's of business administration a few weeks later. He had finished second in the class, with all A's save one course. That Monday examination, Mike would later find out, pushed his score down in that particular class to a B and prevented him from tying for first place with straight A's. To this day, Barb proudly claims that B as her B. But a marriage still going strong after 40-plus years certainly brings the average up to a solid A.

MIKE WALKED OUT THE DOOR of Research Analysis & Development one Friday in March 1975 and promptly started the rest of his life. He was on a full-court press to finish his graduate studies in business at the University of Colorado that semester while sending out resumes. Engineering degrees were still in demand in the 1970s, and even though the Air Force was cutting back, industry was still buying, just a bit more selectively. Within short order Mike was working on three interesting prospects for his next position: TRW (formerly Thompson, Ramo & Wooldridge), Logicon, and General Dynamics. The TRW and Logicon interviews were held near San Pedro, California, outside Los Angeles, while those of General Dynamics were in Fort Worth, Texas.

As life often reveals itself, the Wynnes went from having a little to a lot. It was now June 1975, and they were just scratching by financially. They couldn't hold on to the house much longer, and it was macaroni & cheese and hot dogs for the kids more often than usual. Mike had completed a series of interviews with the three prospects but had not yet received any firm offers. As Mike and Barb grew poorer, his negotiating position grew weaker. Then in one-day, he received an early morning telegram from TRW transported by taxicab, a package from Logicon delivered around noon in the U.S. mail, and a telephone call that afternoon from General Dynamics. From nothing to everything.

Mike leaned toward Logicon, which centered on missile guidance, but he was worried about housing and living expenses in California. Living around the rolling hills of the Palos Verdes peninsula in the San Pedro area of Los Angeles county would be wonderful, but how would he arrange finances? General Dynamics, which involved contracts and cost estimating, offered a nice salary, but Logicon topped it by 20 percent. Besides the financial issues, Mike and Barb had to consider their young children. Barb's opinion was that since they had three girls, she would prefer they started in a location where the kids were not in bathing suits all the time. Could General Dynamics sweeten the pot a little? In the end, General Dynamics narrowed the pay differential and clinched it for the Wynnes to choose Texas rather than California. Mike and his family moved to Fort Worth during the July 4th weekend of 1975.

❧

GENERAL DYNAMICS TRACED ITS ROOTS to submarine building off the coast of New Jersey. The Holland Torpedo Boat Company built its first submarines in the late-1890s and sold the United States Navy its first one in 1900. Similar to corporate machinations seen in the late 20th and early 21st centuries, the original company had experienced name changes, management upheaval, mergers and acquisitions, and various transformations in its business model.

General Dynamics (then called Electric Boat Company) entered aviation when it purchased Canadair in the 1940s. In 1952 Electric Boat became General Dynamics and shortly thereafter purchased Convair, another aerospace company. This subsidiary went on to produce commercial and military aircraft and the Atlas ICBM. Convair rented its main manufacturing facility from the U.S. Air Force, in Fort Worth. Reorganization in the early 1960s saw aerospace activities moved to San Diego, California. A second round of restructuring concentrated aircraft production in Fort Worth, and space and missile manufacturing in San Diego.

When Mike arrived at General Dynamics in 1975, the company already was firmly entrenched as a part of the military-industrial complex. It had been a part of the defense industry long enough to have embroiled itself in a few ethical predicaments. One of many targets of congressional investigation under the auspices of the Truman Commission in the 1940s, General Dynamics predecessor, Electric Boat, had been accused of profiteering and unethical practices. In 1962 the company's besting of Boeing in competition for the TFX tactical fighter experimental also raised suspicions. Neither instance left lasting impairment, just the hint of impropriety.

In the early 1970s, General Dynamics outbid Northrop for the contract to produce the U.S. Air Force's new lightweight fighter. With orders for hundreds of aircraft already booked, General Dynamics was in a hiring mode, right about the time Mike was looking for new adventures. He moved to the defense industry, assuming an entirely different posture for his labor. No longer buying and using weapon systems, he joined the trade that made and sold them.

✣

THE DEFENSE INDUSTRY in the United States has been a work in progress. During America's early days, commercial enterprises would develop a product and sell it to the individual military services, such as the handguns and rifles sold to the Army when the West was still wild. Competing producers would make improvements and enter the market. From Colt revolvers to Gatling guns to Winchester rifles to Maxim machine guns to Thompson submachine guns. The process would continue as private businesses would compete with each other in tailoring product offerings to what the military required. But complications developed.

One can look back 50 years and see when the change occurred. Before then the United States did not have a particularly large professional standing military. Built on the backs of immigrants usually fleeing oppression, the United States was not disposed to have a considerable standing militia—just the bare minimum. The country also was not inclined to join in foreign wars too quickly, assuming an isolationist stance. America had a small cadre of professionals who held the military together during peacetime. The military would remain at peacetime levels until a travesty occurred, such as Pearl Harbor. Then the entire nation, acting as one, would galvanize into action. Private business would be turned into military production creating military might. This paradigm worked for a long time.

The United States was slow to enter World War I, not joining the battle until the final year. By the time America joined, enlisting a huge army through the draft and producing millions of tons of materials through its economic engine, the war was nearing an end. American troops and armaments helped push the Allies over the top in defeating the enemy. The American air effort in World War I was pressed so late, it had little import in terms of equipment. The United States supplied pilots but little in the way of aircraft. Fighting in the air was a new dimension. When the war ended, demobilization took over. The military sent most everyone back home, scrapping or finding alternative uses for the material not stockpiled for the future. The years between the world wars saw technological development in weapon systems, mostly with government financial support, but America did not build up a huge standing army. That would take another war.

World War II arrived, and the United States was basically unprepared. Its isolationist posture had tried to keep it at arm's length from the problems in Europe. The attack on Pearl Harbor changed everything. Then a buildup became meaningful with millions of young men drafted and placed in military service. America's economic engine was once again turned loose to produce what was necessary to outfit the nation for war. In a relatively short time, the United States manufactured more than every other country.

The United States traditionally liked to come from behind, finish strong, and vanquish the enemy that commenced the conflict. This was reflected in the industrial response to war, where America had the time to develop overwhelming numbers of armaments. Americans were used to this pattern, having fallen behind the French and British in aircraft development before World War I and trailed the Soviet Union in the space race in the 1950s. Once galvanized to action, nothing stopped the United States from finishing first. Ever postured as the "sleeping giant," the future would be different.

While World War II did not prove to be "the war to end all wars," it certainly was the last one conducted with millions of men moved thousands of miles in an effort to reassemble entire continents. Instead of massive armies thrown at each other, future wars while deadly in their own right would resemble chess matches, using posturing and politics for stepping stones. One power would begin or threaten a conflict to determine how serious the other was in taking a stand. Viewed through the lens of spreading communism, it was usually the United States squaring off against the Soviet Union.

The Soviet blockade of West Berlin in June 1948 was an early indicator. The United States airlift of supplies for the next 15 months reflected American intentions and finally broke the blockade. The conflict on the Korean Peninsula was different and deadlier.

The Korean War was essentially against North Korean and

Chinese forces, who received material support from the Soviet Union. This conflict cast in high relief the effects of small military budgets after World War II and the resulting American lack of preparation. The Air Force made great strides in Korea, even though nuclear deterrence was still its priority. With the American people unwilling to commit troop levels seen in World War II, Korea was destined to be a containment action. United Nations ground forces fought and died valiantly, but the U.S. Air Force was a key factor in bringing about the eventual stalemate. The United States was fortunate to achieve that.

The Cuban missile crisis also involved posturing, resembling the blockade of West Berlin. It was a test of wills. The Soviet Union threatened to set up nuclear missile bases within 90 miles of the United States mainland, placing America in an untenable position. The Navy's blockade, the Air Force's spy mission pictures, and President John Kennedy's hardline stance forced Soviet Premier Nikita Khrushchev to back down.

Vietnam would be more comparable to Korea, a deadly war where the real combatants battled not in their own country but in someone else's. During Vietnam, with the political unrest and the unwillingness of the American people, victory became impossible. The Air Force was able to command the skies but was unable to compel a win or even a lasting stalemate. Mining the harbors, blockading the ports, and bombing the north are what it took to force a ceasefire, initiate meaningful negotiations, and set in motion the withdrawal of American troops.

In both Korea and Vietnam, the rules of engagement placed a stranglehold on air operations. United States aircraft were not allowed to stray into Chinese airspace. This was in spite of the fact that men and material crossed over from China without restraint, and enemy fighters fought from Chinese airbases. In the 37-month Korean War, the flash point was the Yalu River. During the eight years combat troops were deployed in Vietnam, it was a land border shared with North Vietnam that meandered for hundreds of miles.

Through all, the American military posture has evolved. Larger permanent standby forces and an armament industry to supply those forces have been cultivated. The lead time the United States had to assemble an answer to Pearl Harbor would not again be seen. Future wars would happen more rapidly, and America needed forces on duty to meet those challenges. Knowing it was impossible to come from behind in a nuclear conflict, America avoided one by constantly being ready for it. The mission of the Air Force for decades was to stalemate a nuclear threat, to create an impasse where one side would not launch and the other side would not have to retaliate.

The 20 years between 1945 and 1965 saw the maturation of the relationship between those who fought the wars and those who equipped the fighters—the military-industrial complex of which President Eisenhower warned.[79] Political scientists often refer to this association as the Iron Triangle, where the military meets the defense industry that relies on Congress. In either representation, uneasy lay the alliance between government and commerce, the defense department and the defense industry. Where America once manufactured weapons in quantity tailored to meet a current event, it had evolved with a permanent segment devoted to the production of those weapons. This was the industry Mike Wynne joined in 1975, one whose *raison d'être* was making weapons for war.

❖

BY JULY OF 1975, Mike and Barb had already been a couple for nine years. Similar to his father in 1940, Mike had married soon after graduating from West Point. His marriage to Barbara Ann Hill took place on July 23, 1966. They had waited only a bit longer to marry than his brother Pat had with Nancy. Mike and Barb's friendship had come a long way in just 18 months of dating, mostly carried out long distance.

Their relationship was facilitated by the interlaced careers of their fathers. Barb's dad worked for RCA Services at Cape Canaveral and was deeply involved with activities at the down-range stations. RCA was the subcontractor for Pan American Airways that operated and maintained the recording equipment at the various tracking stations. Mike's dad was the military representative who oversaw the work of the range contractor and its subcontractors. These two men had any number of occasions to work together at the Cape.

Barb's dad maintained the equipment that recorded the data emanating from rockets as they passed the tracking stations. That information was then pumped into the Air Force technology laboratory where Mike's dad was the commander. These two would meet to ensure the data streams were correct and being recorded properly. So the two families were connected on a number of levels, beginning with their fathers' work. On another level, one of Mike's sisters and one of his brothers had counterparts in the Hill family. Mike and Barb didn't really know each other in high school because they were in different years, but the two-year differential in their ages diminished as a factor each year.

Mike met Barb at the end of December 1964 at a Christmas social for college-age children of Patrick Air Force Base personnel. The dance was held at the base Officers' Club. Mike's mother had signed him up to be a host for the Christmas get-together. As it happened, the mother of one of Barb's friends had signed her daughter up to be a host also. Since this daughter did not want to go alone, she called Barb and invited her to come along. So it was a bit of serendipity.

The dance was restricted to those having a connection to Patrick Air Force Base, but Barbara's father's work gave the family an entry. The town was somewhat distant from Patrick, so the base had allowed senior civilians working at Patrick to join the Officers' Club. Barb's dad had done just that. Thus, Barb was eligible to go to the social, and she agreed to go with her friend. When one reflected on the event, it was the mothers who brought the couple together.

Mike was sitting with Kirk Stowers, one of his old high school buddies. Kirk's mom, Bev, was friends with both Mike's and Barb's mothers. Add to this the fact that it was another mom who had signed up Barb's girlfriend to be a host. With four mothers involved, perhaps it was not so much serendipity after all. When Barb came into the dance, Mike asked Kirk, "Who is that?" On obtaining a name to match the pretty face, Mike promptly walked over and cut into the gaggle of her friends.

"Hi, my name is Mike Wynne and I'm a host here. Would you like to dance?"

With the ice broken, later that night the young couple settled on a date for the next evening. Mike met Barb's dad. Twenty-year-old Mike was a junior at West Point, and 18-year-old Barb was a freshman at Florida State. Given her youth, Barb's father did what fathers do and was a bit overprotective, or maybe that is just how the suitor recalled the summit. To set the appropriate mood, her father led off with a polite glower. Barb happened to introduce Mike as Peter's brother, connecting the families through the siblings. After learning that Mike also was the son of Colonel Ed Wynne, whom he knew very well from the base, Barb's father softened but only a bit. Mike taking out his daughter became less "not okay."

They had their first date. With a few days of Christmas break left before he had to be back in upstate New York, Mike ended the first date by asking Barb out for the next evening, but she was already booked. She had a date with an acquaintance of Mike's. This other fellow was on holiday break from the Air Force Academy and had driven home in his new Chevy Corvette, the coming-of-age statement for Air Force Academy seniors. Barb can still tease Mike about what she gave up for him, but that was the last of it and they officially became an item. She would prove to be the perfect foil.

During the next year or so, they only saw each other a dozen times. Barb kept on with her studies at Florida State, and Mike was busy at West Point, often being ferried around the nation for this duty or that. It was a long-distance courtship, at least until Barb came up to West Point for her job in the post exchange during Mike's firstie year. Mike finally had his own coming-of-age automotive statement, a 1966 Oldsmobile Cutlass.

During spring break in senior year, Mike had been invited by his old swim coach from West Point, Jack Ryan, to come to Fort Lauderdale. Through Jack's contacts, Mike had the opportunity to swim in a new international natatorium in Fort Lauderdale; Mike invited Barb to come along for the trip. One of Mike's classmates from the Military Academy, Fritz Ernst, lived in Fort Lauderdale, and the young couple had occasion to be at Fritz's place. It was there that Mike officially asked Barb to marry him. While he had left the engagement ring back home in Satellite Beach, Mike asked and was answered in the affirmative. Fritz hustled up a bottle of champagne, popped the cork, and they shared a toast for the happy occasion. But a little family drama was to come.

On returning from Fort Lauderdale, Mike wanted to surprise his parents. Before he reached home, Mike called his nine-year old brother, Peter, and enlisted him in a conspiracy. Mike told Peter where the engagement ring was squirreled away and asked him to retrieve it with no one the wiser. Mike wanted to give the ring to Barb so she could have it on her finger when she entered the house, making an event out of it. Even though they had dated for awhile, Mike had not told everyone he was going to ask Barb to marry him on that trip to Fort Lauderdale. So while making it official would not be a total bolt from the blue, the timing of the announcement would catch most of them napping. Mike did not take his mother into account.

Peter was a perfect plotter, but his mother stumbled on him rummaging around in Mike's belongings. Having four boys, Mom Wynne sometimes had to guard one son's possessions from another's inquisitive mind and acquisitive hands. So Mike's mom acted as sentinel and stopped Peter dead in his tracks. Convinced he was acting maliciously in taking Mike's ring, she intercepted Peter on his way out and berated him unmercifully. Peter, wanting to preserve the secrecy of his mission, said little and appeared all the more guilty. Mom was being protective of Mike's property, and Peter was shielding Mike's surprise, but neither knew of the other's point of view. It was not a good standoff.

Peter finally exited the house and tearfully admitted to Mike that he had been forced to divulge their secret pact. But he did deliver the ring—mission successful, sort of. Barb put on the ring and in the house they went, finding the place in complete disarray. Now dad was furious at mom for ruining Mike's surprise. As it turned out each family member was on Mike's side, but each in their own corner. While the scheme did not come off quite as planned, everyone found out Mike and Barb were officially engaged. Even with this inauspicious preamble, Mike and Barb did in fact marry.

Fritz Ernst was Mike's best man, and Ray McGarity, a classmate from Mel High and a 1966 graduate of the Air Force Academy, was one of his ushers. The ceremonial sabers from West Point arrived by rail in Florida on schedule for the wedding, Fritz handling those arrangements. Being just 21 and 19, marriage was a leap of faith for Mike Wynne and Barb Hill, but one that proved well worth bounding over. Their marriage was based on a lot of love, a little faith and a load of plans. All still apply.

True to military custom, Mike and Barb's children would each have a different birthplace, three of them at military installations. The first daughter, Lisa, was born on Thursday, June 15, 1967, barely five days after Israel altered the geopolitical landscape in the Middle East with its Six Day War. She arrived at the base hospital at Fort Devens, outside Boston. Her almost Irish twin, Collene, arrived 14 months later, on Friday, August 23, 1968, in Greene County, Ohio. This birth took place while Mike and Barb were stationed at Wright-Patterson Air Force Base, exactly 50 years to the day marking the birth of Mike's father.

Mike was a professor of astronautics at the Air Force Academy when his third daughter, Karen, arrived on Monday, March 29, 1971. She was born at the hospital on the academy grounds. Giving all indications that this was getting to be a common occurrence, Mike almost missed the whole event when he lagged in finishing the academy inter-department volleyball championship game before leaving to meet Barb at the hospital. The last was Laura, born at Harris Methodist Hospital in Tarrant County, Fort Worth, Texas. She would be the second Monday baby in the family, born on September 27, 1976.

❧

BACK AT FORT WORTH, Mike was getting his feet on the ground. When new employees join an organization in anything other than bare entry-level positions, they often bring a few innovations to the business—a few quick tricks. Mike would take advantage of his expertise in computers that he had gained back at the

Military Academy. He started out at General Dynamics as the junior information technology specialist for the cost estimating department, which prepared spare parts estimates for various programs. Hundreds of cost estimates were being worked on at any given time, all done by hand. A squad of clerks produced the estimates, which were subject to clerical errors. This framed the effort a candidate for computerization.

Mike was strong in the science of computers that was just surfacing with punch cards, and key punch and verifier machines. With knowledge of basic computing language, one could harness this technology by developing a simple logic routine, reducing it to a series of machine-readable instructions, and preparing it to be run against any particular dataset on room-sized computers. But this batch-processing technology, which relied on a computer department, was evolving into desktop units, where users performed their own real-time processing. This was the emergence of the personal computer.

After receiving a Computer Sciences Corporation (CSC) terminal, Mike wrote a short computer processing routine that would eventually perform the look-up, accumulation, and printout of the parts estimates. In the beginning, the clerk would reference the spare part information as usual and input the relevant facts and figures into the system, rather than on paper. So the work began as before, with a clerical function. But this time, the program would "remember" the spare part number and the cost associated with it. It did not have to be matched again.

As the cost-estimating program was used, it amassed the parts and prices in memory and could regurgitate the figures in any order desired. In a day when computers were just beginning to make inroads in business, Mike's knowledge from the academy gave him a head start. He became a hero with his first project—automating cost estimating. Spares proposals, which used to take two and one-half months, now took two weeks.

Customer satisfaction improved, and spare parts sales rose. While Mike's superiors saw the internal benefits of freeing up clerks for other work and speeding up the estimating process, the corporate technology people were a bit chagrined. Mike's project essentially took the computer work away from the batch processing of the information technology department and placed it squarely in the cost-estimating department. The information technology people felt diminished, and it would not be the only work removed from their purview.

With so much government work at General Dynamics, a Defense Contract Audit Agency representative roamed the halls at the Fort Worth plant auditing various project elements. On one visit through the cost-estimating group, he noticed the CSC terminal clicking and ticking in the background. The auditor needed a random number table to simplify his task of arbitrarily selecting which program components were to be audited. He inquired about the CSC terminal, which was the essence of an early personal computer, and one thing led to another. Once Mike had the parameters, he wrote a simple routine to generate a random number table. The problem was Mike did it while the auditor stood there, and then found out the auditor had been waiting for six weeks for the same thing from the information technology department. Oops!

The defense contract audit people later sent a letter to the general manager of the Fort Worth plant thanking them for breaking the logjam they had run into at the central processing level. Maybe a quiet "thank you" would have worked better because now the central processing people were in an uproar. The misdemeanor had turned into a felony, and it was time to guard one's turf. The information technology group wanted the CSC terminal removed from cost estimating. They believed those functions should be done in central processing and not in the individual departments. What next, each department doing its own computing?

Mike was on the job just four months, and already his boss was in the position of having to defend him. On the outside, Mike was getting rave reviews. On the inside, a few threatened employees were trying to remove him—the intrigue of corporate politics. Right about this time, Logicon took one more run at hiring Mike. Logicon offered to raise his salary, cover the move to California, and pay any penalties Mike might owe General Dynamics for the upheaval.

Logicon was engineering, General Dynamics was business. Mike was already established in Fort Worth, he liked the people, and he felt a responsibility to stay. He did not want to gain a reputation of jumping from one job to another every few months, solely for a few bucks and a new title. He wanted to settle in and make a significant investment of his time and talent since he felt he could make a difference. So Logicon lost once again to General Dynamics, and Mike and Barb remained in Fort Worth.

Back in estimating, Mike kept his computer terminal and applied himself to the work. He was learning new computer languages and now working on major proposals, not just spare parts orders. He continued helping others with computer projects. One of his friends at the plant was working with a massive batch-processing routine. He would assemble the program and put it in for processing each night. In the morning, he would retrieve the results and usually find out the program had aborted. He would change this or that and rerun it. Next day, same results. He was having the hardest time determining why the program would not run to completion.

Mike showed him how he could input short stop-and-check sequences into the program so it would indicate where a problem was encountered. He also fashioned limits, a way to run parts of the routine instead of entire program. These allowed specific targeting of a remedy when the program failed, instead of trial and error. The program was soon up and running. What took weeks now took days. This was getting to be a habit, and Mike was getting noticed.

It was early 1976 when Mike was called into his friend Bill Mcurdy's office. Seated there were Ralph Stangl, the lead on contracts for the new F-16 program, and Harold McCaslin, head of the F-16 estimating group. Barely past his 31st birthday, Mike Wynne was made the lead estimator on the F-16 program. The F-16 was the project-du-jour at the Fort Worth plant, years in the making and just then reaching production. Mike joined the F-16 program right as it hit the market and revolutionized the fighter business.[80]

Mcurdy, Stangl, and McCaslin would become mentors to Mike in the ensuing years, especially Bill Mcurdy. Mike acquired a better office or more precisely, his own cubicle. He was not in the bullpen of desks anymore, but it would take a bit longer to have real floor-to-ceiling walls. The essential point was that Mike was now on the F-16 production proposal team.

MIKE'S SUPERVISOR WAS HAROLD McCASLIN, but one would not know it on seeing how closely he worked with the contracts lead, Ralph Stangl. Aptly described as the curmudgeon's curmudgeon, Ralph was unforgettable. He was an early devotee of full and complete disclosure and insisted on true transparency in working with the government. He even had his own set of rules to follow, quickly dubbed Ralph's Rules.[81] Ralph felt one should never let a customer leave with a question unanswered, as it would always come back to haunt you. Ralph and Mike began to design the estimating program, and it was none too soon as General Dynamics already had orders in-hand, both foreign and domestic.

Belgium, Denmark, the Netherlands, and Norway had announced their intention to purchase the F-16; these were the first international orders. Years later, Mike would find out that Donald Rumsfeld, the United States ambassador to the NATO in 1973–74, had been working behind the scenes to convince Europeans to buy a common airplane from a NATO member. The suggestion to buy from a NATO member ruled out the French Dassault Mirage family of aircraft and the Swedish SAAB Viggen/Gripen, leaving the American in-the-works F-16 Fighting Falcon from General Dynamics as the only air superiority aircraft from a NATO member nation.[82] With orders booked, Fort Worth had to start work with the estimating.

Estimating for the F-16 was a bit more complex than that for spare parts orders. The F-16 had thousands of components compiled into hundreds of assemblies by dozens of manufacturing companies from a number of countries, all brought together at Fort Worth to construct the F-16. The European production group encompassed four countries, each of which received a slice of the manufacturing for its own gross domestic product. To facilitate this, within three years F-16 assembly lines would be established in Belgium and the Netherlands. Other cost variables were foreign currency translations and interest rates, especially with long-lead financing that applied to deliveries scheduled years in the future.

Herb Rogers, the marketing lead on the F-16 program at Fort Worth, had complained that getting estimates took too long. By the time the variables were considered, a process that took months, prospective buyers were shopping for alternatives. The compounding factor in the matrix of costs was that each European production group country received a variable portion of the manufacturing. Thus, estimating was more art than science, trying to grab a handle on a moving ball of costs. If the process took too long, the ball would move again. Mike had the opportunity to apply his expertise to automating cost estimates on the F-16.

In the end, Mike's automation schedules resembled computerized project management outlines. The routines allowed the change of any variable, and a new cost matrix would be produced. Change the country placing the order, and the division of labor among the European production groups was changed to match, and a new cost matrix was generated. Change the desired delivery date, and a new schedule would be produced with updated cost estimates and manufacturing allotments. Simplifying the estimating sped up the whole process. What used to take almost a year, from intent to bid to estimate to proposal to negotiation to sale, could now be turned around in less than 90 days. Herb Rogers was sold.

Marketing now had something it could utilize in sales. No longer would it take a year to turn around a proposal. Herb liked the model so much, he sent it on to corporate in St. Louis, Missouri. Of course, at headquarters it met with the dreaded NIH syndrome—not invented here. Corporate did not think one could estimate complex aircraft program purchases by multiplying Xs and Ys. They didn't think the mysterious and time-consuming process of estimating could be reduced to mathematical equations. Corporate sent a letter saying as much back to Fort Worth General Manager Dick Adams. But Dick Adams didn't suffer those uncertainties and pressed Mike to "keep up the good work." Herb also chimed in with the request that Mike keep on churning out the proposals. Business was good.

DURING THIS PERIOD, Mike also had occasion to reconnect with his friend, Ron Schillereff, providing yet another opportunity for their careers to intersect. Ron, fresh off his Ph.D. program at the University of Colorado, was in his first teaching assignment, at Texas Tech University in Lubbock. Ron started taking his students on field trips every semester to visit neighboring corporations. It was great exposure to finance and business, out of the classroom and into the marketplace. Mike's being at General Dynamics in Fort Worth, even though it was a journey of 300 miles for the students, was a natural for the class and one more link for Ron and Mike.

MIKE HAD THE CHANCE to mix business with pleasure, his work with F-16s and his relationship with brother-in-law, Al Guarino. In 1975 and 1976, Al was assigned as an operations inspector and T-38 flight examiner to Headquarters Air Training Command Inspector General at Randolph Air Force Base. Randolph was located in Universal City, Texas, about 10 miles northeast of San Antonio. One Thanksgiving holiday, the Guarinos were visiting Mike and his family in Fort Worth. Mike invited Al to the General Dynamics plant to see portions of the design and engineering work on the F-16 Fighting Falcon.

Mike thought having a little informed opinion from an experienced fighter pilot might be helpful, so he had Al sit in the F-16 cockpit mockup. It was simply a matter of giving a user the opportunity to offer pointers on the human engineering side of fighter-aircraft layout. As it worked out, Al did have a couple of suggestions, such as moving the radio switch to be more in line with the pilot's actual cockpit behavior. Mike had been prescient enough to bring along one of the cockpit engineers who took notes as Al went through his comments.

COST ESTIMATING IS A LIVING PROCESS. One is not finished just because a model has been created. Program routines were constantly tweaked and improved as new information was received. What turned out to be a bit of an Achilles' heel for Mike's program was long-lead financing. For any sale, suppliers had to be lined up and placed in the model for various parts and components. Whether the supplier was a large manufacturer or a small operation, they had to forecast engineering and production requirements, tool and die needs, raw material levels, personnel, and the other items that would find their way into the cost-estimating model. These estimates were subject to variation, even more so if delivery was scheduled for years down the road. This is where long-lead financing and its corollary, long-lead liability, came into play.

Early in the order cycle, a manufacturer such as General Dynamics places orders for components with suppliers. The suppliers incur costs as they build to the order, but they don't bill General Dynamics immediately. In scheduling out, General Dynamics does not pay out cash for a period of time but takes on the liability to do so at a later time. On one of the larger component proposals, with a long lead time, related to F-16 product for the United States government, Mike's program routine missed a portion of the cost elements and underestimated the component expenditures by roughly $60 million. In the 1970s, that was still a big number. Unless this discrepancy was fixed, General Dynamics would have to absorb the $60 million loss as the government would not pay the unapproved bill.

Everyone watched to see what would happen to the rising star of the estimating department. Would this be the dénouement of automated costing? Given the complexities of the estimating program routine, it was decided that Mike should go and explain the differences to the government business agent in charge of the overall project including the component parts. Fred Wood, based out of Wright-Patterson Air Force Base, was the government representative on the project in question. Mike arrived, hat in hand, and explained the reason for and the magnitude of the error. In the aggregate, it was long-lead financing that would not have to be cashed out for years and it was but one portion of a much larger project cost.

Fred must have liked what he heard because he said the explanation was adequate and the error understandable. About a week later, Fort Worth received a letter signed by Chesley Holloman, the contracts negotiator for the government. It thanked General

Dynamics for the clarity on the situation. The government agreed to cover the $60 million difference for that component in the next round of bills. Only skeptics questioned the integrity of the costing model, because the problem had been the inputs. In the game of corporate politics, Mike had walked away with a vote of confidence.

Sometime later, Mike was able to return the favor. Mike found out through his contacts that the government had erred in estimating some of the cost parameters. The particular one that matched up Mike and Fred was a situation where the government had misstated the allowable foreign currency exchange on F-16 purchases by Denmark and Norway. The sum and substance of the difference was that the government would be required to pay approximately $20 million extra, to the benefit of General Dynamics. After another meeting at Wright-Patterson, where both the government and the General Dynamics representatives wore their stern game faces, Mike arranged for a contract adjustment that would reflect the true, lower figures. Their relationship was the essence of fair business practices.

IN EARLY 1977 the complete F-16 project cost package was ready for presentation to the government. This was the big one, as the United States government was the number one customer for the F-16 Fighting Falcon. Sometime before the package was presented, Mike had second thoughts. He reviewed the major aspects of the $1.8 billion program and felt uneasy. Something was missing—the total program just didn't feel big enough. The mid-1970s witnessed tremendous inflation, and January to July 1975 was a high-rate period. Mike wanted to rebase the figures.

Mike traveled to Wright-Patterson to press the case with the government representatives, Dick Wyatt and Chesley Holloman. Mike's position was sound enough that he received permission to rework the program costs on the F-16. The agreement allowed him to reset the baseline for the figures from July back to January, the start of the high-rate inflationary period, and bring the data forward using the government's own escalation estimates. The $1.8 billion program grew to $2.05 billion, an increase of about 12 percent. The downside was that every single number and factor in the program had to be changed.

Now the project had to be reworked for presentation. With a project of the F-16's magnitude, this was no small matter. Frank Riney, who worked the cost estimating for the F-111 program, shut down his side of the business and pitched-in with his resources to help Mike churn out the proposal changes. Ralph Stangl was also in on this from the start. Together with an economist from the finance department, Ralph and Mike codified the baseline change and price adjustment into a permanent stipulation in contract work at General Dynamics. They had invented an escalation price adjustment mechanism. Mike's ability to utilize a revised baseline with the F-16 contract rendered the project one of the most successful in the Fort Worth plant's history.

MIKE HAD WORKED LONG AND HARD on the F-16 program, which turned out to be an unqualified success. When he finished up one particular engineering change proposal, the production program for the F-16, he had scheduled in a bit of vacation—down time so he could reconnect with his family. Plans were set, everyone was excited. In a work-hard play-hard business world, it was time to play. A few days before he was due to leave, a senior executive's factotum came into Mike's office to inform him that the company was forming a new team. Mike was to be a member, and a meeting was scheduled for the next day. This team was to work on F-16 support systems, and they were leaving for San Diego at the end of the week to begin. Mike put his foot down and rejected the premise.

Mike countered, "I understand you are just the messenger, but please tell whoever sent you that I leave for a short vacation tomorrow. When I return in two weeks, I will join the team and dedicate myself to the project at hand. If that is not acceptable, I will go on a longer vacation, and when I return, I will join someone else's team and dedicate myself to who ever will have me."

Mike did attend the meeting the next day to hear about the project. Team leaders were waxing eloquently about the new effort, and in the course of their orations revealed the names of everyone on the team. One of Mike's old friends, Herb Rogers, who had become the general manager of the entire division, sidled over to Mike as the speeches continued. He whispered, "Vacations are important. Enjoy yours."

SUCCESS WITH THE F-16 PROGRAM led to other perks. Mike met with the carpenter. It was time for a real office, one with floor-to-ceiling walls. He had "hit it out of the park" with the F-16 program work. No more cubicles, no matter how large. It was four walls with a door. He had wallpaper on the walls and a lock on the door. Everyone thought he was headed for director-level responsibility at the Fort Worth Division, but his stay was destined to be short term. He was leaving Triple-A ball and being called up.

CHAPTER TEN

Unfinished Business

FOR THE EXTENDED WYNNE FAMILY, unfinished business remained. First-born son Patrick had been a downed pilot since 1966. The war in Vietnam had ground to a distasteful end, practically no one happy with the result. Hundreds of prisoners of war had been repatriated, yet not a word of Pat's status. None of the released prisoners had ever seen or heard of Pat while they were imprisoned. By 1974 seven years had elapsed, and silence reigned. How long was too long? How long was long enough? It depended on who one asked.

THE UNITED STATES had always strived to recover and identify its war casualties, and it had become more of a science with each conflict. In World War I it was a graves registration service. With World War II and Korea, trained anthropologists and anatomists were employed for the first time but laboratories were still temporary identification facilities. With the third war in 20 years, the process became more permanent. During Vietnam, Army mortuaries were established in South Vietnam at Da Nang and Tan Son Nhut for the identification of American war dead. Besides processing records for the more than 50,000 casualties, the recovery and identification of remains began.

When the war ended in January 1973, the identification mission was transferred to Camp Samae San in Satahip, Thailand, just outside of U-Tapao RTAFB. Three years later, in line with troop reductions throughout Southeast Asia, this unit was transferred to Honolulu, Hawaii, and officially designated the U.S. Army Central Identification Laboratory. This command was stationed at Hickam Air Force Base in Hawaii.[83]

Once remains were located, the usual procedure was to have them preserved and sent to the laboratory for identification. Depending on the circumstances, information was then requested for the identification staff to conduct research. Once identity was established, the actual date of death was back-dated to the date the remains were recovered. The next of kin was then informed, and the process for the return and burial was handled directly with the family members.

For Pat Wynne, he was classified missing in action as of that fateful day he and his pilot, Larry Golberg, were downed in their F-4C aircraft—Monday morning of August 8, 1966. Pat had been promoted to major effective April 1, 1974. Almost eight years had passed, and the issue was whether to declare Pat legally dead? As with any emotional and troubling question, the answer often was not a simple yes or no.

Pat had married Nancy Opalinski as soon as he graduated from the Air Force Academy. Married cadets were not allowed in the academy in those days, but they could certainly walk down the aisle as soon as they graduated. Pat and Nancy were married on June 6, 1963. They had waited all of 24 hours to make it official, similar to a number of other cadets and their partners.

Pat and Nancy had the opportunity to share a couple of years together, as Pat went to graduate school and then pilot's training. For Nancy, the 30-some months they had spent together married were now overwhelmed by the 90-some months they had been apart. Nancy needed to take charge of her life and sought the guidance of Pat's younger brother, 30-year-old Mike, who now stood in as the elder of his brothers and sisters.

Right around the seven-year anniversary of Pat's crash in North Vietnam and the ten-year mark of his graduating class at the Air Force Academy, Mike talked with Nancy to advise her on the process of declaring Pat legally dead. Nancy did not want to give up her last remaining hope but needed to move forward with her life. The still-young Nancy had moved to Madison, Wisconsin, where she operated a rooming house for University of Wisconsin students. This work and being near college students kept her young at heart and firmly grounded. And she had met someone. The situation brought into sharp relief one of the many seemingly impossible decisions people had to face with the Vietnam War. She needed to declare Pat legally dead, certainly a difficult life's moment.

With full knowledge that his mom and dad would have trouble accepting any action with all the grace one might hope for, Mike counseled Nancy to move forward. She was young and still had a great deal of living to anticipate, another 50–60 years with any luck. Nancy started proceedings to have Pat declared legally dead, wherein his status would change from missing in action to killed in action.

The downside was that she would go from being a partner in an active service relationship, albeit a missing in action relationship, to being a surviving widow as Pat went off the Air Force roster. Her compensation would go from 100 percent of a major's salary to 50 percent or less. After a few months of delay on Nancy's part and of procedure on the court's part, Pat was declared legally dead on May 28, 1974, all of 2,851 days after his F-4C Phantom II disappeared in the forested highlands of North Vietnam. It was only a matter of paper, but it troubled everyone in the family and covered the extremes of emotion.

Pat's mom had the most difficulty dealing with the situation. She couldn't accept that her 24-year old firstborn son had perished so quickly and in such a far-off location. A picture of Pat showing him in his twenties would remain on the wall in their Florida home, surrounded by photographs of his siblings that changed to reflect their growth in the ensuing years, Pat's image frozen in time. One could feel her thoughts. So many unanswered questions lingered. Why Pat? Was he one of the prisoners of war who were rumored to still be in captivity? How come no one ever heard anything of him? Were any of his remains found to prove his death? She knew in her heart that Pat was the best our nation would ever have to offer, but did he actually die and what were the circumstances? Questions remained. She was more comfortable with uncertainty than closure.

Mike's mom denounced Nancy's declaration of Pat being legally dead. A mom just couldn't let go of her firstborn son. Dad was not happy with the situation either, but he was definitely the more pragmatic of the two, and the lives of the Wynne family members continued on. And a few of the questions were destined to be answered.

As Mike finished up his work on the F-16 proposal in early 1977, the Wynne family reached another milestone in closure. Pat's remains had been found and identified. They were returned home to the United States on March 18, 1977. The family planned to have him interred on the grounds of the Air Force Academy.

The elder Wynnes, especially his mom, still had unpleasant feelings from three-years earlier when Pat was declared legally dead. He was of course, but that wasn't the point. It was a situation rife with emotion. As eldest surviving son and still a member of the Air Force reserves, Mike took charge of the funeral arrangements and made sure the ceremony was civil in every sense of the term. He met with the priest and the protocol people before the service, and arranged for the priest at the funeral ceremony to provide two crosses in the casket as mementos, one for Pat's widow and one for his mother. It was the only fair thing to do. Then the burial flag posed a problem.

Wednesday, April 6, 1977, broke bright sunny and altogether more cheerful than the Wynne family might have felt. A thin veneer of snow layered the cemetery grounds; just enough to remind the visitors that winter had not quite finished with the eastern slopes of the Continental Divide. A few hundred square feet of land around the gravesite were swept clean to provide the mourners an honorable place to stand. It was the day Pat was finally laid to rest back home in the United States; he had been gone a long time.

Besides Pat's parents, siblings Mike and Maureen were there,

Burial of Pat Wynne on April 6, 1977, on the grounds of the United States Air Force Academy. *Source:* Wynne Family.

as were Nancy and her parents and brother. Protocol required only one burial flag be presented at the ceremony. Since spousal relationships can and do change but parental bonds never vary, the burial flag from the ceremony ended up with Pat's mother. The flag that had honored Pat's casket was removed, properly folded without ever touching the ground, and with a nod to Nancy presented to Dorothy Wynne.

Patrick Edward Wynne was buried with full military honors in the cemetery located just off the Parade Loop on the campus of the Air Force Academy in Colorado Springs. The academy was a place where both Pat and Mike were comfortable. They had spent wonderful years on the ramparts. Now Pat would rest easy, in a place of honor. This remained a place to which Mike would be comfortable returning anytime.

Even though he was declared legally dead in 1974, Pat's actual date of death was debatable. Early on evidence was found to support the conclusion that he was able to eject from his aircraft before it crashed on August 8, 1966, and that he survived the ejection. On identifying his remains in 1977, the examiners noticed that Pat had broken a small bone in his leg, oftentimes a result of emergency ejection from an aircraft. So he hadn't crashed in his aircraft, he had ejected from it.

So a new line of questions began: If Pat did eject from the F-4C, did he survive the ejection and crash landing? If he did, what were his final hours like? Did he see anyone, was anyone there to help him? Pat's case remained in that posture. While the family knew with surety that Pat had died, how would they ever know the circumstances or the exact date?

※

PAT'S GRADUATING CLASS had been a bit ahead of its time for the Vietnam War but as things developed, they worked through pilot training and gained their ratings just in time for President Johnson's buildup of hostilities. When Pat graduated in 1963, roughly 20,400 Americans were stationed in Southeast Asia. By the end of 1965 when Pat had earned his pilot rating, the number in Vietnam had ballooned by a factor of ten. The Air Force had 5,716 servicemen in Southeast Asia in 1963 and almost 79,000 in 1966.[84] Pat was not alone.

The Class of 1963 had begun with 755 appointees on June 26, 1959, at the newly finished facilities in Colorado Springs. The setting for the Air Force Academy was more than 17,000 acres of pine-laden countryside, bordered on the west by the Pike National Forest. This part of the country sat at the foot of the Rampart Range, a section of terrain between Denver and Colorado Springs with the panoramic Rocky Mountains as backdrop. At an altitude of roughly 7,200 feet, the Air Force Academy locale could take one's breath away literally and figuratively. Of those 755 appointees, 499 would graduate four years later, all but 10 being commissioned into the U.S. Air Force. The Army, Navy, and Marines accounted for the remaining second lieutenants.

Graduation exercises held on June 5, 1963, celebrated the fifth class to complete its studies at the Air Force Academy and the first to have attended all four years at the new facilities. After the commencement address, diplomas to the top 25 graduates and the last to make it through were presented by President John F. Kennedy, the first president to so honor the academy and barely six months before he was assassinated. The remaining diplomas were granted by Brigadier General Robert F. McDermott, dean of the faculty. Commissions were presented by Air Force Chief of Staff General Curtis E. LeMay. The Class of 1963 was the largest yet, illustrating the ramp up in operations at the academy. The first four graduating classes each commissioned approximately 200 second lieutenants, averaging 237. The Class of 1963 more than doubled that with 499 graduates proudly wearing the gold bars of second lieutenants.

The experience of Pat's classmates was typical of the age and the demands of Vietnam. Pat was a member of Cadet Squadron 10 in his final year at the academy, along with 19 other young men. Of these 20, 10 would make the military a career, 8 retiring after at least 20 years and 2 dying in the service of their nation, one in Vietnam and one in an aircraft accident. Four others resigned their commission in the regular Air Force but continued on and rose through the ranks in the Air National Guard or the Air Force Reserves. Two were discharged from the Air Force. The remaining four resigned their commissions in 1969, having risen to the rank of captain.

Given these 20 men in Cadet Squadron 10 came through the Air Force Academy, flying is what most of them wanted to do. Sixteen would continue on to pilot training and earn their pilot rating. Two others would earn navigator ratings. Twelve would serve directly in the war, being stationed in Vietnam or Thailand. Three others would serve in the larger Southeast Asia theater in military airlift and troop transport squadrons, flying out of the Philippines and Japan.

The first of the Academy's "blue line" to give his life in Vietnam was Val Bourque from the Class of 1960, who was shot down in a C-130 just north of Saigon on October 24, 1964. Five more academy graduates died in 1965, and the tally added 22 graduates in 1966. One of those was Pat Wynne, who would be the fourth from the Class of 1963 and the 15th academy graduate of any year to perish in Vietnam. In the end, 18 from the Class of 1963 would not survive Vietnam.[85] Counting those who died in Vietnam or as a result of wounds attributable to the war effort, 151 Air Force Academy graduates earned their way onto the Vietnam Veterans Memorial. What of the rest of the graduates of the Class of 1963?

One of the icons from the Class of 1963 was Ron Fogleman, who would go all the way, rising to four-star general and chief of staff of the Air Force, the first academy graduate to do so. General Fogleman would resign his position in disgust in response to changes in his beloved Air Force. Reports on the circumstances included the general's disagreement with the Pentagon regarding reductions in the Air Force and his concern with a one-star general being made the scapegoat for a terrorist bombing in Saudi Arabia.[86] With the desire to be accountable in all regards, rather than serve under civilian policies he could not counter, Fogleman resigned.

Class valedictorian Sam Westbrook made a career out of the Air Force and rose to major general. A Rhodes Scholar after graduation, he served 28 years in the Air Force, including a stint back at the Air Force Academy as commandant of cadets. Jim Martin, who wrote for the academy's *Talon* with Pat and served as matchmaker in fixing up his classmate with Nancy on a blind date, retired as a brigadier general out of the Air Force Reserves.

Chuck Bush, Pat's debate partner from the academy, fellow graduate student at Georgetown University, and arguably one of his closest friends, stayed in the Air Force until the late 1960s. He worked in intelligence, served a tour in Vietnam, was awarded a bronze star, and resigned as a captain. He followed his service with an MBA degree from Harvard University and a successful business career. Years later, his daughter would become a recording star and return to the Air Force Academy to entertain the cadets.[87]

Pat's roommate in Thailand, Tom Fryer, had graduated with Pat's class from the Air Force Academy with the Order of Merit of 10. He performed graduate work before shipping out with Pat to Vietnam. He returned from Vietnam and eventually notched 21 years in the Air Force. He spent time as an instructor pilot at Williams and Reese Air Force Bases, and taught at the Air Force Academy and an Air Force Reserve Officer Training Corps program at Kansas

State University. After retiring as a lieutenant colonel, he pursued a second career in banking and financial planning.

Hopkins and Dodgen were acquaintances from Ubon RTAFB who were affected by Pat's work on awards and decorations. Bob Hopkins had graduated in the class before Pat's at the Air Force Academy and had taken his pilot training at Webb Air Force Base in Big Spring, located in West Texas. Don Dodgen had come to the Air Force through the Reserve Officer Training Corps program at Texas A&M University; he had earned his wings in pilot training at Laughlin Air Force Base, class 64-E. Both men completed tours of combat in Vietnam and made civilian use of their wings during the 1970s piloting aircraft for Trans World Airlines—the "We Want To Be Your Airline" airline. Furloughs and financial troubles took the adventure out of commercial operations and led them to new careers: Jeppesen Sanderson for Hopkins and Honeywell Aerospace for Dodgen.

Bob Hopkins, with 107 combat missions in Vietnam, was awarded a Distinguished Flying Cross and 13 Air Medals for his service. Dodgen, with 116 missions in the theater, most with the 555th Tactical Fighter Squadron, never did receive his Distinguished Flying Cross. Best guess was that his paperwork, left in handwritten form when Hopkins rotated home on July 31, 1966, was misplaced or forgotten in the shuffle when Pat was lost just eight days later.

What happened to the Georgetown 15? All graduated with advanced degrees and 13 went on to serve in Vietnam. As a class, they would be awarded 14 Distinguished Flying Crosses, one Silver and four Bronze Stars.[88] The Chevy? Nancy kept the 1964 red Corvette and drove it for years. It served its final duty with Nancy's dad, who was handy enough to repair what needed fixing on the, by then, aging and classic Corvette Sting Ray. As for Nancy, she finished what she had started, returning to college and completing her bachelor's degree in Art.

Chapter Eleven

Presentations and PMD

A YEAR AFTER THE F-16 PROPOSAL was firmed up, Fred Wood, who had been the government's business manager on the program, was still at Wright-Patterson in the employ of United States. One weekend while productively engaged mowing the lawn, Fred received a call from Dave Lewis, the chief executive officer at General Dynamics. Dave inquired as to whether Fred might be interested in coming to work for him in St. Louis. Fred put off answering to talk it over with his wife Erma but all was soon made official with a letter from General Dynamics, in which they offered him the position of vice president contracts at corporate in St. Louis, Missouri. One thing led to another, and in short order

he accepted the offer and moved to the supply side of weapons development. The year was 1978. Months later, Mike Wynne had occasion to be at corporate, making a review presentation. Fred was in the room, this time as a fellow employee. After the meeting, Fred challenged Mike, "When are you coming to corporate?" It appeared to be time for a new adventure.

Mike Wynne in January, 1978.
Source: Wynne Family.

MIKE AND BARB moved with their family of four girls to St. Louis, their second posting with General Dynamics. In fact, a number of the people involved with the F-16 program in Fort Worth were on the move, in concert with the success of that product line. As vice president, Fred Wood was Mike's ultimate boss. Bill Mcurdy also had moved to St. Louis, now stationed as Fred's deputy. With so many of the same players, it was beginning to resemble old home week.

Mike's first assignments were to validate projections on major ventures of General Dynamics. He was very familiar with one of the first he had to review, the Fort Worth Division's F-16 program. In essence, part of the team Mike originally worked with in Fort Worth came to St. Louis to substantiate the full-scale development program and earnings projections. Mike then had to present his corroboration of the projections on this program to Dave Lewis, the chairman and chief executive officer.

Lewis, an aeronautical engineer by training, began his business career with the Glenn L. Martin Company and then joined McDonnell Aircraft in St. Louis in 1946. As chief of aerodynamics, he was in on the early development of jet fighter aircraft. In the 1950s Lewis headed up the engineering that evolved into the F-4 Phantom II, which would sell more than 5,000 copies in the ensuing years. The success of the F-4 launched him into management at McDonnell Aircraft. In 1967 McDonnell merged with the troubled Douglas Aircraft, and Lewis was credited with straightening out the division. With founder J.S. McDonnell unwilling to hand over the reins, Lewis resigned and became chairman and chief executive of General Dynamics in 1971. General Dynamics was in the midst of developing what would become the F-16 Fighting Falcon but was having financial difficulties of its own. Lewis was brought in to transform the company's fortunes. This was one of Mike Wynne's first presentations to the chairman, and proved to be memorable.

For some unknown reason, Mike's presentation was terrible. He was out of sync and the projections, which he had gone over numerous times, did not seem to add up. While Mike was a confident and sure speaker, he had trouble with this performance from beginning to end. As he began a slide into discomfort, the exhibition just became worse. He tried to press on.

Finally, at one juncture in the show, Lewis piped in and remarked, "I don't think that's right, Mike." He could see the projections were not holding together and the numbers were not adding up.

With just a bit of awkwardness, Mike acknowledged, "You know, I don't think it is either. But it is a simple math problem. If I can't solve this simple math problem, I ought not to be here. So just give me a minute, and I'll solve this thing."

But Lewis, not willing to let the uneasiness continue, jumped in with, "Oh, hell. Let's just…," offering comments and calculations that helped solve the simple math problem. The aeronautical engineer and the electrical engineer, 30 years apart in schooling, put their heads together and quickly came up with the solution to the mathematical road block. The presentation finished successfully. Dave Lewis was happy. Mike Wynne was happy. Everyone was happy. And in the greater scheme of a career opportunity, even glitches served a purpose. Mike became fairly well known, fairly fast at the corporate level.

ANOTHER REVIEW PROJECT for Mike concerned the *Los Angeles*–class fast attack submarines (SSN-688s), each 360 feet long with a submerged displacement of 6,900 tons. Design work on the SSN-688 program, the intended centerpiece of the Navy's nuclear-powered submarine fleet, had started in the late 1960s. It had developed into a joint program of Tenneco's Newport News Shipbuilding, located at the mouth of the James River in Virginia, and General Dynamics Electric Boat shipyard, on the Thames River at Groton, Connecticut. Newport News had the design contract, its first for a submarine from the ground up. Both Newport News and Electric Boat would receive construction awards.

Electric Boat's first orders for the SSN-688s had come in January 1971, when the Navy awarded it a contract for seven vessels. In 1973 the Navy added another 11 ships to the contract. By 1974 the Electric Boat shipyard was launching *Los Angeles*–class submarines. The first had been SSN-690 *Philadelphia*, which was commissioned on

June 25, 1977, followed by SSN-692 *Omaha* and SSN-694 *Groton* in 1978. By the time Mike became involved in this project, a great deal of murky water had already flowed.

In February 1975, soon after launching its first *Los Angeles*–class submarine, General Dynamics began filing claims against the Navy for cost overruns caused by design problems. General Dynamics followed up with additional petitions, and by 1977 outstanding claims stood at $843 million. In June of 1978, right about the time Mike arrived in St. Louis, General Dynamics and the Navy reached a settlement of $534 million to be paid to General Dynamics.

Compounding the cost overrun problems was the 1977 arrival of P. Takis Veliotis, who transferred over from General Dynamics Quincy Massachusetts Shipyard to become head of the Electric Boat Division. As foil to Admiral Hyman Rickover who still ruled the Naval Reactors Branch of the Navy's nuclear submarine programs, Veliotis was promoted by Lewis to control costs at Groton. Veliotis inaugurated his tenure by laying off thousands of employees.

Part wizard and part villain, both legendary and loquacious, Veliotis worked to straighten out the SSN-688 program, managed the start of the *Ohio*–class (Trident) ballistic missile submarine program, handed out questionable gifts with aplomb, and lined his own pockets with kickbacks at most every opportunity. By 1983 Veliotis would flee to Greece, one step ahead of federal indictments. This was the corporate climate in which Mike worked as a reviewing official for the SSN-688 submarine program.

His expertise in developing cost models and certifying projections would be used heavily during his stay in St. Louis and afterwards. In the flurry of hearings and court proceedings that arose in subsequent years, Mike would testify about costs and pricing issues on a number of occasions. He appeared before a Securities and Exchange Commission panel and testified at a Department of Justice hearing. He even was called to appear before a grand jury in Groton on the subject of General Dynamics submarine and ancillary businesses. These were great life experiences that provided firsthand confirmation on the right way and the wrong way to do business.

OF COURSE, NOT EVERYTHING WAS A BIG EVENT and not everything was on center stage. Work progressed, and Mike settled in very nicely in St. Louis for the next couple of years. In 1979 Mike was even able to help brother Pete find employment with the company. At the time, Pete's career aspirations were sated building swimming pools in Satellite Beach. Single, 25 years old, with a love of the outdoors, what's not to like? But Mike thought his beach-loving youngest brother might move past that. Mike helped Pete arrange an interview with General Dynamics in Fort Worth. Called back for a second interview, Pete received an offer that moved him into office work. His next stop was Texas. Pete ended up in finance in Fort Worth, while Mike worked in contracts from St. Louis. Pete also met a gal, started a family and settled down, supporting the concept of moving past.

Mike was ever the older brother, and had occasion to visit Pete at work in Fort Worth a time or two and continue in his role. In fact, it was Mike who showed Pete the correct way to tie a tie in the business world. While visiting the office in Fort Worth one day, Mike noticed Pete's beach roots were starting to bleed through in his sartorial demeanor. Mike showed him the correct way to fashion a classic tie knot, probably the slightly more assertive half-Windsor, and Pete was on his way.

BEING AT CORPORATE in St. Louis agreed with Mike; he could be involved with everything going on at General Dynamics, even if only on the periphery at times. He was but a heartbeat away from the action, which suited his sense of participation just fine. He was gaining a perspective on the entire General Dynamics operation. As time went on, the company began to groom Mike for more responsibility. In the fourth quarter of 1981, he was chosen to attend the Program for Management Development at Harvard University. PMD-42, the forty-second offering of this management development program, was structured for high-potential executives.

So Mike was off to Boston for 90 days. Besides learning about leadership and vision, Mike met other executives from major corporations around the world. It was a broadening experience and added an international point of view to his knowledge base. While Mike was hunkered down studying by the St. Charles River, General Dynamics Corporate had formed a team to negotiate the possible purchase of Chrysler Corporation's tank works located outside of Detroit.

THE 1960S THROUGH THE 1980S was a period of deal making and corporate restructuring across the United States, as many companies decided they could grow their business faster through external acquisitions than by limiting themselves to internal expansion. Firms generally took one of three tacks when expanding through acquisitions. One option was to gobble up competitors in horizontal integration. The contrasting business strategy was to acquire upstream suppliers or downstream buyers in vertical integration. The third option was pure diversification, where a company would cobble together businesses that operated in different industrial sectors.

General Dynamics, which began as a builder of submarines, had limited experience with acquisitions. The two biggest deals had been the acquisition of Consolidated Vultee Aircraft (Convair) and the merger with Material Services, both of which occurred in the 1950s. With the Republican Party's return to power and newly-elected President Reagan pushing defense spending right from the start in 1981, General Dynamics was in the market looking to expand and diversify. In Michigan Chrysler Corporation was hemorrhaging money in the automotive business and in the midst of borrowing $1.2 billion from the government just to stay afloat in 1980 and 1981. It needed to convert assets into cash. There sat Chrysler's proud tank works, which had been making armored vehicles since 1941.

CHAPTER TWELVE

Chariots of Iron

AT THE ONSET OF WORLD WAR II IN EUROPE, the need for armor, especially tanks, exploded. The United States government began purchasing property for manufacturing resources. In converting American business to a wartime footing, the objective was to have government-owned but contractor-operated facilities to mass produce tanks. The Detroit Arsenal Tank Plant was built in 1940-1941 on government property in Warren, Michigan, and put under contract to Chrysler Corporation. In 1941–42, the Lima Arsenal Tank Plant was constructed in Lima, Ohio, and operations were contracted to United Motors Service. These two plants continued to supply armored vehicles on and off again, long after the armor, artillery, and infantry of World War II returned from Europe.

By the mid-1970s both plants were under contract to Chrysler Corporation, which had been given the charge to develop and manufacture the new XM-1 tank with a 105 mm gun. The XM-1 eventually became the M-1 Abrams.[89] By the late-1970s the Detroit plant was fabricating components and shipping them to the Lima facility for final assembly of the M-1. But the Detroit plant was soon to assemble its own.

WHILE MIKE WAS IN CAMBRIDGE, his contacts back in St. Louis kept him in the loop. Negotiations seemed headed for an acquisition but not one in which he would participate. The other team members intimately involved with the deal making would structure the acquisition and make it work. Mike was happy with that. He and Barb were comfortable in St. Louis, and it was nice being located where the major decisions were made. Every time Mike received a newsflash or an update from the tank work's negotiations, he relayed them to Barb and assured her no one had brought up the idea of a transfer to Detroit. They were thrilled with how things were working out and so far, safe in St. Louis.

Once back from Harvard University, Mike dove right back into work, trying to win his way back into the good graces of the corporation. After all, one of the problems with being away for three months is that everyone starts to see and believe they can do the work without you. So Mike was busy at work in St. Louis while the Detroit negotiations were finalized toward the end of 1981, with closing scheduled a few months out. At about the same time, the General Dynamics Board hired a new president, Oliver C. Boileau, the former president of Boeing Corporation.

In sum and substance, Ollie Boileau was to be the succession plan for General Dynamics. Chairman Dave Lewis ruled at General Dynamics much as his mentor, J.S. McDonnell, had at McDonnell Douglas Aircraft. He did not share power easily. Thus, Boileau was brought in as president to be groomed for the next step. For the interim, he was hired with the express task of making the tank works acquisition a success.

ON A PERSONAL LEVEL, the New Year started out cheerless. Mike's mom died in January 1982, and it hit her children hard. Dot was a few months shy of her 63rd birthday. One of Mike's colleagues, Ed Ewing, passed by one day and saw Mike in a blue mood.[90] On finding out Mike's mother had passed, he offered to support Mike and his family in any way possible. Mike's dad had arranged for interment at West Point and requested no flowers for the funeral. Ewing thought differently and literally buried West Point cemetery under a sheath of flowers, an arrangement from each General Dynamics plant arriving for the appointed day. The dark, dingy ceremony in the winter at West Point was lightened considerably. That was the way it was with the General Dynamics people. Everyone was family and they cared.

ONE DAY IN FEBRUARY 1982 Mike received a call to come up to Boileau's office, ostensibly to brief the new president. As Mike walked in the door, he found arrayed before him most of his erstwhile friends and mentors from General Dynamics, with Boileau holding court at the head of the table. The president began. "You have been recommended by these people to be on the transition team," he said with a wave of the hand. "Welcome aboard. You now work in the Office of the President of the Tank Division." And that was it.

For the next two months, Mike worked for Boileau and his Office of the President of the Tank Division. Mike did receive his fondest wish, to remain in the St. Louis area. He traveled back and forth between St. Louis and Detroit each week, working daily with Boileau on a variety of tank works projects. One of the first things Mike initiated was a survey of the current state of affairs at tank works, to bring him up-to-speed on the business of building tanks.

Remembering his time in Fort Worth and equipped with his own degree in electrical engineering, Mike noticed a disconnect concerning engineers when it came to building tanks. While he was quite sure he was not the first to recognize the disparity, he could detect that the utilization of electrical engineers paled when compared to that of mechanical engineers.

Back in Fort Worth the company was just finishing up development on the second generation F-16, and already had plans on the books to improve that version. The company was working to digitize the F-16 since weapons development was heading toward the use of more electronics and computers. Quite simply, following the pattern, the future of tanks would be in aircraft-style systems. Mike mentioned his views one day in a conversation with the chief engineer of General Dynamics.

"I just wanted to make sure you knew that I'm like the ninth or tenth electrical engineer here in Warren, and I am in contracts," Mike said. "Maybe what we need is a cracker-jack, digitally oriented, electrical engineer up here to run engineering, crafting systems for tanks much like avionics work in the F-16." Sometime later, an electrical engineer named Gordon England arrived in Warren to head up Land Systems engineering. For the moment, Mike was on a different path, as the president had other plans.

IN APRIL 1982, Boileau decided to promote Mike to vice president of contracts for the tank works division. Mike's direct report would be Fred Wood, the corporate vice president of contracts, if they could work out an arrangement. Mike enjoyed employing a few of the skills he had learned at Harvard's management development program to negotiate his package, but in the end his old friend Fred did what it took to make the change happen. He gave Mike what he asked for, save one dollar under his desired salary. For the Wynne family, it was time for an exodus from St. Louis.

The kids were growing up and working their way through school. Their eldest was in high school and beginning to date. Everyone was happy in St. Louis, but by late spring 1982, the Wynne family had to pack up and leave their comfort zone. Mike kept up the commute until the end of the school year. Then it was a series of going-away parties, one of which was in Bill Mcurdy's backyard. With the tank works headquartered in Detroit, the family settled in Sterling Heights, Michigan, one of the largest of Detroit's suburbs. Sterling Heights was but 20 miles north of downtown Detroit, and just a couple of miles from Warren.

Even though they remained in the Midwest, the family went from the climate of St. Louis, moderated largely by the Mississippi River, to the weather of Detroit, which lay at the mercy of the Great Lakes. The Wynnes needed to manage these moves better in the future, as they were developing an unsettling pattern. Fort Worth had annual snowfall of but a spare 2.5 inches, while St. Louis would hobble in with 19.5 inches. The Detroit area, in contrast, weighed in with snowfall exceeding 40 inches per year.

THE NEW TANK WORKS ADVENTURE in Michigan, dubbed General Dynamics Land Systems, embodied a rough start for Mike. Shortly after he became the go-to guy in contracts in April 1982, the United States government derailed operations. Land Systems' number one buyer sent a letter, the essence of which basically shut them down. Mike immediately responded with a missive of his own, rebutting the notice. As it came to light, a portion of the early production turned up with serious design flaws, and the Army refused to accept any more deliveries. The quality departments on both sides of the table were spending more time searching for the guilty than hunting for the solution.

Tank work's quality control people were sparring with their counterparts at the Federal level. It had been a bit cheeky of Mike to reject the government's notice, but his title of vice president carried just enough weight to require attention. The recipients were clearly flummoxed. The government was not used to receiving letters rejecting their rejections, and it served to open a dialogue.

Mike soon met with the Army colonel who was the government's deputy program manager. Having done his homework, the colonel had found out about Mike's roots in the service, which provided common ground. Mike explained that General Dynamics was just starting out in the business and had only been in control for a matter of months. The company was new to the job and up to the task, but this shutdown would undermine the tank works. Mike offered his optimum.

"Look, I'll do the best job I can for you and remedy the problems. But you need this equipment for your soldiers."

The colonel agreed.

Mike reasoned, "Things will only get better if we work together on these problems, not by shutting down the plant and the production line."

The colonel agreed.

Mike told him that as General Dynamics took over the tank works, it had replaced the quarrelsome quality department associate. Now maybe the government might consider doing the same, so the parties could start fresh. Mike pressed, "This is a squabble that will go on forever until we grab control and take charge of it. We need to take it as our own."

The colonel agreed.

So they hammered away at the issues and the government gave Land Systems a work out plan, a chance to fix the quality concerns. When the deputy program manager asked who would sign for the company, Mike said that, as the vice president of contracts, he would. When that raised nary an objection, the deal was done. Within three months, tank works resolved the issues to the government's satisfaction.

Back at corporate in St. Louis, Mike's colleagues were astonished that he had sent a letter rebuffing the government's rejection and that the Army then moderated its position by agreeing to a work out plan. Mike had to admit that his actions, which circumvented the entire bureaucratic custom, were driven by a bit of naïveté and a lot of desire to solve the problems. Later Mike found out General Dynamics San Diego-based Convair Division that worked with cruise missiles, had received a similar letter. It would take that division two years to work out its peccadilloes.

After that rough start, things had to improve, and they did. Mike settled in. His influence began to spread in the defense industry in general and in Michigan in particular. He became president of the National Contracts Management Association of Detroit, a professional development group, and president of the Michigan chapter of the National Defense Industrial Association (NDIA). The NDIA kept the various elements of the defense community— government, military, and defense organizations—working together. Mike was cultivating a network of associates and plowing up a number of interesting deals.

ONE OF THE KEYS to expanding the tank business was creating more chances for friendly countries to domestically produce versions of Land Systems flagship product, the Abrams tank. The linchpin to any deal was Land Systems retaining fundamental technology, some crucial piece of the puzzle, so it could share in the residuals and continue to be involved. Using the same template fashioned for the F-16 program, Mike and his associates would accomplish this by having Land Systems retain the electronics package, while the foreign contractor assembled components. This was the pattern for future international efforts.

The marketing lead for Land Systems, George Psihas, had been working on a deal with Egypt.[91] Together Mike and George finalized arrangements for Land Systems to sponsor a tank plant in Heliopolis, a suburb of Cairo. In that situation, with the understanding put together in late 1982 or early 1983 and operations ramped up in 1988, tank kits would be supplied against Egyptian Army orders. The Egyptians would do the drive train work and conduct final assembly but purchase wiring for the tank commander cupola and turret from General Dynamics. Land Systems retained the basket of electronics and control elements as proprietary components. To oversimplify, it was a plug-and-play design.

The Egyptians would build the tank, then drop in this basket of electronics, and plug in the electronic connections. If one had the insert of electronics plugged in, the tank worked. If one did not have the electronics, the tank did not work. This is what kept General Dynamics Land Systems in the business.

The Egyptian tank plant business arrangement proved to be an even more complex international experience, since transnational agreements with former enemies of Egypt such as Israel had to be fashioned into the overall understanding. In a twist of fate, tank operations were ramped up at a point in time coinciding with the 10-year anniversary of the Camp David accords of 1978. In the final analysis, the Egyptians were the only foreign nation to have the capability to build full-size Abrams tanks, the salient difference being the lack of the specialized depleted uranium armor.

SOUTH KOREA HAD BEEN A CUSTOMER of Chrysler's for years, buying hundreds of M-48 Patton-series tanks. To remain competitive with the threat to the north, South Korea was looking to add a new tank to its inventory. About the same time the new M-1 Abrams rolled out of Michigan, South Korea was evaluating various models that could be domestically produced. Land Systems promoted the idea of building tanks at a plant in South Korea, and Mike and George were able to finalize an arrangement a year after their success in Egypt.

The essence of the proposal was to have Hyundai Precision build a scaled-down version of the M-1 Abrams tank, identical in most respects to the American model. The thought was that the Hyundai plant in Changwon, just outside Seoul, would construct the tanks while Land Systems would supply components and parts and, most importantly, furnish the manufacturing know-how and technology.[92] Hyundai obtained the electronics from German manufacturers. Mike Wynne worked the deal from the contracts side.

Hyundai and Land Systems quickly reached an accord, subject to the government of South Korea buying into the program. As South Korea blessed the pact, a tripartite agreement was signed. Quicker than one would expect, Washington weighed in. Land Systems soon received a letter from the State Department, stating that it was illegal for a private company to endorse an agreement with a foreign country. It was time for lawyers.

General Dynamics counsel knew Mike and George had extended the company into unknown territory. Mike's position was that the contract was between Hyundai and Land Systems, with the South Korean government simply concurring in the action. While even Land Systems' lawyers rolled their eyes at the merit of that kind of interpretation, the agreement did feel right. It was with a friendly country, one which the United States wanted to support with infrastructure, and it was good business for the American company. In the end, even though the signatures of South Korean officials were clearly on the agreement, the State Department agreed it was more akin to a concurrence. With production initiated in 1984, the first vehicles under this pact rolled off the Hyundai line in 1985. The South Koreans designated it the K-1 main battle tank.

AS HEAD OF CONTRACTS at Land Systems, Mike had one major challenge that had escaped him, nailing down a multiyear contract with the military. Up to that time, the Army had rarely signed contracts that extended into consecutive budget years. While a multiyear contract would give the tank operation a steady stream of business and scheduling and financing wherewithal, the real benefit was in the residuals. The Army would be committed to the Land Systems product for both new purchases, and parts and supplies. In 1986 Mike began working on a multiyear contract for tanks.

Mike cultivated relationships in Washington through a series of meetings. He met with subcommittee members of the House Armed Services Committee, chaired by Les Aspin from Wisconsin. He also met with comparable groups of the Senate Committee on Armed Services, chaired by Barry Goldwater of Arizona. Conference work resulted in authorization for the Tank Automotive Command (TACOM) to enter into a multiyear contract, as long as savings remained at least 10 percent.

TACOM was certainly willing to consider a multiyear acquisition program for the M-1A1 tank, which was an M-1 upgraded with the 120 mm smoothbore cannon and advanced systems. With the mandated 10 percent savings, the Army was an enthusiastic buyer and wanted its share of the defense spending spree. The Army signed up to a four-year deal covering 750 vehicles per year, with the possibility of an extra 300 or so. But now with an order covering more than 3,000 units, someone else grew nervous.

Mike had essentially just finished negotiations with TACOM, when his leadership in St. Louis developed a case of anxiety. Whether it was the size of the deal or the 10 percent reduction in price or the uncertain economic times, corporate was nervous. General Dynamics had the added pressure of a marketplace losing trust in the company.[93] General Dynamics new chief executive officer, Stan Pace, dialed up Mike one day and said he was coming to Michigan. "I am getting reports from our senior people that doing this deal would be a mistake. I need you to show me why we should do it."

Stanley C. Pace, a 1943 graduate of the United States Military Academy, had earned his pilot's wings in the Army Air Force. He served with distinction in World War II, flying Consolidated B-24 Liberators, and was interned as a prisoner of war. He also served during the Korean War, rising to the rank of colonel by 1954. Pace resigned his commission and began a long, successful business career with a predecessor to TRW Corporation. In 1985, on the verge of retirement, the board of directors of General Dynamics prevailed upon him to help the company restore its credibility, which was under assault by both Washington and Wall Street for alleged fraud and waste in billions of dollars in defense contracts. Pace, with the mantle of chairman and chief executive officer, was brought in above Ollie Boileau, who had been the understudy. It was Stan Pace, a man of integrity and ability, who arrived with the mission of restoring public trust.

Pace came to Warren and Mike put on a show-and-tell about the multiyear proposal. Just three of them were in the room: Stan Pace, one of his assistants, and Mike Wynne. While the proposed deal would still require the approval of corporate, the chief executive officer sat in judgment with a private, 30-minute briefing because of the influence he wielded. Mike began with the remark that the slides he was going to show had already been seen by the government but not in the order they would be presented in this briefing. With that single caveat, Mike dove right in.

Mike walked Pace down the path that clarified how General Dynamics could sustain a 10 percent price reduction and still have a better-than-even chance of beating profit projections. It was unadulterated economics. Economic realities necessitated a business strategy of locking in future business, even if that meant trading price for volume.

Ronald Reagan was the sitting president, in his second term of office. The economy was in good shape as inflation was under control and unemployment had declined, but the specter of reduced investment in defense programs loomed on the horizon. Reagan and Gorbachev were working to suspend the proliferation of intermediate-range nuclear weapons, a first step in strategic arms reduction and an indication of what was to come. After a significant advance in expenditures during the first half of the 1980s, the future for defense spending looked bleak. It was essential for Land Systems to initial a multiyear contract at the peak of spending, to secure a base level of manufacturing to carry the company through the anticipated slide. Pace became a believer, but one last hurdle remained.

Mike traveled to St. Louis and presented the program to the assembled senior management of General Dynamics. Pace sat back and watched the now-familiar show unfold. Mike summarized that the ground-breaking proposal would partner the Army and Land Systems and would lock in profits for General Dynamics for years to come. The collective wisdom of the group was divided, with predictable positions on each side of the room. Mike's compatriots, Fred Wood and Bill Mcurdy, were steady in support. It ended up a judgment call on whether the savings could be achieved.

Pace did not mind taking on a little risk, and the project was approved. The proposal moved from conception to reality, from contracts to manufacturing. This was the point in the process where Mike had the opportunity to hand off the venture. Mike worked up the numbers, and then someone else had to make the numbers work. Bob Truxell, the general manager in charge of Land Systems, inherited the program and worked his magic. Truxell went out and brought in what was needed to make the project a success. Because of Truxell and his team, General Dynamics corporate had little reason to regret its decision. Neither did the Army, although one would not know it from the response.

In time Mike would receive the equivalent of hate mail from some of his classmates from the Military Academy. They felt that he had stuffed the Army with thousands of high-tech tanks at the expense of the other branches. While armor might be happy for the moment, artillery and infantry were dismayed that tanks monopolized such a major portion of the next four budget cycles. No one could have predicted that within just a few years, 1,904 modern M-1A1 tanks would be deployed in the Persian Gulf, hundreds of which were utilized in making sweeping armored flanking movements around the western edge of Kuwait through the Al-Dibdibah desert.[94]

BY THE TIME THE NEW YEAR ROLLED IN, Mike was firmly established as part of the Michigan defense business and at full stride in his position. As one of the company's *wunderkinder*, Mike received pressure from General Dynamics for another transfer. Even though he had only a few years in with tank works, corporate decided it wanted Mike in San Diego for a new adventure. But Mike's children were at the age where a move would be disruptive, and he felt he had much more to offer Land Systems. Tanks had not yet seen his best. So Mike threw his feet out. His colleagues back in St. Louis thought he was committing corporate hara-kiri, but the company had bumped into his steel again. Mike stayed. With success in contracts, Mike made a transition to business development, and the world of opportunities in tanks broadened.

Possibilities in East Asia involved complicated transnational concerns, nowhere more so than Taiwan. Since 1949 the United States had supported the government of Taiwan. This support embraced armaments including tanks. The Taiwanese had been customers of Chrysler tank works for years and owned large fleets of M-48 and M-60 Patton-series tanks. Due to trade restrictions and treaty regulations, the United States was limited in what new tank equipment could be sold to the Taiwanese. Land Systems marketing and business development came up with a business scheme where the company could fashion an upgraded tank to the Taiwanese and remain in full compliance with Chinese trade agreements.

The marketing department's George Psihas had come up with a plan to take an M-48 Patton-series tank turret, upgrade from a 90 mm high-velocity cannon to a 105 mm rifled gun identical to that found on the M-1, and patch that on to an M-60 diesel-powered tank hull. By adding in improved fire control and other upgraded systems, Land Systems had cobbled together an M-48H tank, designated a CM11 Brave Tiger by the Taiwanese. While the Taiwanese would be given the technology to modify their own tanks years later, the first copies came from Land Systems.

Psihas had marshaled the resources to take the project this far. With international issues cleared, the remaining hurdle barring the sale to Taiwan was certification. This work was done at the Aberdeen Proving Grounds, an Army facility protruding into Chesapeake Bay just northeast of Baltimore, which occupied more than 100 square miles of land. Certification proved more difficult than expected.

While a standard M-48 tank with the 90 mm gun registered a good percentage of first-round hits, the cobbled-together M-48H did not. In simple terms, the M-48H was having trouble hitting anything. The Army did not want to certify the tank, and without certification, no sale.

Boileau dialed up Mike one day and said, "We can't sell these things. I want you to go take over the project." Mike parried that he was in contracts, but the president persisted. Mike became program manager for the M-48H.

Since the problem was target hits or lack thereof, Mike hired a retired gunnery sergeant from Aberdeen to act as an expert consultant. That decision quickly made the Aberdeen rank-and-file defensive. Orders came down that only Aberdeen employees would be allowed on the range. Not to be dissuaded so easily, Mike took it to the range commander.

Distilling the issues, Mike outlined, "Sir, neither you nor I want to be in the middle of an international incident, where the United States offers Taiwan an advanced tank in one breath and then refuses to ship it to them in the second breath. They think we are diplomatically upset with them. They do not get it, that the tank has a problem hitting the target. If you would authorize the use of our retired Army gunnery sergeant, I believe he can help us decode the problems we are having in getting the tank to hit the target one way or another."

More sparing in language, the range commander challenged, "Will it get it off my damn range?"

"I think I can have it off your range faster with my guy," Mike countered.

With authorization, Mike pressed his gunnery sergeant in the mix. Feeling taken down a peg, the Aberdeen people were fuming but they channeled their ire into action and quickly rose to the occasion. The retired gunnery sergeant started out hitting 8 or 9 out of 10 shots. The Aberdeen troops, who warmed to the challenge and made it a competition, started hitting the target with a higher percentage. What had been 2 or 3 out of every 10 shots, rose to 6 or 7 out of 10. They hit enough.

The general confirmed that Aberdeen was willing to certify the tank. "Get your tank off my range."

"Okay, I got it."

"And get your guy out of here."

BUSINESS WAS GOOD at the tank works in Michigan and bound to become even better with the advent of an upgraded M-1A1. This was the digital tank, so advanced it received its own moniker, the M-1A2. This tank was the product of Gordon England's team. He had been brought to Michigan and the tank works in 1986 for the express purpose of guiding the M-1A1 to the next level, and he delivered.

England appeared on the scene in Michigan fresh from his design work in Texas. Mike and Gordon knew of each other back in the 1970s in the General Dynamics hierarchy in Fort Worth but didn't have much contact since they were in different areas. Mike had been in contracts, and Gordon had been in advanced engineering.

England was an electrical engineering graduate from the University of Maryland, with a master's degree in business from Texas Christian University. He started his business career with Honeywell and transitioned to General Dynamics in the late 1960s as a 30-something design engineer. At the time he moved to Michigan, England was just finished laying in upgraded systems on the second generation F-16 at the Fort Worth facility.

The F-16 Block 25, the first copy of which came off the line in 1984, was the latest generation Fighting Falcon. Earlier versions of the F-16 had utilized what was designated as 1553 data bus architecture for its avionics. An upgraded layer, 1760 data bus technology, was introduced on the F-16 Block 25. It was obvious that the future would be fully digitized avionics and systems, and here was a man of the digital age. The company wanted England to repeat his F-16 success with the Abrams tank. What was avionics in the air would evolve into vetronics on land, vehicle electronics.

Electrical engineer Gordon England effectively replaced mechanical engineer Phil Lett, who was promoted up and out. Lett had done yeoman work creating and designing the original M-1.

A larger cannon and numerous tweaks brought about the M-1A1. England would bowl everyone over with the digital version of the tank—the M-1A2. Gordon lined up the leading-edge programmers and avionics experts needed to bring the tank into the digital age, and in the final analysis the M-1A2 probably had more computer code in it than the first F-16s. Now, Mike Wynne and George Psihas had new product to sell.

But then, talk about letting the air out of something. The Army did not want the M-1A2. Was it too fancy and too complicated? Besides the digital developments, this next generation in tanks provided a means for the vehicles to communicate with each other. Welcome the IVIS—the Inter-Vehicular Information System. IVIS, which made its first appearance on the M-1A2 Abrams tank, was capable of communicating with other platforms, such as tanks, Bradley fighting vehicles, and even helicopters in the combat theater. It was the concept of a local area network system, a contained feedback loop, applied to armor. For General Dynamics, this was the application of improvements scheduled for future versions of the F-16 Fighting Falcon to the M-1A2 Abrams. Was the Army's problem the fact that Lett had been superseded, or was it the fact that the M-1A2 was becoming more expensive in the face of defense budgets being slashed? It didn't matter, the Army didn't want it. Mike had his work cut out for him, and he came at it through the back door by way of the Department of Defense foreign military sales program.

Mike sold M-1A2 tanks to the Kingdom of Saudi Arabia, which was the first to place firm orders. While on the surface a simple transaction, this particular case provided Wynne with a taste of politics and a huge dose of international negotiations of a different scale. He worked with the American Israel Public Action Committee and was able to bridge concerns to the extent that the business deal finally went through.

Once the Saudis were committed to the M-1A2, it became a lobbying effort in Washington to bring the deal home. The Army had to purchase at least a battalion-sized unit for evaluation to fully understand the capability. In the end, the Army purchased 60 new

M-1A2s, and they liked them. This also gave General Dynamics a logistics base for international sales. Land Systems did not have to sell brand-new M-1A2s. With an installed base of thousands of M-1s and M-1A1s around the world, as these models came of age for refurbishing, they could be converted and upgraded to the M-1A2 package.[95]

FIRMLY ENTRENCHED ON THE BUSINESS DEVELOPMENT SIDE of armored vehicles, Mike's responsibility now encompassed more than M-1A1/A2 Abrams tanks. The timing was just right in that the Marine Corps appeared a bit disgruntled with one of its long-term suppliers. Whether it was a disagreement about price, the Corps feeling that it should have alternate suppliers, or any of a myriad of other business concerns, the essence of the matter was that the Marine Corps was taking a serious look at options on one of its longest-running inventory items—amphibious assault vehicles.[96]

Assault vehicles had been utilized by the Marine Corps for decades. Food Machinery Company (FMC), a Philadelphia-based, old-line manufacturer of farm equipment, had become the major player in this product line. FMC was contracted in 1941 by the War Department to build a series of tracked amphibious landing vehicles to support the war effort. Designated the LVT and originally intended to be a shuttle for ship-to-shore operations, the number of uses had expanded and the design had evolved over the years. One of the first innovations was adding armor protection.

With LVT-1 through LVT-4 produced during World War II, the LVT-series evolved. The LVT-5 amphibious armored personnel carrier entered service in 1956, capable of carrying 30 troops. FMC followed with the LVT-7 model in 1972. In a purely semantic upgrade, the LVT-7 was soon renamed the amphibious assault vehicle—the AAV. With a crew of three, the AAV carried 25 soldiers, could travel 300 miles, hit 45 miles per hour on land, and conquer most terrain. More than a 1,000 had been produced for the Marines by the late 1980s, when the Corps opened up bidding for the next generation of armored assault vehicles. Originally dubbed the AAAV or advanced amphibious assault vehicle, the latest iteration would emerge as the EFV, the expeditionary fighting vehicle.

FMC and its rival, BMY Combat Systems (formerly Bowen-McLaughlin York), were vying for development contracts. General Dynamics Land Systems, which had experience with tanks but not assault vehicles, thought this could be a logical extension for its business. The new vehicle program with the Marine Corps was at the concept exploration stage. This was the kind of program that would take 20 years to come to fruition, but if a company was not in on the front end, it would be shut out for the entire period.

Land Systems and the other defense contractors had bids in for design and development work on the new generation amphibious assault vehicle. Mike's task was to close the deal so Land Systems received a development contract, even if the company was only one of a number of competitors. The essence of the negotiation was to agree on a range of price for a vehicle with a set range of capability. Successful bidders would then move to the next stage and build nonoperational, full-scale mockups.

Mike's dialogue with the Marines on the contract proposal was fair but far from pleasant. The Marine general's approach to negotiations was adversarial. He ripped Mike up one side and down the other for some time. Rather like taking a shower with a wire brush. The barrier to a deal was price, and the general shredded Land System's bid as exorbitant. The general was intent on taking the price down with Mike in tow. In between words such as ridiculous and excessive, Mike caught the general taking a breath at one point and decided to force a climax.

"General, I am ready to commit the company to the design and development of the armored vehicles you need at the price you stipulated, if you are ready to pledge the Corps to purchasing from Land Systems."

Since the project called for a new vehicle in a product line in which Land Systems had no experience, the general was skeptical. "You don't have the weight to obligate the company. You don't have the authority," the general deflected. But Mike could see the general was giving it consideration.

Pressing his hand, Mike joined the chase, "General, who would satisfy you that the company is committed to investing in the development of a new generation armored vehicle? Would a general manager carry enough weight?"

On getting a yes, Mike worked out the details, asking if he could use the telephone in the general's anteroom. Mike dialed up the magic man who made the multiyear deal with the Army work, general manager Bob Truxell. Mike laid it out for him. Even though the proposal was only for nonoperational, full-scale mockups, it would obligate millions of dollars. Mike admitted it was a scary proposal, since Land Systems had never produced this vehicle and was now proposing to make the next generation version more efficiently than the competitor who built it for years. Scary? Yes. But was it doable?

"I need your title. As a general manager of the firm, please tell the general that I have your full backing and power to commit Land Systems to this development proposal," Mike came to the point with Truxell. "I know it is a bit scary, and I am just as anxious, but we have an opportunity here. We don't know every contingency, and we don't know if we can produce for this price, but we have an opportunity here."

Truxell cut to the quick, "How much will we lose on this deal?"

"Trust me, Bob, you don't want to go there or it will ruin this conversation."

For 50 years, FMC or one of its subsidiaries had been producing landing craft for the Marines. During the last 18 years, it had been versions of the LVT-7. Now Land Systems was being given the chance to enter in the game on the next generation of amphibious personnel carriers. This was not an opportunity that came up often. Mike went with the tide, "You're right. I guarantee we will lose money on this development program, but it puts us in the picture for manufacturing amphibious armored assault vehicles, a new business line for the company. If successful, the arrangement would extend to residuals, follow on orders and parts, and that is what we want."

The call was picked up in the general's office, and Bob Truxell did Mike proud. He told the general that Mike's word was all he needed for this project. Land Systems would be committed. In that instant, the nub of the negotiation shifted to the general's side of the table. The general called his clerk and had the contract guys brought in. "I just negotiated this deal. Let's put it to paper." This would be one of Mike's last business development deals representing tank works.

Land Systems would acquire the business, moving from nonoperational, full-scale mockups to fabricating full-scale prototypes and more, but it would be other men to move the project to those milestones.[97] The company grapevine gossiped about Mike being in the running for general manager of the tank division, and these rumors had been flying since the fall of 1990. After nine years, Mike had become one of the elder statesmen at tank works. Several people were on the move in the organization.

THE LATEST DEVELOPMENTS in corporate succession at General Dynamics had William Anders replacing Stan Pace as chair, and James Mellor rising to president. Anders, a graduate of Annapolis and the Air Force Institute of Technology, brought an impressive resume including former Air Force officer and Apollo 8 astronaut. Mellor, a University of Michigan electrical engineer with a specialty in digital computing, brought experience from Hughes Aircraft, Litton Industries, and AM International. Both men would stamp their mark on the organization.

Nice resumes aside, Anders and Mellor were brought in as agents of change, one from the outside and the other from the ranks. General Dynamics registered an operating loss of $587 million for 1990, and the board wanted nothing less than a transformation in operations. It was none too soon, as world events would coalesce into a new order in 1991. The Gulf War ended, the Warsaw Pact dissolved, the Cold War ceased being relevant, and the Soviet Union collapsed. General Dynamics needed to match its structure to a new reality.

The rumors of Mike taking charge of tank works came to a head one day in late 1990. With the general manager at Land Systems scheduled to retire at the end of the year, Gordon and Mike were the two heirs apparent, each with his own cadre of partisan supporters. Jim Mellor called and let Mike know that he was not getting the promotion. It was not the first time Mike had a disappointment and it would not be the last, but it still stung. The general manager's position was going to Gordon England. If Mike could not have the job, he had to admit Gordon was an excellent candidate since he had done a wonderful job marshalling the new digital design concept on the M-1A2.

Jim Mellor also mentioned to Mike that he should not become too excited about being passed over. While it might be little consolation, now that Mike worked for Gordon, even Gordon wanted to make sure Mike didn't leave. Mellor stated that Gordon wanted to expand Mike's area of responsibility into managing the independent research and development of the division. This was advanced design and engineering. Mike would also be getting a raise and, more intriguing, the board had bigger things in store for Mike which they were not at liberty to discuss just as yet. So Mike stayed put. Gordon and the company stayed true to their word, and Mike's sphere of influence grew.

In February of 1991 Mike and Barb were headed to Orlando, Florida. Mike was off to the Association of the United States Army (AUSA) winter symposium. This show was a meeting of Army, Department of Defense, and industry leaders, which provided a forum for dialogue on and development of current issues impacting the Army. Government contractors, such as General Dynamics Land Systems, exhibited their wares during the symposium. Mixing work and play, Mike and Barb had allowed for a few days vacation.

They had driven down from Detroit so they would have a chance to swing by and visit family, especially his dad who was retired in Satellite Beach, east of Orlando, and a few of Barb's relatives in Clearwater, on the west side of the peninsula. Headed for the Gulf side of Florida, Mike had pulled over to a road-side telephone and placed a call to his dad. Mike's dad told him that corporate in St. Louis was trying to reach him; Arch Rambo from personnel had telephoned and asked that Mike return the call. Mike followed up with corporate, "Arch, what's up?"

"Mike, we know you're not really happy with the outcome at Land Systems," Arch started in, giving Mike a hint of the topic.

"Well I'm coping. We have a number of meetings down in here in Florida, and that's nice. So, I guess, when you consider everything, it's working out."

Niceties out of the way, Arch came to the point, "Bill Anders would like you to come up and have a conversation."

With the AUSA meeting scheduled, but no presentations from Mike on the docket and deputies available to work the exhibit, Mike tried to gather a sense of how keen everyone was for this conversation. "When might you like me to be in St. Louis?"

"It is sort of important," Arch temporized.

"Well, is it important enough for Barb and me to fly first class to St. Louis?"

"Yes, I think it is that important."

With an affirmative, Mike and Barb were back on the road. Originally headed for Clearwater, they stopped short and diverted straight to Tampa International Airport. They made St. Louis by late afternoon, and Mike was front and center with Bill Anders first thing the next morning.

Mike went into the chairman's office. Anders, the chief executive trying to restructure an entire organization, went to the heart of the matter, "I'd like you to go take over the Space Systems division of General Dynamics in San Diego."

Mike was floored. He had grown up with rockets, watching his dad manage the tracking stations lining the range south southeast out of Cape Canaveral. He had studied and taught astronautics. Jets and tanks had been fun, but now he had the chance to go back to his roots in space. "Well, you're not going out there for that," Anders punctured his bubble. "Everyone says you're one tough son of a bitch, and that's what we need out there.[98] You were destined for this, and you'll do a fine job." So his role was cast.

Fully half the company's loss of the prior year was attributed to the Space Systems division. Hemorrhage was not too strong a word. Employees at the San Diego facility would be nervous with the change. When news of the management shift hit the *St. Louis Post-Dispatch* that Tuesday, February 19, 1991, the pictures of the principals gave the impression of being cast in Hollywood roles.

Depicted were 61-year old grandfatherly Al Lovelace, a former NASA administrator, pleasantly pictured with a faint smile and on the way out, next to the 46-year old no-nonsense replacement, Mike Wynne, a tank guy with lips pursed as a preview of things to come. While both individuals were really being reassigned, Mike was positioned to come in and save the day, to be a hero. He promptly witnessed the rocket from the first missile launch under his purview tumble into the ocean. With this introduction to Space Systems, it was going to be a unique journey.

CHAPTER THIRTEEN

Rockets and Russians

MIKE WYNNE'S BUSINESS SKILLS had matured through his early years in the corporate world. As he stepped up to the Space Systems position, he would need them. His profession had now advanced to the point where it was more than just managing projects and presentations. He was going from being a manager to becoming a leader. Hiring and firing, vision, and accountability rose to the fore. But Mike was ambitious, driven, and capable, similar to his father. Neither had left their career to chance.

The missile business to which Mike returned in 1991 had progressed since his father's tenure at Patrick Air Force Base back in 1958. Missiles dated back even farther than that. At the conclusion of World War II, missile development in the United States began in earnest, exploiting German missile expertise. Missiles and the U.S. Air Force had been inextricably entwined since the beginning, envisioned as a nuclear weapon delivery system.

THE SOVIET UNION became the second nuclear power when it exploded its first fission weapon in August 1949, four years to the month after Hiroshima and Nagasaki. Thirty-eight months later the United States upped the ante by detonating the world's first thermonuclear device on Enewetak Atoll in the Marshall Islands. In November 1955 the Soviet Union once more matched America when it set off a nuclear fusion device. With this pattern of one-upmanship, the United States soon fixed on the concept of nuclear deterrence, which became the centerpiece of the Air Force mission: sword and shield, offense and defense, retaliation and deterrence.

The Air Force carried out its mission by having men and material ready to respond to a nuclear threat on minutes notice. This became the primary function of the Strategic Air Command (SAC), which arranged for a nuclear response to be deliverable through either bomber aircraft or strategic missiles. These were the early ICBMs. The addition of missiles to the Air Force inventory was an evolutionary change.

Air Force General Bernard A. Schriever advanced missiles along the learning curve into ballistic weapons. The early ICBMs were structured to be weapon systems, along the lines of the German V-2 rockets. Since both the United States and the Soviet Union were developing missiles, it became a race of some consequence. The military believed no defense against an ICBM existed, other than the retaliatory counterpunch of another ICBM. Thus developed nuclear proliferation.

Spurred by the need for nuclear deterrence, the Air Force pursued four missile systems in the 1950s. The Atlas program led the way, with Convair awarded the assembly contract. An Atlas missile had the range to reach the Soviet Union. Atlas spawned the shorter-range Thor missile program of Douglas Aircraft. The intermediate-range Thor could reach the Soviet Union from England and other NATO pact countries. But when it came to intercontinental reach, the Air Force wanted to spread its bets around.

An alternative and backup to the Atlas program came in the form of the Titan, a Glenn Martin Company project. The Titan was the first multistage rocket effort by the U.S. Air Force with the scale to reach the Soviet Union from the United States. Lastly, Boeing Airplane entered into the mix with the lead on the Minuteman program, the Air Force's first solid-fuel rocket with intercontinental range. Neither the Atlas nor the Titan were quick-launch systems and thus of dubious menace in deterring nuclear threats. The Minuteman was a solid-fuel missile and could be launched at the turn of a key. The Soviet launch of Sputnik in 1957 did nothing to cool the pace of exertion.

The spectacular news of the Soviet Union launching Sputnik and beating the United States into space was but one indication of how far behind the United States was in capability. The Soviet nuclear threat with its accompanying missile buildup forced the U.S. government to give the Air Force the resources to compete. Looked at in a larger context, Sputnik did more than generate the space race. It spurred progress in the United States Air Force.

Development of the Atlas missile family dated back to the mid 1940s, when research projects for more sophisticated versions of the German V-2 type missile were funded by the Army Air Forces. These futuristic projects were soon the target of budget cuts. Undeterred and quite possibly sensing the future, a few contractors such as Convair continued exploration of these long-range missiles using unexpended funding.[99] In 1951 Convair was rewarded for its patience and persistence with a feasibility contract for a missile with a range of 6,000 miles. Officially Project MX-1593, it was with just a smidge of pilot hubris that the Air Force tagged it the XB-65. XB cast the 90-foot long projectile as an experimental bomber, albeit one without a pilot. While budget concerns and Korea would slow the process, the Atlas program continued.

With operational missiles on the horizon, the Air Force began structuring warhead delivery systems to partner with the long-range bombers as a means of nuclear deterrence. SAC activated its first missile wing in 1958. More than 100 Atlas missiles would be produced before deactivation in 1965. Nuclear deterrence would be taken over by the Titan and Minutemen arsenal. Each had its advantages. The Titan could carry a larger payload, and the Minuteman could be launched in seconds, rather than minutes.

The glory days of the Atlas had come and gone, at least as a weapons system. Still, the missile had its two sides of the coin. As a liquid-fueled rocket, it took too long to ready for launch, but as a light-weight rocket, it provided near single-stage to orbit performance. As time passed, the use for the powerful Atlas rocket system broadened from nuclear warheads to satellite platforms and finally to launch vehicles for astronauts and space missions.

As the technology of a complex Air Force expanded, so also did the process that evolved into a systems approach. Rather than simply ordering a number of aircraft from a single manufacturer, the process became one of bringing together engineering and parts and components and scientific direction from a variety of organizations into an assembly point that often involved yet other parties. In each case, primary and secondary suppliers were lined up to lower the overall project risk should a manufacturer or contractor fail in its responsibility. As systems grew even more complex, international sourcing became part of the equation. It was not unusual for a more than a dozen prime contractors and scores of subcontractors to be involved in programs. In the end, the Air Force development of the Atlas missile program was but a short hop from the beginnings of the aerospace industry.

❦

MIKE WYNNE'S RETURN TO ROCKETS in 1991 was a homecoming to the United States' first ballistic missile weapon system, the Atlas rocket of his father's day. General Dynamics had acquired Convair in the 1950s and had continued development of the Atlas system during the next 35 years.[100] When Mike came back, the venerable system still retained its one and a half stage, booster-sustainer propulsion system. The current generation was called the Atlas-Centaur series, as it was topped with a Centaur rocket. A number of distinct models would be advanced.

What changed the rocket world was NASA getting out of the commercial launch business in 1987, in response to the space shuttle *Challenger* disaster of January 1986. Comparable to aircraft development, private business took over the task. Government would help with funding, but much of the future development and manufacturing would be shouldered by industry rather than the military. While the military and the government continued to control the launch sites, rockets were now a business, with the Air Force and NASA as customers. The launch systems themselves were operated by major aerospace corporations, such as General Dynamics, Martin Marietta, and McDonnell Douglas.

In this new for-profit marketplace, competition quickly broke out for the available business. Foreign competition would be the stiffest because of foreign government price supports. The French consortium Arianespace was founded in 1980 as the first commercial launch provider. Arianespace utilized the Ariane family of rockets, a product of the joint efforts of the European Space Agency.[101] The company's first successful commercial launch was in 1983 and took place at its space center in French Guiana. In America, it was competition among the General Dynamics Atlas system, the Martin Marietta Titan system, and the McDonnell Douglas Delta family of rockets. The Delta system was a multistage rocket that utilized the Thor intermediate-range missile as its first stage.

With NASA dropping out of the commercial launch business in the mid-1980s, General Dynamics had changed its leadership at Space Systems in San Diego. They had hired a former Air Force officer and NASA administrator, Alan Lovelace, to run operations in the brave new world. After five years, the General Dynamics Board decided to change management at Space Systems once again. Lovelace, who had been steeped in NASA, launch vehicles, and satellites, was the antithesis of Mike Wynne, who still called them rockets. Archaic? The people at San Diego were thrilled, as they felt they had someone who spoke their language.

Arriving in San Diego during March 1991, Mike started out his term as general manager by sending a two-page letter to the employees, welcoming them to the new Space Systems division. He outlined goals and objectives and process, easily summarized as being the best in space. Six weeks into his new position, on April 19 Space Systems had a scheduled launch at Cape Canaveral of an Atlas-Centaur I topped with a Japan Broadcasting Corporation satellite. The upper stage failed after liftoff.[102] Beautiful launch but the satellite was not delivered into orbit. The rocket was destroyed by range safety and plunked into the water.

Mike immediately began talks with the Japanese representatives, reviewing the company's quality program, in as much detail as he had a handle on that early in the game. Dick Adams, of Fort Worth fame from Mike's past, ran the failure board to organize the review of the missile malfunction. Although the failure board worked for months to determine the cause of the disappointment, in the end, its members had to admit they had absolutely no idea why that rocket ended up all wet. The only inkling they could find was a bit of foreign debris being picked up in a pump. Operations had to continue.

After the failure board completed its work, Space Systems launched five more rockets from Cape Canaveral launch complex 36 with success, before another Atlas-Centaur I plummeted from the heavens. On August 22, 1992 range safety was forced to destroy the rocket. This time the cargo was a cable television relay station. The rocket launch flopped after one of the second-stage engines failed to fire.[103] Now it was getting serious. Two break downs in seven flights would not cut it. This was not the way to turnaround a division. Chairman Bill Anders put himself in the middle of the conversation and wryly mentioned, "General Dynamics made practically every weapon system known to man except torpedoes. Please don't tell me our rockets are now torpedoes."

Former Air Force Lieutenant General Forrest McCartney, recently retired as the head of the Kennedy Space Center, ran the second failure board of Mike's tenure. This board achieved success, figuring out the problem that turned out to be the root cause downing both rockets. The problem was traced back to a NASA engineering change proposal issued in 1967, which set the stage for this possible catastrophic breakdown.

The particular combination of physics was a gas transforming into a solid without passing through the liquid stage, a phenomenon called deposition or desublimation. In thermodynamics it is called a triple point where, at a certain temperature and pressure, all three phases of a substance can coexist. In the two missile failures, this event occurred as material flashed through a valve, causing a disruption. This perfect storm of physics had not caused a problem until these two launches.

Immediately after the second failure, it was time for damage control with the employees. Mike spent a period visiting the workers to ensure they knew the two mishaps were not their fault. Mike was the company's cheerleader, and he knew the importance of company morale. He told them they could take a day to feel gloomy and miserable, but then everyone had to jump back to the job at hand to become the best in space. "Let's control what we can control."

Confirming the notion that things run in threes, on March 25, 1993, an Atlas-Centaur I rocket lost power 24 seconds into launch. The result was that a United States military communications satellite was placed in a useless orbit.[104] Two good outcomes resulted from this letdown. First, the team immediately knew what went wrong since it was a malfunction in the first stage. The failure board for this flop took only weeks to confirm the cause: a tiny screw loosening on the propellant tank. The other good turn of events was that Mike's team did not suffer another failure in dozens of launches.[105]

BESIDES HITS AND MISSES during his first three years with missiles, Mike began digging the footing for a joint effort that would progress slowly but prove to be inspired. Early in his first year at Space Systems, he instituted production efficiencies to cut costs at the fabrication facilities. The fact of the matter was that the Atlas delivery system was expensive, and to stay competitive the company had to trim expenses. Mike instituted a number of productivity improvements, similar to just-in-time manufacturing and the kanban system brought to the United States by Toyota. The efficiencies paid benefits, and Space Systems was the beneficiary of positive press.

In mid 1991, while Mike was working to drive down costs, a State Department tour came through Space Systems that included scientists from the Russian space industry. Since Mike had spent some time with Russian engineers while at tank works in Michigan, it was an easy transition to join in discussions with those from the missile business. One of the Russian scientists was Boris Katorgin, the 57-year-old deputy chief designer of NPO Energomash, a Russian manufacturer of rocket engines. Mike Wynne and Boris Katorgin would begin their own variety of détente.

At the end of World War II, a rush had occurred to acquire German rocket expertise, engineers, and scientists centered around

Peenemünde, Germany. The United States was able to secure many of the leading scientists such as Wernher von Braun and his team, and the Soviet Union sheltered most of the others. Several of the scientists gained by the United States happened to be involved with the guidance side of rocketry, while a number that the Soviets procured were involved with the propulsion side. This is part of the reason why the United States was able to control its space flights with relative accuracy, while the Soviets could carry larger payloads earlier than anyone else. Viewed simplistically, not much had changed in the intervening 40 years. Only the Americans could land on a dime 200,000 miles from Earth, and the Russians still had the heavy-lift capability.

Wynne and Katorgin broached an interesting possibility. Katorgin's company produced the rockets that facilitated heavy-lift capability. The two men tossed around the idea of taking an Atlas missile and retrofitting the first stage with a geared-down version of the NPO Energomash RD-170 four-motor rocket engine. The RD-170 put out almost 1.8 million pounds of thrust and it was assumed a two-motor version would generate roughly 900,000 pounds of thrust. This hypothetical output stood out against Space System's Atlas-Centaur IIs, which produced thrust usually amounting to less than 500,000 pounds.

While this was just the start of a project that would take years, nine years in fact, Mike and Boris laid much of the conceptual groundwork. In their rough-and-dirty analysis, a two-bell version of the RD-170 appeared to be of a size that could be accommodated by the Atlas-Centaur II. This would result in a two-across rocket engine to replace the current three-across engine. Mike and Boris would continue the conversation on and off during the next year and a half into 1993. Politics, of course, would have to be dealt with on both sides, but that was left to other men for other times.[106] Mike continued exploring the art of the possible, as Otto von Bismarck would say, quietly funding the project out of petty cash.

As a quid pro quo offered to show good faith during this period, Mike was able to arrange for the Russian scientists to view a Titan and an Atlas launch at Cape Canaveral. As both the Americans and

Russians knew, each country had a very different process. With full knowledge that neither would change the culture and process of the other, they agreed to proffer suggestions that might engender incremental improvements in either process. Toward that end, the Russians later presented Mike with a report that resembled a management consultant study. Their survey suggested process improvements and in the end Mike was able to use several of the ideas. For the time being, the American and Russian organizations agreed to look a little deeper into the possibility of a new engine.

WITH TIME THE ATLAS-CENTAUR I problems were settled, and a period of successful launches with the Atlas-Centaur II took center stage. The Space Systems division settled into a successful streak and in the parlance of Wall Street appeared to be turned around. In spite of this, the General Dynamics board decided it had had enough of the space business, believing the line monopolized too many corporate resources to be continued.

The missile fizzles, the financial losses incurred before Mike arrived, and the withering competition for each commercial launch encouraged corporate to exit the market sector. In 1993, after the third rocket failure, Mike told Bill Anders that the company had put that in the rearview mirror. Even though General Dynamics had invested the seed money to perfect the system and appeared on the brink of success, Anders was directed to sell. A new fervor in Washington storming through the defense budget settled the issue.[107]

With the dismantling of the Berlin Wall in 1989 and the dismembering of the Soviet Union in 1991, defense concerns had changed and the defense industry followed suit. In 1993 Deputy Secretary of Defense William Perry hosted a Pentagon dinner for a number of industry leaders, a meeting which would earn the sobriquet "The Last Supper." With defense budgets in freefall and overcapacity weighing heavily on the industrial base, consolidation and restructuring were encouraged by the Defense Department. Thus warned, it became open season for mergers and acquisitions. It was the de facto deregulation of the defense industry.

Deregulation promised a new paradigm. For decades, the industrial base had been safeguarded by the allocation of government expenditures among a large number of defense contractors. With deregulation, government spending would be concentrated in fewer companies, resulting in less competition. In fact, the possibility of sole source contracts rose, where only one defense contractor might bid on and produce select items. But the defense industry was just the latest in a series of business sectors going through deregulation.

The transportation industry had gone through the process earlier, and the financial trade was in the throes of being deregulated piece by piece. The move toward liberalizing the economics of certain businesses was couched in the free market theories of Milton Friedman and Alfred Kahn. While the earlier moves were aimed at lowering the barriers to entry and promoting competition, what was being proposed for the defense industry was the invitation to create oligopolies. While the consolidation of power in few defense corporations would be a challenge for transparency, General Dynamics was intent on being part of the handful of contractors that would result and began its own transformation.

Bill Anders had been brought in to turn around General Dynamics fortunes, and he was going at it with abandon. Prior management had run a little too fast and loose for the board's comfort, and Anders was in the process of redressing those oversights in addition to sizing the company to address the new model. He sold Cessna Aircraft back to Textron for $600 million in cash, tactical and cruise missile production to Hughes Aircraft for $450 million in stock, and the Fort Worth aircraft operation to Lockheed for $1.525 billion in cash. The company had reduced its employees from 80,600 at the end of 1991 to 30,500 by the end of 1993.[108] The company intended to focus on nuclear submarines and armored vehicles, which meant it now was Space Launch Systems' turn to be part of the solution. They chose Mike to retail the rocket company.

On the premise that consolidation was the future, Mike approached the other two major players, Martin Marietta and

McDonnell Douglas. He believed that the culture at Space Systems was more akin to that of McDonnell Douglas and promoted that fact. The culture at Martin Marietta was not quite as good a fit in his estimation, but then Mike didn't close on these prospects. He pitched the deal, and corporate closed. The ever-consolidating aerospace industry was flush with takeovers and acquisitions.

MARTIN MARIETTA WAS A BUSINESS formed in the early 1960s out of the merger of the Glenn L. Martin Company and American-Marietta. During the 1980s, Martin Marietta had successfully transitioned its Titan ICBMs from weapons systems to launch vehicles. When General Electric was peddling its aerospace division in the 1990s, Martin Marietta was just the company to pony up $3 billion for it. The acquisition formally joined Martin Marietta's Titan launch rockets with GE Aerospace's satellites, effectively doubling the size of Martin Marietta. The companies had become close associates in 1992 when a Martin Marietta Titan III rocket topped by the GE Aerospace satellite Mars Observer was launched on a voyage to the red planet.

McDonnell Douglas was also a business formed in the 1960s through a merger, this one involving McDonnell Aircraft and Douglas Aircraft. Preferring to grow internally, McDonnell Douglas' only large acquisition in the 1980s was that of Hughes Helicopter for $500 million. While rockets seemed destined for destruction in 1981 with the arrival of the space shuttle program, President Reagan's 1986 announcement that the shuttle would not carry commercial payloads changed the rules for everyone. The McDonnell Douglas Delta rocket system was able to make the same leap from ballistic missile to launch vehicle.

BY THE END OF 1993, General Dynamics had signed a tentative deal with Martin Marietta for the transfer of the Space Launch Systems division. In an agreement valued at $209 million in cash, the transaction closed a few months later on May 1, 1994.[109] To help navigate any government concerns, Martin Marietta had agreed to split savings generated by its takeover of the Atlas program with

Major players in the rocket business during the early 1990s include (left to right)
Jim Mellor and Bill Anders from General Dynamics, Norm Augustine from
Martin Marietta, and Mike Wynne who would over time work for each of them.
Source: Wynne Family.

the government. In return, the government provided $50 million in
funding. Now to make the acquisition work for all vested interests,
Martin Marietta had to consolidate facilities.

Not counting launch services, the old Space Systems of General
Dynamics was spread over three locations and 2 million square
feet. The main stage of the Atlas missile was assembled near the
San Diego airport in the original Air Force Plant 19 complex, where
Convair used to manufacture four-engine B-24 Liberators during
World War II. The Atlas-Centaur upper stage came together in
a clean room final assembly area at the company's Kearny Mesa
operation north of San Diego, where engineering services was
located along with the division headquarters. The third operation

was at Harlingen, Texas, where payload fairings and adapters, thrust structures, nosecones, and other items for the Atlas-Centaur system were fashioned.

In consolidating after the Martin Marietta takeover, the Kearny Mesa operation moved to Denver, beginning with administrative and engineering forces. Rocket assembly was soon combined at its Waterton Canyon facility southwest of Denver. Martin Marietta's chief executive officer Norm Augustine, along with acquiring the space launch systems, took on Mike Wynne with the deal. Mike went from vice president of General Dynamics and president of the Space Systems Division to vice president and general manager for launch vehicles at the Martin Marietta Astronautics Division.

So Barb and Mike now with four girls in the family were on the move once again, but this time it was back to familiar territory. Mike would be launching Titan and Atlas systems, and it was up to him to make the cost savings estimates of the combination a reality for Augustine. Then Mike's plans were interrupted for a message from his Maker.

HEART PROBLEMS HAD STARTED in San Diego, but there were only hints at the concealed commotion. Mike Wynne led a full and busy life. While still in California, every once in awhile he would spike a low grade fever at night, but Mike and Barb did not think it was a symptom of any underlying problem. It was more akin to being under the weather or maybe coming down with something. The problem always seemed to resolve itself pretty quickly, and he would feel better in the morning. Feeling "one off" would go away for a week or two, and then return. They chalked it up to stress.

These short sessions of feeling under par occurred right about the time Mike was traveling back and forth to Russia on Space Systems business, long arduous flights of more than 6,000 miles in length. Pile on the responsibility for marketing the company, followed soon thereafter with moving the business and family to Denver, and Mike was crossing an unseen line in the sand. Right about the time the Wynne family's boxes arrived in Denver, delivered but not so much unpacked, Mike would become sick for real.

Within a week or two of the boxes being piled in the garage and in rooms throughout the house, Mike had to travel to a quarterly review session, this particular one held in Naples, Florida. The review was timed to coincide with a Space Systems rocket launch at Cape Canaveral space launch complex 36. Even though Mike had a company plane available, he still racked up the hours as he tried to participate in the quarterly review and oversee the launch, which was scheduled to blast off shortly after midnight. Twenty-four hour days soon were not enough.

In Naples Mike attended the first day of meetings, grabbed a bit of shut eye and then drove to the airport for a quick flight to the Cape. He was present and accounted for at the launch, but it was scrubbed. For Mike, it was grab a couple more hours sleep, back to Naples, more meetings, a bit more sleep, another jaunt to the Cape, finally a successful launch, and then back to Naples. After a nap it was more meetings.

At the dinner that evening one of the company's plant managers Dain Hancock, a friend of Mike's from his Fort Worth days where they had both started as rookies, saw him and immediately remarked, "You look like hell. You have to go home."

Mike was quick with the "I need to stay," but his pallor screamed otherwise.

"No, you don't. You need to go home," insisted his friend. And that is what he did.

He arrived in Denver determined to see a doctor. Trouble was, being in Denver but a week meant the family was not on any medical group's radar. No relationships had been established. Mike and Barb tracked down the medical practice most company employees used and tried to schedule an appointment. Mike had never been to this practice, so as a new patient he could not maneuver his way around the physician's assistant (PA) who wanted him to have a complete physical first. Mike agreed, "Fair enough, let's schedule it."

When the PA said, "We can't get you in for six weeks," Mike was about to become a statistic of the system. Believing he could be dead in six weeks, he made the next stop the emergency room where he could be looked at in real time. Welcome to the hospital zone.

The young emergency room intern listened to Mike's heart and said it sounded similar to mooing. In professional parlance, a weak valve produced substantial mitral regurgitation that made a noise resembling cows mooing. After blood tests and cultures, the staff decided he did not need to be admitted. The intern helped set up an appointment with Mike's practice doctor for the next day.

Tomorrow could not come fast enough and by the time Mike arrived for his appointment, he was doubled over in the waiting room. Seeing that Mike was ready to pass out, the receptionist took matters in hand and positioned him in a room, lying down. The doctor examined Mike and immediately concurred with the intern, "Yep, you have a problem. You need to go home, pack a bag, and I'll meet you at the hospital." Mike was admitted and started on a course of antibiotics. He soon met the cardiologist and the infectious disease specialist. An echocardiogram confirmed the mitral regurgitation, while blood tests confirmed an infection. Mike had a raging case of endocarditis.

Late that night, once Mike was stabilized, Barb went back to her empty house filled with boxes and cried until the sun rose. She was alone. The girls were away with their own lives. Mike and Barb didn't even know their neighbors.

The next morning the two specialists returned with stern faces and severe frowns, listening to Mike's heart again and again. The doctors looked back and forth, at each other and Mike's chart. They noticed his address, "Oh, you live in Glenmoor. So do we, except not on the course." Mike and Barb, who had purchased a home in Cherry Hills Village on the 17th green of Glenmoor Country Club outside Denver, had just made the acquaintance of a pair of their neighbors. Doctors first and golfers a close second. They were also interested in looking at the Wynne's house, if they ever decided to sell.

The doctor-duo pronounced the ageless "good news, bad news." The bad news was that left untreated his condition was 100 percent fatal. The good news was that his condition was treatable. "We think in the long run he'll be fine." Nuclear X-rays revealed he had been lucky. The infection was confined to the heart and had not spread and it was related to strep microorganisms rather than staph bacteria.

So began a month for Mike in cardiac intensive care with a shunt up his arm opening a pathway to the heart. The cocktail of antibiotics he received every four hours wreaked havoc with his blood vessels but began to take hold. After four weeks, he graduated to a rehabilitation floor. Six weeks into the adventure, he went home and recuperated for an additional week, even helping unpack a few of the boxes that remained.

Mike's doctors left him with the prognosis that nine out of ten times the condition would return, and the patient eventually would have the valve replaced. While the doctors recommended replacing it right away, Mike chose to delay as long as possible. With a bit of luck, he hoped to manage the heart condition similar to his dad who had mitral valve prolapse yet was able to avoid surgery. Mike also knew waiting brought the possibility of advances in medicine. Since Mike passed his stress test, albeit with a D-minus, he had a certain foundation for delaying valve replacement. "Not until I fail a stress test. I'll be back in six months for another test." Then it was back to the rocket business. Mike still had to make the recent combination of rocket systems work for his new boss, Norm Augustine.

AUGUSTINE WAS A PHI BETA KAPPA aeronautical engineer from Princeton University. With experience at Douglas Aircraft and LTV missiles, he served in the Department of the Army in a number of roles including assistant, under, and acting secretary of the Army. He joined Martin Marietta in 1977 and 10 years later having directed the company into a strong market position, was the chief executive. He engineered the acquisitions of GE Aerospace and Space Launch Systems. Not the shy and retiring type and having invested hundreds of millions of dollars in the business, Augustine lobbied long and hard for a leveling of the launching field in commercial rockets.

In January 1994, just before closing the Space Launch Systems deal, Augustine was quoted in the *Washington Post* stating that the foreign-subsidized competition provided by the Russian, European, and Chinese rocket programs would destroy the American effort.[110] Mike had come to a similar conclusion, testifying six months earlier in May 1993 on the competitive conundrum before the House Subcommittee on Space.[111] The sum and substance of their argument was an appeal for all American payloads to be launched on all-American rockets, even though that would cost more.

The satellite makers were against this appeal because they wanted the option of choosing the lowest-cost launch alternative, but the rocket makers had to have "Buy-American" if they were to survive.[112] Such was the competitive climate in which Mike busied himself during the remaining months of 1994. But changes were in the offing. Martin Marietta including its launch systems was not long for the independent business world.

It is unknown how much the seemingly unfair competitive environment or the leverage taken on in the acquisition of GE Aerospace influenced Martin Marietta, but the company remained active in the consolidation game. The stock market had given Martin Marietta a stock price boost for its acquisition of GE Aerospace, and it had achieved a portion of the expected savings through the layoff of thousands of employees. Martin Marietta had even gone after Grumman, although it lost in a bidding war with Northrop. Then right in the middle of a market period intent on business restructuring, where big fish seemed to have an insatiable desire for smaller fish, Martin Marietta entered discussions with someone its own size—Lockheed Corporation.

Martin Marietta and Lockheed began discussions, initiated by Lockheed's Daniel Tellep, in March 1994, even before the close of the Space Launch Systems deal. The two companies announced their merger intentions in August 1994.[113] After a series of negotiations and government reviews, Lockheed Corporation completed the merger with Martin Marietta in March 1995, in a transaction valued at $10 billion. The merged company soon changed its name to Lockheed Martin.

Mike Wynne had gone from "Tinkers to Evers to Chance," from General Dynamics to Martin Marietta to Lockheed, in the space of less than 11 months. He kept the same function. Only his letterhead changed. Thus, in an encircling maneuver, Lockheed had taken over General Dynamics F-16 production and space launch systems. Mike remained in rockets but his geography had changed. He had stayed with missiles, but those missiles now tracked back to the mountains around Waterton Canyon.

The Waterton Canyon facility of the Titan missile operation was a fortress on the Front Range of the Colorado Rockies, situated at that location long ago as a concession to the federal government. In the early days of ballistic missiles, with two of the nation's primary rocket operations located in California, the government wanted a facility sited in the interior, as an added measure of safety and security. The Titan missile operation dated back to 1956 when the Glenn Martin Company built a rocket factory in the Denver area. In spite of the many corporate changes, operations remained. With his move, Mike made sure that important alliances were advanced.

Mike kept pushing ahead on the joint effort with the Russian engine builder, NPO Energomash. If it appeared a bit incongruous for Mike to lobby for all-American in one breath while working to develop a Russian rocket engine option for the Atlas in the next, it was. One had to keep all doors open. As Mike once framed it, "Remember what parade you're in, and bring the right signs."

EARLY IN THE TAKEOVERS involving Space Systems, Mike had wangled the authority to spend up to $1 million on feasibility and development of the proposed two-bell Russian rocket engine. This first tranche of money was part of a one-five-ten arrangement, where only the $1 million was committed. The $5 million was an option for further development work, and the $10 million option would result in an actual test engine. The gist was Mike had something in hand to market.

Once the general feasibility of a Russian-powered Atlas was ascertained, Mike had to line up an American sponsor and an American rocket engine manufacturer as customer and coproducer. Mike started his effort with Lieutenant General Thomas S. Moorman Jr., who had been instrumental in establishing the Air Force Space Command. Working on a parallel course, Mike had three rocket engine manufacturers compete for the engine coproduction partnership.

The Air Force eventually stood in as a sponsor, and after a spirited competition, Pratt & Whitney carried the day as the American coproduction partner on the Russian engine. Another stepping stone was set in mortar when NASA in Huntsville, Alabama, was selected as the certification lab for the Russian engine. NASA would fire a number of engines en route to determining they would not blow up on the launch pad. In due course, the foundation Mike Wynne and Boris Katorgin laid resulted in the RD-180, a two-motor version of the Russian RD-170.[114]

The RD-180 engine being tested at the Marshall Space Flight Center on November 4, 1998. Powered by kerosene and liquid oxygen, the RD-180 produced 860,000 pounds of thrust. *Source:* NASA Marshall Space Flight Center (reference MSFC-75-SA-4105-2C, negative 9808476).

Maybe it was not so incongruous in the end—the drive to save money with competitive delivery options while preserving the American launch system. Costs were saved with thousands of fewer parts in an RD-180–powered Atlas, and this was linked to a much shortened development schedule. And what about the health of the American launch business?

IN THE ROCKET BUSINESS, industry consolidation was in lock-step with the advance of technology. U.S. launch capability had developed a split personality, the reusable space shuttle and the expendable launch vehicle (ELV), such as the Delta, Titan, and Atlas systems. The need for both launch options was driven home by the *Challenger* disaster, which effectively had shut down shuttle operations for almost three years. To keep pace in this bifurcated business, the commercial space launch companies had to evolve and the product had to be less expensive and more reliable. Mike could see the wave coming when in May 1994, the Department of Defense released its Space Launch Modernization Plan, a study that had been chaired by General Moorman. The Air Force would soon follow with the announcement of a competition for an advanced launch vehicle.

Mike's approach with his people in Denver was the same as always, to bring them into the conversation early and completely. He called a meeting of the merged ranks, both from the Titan rocket side and from the Atlas rocket side. Even the government inspectors and monitors on the property showed up. The meeting was held outdoors, between two of the larger buildings on the property. Mike had made provision for audio equipment lining both sides of the area, and he did not play down the situation.

"Such is the life of a government contractor," Mike began. "I wanted you to hear it first and hear it from me that the government just announced a competition for the future rocket. The reason I want you to hear it now is because the competition means all of us have basically been fired. While it may not be phrased in those terms, that's what's happening."

As Mike immediately knew when he heard of the competition, what the company manufactured in Waterton Canyon now was the old rockets. They were producing the rockets of the past and might not be a part of the rockets of the future. While the change would not happen overnight and, in fact, would take years, it was a transformation that was going to affect everyone. The good news was that the company had an extraordinary team working to procure the contract on the next-generation rocket.

Mike drove the company to manufacture rockets for the existing program with optimum quality. He wanted the customer to admit when the program ended that it had been a great program. The company goal was to provide a reliable ride, on time and on target. Mike felt that with these objectives, the company might even receive extensions on the existing program to keep the lines going longer. To jump-start the quality program, he resolved the classic difference between manufacturing and operations. He had manufacturing personnel deliver and assist in the setup of each rocket at the launch facility, and he had launch employees work side-by-side with manufacturing in assembling the vehicles before delivery. Each learned the other's concerns.

It would take years for the results of the competition to come in. The contest was consequential, enough so that a bit of deceit and cheating took place as one of the competitors, Boeing, was charged with stealing trade secrets from Lockheed Martin.[115] In time, the Lockheed Martin Astronautics operation won a major part of the advanced launch vehicle contract. What began as a winner-take-all competition ended up a split award, with roughly 60 percent granted to Astronautics. It was dubbed the EELV—the evolved expendable launch vehicle. American-built launch systems coalesced into two options: the Delta IV and the Atlas V, the Atlas V powered by the RD-180 engine.

AS GENERAL MANAGER for Martin Marietta Astronautics and then Lockheed Martin, Mike still assembled rockets for space and found ways to connect back to his Air Force. He and an old teaching associate from his academy days, Chuck Fosha, came up with an approach to advance the education of Air Force Academy students, to show them Air Force didn't mean just pilots, it also meant space.

Mike was able to sponsor the students in the Centaur program, his version of Frank Sinatra's "Come Fly With Me." The plan was to provide space in the Centaur vehicle for an academy module to accompany a satellite launch.

Mike's engineers designed a special compartment that allowed just enough room for a small module of instruments. The engineers did the weight balance calculations, and when Astronautics had a rocket launch that came in under the performance allowance, Mike was able to add on the academy module and let them fly along virtually free. The Air Force Academy module did not separate from the Centaur stage of the missile as did the satellite, but since the vehicle stayed in orbit for roughly 90 days after launch, it provided students with the ability to accompany these rockets and conduct experiments in space. Mike gave the academy students ride after ride in this fashion and showed that, even when he wasn't in the Air Force, he still was with the Air Force.

MIKE HAD MOVED TO DENVER and worked hard for three years to effect the consolidation savings. Martin Marietta and Lockheed had done their deals, and Mike had played his part to make them work. He had been successful, but now it was just a job. It was now a maintenance position, and his wanderlust returned. It just was not fun anymore. Lockheed Martin did not seem to be mounting a charge to make Mike the president at Aeronautics but seemed to be using him to train future division presidents, so he started looking at his options. While not the president's position, the company did offer an alternative.

Lockheed Martin people asked if Mike would consider going down and taking charge of the tactical missile operation in Dallas, Texas. This was one part of the old Vought Aviation division of LTV, which had been one of the early players in conglomerates.[116] This division now produced the Theater High-Altitude Area Defense system (THAAD). Mike went and interviewed with Tom Corcoran, who had come up through the GE Aerospace side of the business. At the time Mike interviewed, Corcoran was president of Lockheed Martin's electronics sector.

Corcoran quickly figured out Mike was a General Dynamics guy and not a Martin Marietta guy. As interest rose, the Dallas personnel people called around for references on Mike. One person they called was Jim Mellor at General Dynamics. Mellor had risen to chief executive and chairman of the company. His response was interesting and all it took to engender a new adventure.

"I am pleased to hear you're considering Mike Wynne for other positions. Does this mean you won't be using him in space and rockets anymore?"

"It doesn't appear so," was the personnel department response. "The Dallas position is more involved in tactical Army missiles."

Mellor finished the conversation with "Thank you very much." He hung up and immediately called Mike in Denver. "You are not taking that job in Dallas."

"I'm not?"

"No. You and Barb are coming with me to on a trip to the Middle East in two weeks. And you're coming back to General Dynamics to work for me."

CHAPTER FOURTEEN

Big Business, Small Business

JIM MELLOR WAS CHAIRMAN AND CHIEF EXECUTIVE OFFICER of
General Dynamics from May 1994 to May 1997. He then stepped
up to the board of directors. Getting Mike back in February 1997
was one of Mellor's last official duties. The Wynnes would move
to Washington with the work. While Mike had been occupied
with rockets in San Diego and Denver, General Dynamics had
moved its corporate headquarters from St. Louis to Falls Church,
Virginia, outside Washington. One other thing was in a state of
flux, leadership. A few months after Mike returned, Mellor stepped
up at General Dynamics and the company turned to a new chief
executive officer, Nicholas Chabraja.

Chabraja didn't fit the pattern when he rose to CEO of General
Dynamics in 1997. He followed a series of engineers and military
academy graduates into the chief executives office. A graduate of
Northwestern University School of Law, Chabraja did not work his
way up through the ranks at General Dynamics. Rather, he was
a partner with the Jenner & Block law firm in Chicago where he
worked for years on Crown family and General Dynamics business.
At the time Chabraja was elected chief executive officer, General
Dynamics had just completed its business contraction under the
Anders and Mellor administrations. Mellor's hiring back of Mike
Wynne would prove to be more of a homecoming than anyone
could have predicted.

THE WYNNES HAD GONE on that trip with Jim and Suzanne Mellor. In the end, Mike came back to General Dynamics as the corporate senior vice president international, planning and development. This relatively nebulous title included strategic planning. In essence, Mike was brought back because Mellor thought he was a key player who could help the company with growth and strategic plans. Mellor could not touch Mike while he worked in rockets, undoubtedly part of the employment restrictions of the original transaction. But with Lockheed Martin's taking Mike out of rockets, possibilities had opened up. Mike was not the only one. Lockheed Martin was apparently putting its own people in the top jobs at the businesses it had acquired during the buying splurge of the early 1990s.

Literally the day Mike walked back into General Dynamics corporate in Falls Church, Gordon England passed through the same revolving doors. Mike returned as a new senior vice president and Gordon reprised his role as a new executive vice president. Mellor essentially reunited the team that had such success at tank works a decade earlier. England came back just a step ahead of Mike, once more.

England was seven years older, to the month, than Mike Wynne. Their relationship dated back more than 20 years. Due to his seven-year head start in the business world, Gordon always remained one step ahead of Mike on the promotion schedule. They had both been in the running for the same jobs a number of times. This was repeated at tank works and once again in returning to corporate. But they remained friendly competitors on the field and friendly contacts off the field. They had been to each other's children's weddings and would be at more family events.

While Mike had departed General Dynamics with the sale of the rocket business, Gordon had made the switch even earlier when General Dynamics sold off the F-16 operation. Mike transitioned to Martin Marietta and Gordon ended up at Lockheed. When Martin Marietta and Lockheed merged, the two were reunited under the Lockheed Martin umbrella. Both soon departed Lockheed Martin in the management churn going back to positions at General Dynamics, Mike in international and Gordon at Land Systems.

Soon after they settled in, Nick Chabraja became their new leader. As senior executives, Mike and Gordon would be involved in many corporate decisions.

As had been their experience, Mike and Gordon came down on the same side of many issues and on opposite sides of others. Since the size of the company had been compressed by previous administrations, General Dynamics was in a rebuilding mode, a buyer and looking to expand. In one early merger and acquisition meeting, Mike and Gordon disagreed on a particularly strategic target. Mike knew that the company was interested in buying an ordnance venture and, having spent time in the tank operation, believed he understood ordnance pretty well. Mike recommended to Chabraja that the company consider acquiring Alliant Techsystems out of Minneapolis in a stock transaction.[117] This company seemed to be in line with General Dynamics growth plans, and Mike pressed his case. His proposal was turned over to Gordon's area of responsibility but Gordon was not in favor of the acquisition and in the end the company did not pursue Alliant Techsystems.

Mike's rationale had been that Alliant Techsystems' blend of tactical weapon munitions, laser/radar technology smart weapons, unmanned aerial drones, and solid rocket propulsion systems would be an attractive operation for the new General Dynamics. Alliant Techsystems business sectors included information systems technology, which positioned it for the future and fed directly into General Dynamics embryonic Information Systems and Technology unit. Mike also felt that the acquisition addressed the upgrade market. He had written an internal report outlining how the Pentagon in all likelihood would be shifting its narrowing budgets toward weapon upgrades rather than new hardware. He believed the Pentagon was looking for ways to enhance what they had rather than develop and deploy entirely new systems, and Alliant Techsystems' products suited this new paradigm.

One of Mike's weaknesses and strengths was his vision, his long-term viewpoint. At times he would delegate the interim steps of moving a project from A to B to team members, but his visualization of the future, where he wanted to take the organization or where he thought it should extend, could be inspired. Wynne was not successful in getting the company to acquire Alliant Techsystems, but General Dynamics was moving toward those businesses. General Dynamics would go after other companies in the advanced information technology business sector. For the time being, Mike worked on international projects, a few of which were a return to his old haunt tank works.

Mike was back working with the Egyptians to progress their Abu Zaabal tank plant, located outside Cairo, into operations once again. The Egyptians took on the assembly of an additional 100 tank kits for the M-1A1/A2 Abrams. Mike also was involved with the Spanish tank industry, arranging for General Dynamics to take over the established Santa Barbara Sistemas factory outside Seville. This facility and others comparable to it throughout the country was owned and operated by the Spanish government and assembled Spain's main battle tanks and other armored vehicles. These vehicles were not necessarily General Dynamics or American designs. The takeover involved the manufacturing operation being outsourced to private industry. Mike reached almost the same point with an operation in Australia but was stopped short. While Chabraja appreciated all that international could bring to the company, he really wasn't a proponent of operating half way around the world. The Australia deal never came to fruition because Mike was not long for the job and his replacement was not given the task of completing it.

MIKE HAD RETURNED to General Dynamics at the invitation of Jim Mellor, who subsequently moved up to the board and out of daily operations. The new chief executive after a short interval gave all indications that he wanted to run the strategic and international areas in a different fashion. It wasn't that Chabraja had a problem with Mike's work but rather he was looking for different things from a position his predecessor had created.

Mike had strayed pretty far from his portfolio in pushing for the takeover of Alliant Techsystems. That was more a long-range call than an international opportunity, and the proposal had been a risky one, albeit with the potential of a big payoff. In the months that followed, General Dynamics acquired a number of companies in cash transactions, all the while the price of Alliant Techsystems stock climbed steadily. As it increased, so did the inkling that maybe Wynne had been right. For Chabraja this might have cast a shadow over the executive floor in Falls Church. And Mike had trouble separating himself from planning.

At his roots, Mike was more of a strategic thinker than a tactical operator. Chabraja in contrast, was schooled as a lawyer and consumed with tactics. So a clash of styles emerged. Even when Mike stayed within his portfolio, as he had with the opportunity in Australia, it didn't seem to be what Chabraja was looking for. They didn't even play golf with the same approach, Chabraja was passionate and Wynne was nonchalant. And way down deep, it might also have been a case of the new guy wanting his own guy. While Chabraja would prove to do a brilliant job rebuilding General Dynamics, it was destined to be without Mike Wynne. In September 1999 Chabraja had a meeting with Wynne and worked out a package for the orderly transfer of those roles.

In all likelihood, Wynne and Chabraja would have developed a nice relationship had they had a little more time to become acquainted with each other and work together. But such was not the case. It was time for change. Mike left with a nice firm handshake and a nice financial package. Chabraja allowed Mike's stock options to automatically vest, so he could leave General Dynamics with no strings attached. Chabraja was an important contact and would prove to be involved in Mike's future in more ways than this 1999 management change. This parting of ways was on good terms from start to finish.

❧

MIKE WAS 55 YEARS OLD and out of General Dynamics after a career whose pieces and parts added up to more than 20 years. While it was too early to call it retirement, he was in for a period of employment unlike his former days. In the past, he had always been a part of a major corporate entity, one listed on the New York

Stock Exchange, with billions of dollars in sales and thousands of employees. Upon leaving General Dynamics for the second time, Mike changed his pattern and dropped off the big corporate merry-go-round. He also changed another habit.

Mike and Barb made the decision to stay in the Washington area. Mike felt he had asked enough of Barbara in picking up and moving the family so often in the past. She liked the Washington area and was happy there. So after marking years in Massachusetts, Ohio, Colorado, Texas, Missouri, Michigan, California, back to Colorado, and now Virginia, they decided to stay put. Mike had spent his entire professional career in the military and defense industry, and Washington had enough action in those areas to keep him engaged and challenged. So as his first attempt at retirement, Mike became involved with a boutique investment firm that provided seed financing to start-up businesses in the technology sector.

Following the broad trends in finance, after the leveraging that took place in the 1980s, the 1990s were a period of re-equitization. Companies tried to pare debt and raise equity to more properly balance their financials. The Anders and Mellor leadership had done precisely that with General Dynamics during the early 1990s. With leverage out of favor, equity became the coin of the realm. The fact of the matter was that anyone with cash was now in demand. With cash, one could shop the market of business opportunities that was looking for equity players. This was the genesis of NextGen Capital LLC, Mike Wynne's first stop after his grand departure from the defense industry.

NEXTGEN CAPITAL LLC managed venture capital funds. The typical NextGen Fund was structured so that each of its partners put up a basic level of capital, ranging around $250,000. These assets collectively were used to finance investments in early stage technology-based operations. A NextGen Fund was essentially an executive committee of principals that would meet to select investment candidates. The fund would invest the first tranche of venture capital, and then any partner could invest additional funds in opportunities that were particularly attractive. In select cases, NextGen Fund principals would join the staff of the start-up company to lend business experience and counsel to the operation.

These technology companies generally were new operations that could not arrange financing at attractive rates or already had debt levels that required additional equity participation. NextGen Fund functioned similar to an investment club. Mike was a limited partner with NextGen Funds from late 1999 through early 2001. One of the companies in which the fund took an equity position was of special interest to Mike, and he took a more significant role in its operation. That was RFP Express.

RFP Express was a publicly traded company on the over-the-counter market. NextGen Fund became the majority shareholder, and Mike a part owner in RFP Express in 2000. He was installed as chairman and chief executive of the company with the intent of developing business operations, hoping to move the company onto a larger stage. Mike drew an annual cash salary of one dollar. He garnered a significant number of options in company stock but nothing with which he could pay bills. Mike commuted weekly from his home in Washington to the company's location in San Diego and was reimbursed for travel.

RFP Express prenegotiated lodging reservations with a network of hotels and then offered those blocked reservations to a number of Fortune-500 companies that booked substantial amounts of travel. The large corporations RFP Express targeted were those that required lodging and other hospitality services at numerous places around the country and even internationally. The Internet was used to match up both ends of the travel reservation contract. RFP Express would offer tailored programs to travel managers at the major companies who subscribed to RFP Express services.

RFP Express was typical of small start-up operations, where they often were long on name changes and restructuring but short on consistent operations. This occurred as fledging companies tried to find their market niche. SecurFone America was a company that marketed prepaid wireless products. It acquired IXATA, Inc., which operated Internet-based electronic commerce services.

This morphed into RFP Express, IXATA's primary service, which specialized in the travel and hospitality market. RFP Express generated revenue through subscription and transaction fees.[118] These business maneuvers took place before Mike arrived on the scene at RFP Express. He was there to make the promise of the future a reality.

Mike also had invested in a number of other small venture capital opportunities, some through the NextGen Fund and some on his own. Extended Reach Logistics was one opportunity in which Mike had invested personally. This company utilized electronic commerce to match up parts supply with demand from companies holding government contracts. Extended Reach Logistics was an early Internet-based application of e-commerce to supply chain management, in this case focused on military procurement.

The Defense Logistics Agency in the Defense Department was responsible for the procurement of most military parts. In practice, small orders usually ended up on the bottom of the logistics pile. The agency and its supply routines were unwieldy and slow. With more than 20,000 employees responsible for more than 5 million parts spread across 48 states, it was always looking to consolidate orders to maximize throughput. Thus, low volume orders could take months to achieve fulfillment. Companies such as Extended Reach Logistics filled the gap.

Extended Reach Logistics, in its purest form, simply took orders and arranged for delivery of product. Its business plan achieved for the military parts procurement system what Amazon.com accomplished in matching orders and suppliers in the book trade. Extended Reach Logistics could compete with the Defense Logistics Agency because it had an edge in using the technology of the Internet, which allowed it to treat every order the same. Similar to RFP Express, Extended Reach Logistics stayed a small operation and was not a huge commercial success. The company was later sold to Stewart & Stevenson for about what had been invested in it.

This period in Mike Wynne's life would turn out to be just a placeholder in his career. He had a little fun, and he and Barbara had the opportunity to enjoy a bit of travel around the country.

They had caught their breath after getting off the corporate merry-go-round. True to his decision to remain in the Washington area, Mike turned down a few major corporate opportunities that would have required moving. But with only small venture investments such as RFP Express and Extended Reach Logistics, Mike could not find a great fit for his energy. He had substituted activity for purpose. Barbara would call this period "Mike's first failed attempt at retirement." Other options were brewing, and they began with a call from an employment recruiter, in early 2001.

Chapter Fifteen

Launching Government Service

Beginning January 20, 2001, a fresh breeze swept through Washington with the arrival of a new administration, bringing with it far-reaching change. In the 20 Congresses from the start of John F. Kennedy's presidency to the beginning of George W. Bush's, from the 87th through the 106th, the Republican Party held a majority of the House of Representatives during only three of those periods. The tally was 6 out of 20 in the Senate. President George W. Bush began his term with effective control of both, a majority in the House and an even split in the Senate.

President Bush arrived in Washington on the swell of a conservative wave, a ripple of which promised to transform the military and the Defense Department. As the new president put together his cabinet, he selected Donald Rumsfeld as secretary of defense to execute that transformation. Rumsfeld quickly set about designing a change in military strategy and weapons programs. In a town where change was a biennial affair, everyone was confronted with it once again and nervous about it. Overarching the shifting current in strategy was Rumsfeld's plan to make the Defense Department operate more akin to a business, something that would be coined "Defense Inc."[119] This translated into more civilian control, with less congressional and military influence.

As with any transition, Washington was abuzz with news and natter, and reports and rumors. Headhunters were shuffling through their Rolodexes calling contacts, and interviews were taking place throughout the city. Over at Defense, Secretary Rumsfeld was beginning to stamp his mark on the department. Mike Wynne would end up in the thick of it but first he would make the acquaintance of the other players: Paul Wolfowitz, Marty Hoffman, and Jerry Jones.

WITH DONALD RUMSFELD as secretary, Paul Wolfowitz staged his own return to Washington. Wolfowitz had received his introduction to the inside years earlier, working for long-time Senator Henry "Scoop" Jackson from the state of Washington. This led to positions in the Nixon and Ford administrations and on to the Pentagon during Jimmy Carter's. Twenty years later, with experience as assistant secretary of state, an ambassador, an under secretary in defense for George H.W. Bush, and a stint teaching at Johns Hopkins, Wolfowitz returned for George W. Bush as deputy secretary of defense in Rumsfeld redux. With degrees from Cornell and the University of Chicago, Dr. Wolfowitz was smart and savvy and few outworked him.

The White House transition team in Rumsfeld's Department of Defense was orchestrated by a friend from his college days, Marty Hoffman. After college and a stint in the Army, Hoffman had earned a law degree and begun practice. Over time, his work connected with a variety of Washington-related positions. Hoffman was general counsel to James Schlesinger, when the latter was chair of the Atomic Energy Commission. He followed Schlesinger to Defense as special assistant, when he became the 12th Secretary. Hoffman rose in the Defense firmament when he became secretary of the Army in Rumsfeld's first tour in leadership. Hoffman left the Defense Department with Rumsfeld as the changeover in administrations took place in 1977. When Rumsfeld returned 24 years later, he began reconstruction with the aid of his longtime associate, Marty Hoffman.

When it came to personnel matters in the transition, Rumsfeld and Hoffman tapped another associate dating back to the Nixon and Ford administrations. Jerry Jones, whose family roots traced back to west Texas, worked on the personnel facet of the 2001 changeover in the Defense Department. Holder of a Harvard MBA and experience with management consultant McKinsey & Company, Jones also spent time working in the Robert Dole presidential campaign, as had Wolfowitz. Jones would be one of two bridges into the Wynne's life.

WITH THE WYNNES decision to stay in the nation's capital, the couple now lived in the hub of national politics. Barb had one wish and with the arrival of a new administration, the possibility of having it granted opened up. While Barb had enjoyed many opportunities in traveling the world with Mike, she had one desire much closer to home. Just once in her life, Barb wanted to attend an inaugural ball. But this required an invitation from the Presidential Inaugural Committee, and the Wynnes hadn't been very active on the political front.

While decidedly conservative, Mike and Barb pretty much kept their politics to themselves. Employment in the defense industry required the ability to work across party lines. Every Senate and House committee included members from both major parties. No matter what political group was in power at the moment, businessmen had to adopt the long-term view. During Mike's years with General Dynamics five different presidents had been in the White House, three Republicans and two Democrats. But the most recent election was bringing in another Republican, and it just so happened that the chair of the Republican National Committee (RNC) during the 2000 election cycle was a friend of the Wynnes from their years back in Denver.

Mike and Barb's Denver home in Cherry Hills Village had been the source of many new acquaintances, especially because of their location on the course at Glenmoor Country Club. The Wynnes never were scratch golfers, more like duffers, but they enjoyed the camaraderie of the game and the clubhouse. Every so often the club would hold a couples night, where members were partnered in mixed foursomes and played with strange handicaps, such as teeing off giant tees or driving golf balls with a baseball bat. This event was one more way for the membership to interact. On one such occasion the Wynnes were matched with a couple named Jim and Suzanne Nicholson, and they had a wonderful time together.

While the Nicholsons did not live in Cherry Hills Village, they were club members and shared some background with the Wynnes. It turned out that Jim and Mike were both military academy graduates from the 1960s, and the two families were both Republican and Roman Catholic. They later discovered that Mike and Suzanne had actually attended the same kindergarten when Mike's dad was teaching at the military academy. Suzanne had the picture to prove it.

The families socialized a number of times while together in the Denver area and even shared a Colorado Rockies game from time to time when Mike was still with Lockheed Martin and Jim with his residential development and construction operation, Renaissance Homes. While Jim was not a politician, he was close to the action. He represented Colorado on the RNC. Time passed and the Wynnes relocated to the D.C. area in early 1997.

Attending Mass at their local Catholic church one Sunday, Mike noticed two people behind them in bright purple Rockies jackets. After a double-take or two, he recognized the Nicholsons who also had transferred to Washington. Jim had continued in his role of fundraising for the RNC but had been promoted to chair of the organization right about the time the Wynnes had moved. Geographically close once again, they arranged occasions to be together.

In one instance Mike invited a number of area businessmen to a General Dynamics corporate outing at a Redskins game, and he included Jim Nicholson. While most of the group traveled between the feast and the football in a bus provided by General Dynamics, Nicholson rode in a private car so he could work the telephone for contributions. Riding with Jim, Mike gained a new appreciation for fund raising as Nicholson seemed to effortlessly raise $25,000 contributions for the RNC from more than one benefactor on the trip to the stadium. Jim reciprocated the junkets and on one occasion invited the Wynnes to a party that turned out to be a dinner with a number of Republican Eagles, the major political backers. So Mike and Barb, who were sort of the Nicholsons' nonpolitical friends, had the opportunity to meet some of their very political friends.

Mike and Barb contributed to the Republican effort in the year leading up to the swearing in of George W. Bush as president.[120] With their party support and a little help from their friends, the Wynnes were invited to one of the eight official inaugural balls that the new president attended in January 2001. Barb had her wish granted. In the larger perspective, party backing and presidential balls undoubtedly played a part in putting the Wynnes up on the radar screen for possible employment in the new administration. Jerry Jones placed the call to Mike Wynne.

THE HEADHUNTER CAUGHT MIKE on a Friday, just as he returned from his weekly circuit to San Diego. While Mike professed a bit of fatigue and knotty schedule hurdles, Jones pressed him to come in for an interview. All Mike could glean from his rejoinder of "Interview for what?" was that it wasn't a specific opening but several were available in the Department of Defense. The changeover in administrations entailed the added dimension of a switch in political party which increased the number of vacancies that had to be populated. It would take many candidates to fill the available seats. The caller had offered that Mike's name had been recommended by a half-dozen sources. Secure in his station and standing but always open to adventure, Mike told Barb he was going to the Pentagon "to have some preliminary conversation."

"I should be back in an hour or two." It was more akin to seven.

Barb was thoroughly caught up in the excitement and quizzed him on the cell phone as he drove home at the end of what turned out to be a long day, "So, what was it like?"

"I don't know any other way to explain it, but it was exactly like the old Ralph Edwards television show *This is Your Life*. After talking with the recruiter, I went into this room and found all these friends and associates from my life. Brad Parkinson and Pete Aldridge were there, as were people from my days teaching at the Air Force Academy, folks from my years at General Dynamics, and still others from my work with missiles. It was like old home week. It was surreal."

Mike explained that he had started a round robin with Jerry Jones, who didn't show many of his own cards during the interview. Jones had done his homework though and knew that Mike had been an Air Force officer and educator, had experience with numerous research projects such as the snap-shoot gun sight and AC-130 gunship, and had been involved with major defense systems such as the lightweight fighter program, *Los Angeles*–class fast-attack submarines, M-1 main battle tanks, and the ballistic missile program. For a guy who had never worked in government, Mike Wynne surely had a great deal of experience with a number of significant government programs covering air, land, and sea. After talking with Jones, Mike ran a gauntlet of four additional interviews, before calling it a day.

"So what happens next?" Barbara couldn't wait to hear.

"They want me back next weekend. They said I need to interview with Paul Wolfowitz, the new deputy secretary of defense. I guess I cleared the first hurdle."

The following weekend, Mike met with Wolfowitz. The two of them had an interesting give and take. Wolfowitz was officious in positioning the possibilities as an important event at an important time, a big deal. Mike was playing it down, that it might be more comparable to summer help coming on the scene as titular head. But Wolfowitz insisted that was not how it was going to be. The new-look Defense Department was going to change how things were accomplished, and Mike might be a part of that.

"Well if the new players are really serious, there are a few things I'd like to do and some others I'd like to see done." Mike laid out his view of the world.

Mike finished up with Wolfowitz and returned to Jerry Jones. He'd had his interview, and now it was time to hurry up and wait once again. Or not. Jones asked if Mike had a few minutes to see Rumsfeld.

If he had started at the Pentagon's central A-ring, it would have been up to the 3rd floor, down the 8th corridor out to the E-ring on the riverside entrance of the building, with a right turn down to Secretary Rumsfeld's bay, Office 3E880. Mike was whisked into the green-hued anteroom outside the secretary of defense's office. Keyed up for his interview with the secretary, Mike noticed a book on the lamp table in the waiting room. He thumbed through it and saw that people signed in on their visits. So-and-so general had signed in, as had the minister of defense of such-and-such a country. Mike picked up the pen and signed in. After all, he joked to himself, "This could be the pinnacle of a relatively mediocre career."

Mike had his interview with the secretary, and everything seemed to go well. It was short, but this was the secretary of defense who did not have the whole day to spend with one interviewee. It was just long enough for the secretary to capture a measure of the man. Now it was a matter of letting the wheels of government crank away. Mike returned home and shared with Barb what had transpired. They were both interested to see what would happen next.

That night Mike answered the telephone and heard the incredulous statement, "You signed in!"

It was Gordon England.

"Well, yeah. It was a guest book and was there for visitors to sign in. I figured I might not be back this way, so I chiseled my name in the pantheon of visitors to the Defense Department. But even more intriguing, how did you come to see that I signed in?"

"I was there about two people after you."

Mike caught just one breath, as he wondered about protocol and rules of etiquette. How do you spell faux pas, he thought to himself? "Did anyone else sign in?"

"Oh, hell no!"

NEXT UP WERE the Republican screeners. These people made sure that probable candidates supported conservative causes and conservative people. The screeners culled through each prospects background to look for anything untoward. They didn't want any closet Democrats in the new administration. In Mike they actually found items that required explanation. A review of Mike's political contributions revealed mostly mainstream donations to the RNC, but a few glaring alerts showed up in his record during the 1990s.

Managing the rocket business in Colorado for what had become Lockheed Martin by the mid-1990s, Mike found out that the president and vice president—Bill Clinton and Al Gore—were scheduled to visit the Denver area for a Democratic fundraiser. Mike inquired as to who was attending the fundraiser to represent the company and heard, "No one." While not of Mike's political persuasion, this was still an important event as Clinton was the sitting president and Gore, during the eight years he was in Congress, had sat on what was then called the Committee on Science and Technology.[121] These two men may not have been members of Mike's political party, but they were important to his industry. So Mike and Barb were drafted for the job. They purchased the $1,000 per person tickets and attended the event, representing the astronautics business of Lockheed Martin. While it was nice to hear the nation's leaders speak, the unintended consequence was that Mike and Barb were later chronicled as major contributors to the Democratic National Committee. This would have to be clarified.

A couple of warnings also showed up in Mike's record with the Federal Election Commission Campaign Finance Reports when he was back with General Dynamics. One contribution was to Senator Patrick Leahy of Vermont and the other was to Senator Diane Feinstein of California, neither of which could be called conservative. While the former was a progressive and the latter was considered somewhat moderate in political leaning, both were devoted Democrats, which is why they popped up on the screeners' watch.[122] Mike's contributions to these Democratic candidates, for which he had to account, traced directly to his time at General Dynamics with Nick Chabraja—a Chicago Democrat resettled in Washington. In both cases, Chabraja had sponsored fundraisers for the candidates and attendance was required, as was a donation to the reelection campaign. In the end, the explanations were readily accepted and it was simply one more hurdle.

IT WAS THROUGH the back door that Mike found out he was

being interviewed for one of the service secretary positions. Initially, they were looking at him as a possibility for secretary of the Army because of his background from the U.S. Military Academy. As they reviewed his broader civilian background, they noticed his experience in acquisitions and contracts. The Defense Department had problems in the acquisition division at the change in administrations due to overzealous workforce reductions that had been taken in response to Cold War realities. The remaining staff was having trouble getting the job done.

Donald Rumsfeld had begun a process of bringing in business minds to run the Pentagon, reasserting civilian control. The secretary wanted to negate or at least balance out the influence of Washington insiders, politicos, and military leaders. Secretary Rumsfeld was far less concerned with hiring individuals with political background and sought out citizens with industrial experience. The transition to a more corporate approach was revealed by his eventual nominees.

Four of the key positions in the Defense Department for which the secretary had the authority to nominate candidates were the three service secretaries in charge of separate military departments and the all-important under secretary of defense for acquisition, technology and logistics (AT&L), the head weapons buyer. As Secretary Rumsfeld disclosed his cards, he installed James G. Roche as secretary of the Air Force, Gordon R. England as secretary of the Navy, Thomas E. White as secretary of the Army, and Edward C. "Pete" Aldridge as under secretary for AT&L.

Roche, a commissioned naval officer who retired with the rank of captain after 23 years service which he had followed with a 17-year business career at Northrop Grumman, became the 20th secretary of the Air Force. England, with more than 20 years at General Dynamics and Lockheed Martin but no military experience, became the 72nd secretary of the Navy. White, a graduate of West Point, a retired Brigadier General, and an 11-year employee of Enron, was sworn in as the 18th secretary of the Army. Aldridge, who had worked at LTV Aerospace, McDonnell Douglas, and the Aerospace Corporation, in addition to having been the 16th secretary of the Air Force, became the under secretary of defense for AT&L. While

this cast of characters left just questions for Mike Wynne, it spoke
volumes about Secretary Rumsfeld.

President George W. Bush (far left) congratulates (left to right) James G. Roche,
Gordon R. England, and Thomas E. White following their swearing-in ceremony
in the White House Oval Office on June 18, 2001. *Source:* Department of
Defense photo by R. D. Ward. Released at www.defense.gov/dodcmsshare/
newsphoto/2001-06/010618-D-9880W-105.jpg.

RUMSFELD WAS A GRADUATE of Princeton University, where he
had participated in the Naval Reserve Officer Training Corps
program. During the mid-1950s, he was a naval aviator and flight
instructor. Joining the reserves, the future secretary worked as
assistant to congressmen in Ohio and Michigan, and then ran
his own campaign for the United States House of Representatives
for Illinois' Thirteenth Congressional district in 1962. Rumsfeld
resigned from Congress during his fourth term to join the Nixon
administration. After a stint as ambassador to NATO, Rumsfeld
returned to Washington with the Ford administration, becoming
chief of staff for his friend from their days together in Congress.
Rumsfeld would hand the mantle of chief of staff to Dick Cheney
in 1975, on becoming the 13th and youngest secretary of defense.

Leaving Washington when President Jimmy Carter took office
in 1977, Rumsfeld embarked on a career in business, beginning as

president of G.D.Searle, a pharmaceutical company. Within eight years, Rumsfeld engineered the sale of G.D. Searle to Monsanto. He moved on to General Instrument as chief executive officer and took that company public on the New York Stock Exchange two years after it had been involved in a leveraged buyout. Rumsfeld's next move was to Gilead Sciences as chairman.

During this period, Rumsfeld held a number of board directorships that kept him in circles of power. He was a director of Gulfstream Aerospace from 1993–99, when the company was merged with General Dynamics. Besides Rumsfeld, Gulfstream had connections in Washington through other board members, such as former Secretary of State George Schultz and former Chairman of the Joint Chiefs of Staff Colin Powell. After General Dynamics and Gulfstream merged, Rumsfeld dropped off the board, but he had developed even more contacts who could offer references.

Rumsfeld retired from his business career when he reprised his role as secretary of defense, this time as the 21st and oldest in succession. It was with these experiences in business and industry that Donald Rumsfeld set about restructuring the Defense Department in January 2001. Mike Wynne was destined to be a part of it all.

RIGHT WHEN THE TOP POSITIONS seemed to be taken, Mike received a call from Pete Aldridge. At the time Mike finished the interview sessions with Jerry Jones, he had been told to just wait. He did, and Pete Aldridge was the next contact point. Aldridge telephoned and offered Mike one of the deputy under secretary positions in AT&L. While Mike had secretly harbored the wish to have one of the top six positions under Secretary Rumsfeld, it took Barb to reorient him.

First of all, with no previous government service on his resume, he had to keep his ego in check. Second, as under secretary, Aldridge was number five. While Mike entertained the idea of declining the offer, Barb was in support of giving it a try. After all, acquisitions and contracts was what Mike had trained in most of his professional life. Mike accepted.

With the preliminaries in his rearview mirror, Mike Wynne

was nominated to be the deputy under secretary of defense for acquisition and technology (A&T), working for Pete Aldridge. Mike's nomination, PN502-107, reached the floor of the United States Senate on June 12, 2001, and was promptly referred to the Committee on Armed Services. During the period between referral and actual hearings, Mike worked his way through interviews with the committee members and their staffs regarding policy questions. He also provided a written response to a series of prepared questions from the Committee. These would be entered into the record at the hearing.

Hearings before the Committee on Armed Services regarding Mike's nomination and four others, took place at 9:30 in the morning on Friday, June 22, 2001, in Room SR-222 in the Russell Senate Office Building. This hearing before the committee was chaired by Senator Carl Levin of Michigan with Virginia Senator John Warner as ranking member. It took place during the first session of the 107th Congress. Other committee members in attendance were Senator Jack Reed of Rhode Island and Senator James Inhofe of Oklahoma, both of whom had served in the Army.

While it could have been just the thrill and excitement of the moment, the meeting room seemed crowded. SR-222 was a bit on the small side, the space dominated by a huge V-shaped table. The committee members sat along the two sides, while the nominees were juxtaposed in the open end of the V. Staff members lined the walls and the back of the room. Only a few dozen guests could be accommodated, and with five nominees in attendance, the room was full.

The hearing began with an opening statement by Chairman Levin, introducing the nominees and allowing each the opportunity to introduce family or friends who accompanied them. Mike proudly introduced Barb, his wife of 35 years, and his brother Peter, who stood in for his siblings. Senator Levin's opening was followed by that of Senator Warner. With a vote scheduled at 10:30 in the morning on the Senate floor, Senator Levin laid out the committee ground rules. This entailed a series of standard questions for nominees, opening statements by the nominees, and an initial round of questions not to exceed six minutes for each committee member, hopefully finished before recess for the scheduled vote.

After the opening statements, the committee members worked through a round-robin of questions, not all directed at each nominee. During this period Mike was asked general questions about his position on restructuring of the military under the base realignment and closure (BRAC) process, Department of Defense "best practices" in contracting with the private sector, the survivability of the industrial base that supported defense, and the need for a sense of importance in modernizing the armed forces. The committee adjourned a bit after 10:40 a.m. with the determination that it did not need a second hearing.

Nineteen days later, committee action was "ordered to be reported favorably." On the following day, July 12, 2001, Michael Walter Wynne was confirmed as deputy under secretary of defense for A&T by a voice vote on the floor of the United States Senate.[123] Now life would move a bit faster.

Secretary of Defense Donald Rumsfeld (center) conducting a swearing-in ceremony on July 16, 2001. Left to right: Thomas P. Christie, director, Operational Test & Evaluation; Dr. Peter W. Rodman, assistant secretary of defense, International Security Affairs; Michael W. Wynne, principal deputy under secretary of defense, Acquisition & Technology; and Douglas J. Feith, under secretary of defense, Policy. Christie was one of the defense analysts associated with John Boyd's "fighter mafia" in the 1960s (see note 80). *Source:* Wynne Family.

CHAPTER SIXTEEN

A&T, E-mails, and Appointments

THE AT&L DIVISION was concerned with weapons systems, and Mike Wynne certainly had background. From his perch in A&T, he could influence systems and purchases. While he was but a medium-sized fish in a gigantic bowl, he was nearing the top of the food chain in weapons procurement.

Besides its direct report, A&T was cast with the responsibility of advising the secretary of defense and his deputy on matters related to the acquisition of weapons systems. A&T provided oversight and policy direction, and its span of control reached more than 10,000 personnel. A&T's mission encompassed acquisition process improvement, engineering, testing, contracting, and preparedness related to weapons systems. A&T's charge was to consistently provide the nation's warfighters with what they needed. Now Mike wouldn't just work with the bureaucracy, he would manage it.

From the outside looking in, the public saw a murky bureaucracy occupying the Pentagon and the individual service branches. Plans and programs passed into the Pentagon and bounced around the offices for months and sometimes years before finally reappearing, often not looking anything akin to the original idea. From the inside looking out, the professional staff knew that a large part of the bureaucracy was the constant changeover of leadership as administrations came and went. The Pentagon was a full-time business, and the injection of new straw bosses on a regular basis was antithetical to achieving consistent and measurable headway.

In 2001 the Pentagon bureaucracy was a bit stunned when the Republicans showed up after eight years of Democratic leadership. The new guys arrived with plans and a purpose. The Pentagon ship had to alter course somewhat. The great majority of employees at the Pentagon, those who showed up for work every day no matter what administration was in at the top, were the people who made it work.

Mike experienced a professional staff that was exceptionally responsive. Soliciting their thoughts and opinions proved fruitful. Open to staff commentary, he found they were full of initiative. They had nurtured and cultivated many ideas over time. Their suggestions had been polished and rethought and reworked. When leadership allowed the ideas to bubble to the top, the staff's designs were often well developed and right on target. But leadership had to seek out those opinions and ideas.

Once in the flow at the Pentagon, Mike instituted practices that had worked well in business. Wynne changed the prevailing modus operandi from one of "need to know" to "need to share." He wanted to widen the circle of those on the inside, rather than narrow it. This attitude dovetailed perfectly with the state of information technology in the private sector.

When Mike started as deputy under secretary, he led off with an improvement group. This provided the setting for everyone to become comfortable with the new leadership, while presenting a forum for staff to proffer suggestions as they did so. With the aim of "little-steps for little-feet," the only requirement at that early stage was to have people show up. In working with Pete Aldridge, Mike had isolated a little money to invest in ideas. It was up to the improvement group to come up with schemes to try out. Mike organized the meetings to be productive, so that they didn't analyze things to death. If someone had a great idea and the group agreed, implementation moved relatively quickly.

The group began with just eight or so staffers, and about as many ideas. As they achieved a bit of success and notoriety, the group started to take on a life of its own. Soon it was up to 20 staffers. Finally it reached 40. They were meeting every Friday and brainstorming. As the facilitator, Mike would temper this or that facet of one idea and position other suggestions in the appropriate manner. Success bred more success. Soon the ideas and suggestions were flowing. Mike would be the first to admit he was getting credit for the work of his staff, but things were getting done. The process was being improved.

Mike also crossed over into related areas from time to time, such as where A&T intersected with logistics. He believed retail marketing in the business world had relevance in defense areas. For example, an automobile was simply plugged into a computer when brought in for service, its system checked automatically. He wondered, in a similar fashion, why an aircraft engine couldn't be programmed to tell the maintenance crew when it was due for change-out or what specific service was needed, all the way down to ordering parts?

Having years of practice in the defense business, where just about everything moved along a slow and deliberate development curve, Mike knew that he probably would not see the results of much of what he might initiate. Even so, he became the consummate starter, for example, bringing barcode and radio-frequency identification technologies to a myriad of new applications in the Defense Department. To some, Mike had become the consummate bomb thrower. He would throw out ideas and push to have projects started, while moving on to other areas that needed attention. He was a man on a mission.

For Mike, many of these projects were a revisiting of the feedback loop, much as he had done with the snap-shoot gun sight in the Air Force and supply line management at Extended Reach Logistics. In the end, the Pentagon's Defense Logistics Agency and the individual services helped push applications of these concepts forward. While at A&T Mike worked with Navy Vice Admiral Keith Lippert, the director of the Defense Logistics Agency, to bring about dramatic change.

With the military departments dissatisfied with defense military procurement, it was a period when the secretary of defense was considering dropping the agency altogether. Supporting Lippert's efforts, Mike helped streamline operations and reduce overhead. As the process improved, they increased material flow without adding positions, which heightened morale. They had applied retail technology architecture to areas in defense acquisition. It worked. But Mike's early success was tempered with a dose of reality as his heart problems returned. In truth, he had experienced a couple of warning signals.

LATE IN THE GAME at General Dynamics in Washington, Mike's health concerns had returned for a time. He would come home from work every so often and be mortified as he shared with Barb that he had been sitting at the computer terminal productively engaged and suddenly just dozed off. Ever so slowly, since that time in Denver, his heart had been degenerating. The mitral valve had not been replaced in 1994 and the already fragile valve continued to weaken. It was hard to determine how much his heart issues had affected his work performance and if it might have played a role in his retirement from General Dynamics, but retire he did. He also returned to a cardiologist.

The Washington-area doctor rendered the news that Mike probably already guessed, his mitral valve was in failure. Mike essentially was approaching heart failure. As an interim measure, the doctors put Mike on the anticoagulant warfarin (Coumadin). This was 1999, five years since he had had a bout of endocarditis in Denver. In those intervening years, Mike had follow-up stress tests and exams. He had taken the precaution of using antibiotics before every visit to the dentist. But these were palliative measures as the valve continued to weaken. Now he was on blood thinners. By end of 2000, after almost two years on Coumadin, Mike was looking at alternatives.

For those two years, even though on Coumadin, Mike's energy level remained very low. His eyesight, which had not been that good all along, was getting worse. Mike was not the same person, and his stamina was dropping. The degeneration continued, and Mike was losing confidence in his physician. Mike was starting to have trouble keeping up. Then his government service started in 2001. Life was getting faster and stress was rising. Months into the job, he finally had to deal with the mitral valve. He had two reminders of his shortcoming.

Mike had been on a trip in Australia where he was delegate lead for a group of 35. Thousands of miles from home, he developed breathing problems and experienced fatigue. While he thought it might be rooted in allergies or a spring cold, antibiotics didn't solve the problem. A visit to the doctor confirmed that he had fluid buildup in his lungs. The second occasion was stateside, when he was giving a speech to the Northern Virginia Technology Council. During his speech, his words would not come at the right pacing. Mike was out of phase, his brain at one point in the presentation and his words lagging a bit behind. Only by slowing his performance could he move back into sync. After Mike's presentation, the man who had introduced Mike to the meeting said, "Something is dreadfully wrong with you. If I were you, I would go see a doctor as soon as possible."

At the cardiologist, Mike learned that his heart was operating at roughly 40 percent of its capacity. He was lucky that he had not been out jogging or performing other strenuous physical activity, where he might have dropped to the ground with complete heart failure. Instead, he had just experienced breathing and communication problems. He was not dying, but he needed to address the problem. Delay was not an option anymore.

Barb had already researched the major heart centers in the United States and had narrowed their list down to two, one in Houston and one in Cleveland. When they found out that many foreign patients routinely flew to the States to be served at the Cleveland Clinic, that was all the recommendation they needed. Just months on the job, Mike was off to the world-renowned Miller Family Heart & Vascular Institute at the Cleveland Clinic. They checked in at the clinic on December 7, 2001, the anniversary of Pearl Harbor.

The engineer in Mike had been correct; advances in this particular field of medicine had taken place. Mitral valve repairs with a flexible band had become a wonderful alternative to replacements with a pig valve, and the Cleveland Clinic had the creator. The procedure—a mitral annuloplasty— implanted a device called a Cosgrove Ring, invented by the Clinic's own Dr. Delos M. Cosgrove III. Mike loved the fact that the architect was on staff but eschewed having him do the procedure. Mike preferred the fast hands of a young surgeon using the marvelous technology of the old master, and in stepped Yale-educated and Johns Hopkins-trained Dr. A. Marc Gillinov.[124]

The doctors surgically placed the ring around Mike's mitral valve to strengthen the area and trimmed off about three-fourth inch of excess valve tissue to allow the leaflets to close tightly. When Mike later asked about the prognosis for longevity, the doctors had to admit they did not know. The clinic had only been doing the surgery for a few years, but projections looked excellent. For the time being, no more Coumadin and no more worries. Mike went in on December 7 and returned to Washington the week before Christmas. His plan was to show up at the Pentagon that week.

Mike knew the Pentagon had a couple of odd conventions. One was showing up before a holiday break. If an employee put in an appearance at the Pentagon the week before a holiday, even if only for a short visit, everyone would remember you were there, almost as if you had never left. Conversely, if one did not show up the week before the holiday, it was as if you were gone for the year. So Mike made a point of coming back and visiting the Pentagon the week before Christmas.

His executive assistant, Caroline Wilson, arranged for a motorized-scooter so Mike could actually make the rounds. They wished him well and he wished everyone a wonderful holiday season. Mike returned home and finished his recovery. He would not return to his office until mid-February, but they remembered that he had been back.

MIKE BECAME INVOLVED in the flow of important decisions at AT&L early on. His boss, Pete Aldridge, spent the majority of his time traveling around the country on AT&L business. Aldridge was the front man for the department and rarely in the office. This left Wynne back home in Washington keeping the operation running.

Aldridge was the traveling rock star, doing the photo-ops, and Wynne was the guy in the background. But this positioned Mike as if he was the AT&L chief of staff. Even when back home in Washington, the Aldridges didn't partake in much of the social scene.

With the under secretary often unavailable, Mike had the opportunity to represent AT&L in Defense Department meetings. He was found to be knowledgeable on a variety of programs and a quick study on the others. Determined to be more than the average political appointee, Mike naturally became a prominent figure in acquisition discussions, especially in meetings with Secretary Rumsfeld and Deputy Wolfowitz.

Defense secretary Rumsfeld had returned to Washington as the instrument of President Bush's promise of transforming the military, melding the advances of technology into nothing short of a revolution of the armed forces. It was intended to be much more than a series of incremental advances. Things started slowly because of the peacetime power of military leadership, but 9/11 changed the situation. Transformation became more than just a political catchword, and with the probability of retaliation and the prospect of war, the balance of power shifted toward the secretary of defense. But the actual makeover of the military had yet to take place.

A more agile and advanced defense initiative required changes in existing programs. In a September 1999 speech at The Citadel, candidate George W. Bush had phrased the mission as leapfrogging a "generation of technology." This would be accomplished in part by "replacing existing programs" of Cold War weapons systems in favor of shifting funds to new technologies.[125] Two years later, as president, his Defense Department had to make the hard decisions as to which programs would be curtailed to make room for those to come.

When the Defense Department looked at its range of major weapons systems, trying to decide which could be used as a test case for advancement or cancellation, it had trouble singling out one. Budgets were tight and programs sacred, but redirecting limited funds to more promising and technologically advanced systems was the grail. Eventually a program was selected and assigned to Mike's sector for review and analysis. The candidate was the Army's Crusader artillery system, suggested for cancellation by one of Deputy Secretary Wolfowitz's special assistants.

As the Army's latest artillery system, the Crusader had been a work in progress for years. With more than $2 billion already invested in development of the system, and the prospect of another $9 billion to go, it was studied as part of the transformation of the military. Once put on the table for consideration, it became Mike's job to formulate the argument, validate the decision, and sell the conclusion around the department. Since cancelling multibillion dollar programs always incurred someone's enmity, reminiscent of the *Life* cereal commercial from the 1970s, everyone let Mike do it.

With the overarching Army ambition of going light and lethal, the almost 80-ton, two-vehicle Crusader system just didn't fit the future. While the Crusader had much improved range and accuracy, it still lacked the precision sought in new weapon systems. Mike fashioned a tight and relatively impenetrable presentation, similar to what he had done at General Dynamics when he justified the multiyear tank contract with the Army. But this time Mike was slashing an Army program. On top of that, the Armed Services Committee was not happy with the Office of the Secretary of Defense.

Development of the Army's advanced artillery system had begun in 1994 and had been part of each succeeding annual appropriation. In February of 2002, Congress received the president's budget for fiscal 2003, which allocated $475 million for development of the Crusader program, presumably at the request of the Defense Department. In April, it was reported that the department was reviewing a number of programs for the fiscal 2004 budget, one of which was Crusader. A decision was expected around September 2002.

On May 2, Secretary Rumsfeld was reported to have asked for a look at alternatives to the Crusader program within 30 days. Six days later, the secretary canceled the program. The Crusader program had gone from a half billion dollar line item to zero in a short 13 weeks. The nub of the problem was that this took place without any consultation with the Senate Armed Services Committee. They had been embarrassed by the Defense Department.

Hearings were called for May 16 with two panels scheduled to testify. The first panel was led by Secretary Rumsfeld, with Deputy Wolfowitz and Under Secretary Aldridge in support. The second panel was led by Army Chief of Staff General Shinseki. In attendance and sitting in the audience at the hearing was Aldridge's principal deputy, Mike Wynne. After presentations and statements by the three Defense Department civilian leaders followed by a spirited question and answer period, the panel soon ran out of words. The committee's ranking member, Senator Warner, looked over the panel members and noticed Mike Wynne in the background. The senator asked Secretary Rumsfeld if he would have Mike come forward to show on the presentation charts where the money saved would be redirected to other programs. So it was that Mike's government service was launched and he began to operate on a larger stage.[126]

IN TRANSFORMING THE MILITARY, not everything involved a reduction. The constructive and gratifying work in A&T was the ability to review and accelerate the more promising ideas along the development curve. From Mike's background work on the AC-130 gunship autopilot and the snap-shoot gun sight, he knew just how critical the feedback loop was to a weapon's effectiveness. One of the ideas Mike found bubbling around A&T in 2002 was an Air Force project on remote views of the battlefield.

Front-line experience in Afghanistan had raised concerns about the ability to view a field of combat from above, a bird's-eye view. This facility would greatly enhance the on-the-ground warriors' ability to respond in a fluid situation. Being able to see the battlefield in its ever-changing configuration might provide the decisive edge in the insurgent wars.

With the Air Force Predator, an unmanned aerial vehicle, filming the battlefield, its signal picture was being transmitted back to the United States to the remote pilot-operator for review. The field was also being recorded by AC-130 gunships, whose crew viewed the pictures. The logical extension was to have the pictures linked to the ground troops' theater commander or even better to the ground troops themselves. This would provide a real-time video of the combat zone. As the front-line conditions changed, the troops would know immediately. This would be a dynamic battlefield.

A&T in Don Rumsfeld's Defense Department was able to devote funding to help push the development of this technology and became a driving force in the intelligence, surveillance, and reconnaissance (ISR) revolution. One of the primary defense contractors working with the Air Force was L3 Communications, a product of the consolidation in the defense industry.

Lockheed Corporation had merged with Martin Marietta in 1994 and Loral Corporation in 1996. To focus on its core business sectors, the new Lockheed Martin subsequently disposed of 10 commercial lines in advanced electronics. These electronics units were merged to form L3 Communications in a leveraged buyout in 1997 by two former executives of Loral with the financial underpinning of Lehman Brothers. L3 Communications would become a significant factor in ISR capability.

Conceptually, providing a bird's-eye view was easy. The aerial vehicle filmed the battlefield and downlinked the information to ground controllers. It was but a short intellectual hop from providing ground troops with an overhead view of the battlefield to linking air, space, ground, and sea-based efforts with the same information stream. The ground warriors' ability to send information back to the aerial vehicle provided two-way communication, completing the feedback loop. While it would take time to flesh out this technology in all its pieces and parts, this was the foundation for the Remote Operations Video Enhanced Receiver (ROVER).

The battlefield information proved easy to obtain. Sharing it was the stumbling block. In time, ground-based receivers would evolve from Humvee-carried units that were anything but portable, to laptop-sized backpack receivers, to the promise of handheld sets. The dispersal of video feeds from unmanned aerial vehicles to fighters, bombers, ships at sea, and satellites allowed the technology to proliferate.

On the horizon, as the reception and response at ground level moved from theater commanders to platoon sergeants, foot soldiers would be able to pinpoint and confirm targets back to aerial resources. While this would take time, it was the ambition of the technology—spherical situation awareness. The key for Wynne was that A&T could propel this technology down the learning curve. The developing ROVER platform would follow Mike throughout his time in government service, he being its advocate at every stop along the way.

WORKING IN A&T also involved bringing parties together to further programs and sometimes settling disputes. Common ground was not always easy to find. As principal deputy for A&T in 2003, Mike was appointed director of a Defense Department task force charged with establishing a joint Air Force–Navy program office for the development of unmanned combat aerial vehicles, the unmanned vehicle concept taken one step further with weapons delivery. But the Air Force and Navy didn't always play nice together.

Establishing the program office had a measure of time pressure, as it had to fit within a fiscal year budget allocation. At a briefing for Wynne on April 16 sponsored by the two services and the Defense Advanced Research Projects Agency, it was obvious the attendees were working at odds to organize the program office. The services' resistance was a fear that unmanned combat vehicles would compete for limited dollars needed by other programs. Despite the fact they could not agree on the concept, they also could not see eye to eye on where to put the development office. Mike had enough.

He could tell the difference between objection and obstruction, between bona fide and BS. The oftentimes laconic principal deputy became even more so, cutting short the presentation and throwing the briefing book down the length of the table.[127] Was it full-blown frustration or feigning furious to center the groups' attention? It didn't matter, as he made his point and things started moving. One couldn't wait to see what the Army postured when it entered the fray.

❧

ALL THE WHILE MIKE WYNNE was getting started in A&T, a

troubling undercurrent existed concerning Air Force acquisition programs in the Defense Department. This had not yet monopolized oversight's radar but had been simmering in the background for years. While the problem exploded with a specific case in the headlines in the new millennium, its roots were back in the 1990s. It involved influence peddling and acquisition irregularities, problems that surfaced from time to time in the multibillion dollar defense acquisitions business.

The triad formed by the government, military, and industry produced strange bedfellows. Each relied on the other. The military was highly dependent on private industry for the leading technology that arose out of independent research. The major contractors were highly dependent on government for funding their projects, many of which would not be undertaken without the existence of a known patron. At least this was the case in the American system of free enterprise.

With military procurement, the usual practice was for the Defense Department or a particular military service to state its program specifications. A group of contractors bid on making that particular armament or process. After the contractors' bids were reviewed, either a winning bid was chosen or a select few were picked to produce a prototype. Either way, the field of contractors was narrowed. If several prototypes were developed, they were compared and contrasted and after an exhaustive review one was chosen. Thus, major defense procurement programs were generally narrowed down to a winning proposal and prototype.

Because of the size of these programs, the winning bid generally entailed a mix of defense contractors taking specific responsibility for various portions, with one chosen as lead contractor. The dark side was that a single program could sometimes make or break a company. Huge expenditures during time of war were counterbalanced by huge defense spending cuts in time of peace, making the competitive environment even more heated. Given these pressures, major contractors competed hard to win and sometimes competed unfairly. The normal dynamic between government and industry was ripe for plundering on occasion, but this was not new.

The Truman Commission investigated the National Defense Program beginning in March 1941 and highlighted many of the problems in the military procurement process. In military acquisition, especially during times of war, not every supplier had altruistic intentions. The whole concept of competition among suppliers for government largess set the stage for a troubling dynamic. While on one hand, it positioned the military to acquire the best and latest technology, it set up concerns for overpaying and favoritism. President Dwight Eisenhower aptly tagged this dichotomy the military-industrial complex. This "complex" brought with it many concerns that still exist. The defense debacle du jour that loomed when Mike Wynne stepped in at A&T concerned irregularities with Air Force acquisition programs, which would blossom with the Boeing tanker deal in the ensuing years.

THE BOEING COMPANY whose lineage traced back to the end of World War I was a fierce competitor and had become one of the largest defense contractors. While its founder exited the company in the 1930s during an active period of mergers and breakups, the firm continued to flourish. Early on, Douglas Aircraft had the lead in commercial aircraft with its DC series of planes, but after World War II Boeing became a challenger in jets with its introduction of the Boeing 707. Douglas Aircraft slipped from first place trying to compete with its offering, the DC-8 jet airplane.

Boeing's innovation of the "flying boom" in the late 1940s made aerial refueling practical. It followed with the first production refueling tanker, the KC-135 Stratotanker. Deployed starting in 1957 it formed the base of the country's refueling fleet ever since. It was a KC-135 that refueled Pat Wynne's F-4 Phantom II in 1966 on its way to the Red River Valley. When Mike entered government service the KC-135 tankers, with an average fleet age exceeding 35 years of service and countless refittings, were in need of replacement.

While the Air Force had not expressed any urgency to replace its KC-135 tanker fleet as of 2001, a weakening economy and 9/11 altered the playing field.[128] The Federal Reserve cut key interest rates 11 times in 2001, trying to stem the cascading markets. The

White House was willing to open up capital spending to prop up the economy but had to find a way to accomplish that in the face of huge cash drains. To address this, the option of replacing the Air Force tanker fleet through lease was studied.

In any lease-versus-buy analysis, the lease option is generally more expensive. This is by definition, since the faction that funds the lease has to receive a return on its investment. Instead of a two-party deal, it becomes a three-party deal. While a lease is more expensive as time goes by, the initial investment is usually a fraction of an outright purchase. The sum and substance of the problem with the Boeing tanker transaction was the size of the lease-versus-buy difference. The U.S. General Accounting Office estimated a lease for the first 100 units would cost roughly $5.5 billion more than an outright purchase.[129]

Even the financing was suspect—others would call it replete with smoke and mirrors. To allow the Air Force to acquire the aircraft at the lowest upfront cost while providing Boeing the cash needed to underwrite construction, a controversial financing structure was proposed. Boeing would sell the aircraft to a nonprofit Delaware business trust managed by the Wilmington Trust Company, which in turn would lease the tankers to the Air Force. The trust would raise capital in the institutional market to fund Boeing and would be reimbursed for expenses through lease payments from the Air Force. The trust arrangement disguised the true costs.

Even though priced at a lower opening cost, the lease obligated the Air Force to a much higher total expense spanning a number of appropriation years. And if the Air Force began retirements in anticipation of the replacements, the whole artifice became a *fait accompli.* The Defense Appropriation Act for fiscal 2002 authorized the Air Force to move forward with a lease, but when it approached Congress for approval in 2003, it hit a roadblock.[130] The lease plan just didn't pass the "smell test."

THE ROOT OF THE PROBLEM traced to one Air Force acquisition executive, around whom a whiff of controversy had settled previously with regard to a different program, the C-17 Globemaster airlift. As the Senate Armed Services Committee would ask, "How could one person accumulate so much power?" It was always a risk. A fine line existed between checking everything staff produced and moving forward without giving it a second look. This line was crossed.

The flip side to having a professional, full-time staff occupying the Pentagon and the individual service branches in the face of revolving door leadership was that personnel had the opportunity to acquire significant influence. In a game of checks and balances, at times the checks were changed too often to have any real consequence. Permanent staff generally knew more about individual programs than the interim leadership, and this could have both positive and negative effects.

Darleen Druyun, a member of the Senior Executive Service with a civilian Air Force career dating back to 1970, was named the principal deputy assistant secretary of the Air Force for acquisition and management in 1993. As principal deputy and with little consistent leadership, Druyun acquired considerable authority over Air Force programs and the contractors behind them.[131] While she could be hard-nosed with common contractors in fighting for the best deal, she also had the opportunity to go easy on select suppliers in exchange for favors. The absence of supervision was problematic.

From 1993 when Druyun stepped up to principal deputy in charge of negotiating contracts to her retirement in 2002, she worked with four different secretaries of defense, four Air Force chiefs of staff, three secretaries of the Air Force, and at least four assistant secretaries of the Air Force for acquisition.[132] These numbers do not include various under secretaries of the Air Force and those who served in an acting capacity for any period of time. She was the only constant.

During nine years of responsibility for multibillion dollar Air Force programs, Druyun had at least four direct supervisors and almost a dozen other senior people who could have influenced her work. While a few of her overseers recognized her unusual control across programs and contractors and even tried to negate her influence, none were in position long enough to change the course of events. When Mike stepped into A&T at Defense, Druyun's direct report in the Air Force was to the head of acquisitions, Marvin Sambur.

As an independent military department, the Air Force ran its own show on the tanker deal with assistant secretary Sambur the nominal lead. Sambur reported administratively to Air Force Secretary James Roche and had a dotted-line reporting relationship to Under Secretary Pete Aldridge at AT&L for matters concerning acquisition management. Aldridge was the Department of Defense acquisition contact for the tankers.

THE NEW ADMINISTRATION wanted to resurrect the financial markets and the economy by opening up capital spending, and Roche and Sambur counted on that desire to support their deal. Few disputed the need for replacing the aging refueling tankers of the Air Force at some point in time, but as the program transitioned from a purchase to a lease it changed complexion and increased in price by $5 billion. Roche and Sambur arrived at Congress with what they thought was a lay down hand.

The refueling tanker deal, which began as a purchase of 100 units to set in motion the replacement of more than 400 in the active Air Force, had changed by 2002 to a proposal to lease 100. When congressional approval was not forthcoming in 2003, it became a mix of 80 purchased and 20 leased. When the hint of irregularities materialized that same year, the program was frozen to initiate a search for the guilty. Eventually Congress, the Pentagon, and the Justice Department began investigations, all because of Druyun's influence peddling with Boeing.

Boeing Company's operations had been pummeled by the downturn in airline business since 9/11, and Druyun had exploited its disadvantage. Boeing needed the tanker replacement transaction to resuscitate its business and keep its wide-body, twinjet 767 assembly lines operating. For her part, having arranged for employment at Boeing for family members, Druyun concluded her government service by arranging a position for herself. She retired from the

Air Force in December 2002 and started at Boeing the following month. In essence, she had left a mess.

Over and above the fact that Druyun wielded too much influence and eventually squeezed favors out of all-too-willing contractors was the fact that out-of-touch leadership, such as Air Force Secretary James Roche, tried to hurry the tanker deal through Congress. Roche's heart was in the right place in trying to provide the Air Force with needed equipment, but his energy was misdirected in pushing a flawed hand. In hindsight, with that single project amounting to almost an entire year's worth of capital expenditures for the Air Force, leadership should have exercised more oversight.

When the usual questions were raised by Congress, primarily in the Senate, Air Force leadership bristled. Trusting they had the unconditional support of the White House, they overplayed their hand. Instead of diplomacy, they used indignation. The four congressional committees with oversight responsibility were approached. Three panels, the House and Senate Appropriations as well as the House Armed Services, endorsed the deal, two of them without ever holding a single hearing. Getting the fourth committee to pass on the proposal would prove to be a bridge too far. In short order, the Senate Armed Services Committee led by chair John Warner of Virginia, ranking member Carl Levin of Michigan, and member John McCain of Arizona made sure everything screeched to a halt.

MIKE HAD ONLY BEEN INVOLVED on the periphery of the Boeing tanker transaction in 2001 and 2002 since Sambur and Aldridge were the two political appointees most connected with the proposal. Darleen Druyun, the professional staff member in charge of the tanker negotiations, was the chink in the acquisition armor. When she arranged a transaction that was not in the best interests of the United States, Sambur and Aldridge unknowingly became enablers. They assumed they had the best deal and were comfortable cutting corners and disregarding policy to expedite the transaction. Sambur's supervisor, Secretary James Roche, fell into the same trap but compounded the problem with a bit of his own influence peddling. When the deal soured, the policies less traveled became a flash point.

A review by the inspector general of the Department of Defense allocated primary accountability for the tortured tanker transaction to four individuals. The Inspector General stated, in part:

> …we concluded that Mr. Edward C. Aldridge, Jr., … Dr. James G. Roche, … Dr. Marvin R. Sambur, … and Ms. Darleen A. Druyun … were the primary decision makers within the Department of Defense and the Air Force who allowed the Boeing KC-767A tanker aircraft lease to continue moving forward.[133]

Under Secretary Pete Aldridge had signed a decision memorandum on the tanker transaction on May 23, 2003, approving the Air Force request to lease. Four days later, Aldridge resigned and Mike Wynne was appointed acting under secretary. The following day, Mike forwarded the decision memorandum, now under his signature, to the Office of Management and Budget. Caught in the switches as he transitioned to his new role, Mike was considered in the wrong for tacitly accepting Aldridge's decision.[134]

The review by the inspector general would pat Wynne on the back for raising concerns when he was principal deputy and slap him on the wrist for moving forward with the decision memorandum as acting under secretary. The inspector general stated:

> Additionally, Mr. Michael W. Wynne, as the Principal Deputy Under Secretary of Defense for Acquisition, Technology and Logistics raised concerns about the unit price and the conduct of an analysis of alternatives. However, he did not require the Air Force to follow the DoD Directive 5000 series after assuming the acting duties of the Under Secretary of Defense for Acquisition, Technology and Logistics.[135]

Had the Air Force performed an analysis of alternatives, it would have placed its proposal on the high road. Since it did not have an analysis of alternatives, little opportunity existed to evaluate Druyun's tanker lease before pushing it forward. Absent an analysis, the Air Force could have bolstered its position with a fairness opinion, a financial construct performed by an independent body that rendered a judgment as to whether an action appeared fair in light of the overall situation. Either an analysis of alternatives or a fairness opinion would have provided firmer ground for the Air Force and might have uncovered Druyun's influence peddling. But Air Force leadership did not want to slow down the tanker deal by waiting for an analysis of alternatives or any other review.

Up to the time that Druyun left the Air Force, the only substantive outside look at the tanker deal was a simple cost review by the Institute for Defense Analyses, an independent think tank. Issued in late 2002, that report advised that the Boeing deal appeared to be overcharging by about $21 million per aircraft. As a simple cost review and not a detailed analysis of alternatives, it was initially marginalized and ignored. The timing of the report also was problematic, as Druyun's negotiations had essentially preset the program—the die had been cast.

The reckoning? Druyun went to prison for her improprieties. Roche resigned as word of military ethics rules violations surfaced. Sambur, who would be challenged more for being careless than corrupt, followed Roche out the door. Michael Sears, chief financial officer of Boeing and Druyun's partner in crime, received a prison sentence. Phil Condit, Boeing's chief executive officer, resigned under a cloud of bad press. And the tanker project? It appears to be lurching to a conclusion.[136] What of Aldridge, the last of the four Defense Department individuals with primary accountability? He was the first to depart.

Edward C. "Pete" Aldridge was an intriguing fellow. An aeronautical engineering graduate of Texas A&M and Georgia Tech, he had been in and out of government service and defense industry positions for years. He became under secretary of the Air Force in 1981. In the mid-1980s, Aldridge was in training to be a space shuttle astronaut aboard the first launch from Vandenberg Air Force Base in California, but his mission aboard *Discovery*, STS-62A, was canceled after the *Challenger* disaster. He was promoted from his position as under secretary to secretary of the Air Force when the 15th in line resigned for personal reasons after only four months in office. Aldridge was the 16th Secretary of the Air Force, serving from 1986–88. He stayed until that December, bailing out just short of completing President Reagan's term.

He returned to government service 13 years later, under President George W. Bush but once again did not stay long. He served as the under secretary of defense for AT&L from May 2001 until May 2003. Aldridge leaving early was not a big surprise to many of the professional staff, since they knew from experience that a portion of political appointees would exit after the first 18 to 24 months.

No one was quite sure why Aldridge resigned. The military campaign in Iraq, the companion conflict to that going on in Afghanistan, began in March 2003. Undoubtedly, most of Secretary Rumsfeld's time was spent managing the wars from Washington. Aldridge might not have had a significant role in that effort and possibly felt left out of the major decisions and strategy sessions. So Pete Aldridge had his second short stay in the Office of the Secretary of Defense, but he left with a flourish.

While insiders had known for a period of time that Aldridge was leaving the Defense Department in May, just about none of his staff knew the announcement of a final lease agreement was coming. They found out the Boeing tanker lease was a done deal the same way everyone else did, by watching the announcement on television. Ninety-six hours later, Aldridge exited the building. While it was hard to make out why Aldridge left the stage in the middle of the first act, he had in fact walked off the field before the fight. And someone knew exactly how to orchestrate the approaching brawl.

ACTING FOR THE ARMED SERVICES COMMITTEE, Senator John McCain had cast a wide net in his investigation of the tanker dealings, trying to reel in everyone involved. In mid-2003, McCain was able to force out hundreds of damaging e-mails from the Boeing Company regarding the tanker negotiations. These e-mails, which showed Air Force leadership cozy with Boeing and biased against any alternative, cast the transaction as something less than arm's length. The e-mails also documented the fact that Mike Wynne had raised questions about the transaction.

Mike, who had become heavily involved in the tanker discussion by April 2003, had earned a measure of high ground by raising the issue of price on a number of occasions, both as principal deputy under secretary and even later as acting under secretary. The fact that Air Force Secretary Roche asked Boeing's help in pressuring Wynne framed Mike's position as more righteous than most.[137] But holding a patch of high ground did not mean Mike escaped the inevitable inquisition. The confrontation took place in September and November of 2003, when he appeared before the Senate Armed Services Committee, John McCain's home turf.

Mike provoked Arizona's senior senator on the issue of whether e-mails were subject to subpoena. While McCain was able to force out internal e-mails from Boeing, he was having less success with the Department of Defense. Whether Defense Department internal e-mails were subject to subpoena had not yet been decided in the courts. Mike's slice of the Boeing blame game was found to be just shy of inconsequential, but his position on e-mails would rouse the wrath of Senator McCain.

The Senate Armed Services Committee Hearing on September 4 was devoted solely to the lease of aerial refueling tankers. The hearing was split into two sessions, one open and one closed. At the open session, two panels of interested parties testified, placing prepared statements into the record. James Roche, Mike Wynne and the deputy director of the Office of Management and Budget made up the first panel. In closed session, Senator McCain grilled the parties on specific Boeing e-mails, such as one from June 23, 2003 that discussed putting pressure on Wynne. Subsequent to the September 4 hearing, the Armed Services Committee asked for Department of Defense e-mails on the subject. When the issue first reared, Deputy Secretary Wolfowitz set the policy of not sharing internal e-mails.

With this directive, it was not Mike's prerogative to release e-mails demanded by Senator McCain, and he did not. While Defense shared approximately 200 documents with the Senate

Armed Services Committee, it did not share pertinent internal e-mails. When a hearing on Wynne's nomination to be permanent under secretary of defense for AT&L was scheduled for Tuesday, November 18, Mike knew the subject would come up again.

He worked with the Pentagon deputy counsel to fashion a response for the committee. During the nomination hearings, McCain demanded release of the internal e-mails and Mike read his two-paragraph prepared statement, parroting Wolfowitz's policy.[138] While most senators on the committee quickly figured out Mike was responding with the advice of counsel, his answer still suffered the Sturm und Drang of John McCain. Senator McCain was infuriated, enough so that he suspended senatorial civility for a second, throwing a crumpled wad of paper in the nominee's direction.

JOHN MCCAIN WAS A MODEL to some and a Machiavelli to others. No matter the opinion, McCain was a force to be reckoned with in Washington. He was powerful, persuasive, and political. Senator McCain hailed from a family that had invested generations in the military. He could be petulant and picky, even prickly at times, but he was a man of much courage who made a down payment on his silver eagles as a prisoner of war in Vietnam.

With the standard six year term in Republican leadership on Armed Services looming, Senator John Warner was scheduled to step down as chair of the committee, making way for a new senator to lead, John McCain. Quite possibly, with an eye to becoming the party lead on the Armed Services Committee, McCain took a much greater interest in Mike Wynne's hearings before the committee for Pete Aldridge's seat as under secretary. When thwarted, Senator McCain's backup style was nothing but personal recrimination, where he used his political weight to crush people who stood in his way. Even though enough votes might have been found to clear Mike, McCain was having none of it. In fairness, Senator McCain was not the only one with a problem.

CHAIRMAN WARNER, ranking member Levin and other committee

members also expressed displeasure at the Defense Department for being nonresponsive. But the real hunt was undertaken by Senator McCain, who reserved nothing in his press to ferret out the e-mails.[139] Imagine Senator Levin's political reverie as he watched Republicans chew out other Republicans. It had to bring a smile to his face. In the end, Senator Warner appreciated Mike's quandary, noting that the decision was understandably "above your pay grade with the Secretary and the Deputy Secretary."[140]

Mike's position on the internal e-mails, certainly nonresponsive as far as John McCain was concerned, was undoubtedly part of the reason Senator McCain worked hard to hold up Wynne's promotion from acting to permanent under secretary for AT&L. In point of fact, with Defense holding e-mails hostage and the Air Force trapped in a shady tanker transaction, John McCain began holding up most civilian Pentagon nominations that fell under his purview. Mike Wynne was in a no-win situation.

WITH GOVERNMENT GRINDING SLOWLY to sort out the impasse on e-mails, Mike had work to do. After his rough go at confirmation in November 2003, he returned to his duties at AT&L and continued as acting under secretary. Secretary Rumsfeld asked him to focus his energies on the BRAC work for the department. Mike had worked around the edges of this program during the last half of 2003, organizing the department effort, but now he would take an even more active role as the primary effort quickened.

Mike originally came to be involved in the BRAC activity through the back door. Secretary Rumsfeld had written a memorandum on November 15, 2002, organizing the 2005 BRAC effort under two committees. He charged the Infrastructure Executive Council, chaired by Deputy Secretary Wolfowitz, with oversight and policy making. He gave responsibility for operating policies and direction in conducting the analyses to the Infrastructure Steering Group, chaired by under secretary of defense for AT&L Pete Aldridge. Aldridge circulated a letter on April 16, 2003, laying out the first in what was expected to be a series of policy memoranda implementing Secretary Rumsfeld's directions. Aldridge resigned his position the following month and by June 27, it would be Acting Under Secretary Mike Wynne issuing memoranda on BRAC 2005.[141]

BRAC's purpose was the rationalization of the nation's military infrastructure. Due to the change in defense requirements brought on by the end of the Cold War and the politics involved in transforming the military, Congress had set up a series of commissions to review the country's inventory of installations and recommend action. This was realignment and closure. It was an evergreen project, reinstituted every few years after the Pentagon had a chance to implement the changes recommended by earlier commissions. Process was the linchpin, as the aim was to have more transparency in deliberations conveyed through a series of meetings and reviews with the communities. This was especially necessary because any changes, especially closings, often had dramatic influence on the surrounding community and impacted jobs, commerce, and federal funds flowing into the area.

The first commission was established in 1988, followed by commissions in 1991, 1993, and 1995. The fifth and most recent iteration was charged with instituting a round of realignments and closures in 2005. The process called for the Department of Defense to recommend a package of closures and realignments. The list would be forwarded to an independent commission appointed by the president for analysis and review. The commission's work included holding public hearings and making site visits to the installations under review. The commission forwarded a revised and final list to the president for his approval, after which the package was sent to Congress. Mike's job had been assembling the vested interests and marshaling the internal Department of Defense effort to develop the background work in preparation for the recommendations.

As chairman of the Infrastructure Steering Group, Mike orchestrated the endeavor through a series of meetings, knowing full well that, if he wanted to retain the decision-makers and influence centers, he had to control the meetings. At any particular time, hundreds of meetings were being held in the Pentagon. If he expected the major players such as the military department assistant secretaries and the service vices to attend his, Mike had to ensure meetings did not dissemble into long, drawn out affairs where little was accomplished. If that happened, Mike knew he would secure the vice chairman of the Joint Chiefs of Staff, at that time General Peter Pace, only once or twice before the vice chair would begin sending proxies and deputies. Mike started off on the right foot and never had to turn back.

Mike launched the effort with weekly meetings, keeping them to 60 minutes in duration. Mike did not play games when it came to BRAC, he took the commission's work seriously and made sure everyone else did too. Mike wanted to push past the paper and accomplish something lasting. He would allow nothing to vitiate the work of the commission.

Not exceeding one hour became an obsession, but it earned the respect and unreserved commitment of the participants. Most of the organizational effort came in late 2003, and the real ground work was fashioned in 2004. With background material in hand, the individual military departments were able to develop their plans and programs for closures and realignments.

ONE DIFFERENCE WITH the latest iteration of BRAC was the careful consideration of the concept of joint basing. This notion essentially meant combining the administrations of two or more operations to garner savings, which fit right in with BRAC deliberations. In studying opportunities for realignment or closing, it became obvious that many different service installations were within fence-line proximity to each other. If joint administration arrangements could be reached, savings would result. But dissimilar operations and cultures often barred the way to achieving success.

Army units generally train on a particular base and then decamp and deploy in operations around the world. Air Force units often train and operate out of the same home base. For the Navy's part, units generally train and operate out of carrier-based fleets, rather than land-based airfields. Emotions, rivalries, and loyalties all come into play in any discussion of joint basing. In time, 26 installations would be realigned into a dozen joint-base operations but not without a great deal of negotiating about the cultures and customs.

Hickam Air Force Base and the Navy's Pearl Harbor, essentially a fence apart, exemplified the philosophical hurdles. Pearl Harbor was a deep-water naval base and shipyard. The Navy's primary concern was the 39 ships and submarines that called Pearl Harbor home. The Navy wanted the Air Force to just transfer Hickam to their care. The locus of the cultural divide addressed air operations. Most Naval air operations were performed from carriers, while the Air Force operated solely out of airfields such as Hickam. The Air Force maintained Hickam in immaculate shape, since they needed to ensure their aircraft didn't ingest anything into the engines. This clean culture had to be maintained.

Differences were worked out, and Joint Base Pearl Harbor-Hickam, with the Navy in the lead, resulted. As lead, the Navy was charged with providing installation support for the entire joint base. In the larger view of things, everyone shared. Each service department gave up control at select installations and increased responsibility at others.[142] Much of the early discussion on joint basing took place while Wynne was de facto head of AT&L.

As the individual plans and joint basing evolved into a department program, Secretary Rumsfeld gave his blessing. President Bush then recess-appointed the BRAC commission for review. The president appointed Anthony Principi, his former secretary of veterans affairs cabinet member, as chairman of the 2005 BRAC commission. Mike Wynne changed hats and became the advocate, delivering and defending the recommendations to Principi and his BRAC commission. Mike had a bit of history with Tony Principi.

PEOPLE OFTEN RECALL their whereabouts during momentous events, such as President Kennedy's assassination. Mike had a clear recollection of his activities on September 11, 2001—cast as 9/11 forever after. Mike was at Edwards Air Force Base north of Los Angeles that day discussing acquisition programs and planning F-22 Raptor testing. Principi was on vacation in San Diego, about 200 miles to the south. As a cabinet member, Principi was immediately recalled to Washington for a meeting scheduled for September 12,

Under Secretary of Defense for Acquisition, Technology, & Logistics Michael Wynne briefs reporters on the BRAC recommendations at the Pentagon on May 13, 2005. *Source:* Department of Defense photo by Tech. Sgt. Cherie A. Thurlby, United States Air Force. Released at www.defense.gov/dodcmsshare/ newsphoto/2005-05/050513-F-7203T-008.jpg.

but getting a flight was problematic on the 11th when the entire airspace over the United States was locked down. Mike faced the same difficulty, but it turned out they had a common denominator.

Principi was friends with one of Wynne's neighbors from Mike's rocket days at Space Systems in San Diego, so the two men already knew each other. Mike called flight operations at Edwards to see if anything was going east and found out that Principi had commandeered from the Marine Corps a brand new Cessna UC-35 Citation to fly back to Washington. After a telephone call or two, Principi graciously agreed to travel via Edwards and collect Mike for the trip back east. The pickup was made, and the two were en route to Washington when they encountered mechanical trouble with a brake line on the UC-35. The Marine pilots headed for Whiteman Air Force Base outside Kansas City, Missouri, where the B-2 Spirit stealth bomber fleet was based with some of the longest runways available. Once grounded, they were safe and secure but still only halfway to Washington.

As Principi reviewed the dwindling alternatives, along came a

Lockheed C-130 Hercules fluttering through the air with a shipment of medical supplies headed for Dover Air Force Base in Delaware, less than 100 miles east of Washington. As it was the only aircraft headed east, Principi and Wynne climbed aboard for the 1,100 mile outing. They flew the night sky in that four-engine propeller aircraft, droning on at a cruise speed of barely 300 miles per hour and arrived at Dover in the early morning hours of September 12. Principi had a car waiting for him and headed off to Washington. Mike found some place to lay his head at the Air Force base, undoubtedly with a smile as he remembered his work as a young Air Force officer on the gunship version of the C-130 airframe. Mike had shared an adventure with Principi, someone who would turn out to be his BRAC evaluator four years later.[143]

WHILE MIKE WORKED on BRAC duties throughout 2004, his nomination floundered in a parallel world, mired in the e-mail dispute between the Defense Department and the Senate. Ever since Mike's confirmation hearing in November 2003, Senator McCain continued to press for release of the e-mails in question. A few months after the hearing, the Arizona senator put Secretary Rumsfeld on the record regarding the e-mail policy. Rumsfeld laid out the Department of Defense position in hearings before the Armed Services Committee on February 4, 2004, saying in part:

> There is a longstanding practice in the Department of not turning over internal documents that reflect the opinions of our employees as they advise senior decision-makers. Electronic mail, like any other document, is subject to this principle.[144]

Senator McCain had been in pursuit of the truth about the Boeing tankers for two years before Secretary Rumsfeld's statement. This dated back to February 12, 2002, in hearings with Secretary Roche and March 19, 2003, with Under Secretary Aldridge. After February 2004, Senator McCain continued the quest, submitting written questions for Mike Wynne in hearings before the Senate Subcommittee on Readiness and Management Support held on

May 13. The relentless attention Senator McCain paid the tanker lease finally softened the Defense Department position on e-mails.

After Mike's testimony in May 2004, Deputy Secretary Wolfowitz changed the policy and approved the release of internal e-mails, with the names of federal employees below the decision-making level redacted. Taken together, the Boeing and Defense Department e-mails did not display Air Force leadership of Roche and Sambur in a favorable light. Senator McCain, under postcloture debate before the full Senate on November 19, 2004, laid out the entire mess with the Boeing tanker lease.[145] Coupled with the holdup of civilian nominations, the e-mails eventually helped force the civilian leadership of the Air Force out of government the following January.

DURING THE FIRST QUARTER of 2005, as much of the smoke from the Boeing tanker debacle dispersed and a large part of the BRAC work was completed, Mike began looking at his alternatives. He had been principal deputy for A&T for two years and acting under secretary for AT&L for two more. He had essentially had a hand in running the place for four years by this time. With the Armed Services Committee holding up important Defense Department personnel decisions, it did not appear Mike was ever going to be named under secretary.[146] Given the circumstances, he considered offering his resignation to Secretary Rumsfeld to do his part to resolve the impasse.

Mike had a meeting with Secretary Rumsfeld, "I have some news to share."

Rumsfeld responded that he also "had something to say."

Ever the parliamentarian, Mike allowed the secretary to go first. Rumsfeld began talking about nominating Mike to secretary of one of the military departments, possibly the secretary of the Air Force position that had been open since January. Mike parried with the obvious fact that they were having trouble achieving under secretary and that he should probably make room for other nominees. Secretary Rumsfeld rejected the notion out of hand and offered that he could procure both under secretary for AT&L and secretary of a military department for Mike. "You've earned them."

Mike had become a cog of some import in the Pentagon machine.

After so many retirements in the Air Force, forced or otherwise, leadership in the service was lacking. Operating with its second acting service secretary in 90 days and no confirmed under secretaries for space or acquisitions, the Air Force needed a measure of acquisition acumen. To address this, Mike at A&T was assigned decision-making authority on 21 major acquisition programs of the Air Force.[147] While Rumsfeld worked on Wynne's prospects, Mike focused on Air Force procurement. The secretary of defense had a plan.

To fill a portion of the vacancies so that the government could keep functioning, President Bush relied heavily on recess appointments when nominations were being held up. During the administrations of both President Clinton and President Bush, partisanship in Congress was so bitter that each side often had trouble achieving confirmation for its nominees. Both President Clinton and President Bush each recess-appointed more than 100 positions during their eight years in office.[148] So recess appointment was more than a rarely used prerogative. Many believe that the power of recess appointment granted by the Constitution (Article II, Section 2, Clause 3) allowed nominations stymied because of politics to be advanced on merit. Secretary Rumsfeld kept his word to Mike Wynne.

Rumsfeld talked with John Warner and Carl Levin of the Senate Armed Services Committee regarding his recommendations to the president for the under secretary of defense for AT&L position. Senator McCain was also brought into the discussion. Mike had been the acting under secretary since 2003, and his nomination to permanent under secretary had languished in front of the Senate Committee and was eventually returned to the president. The president now wished to nominate Ken Krieg, the director of program analysis and evaluation, to the position. So the wheels of government were set in motion to recess-appoint Mike Wynne, without objection, to permanent under secretary of the area he had been managing for the last two years, and simultaneously nominate his replacement.

Senator McCain had played a major part in holding up Mike's nomination to permanent under secretary. It had been one more bit of pressure he could exert. But with the Air Force secretary and assistant secretary out, McCain eased up on the harangue. The senator wasn't comfortable reversing his position on Mike's nomination, but he did not object to Wynne's recess appointment. Mike Wynne was recess-appointed by President Bush on the first of April 2005. His appointment represented one of 33 nominations during President Bush's term that previously had failed to be confirmed by the Senate and had been returned to the President.[149]

At the same time Mike was recess-appointed, President Bush announced his intent to nominate Ken Krieg as under secretary of defense for AT&L. Krieg was one of the Defense Department employees Roche and Boeing had tried to silence. Similar to Mike, Krieg had come out against the Boeing lease. For the time being, Mike was the full-time under secretary of defense for AT&L. He officially had moved up to number five in the starting rotation, a position of some note. As observed in *Technology Review*, published by Massachusetts Institute of Technology, Mike was one of six men who collectively oversaw "more than $120 billion in research and technology investments in the United States."[150]

McCain seemed to want to put right parts of the past. In hearings before the Senate Subcommittee on Airland held on April 6, 2005, during a pause in the proceedings Senator McCain went on the record.

> As the witnesses are taking their seats, I would like to just make a personal comment to Secretary Wynne. I thank you for your service. I appreciate your willingness to stay on in your position. We may have had differences from time to time, but I think you have always been honest and honorable in your attempts to do what's best for the United States and the taxpayer, and I thank you, Secretary Wynne.[151]

MIKE'S NOMINATION, failed confirmation, and subsequent recess-appointment represented the machinations for just one nominee during an active period in President Bush's administration, especially as it concerned the Department of Defense. During the month before Mike's recess appointment, the president had nominated Deputy Secretary Wolfowitz to the World Bank. When Wolfowitz was confirmed in June, the president promptly nominated the sitting secretary of the Navy, Gordon England, to replace Wolfowitz. While retaining leadership of the Navy department, England immediately took up the mantle of acting deputy secretary of defense under Rumsfeld. England remained one step ahead.

The other half of Mike Wynne's conversation with Secretary Rumsfeld—secretary of one of the military departments—still lay on the table. While Mike's name was reportedly bandied about for secretary of the Navy, England's influence as deputy secretary probably encouraged Rumsfeld to focus on the Air Force. After all, a house-cleaning had occurred in the Air Force. During the months following January 20, 2005, when James Roche resigned his secretariat, there had been four different acting secretaries of the Air Force: Peter Teets, Michael Montelongo, Michael Dominguez, and Pete Geren.

In the end, Ken Krieg was confirmed and appointed under secretary for AT&L effective June 6, 2005, relegating Mike back to principal deputy under secretary for A&T, a position he had not yet vacated. Wynne's term as full under secretary spanned from April 1 to June 6, 2005, a period of but nine weeks, even though he had been the de facto head of the department for more than two years. Placing country first, it was to Mike's credit that he agreed to step back down and remain in his position as principal deputy. He was also following the advice of others.

Once the new under secretary was seated, it would just be a matter of time before Mike looked to the future. The secretary of defense prevailed upon him to remain in place. The possibility of a service department was enhanced if one was currently serving in a senior Pentagon position. Ten weeks later, on August 16, 2005, President George W. Bush nominated Mike Wynne to be the next secretary of the Air Force. On September 6, two days after Mike's 61st birthday, his nomination was sent to the United States Senate, whereupon it was immediately referred to the Committee on Armed Services.

TRUSTING PERSONAL DUTIES only to his closest friends, Mike asked his old pal, Ron Schillereff, to sit with Barb through the confirmation hearings for secretary of the Air Force, just in case they were as feisty as the last ones. Mike's and Ron's paths had intersected once again, this time in the Washington area, right at the turn of the millennium. The thread that kept the families connected through the years was Barb's Christmas letters. When the two families met again, it was as if they hadn't missed a step. Barb's seasonal letters had anchored their relationship. Ron had served as one of Mike's personal references when Mike began in the Department of Defense. For these latest hearings, his job was to remind Barb every once in a while during the confirmation to breathe and relax.

THE SENATE ARMED SERVICES COMMITTEE held hearings on October 6, 2005, for both Mike Wynne's nomination to secretary of the Air Force and Don Winter's nomination to secretary of the Navy. Only a select few will ever know what lobbying went on during this period, but it is certain some took place. It could be that people with whom Mike shared a little history, such as Nick Chabraja or retired General Gordon Sullivan, both General Dynamics board members, might have come out in support of his nomination. After all, they probably played a part in Mike's introduction to government service. These leaders knew their way around Washington and carried influence.

On October 27 the committee ordered the nomination to be reported favorably, which Committee Chair John Warner did on the floor of the Senate that same day. On October 28, 2005, Mike's nomination was confirmed by the Senate in a voice vote. Now confirmed, he entered political limbo. The president nominates, the Senate confirms, and then the president officially appoints. Consented by the Senate, Mike was in an indeterminate state awaiting the president's finishing stroke.

By early 2006, the Secretary of Defense had changed his military department leadership. Left to right: Francis J. Harvey, 19th secretary of the Army, began in his post in November 2004; Michael W. Wynne, 21st secretary of the Air Force, started in November 2005; Secretary of Defense Donald Rumsfeld; and Donald C. Winter, 74th secretary of the Navy, assumed his station in January 2006. *Source:* Department of Defense photo courtesy of Wynne Family.

Chapter Seventeen

Nudging Serendipity

When Mike passed the confirmation stage on Friday October 28, 2005, he was in Washington. He knew that President Bush usually took care of personnel matters on Tuesdays, which would be November 1 at the earliest. Mike figured, with a bit of planning, he could be sworn in as the secretary of the Air Force (SECAF) during the first few days of November at a place of his choosing. He knew just the place.

Still acting in the capacity of principal deputy for A&T, Mike had been scheduled to give a speech in California during the last weekend of October. It was a simple matter to add a side trip on the return flight. Mike arranged a stop at the Air Force Academy as a civilian visitor to review the academy research laboratories. He landed alongside the Colorado Front Range on Tuesday, arriving late in the day. He had set aside the remainder of the week in Colorado Springs.

As expected, the president handled personnel matters on Tuesday, and Mike Wynne's official appointment was announced by the White House on Wednesday, November 2. Mike had put Barb on notice of what might happen, so it was with relative ease that the arrangements fell into place, with a big assist from Acting Secretary of the Air Force Pete Geren.

Geren had a car swoop by and pick up Barb on Thursday morning, bright and early. After a short drive to the airport, Pete accompanied

Barb on the flight to the Air Force Academy in Colorado Springs. Arrangements were made for Mike to be sworn in on Thursday, November 3 at the noon meal formation, certainly a first. The plan was for the swearing in to be held in front of the entire cadet wing, 4,200 of the nation's finest. As it happened, even more people attended.

General T. Michael "Buzz" Moseley, who had been a partner with Mike on the leadership committee for BRAC hearings, had been sworn in as the chief of staff of the Air Force two months earlier. General Moseley, soon to be Mike's partner once again, had called a meeting of his four-star generals to be held at the Air Force Academy right around the time his friend was awaiting the president's appointment. General Moseley and his four-stars were at the academy for the swearing-in of Wynne as the new SECAF.

Pete Geren, as the acting SECAF, introduced Mike to the cadet

Acting Secretary of the Air Force Pete Geren performs the official swearing in for the new secretary Michael Wynne on November 3, 2005, with Wynne's wife, Barbara, holding the ceremonial Bible. In remarks about the occasion, Geren noted to the assembled crowd that this was hallowed ground for Wynne, inasmuch as his brother lay but a half a mile away in the academy cemetery. It was nice of Geren to mention this connection because Mike probably would have struggled with such an emotional statement.
Source: United States Air Force photo by Charley Starr.

wing and then conducted the swearing-in before the assembled group in Mitchell Hall on Thursday, November 3, 2005. While another swearing-in ceremony would be scheduled back at the Pentagon in Room 3E869 for Monday, November 28 to accommodate family and friends and associates who had missed the Colorado Springs event, the November 28 festivities were really just a Washington welcome reception.

Michael Walter Wynne now held the highest civilian job in the Air Force department, responsible for 370,000 active-duty servicemen and women, another 180,000 in the Air National Guard or Air Force Reserve, and a complement of 160,000 civilian employees. Responsibility for a military community of more than 700,000 called for a leader of substance.

With Secretary of Defense Donald Rumsfeld looking on, Under Secretary of the Air Force Ronald M. Sega administers the second swearing in of the new secretary of the Air Force with Barbara Wynne once again holding the ceremonial Bible. This occurred at the Pentagon on November 28, 2005.
Source: Department of Defense photo by Robert D. Ward. Released at www. af.mil/shared/media/photodb/photos/051128-D-9880W-035.jpg.

MIKE ALLOWED HIMSELF a weekend of euphoria and then dove back into work, none too soon it turned out. One of the first things to reach SECAF Wynne was a political projectile, a personnel problem that threatened to undermine much of the work at the Air Force Academy. The academy had from time to time been accused of discrimination, racial and religious. Cadets also had been accused of cheating on tests and, on at least one occasion, of sexual assault. These were serious breaches that threatened to damage the academy's reputation. As Mike Wynne rose to SECAF, claims of intolerance also reached a pitch. It revolved around an academy legend, Coach Fisher DeBerry.

Fisher DeBerry, the head football coach at the Air Force Academy, brought fame to the program in winning more than 160 games during a 23-year span. A deeply religious man, DeBerry had caused difficulty for academy leadership by proselytizing to student athletes in 2004. During the football season, he had even placed a poster in the locker room referring to Team Jesus Christ. This was done during a period when the academy had already been accused of religious intolerance. Jump forward to October 2005, on a football weekend when Air Force lost to Texas Christian University, Coach DeBerry made a few postgame remarks that were considered racially insensitive—shades of Jimmy "the Greek" Snyder.

General John Regni, newly installed as academy superintendent and a former student of Mike Wynne's, became heir to the issue. The problem had to be attacked on two fronts, one at the academy level by the superintendent and the other across the entire Air Force by the SECAF. Regarding the former, the superintendent suspended Coach DeBerry and after another occurrence, ushered in his retirement, which quietly came to pass in late 2005. With respect to the latter, SECAF Wynne also had some work to do.

Claims of religious intolerance had been around for a number of years but seemed to reach a crescendo when Mike became SECAF. As a religious war, it was a crisis that had to be waged and won. Mike worked with his staff and brought in outside counsel including a variety of non-Christian advisors. He knew that what they came up with had to pass muster with the commanders in the field. Taking his cue from the founding documents of our nation, to neither promote nor suppress, Mike worked hard to frame tight regulations against religious intolerance of any kind. His staff's first draft of more than seven pages was trimmed, cropped, and slashed to a single page. After all, it had to be brief and intelligible as posted in orderly rooms around the world. If no one read it, and they would not read seven pages of regulations, the effort would be useless. Mike believed one could not legislate religious tolerance, not even in seven pages. He sent his one-page revision back to the staff, and they were horrified as he had usurped their prerogatives.

Mike received feedback from General Moseley, who felt the dispatch a bit confusing but believed that the message was something with which all commanders could cope. Buzz Moseley had read it—one commander down and a few hundred more to go. Mike had the document stamped draft even though he would not entertain changes and sent it out. It never came back. He intended to review it one year out and then two years out. It never came back. He had drawn a line in the sand.

MIKE HAD ALWAYS BELIEVED that leadership could not fairly take credit for achievement unless they began with goals. That is just how he acted early in his secretariat, listing eight goals on a laminated card that was distributed to every member in the service.

… Foster Mutual Respect and Integrity
… Sustain Air, Space and Cyberspace Capabilities
… Provide Persistent Situation Awareness
… Joint and Battle Ready Trained Airmen
… Continue to improve the Total Force quality of life
… Open, Transparent Business Practices; Clean Audit
… Foster AFSO21 across the Total Air Force
… Every Airman an ambassador to all we meet and serve

Success then was a simple matter of rising to one's own standard.

As Mike progressed in Pentagon positions through the years, his expertise had become more of a flow of ideas. As he rose, it was less of the day-to-day hiring and firing and more of the broader envisioning of the future. Mike had grown with his positions. While he may not always have verbalized an intention perfectly, he knew exactly where he wanted to take his Air Force. Mike could just as easily discuss world events with a four-star general as he could inquire about a certain procedure with a tech sergeant on the flight line. Through it all, most everyone could find some level at which they could connect with Mike.

ANOTHER EARLY ISSUE during Mike's secretariat was the Air Force budget, but he already had done preliminary work in this area. Between his nomination and swearing in, he had taken the liberty of having a budget conversation with Gordon England, the acting deputy secretary of defense. Mike knew that with a little luck in front of the Armed Services Committee England would soon be his boss. Put plainly and directly, Mike had asked Gordon what he expected to see in the next Air Force budget. The deputy secretary felt the Navy and the Air Force were too big and that human resources in both the active duty and national guard had to come down. Mike had provisional marching orders.

His next step, still in the interim period, was to explore options with the Air Force staff. Since Mike was not yet official, the work was done on the basis of comments he might have made, if asked, with respect to various budget items. Mike offered suggestions, and the Air Force could then take whatever action it thought best. At least the service had the benefit of knowing what side he would come down on with regard to fundamental questions. In the end, Mike had the opportunity to make a series of comments and suggestions as the 2006 Quadrennial Defense Review of the military department was put together.

Once official, Mike reconnected with staff and progressed immediately to the nub of the now-familiar budget issue. In conjunction with Chief of Staff General Moseley, they sketched out the manpower decline that would be enforced across the active duty roster and through the national guard ranks. The reduction entailed approximately 40,000 airmen. In addition to the retirement of hundreds of aircraft, numerous productivity efficiencies would be undertaken to make up for the workforce changes.

Leadership instituted the companion program, Air Force Smart Operations in the 21st Century—AFSO21. This was the process improvement and culture change that was packaged with force reductions to generate efficiencies. Mike knew that cutting personnel did not mean pilots just fly longer. He and Moseley were also banking on the fact that the deputy secretary had indicated the Air Force could keep the savings generated and apply them to the many other areas of need.

What of the deputy secretary who was still operating as the acting? He had been nominated to permanent deputy in June 2005, but his nomination had pined away for six months. Finally, in 2006 the president resolved the impasse and recess-appointed Gordon England to the position, effective January 4, the Wednesday after New Year's Day. With new Navy and Air Force service secretaries and a new permanent deputy secretary all within 60 days, the president had changed a significant part of the leadership in the Defense Department. Little did anyone know but within the year the defense secretary himself also would be replaced.

❧

THE AIR FORCE MIKE WYNNE FOUND when he stepped in as secretary at the end of 2005 was much changed from that of Vietnam War vintage of 1973 when Mike last served as an active-duty Air Force officer. Since that war, the Air Force had participated in a number of conflicts and skirmishes around the world. While the small conflicts in Grenada, Libya, and Panama in the 1980s had little need for major deployments of Air Force assets, the larger conflicts of Desert Shield and Desert Storm in the Persian Gulf War, the Yugoslav War, and the Kosovo Conflict during the 1990s saw more participation. War was now practiced from a strategic standpoint. Concepts such as mobilizations and partnerships rose to the fore. Everyone sought swift success and direct disengagement.

With Iraq effectively bankrupt after a decade of fighting with Iran, it wanted to rejuvenate its finances by cutting oil production and driving up prices. When its Arab neighbors rejected the plan, Iraq came spoiling for a fight and took up arms against next-door nation state Kuwait. The opening thrust of the military response—Operation Desert Shield—was a defensive move by the United States to prevent Iraq from extending its conquest into Saudi Arabia. This 24-week-long protective umbrella also safeguarded the buildup of armed forces in the region. The second phase—Operation Desert Storm—was a United Nations–sanctioned coalition of 34 nations whose purpose was to liberate Kuwait. The action began with 38 days of sustained aerial bombardment leading to a ground assault. The air operation entailed more than 100,000 coalition sorties. The U.S. Air Force deployed more than 50,000 servicemen and 25 fighter squadrons, mostly stationed at air bases in Saudi Arabia. The land campaign that followed was a short one, as it took but 100 hours for the assembled coalition to drive Iraqi forces from Kuwait. Iraq was defeated, but Hussein was left in power. Following the ground offensive, the Air Force would partner with allies in patrolling two United Nations–mandated no-fly zones—Operation Northern and Southern Watches—for the next 12 years.

The conflicts in the Balkans had been centuries in the making and played out through much of the 1990s. Marshall Tito had held sway over Yugoslavia since the conclusion of World War II with an iron rule. With his death in 1980 a power vacuum arose. No one proved able to hold together the federal units of Yugoslavia: Bosnia and Herzegovina, Croatia, Macedonia, Montenegro, Serbia, and Slovenia. After years of skirmishes, a more organized effort at ethnic cleansing took place during the Yugoslav War between 1991 and 1995, much of it centered in the war in Bosnia and Herzegovina. Repression reached a new flash-point with the diaspora of tens of thousands of ethnic Albanians fleeing hostilities in Kosovo in the late 1990s, leading to the Kosovo Conflict in 1999. In both periods of cruelty, NATO forces undertook the enforcement of no-fly zones, provided close air support for ground troops, and eventually scheduled outright bombing operations. NATO intervention in the Balkans during the decade would record more than 100,000 air sorties. These included a major role for the U.S. Air Force, largely with aircraft from air bases in Italy.[152] Political pressure and the bombings eventually compelled a peace.

The new millennium found the Air Force on the wing and once again engaged in combat, with war in Afghanistan in 2001 followed by Iraq in 2003. Whether routing out al-Qaeda operatives such as Osama bin Laden and Taliban supporters, searching for weapons of mass destruction, or chasing Saddam Hussein underground, both wars were a response to the September, 2001, terrorist attack on the twin towers of the World Trade Center in New York City. All along the continuum from the Vietnam War, the Air Force had moved steadily up the technology curve, always on the ready.

In Afghanistan U.S. Air Force units were heavily involved in eliminating Taliban targets and providing close air support for American and British ground troops working with the Afghan Northern Alliance, all aimed at ousting the regime. As Kabul and Kandahar fell, militants fled east into the rugged mountains bordering Pakistan. While the battles continued to ebb and flow, the main thrust of the Air Force mission diminished. The war would progress in cave complexes and mountainous regions where ground forces took the lead. By the end of 2005, the U.S. Air Force had flown thousands of sorties in Afghanistan, mostly during the opening months of the campaign. Its force would have even more application in Iraq.

In Iraq, Air Force units played a significant role early on in neutralizing threats, especially command and control centers, with an opening thrust under the soon-to-be-famous moniker of "shock and awe." Air Force technology had figured out how to see through sand storms, easily taking out Iraqi armor in the desert and stopping any Revolutionary Guard movement. Instead of calling in field artillery, friendly ground forces simply called in air strikes to deactivate the enemy. With fertile lands between the Tigris and Euphrates rivers delineating much of ancient Mesopotamia, Iraq was otherwise pool-table flat until one reached the northern mountains of Iraqi Kurdistan. Absent a place to hide, the hunt quickly moved into the cities where it became house-to-house warfare. The beginning of hostilities in Iraq was an air war with thousands of sorties, but once fighting moved to the cities, the Air Force role decreased.

The wars in Afghanistan and Iraq were shaped by the power of the Air Force. The enemy hid in caves, traveled in small groups, and came out mostly at night because the Air Force ruled the skies. The Air Force had risen to the point of being able to wage war on the enemy almost invisibly. This was the state of affairs in the Air Force as Mike Wynne rose to the leadership with General Moseley

❖

EARLY ON AS SECAF, Mike found an Air Force under assault by a system that essentially had forgotten why it needed an Air Force. Part of this could be traced to the fact that the Air Force by dint of its technological advancements had somewhat distanced itself from the other services in its approach to accomplishing warfare. What differentiated the Air Force from the other services was its reach, aptly described by its moniker "Global Reach...Global Power." Each of the services had power, but the Air Force could deliver its particular brand of power anywhere and on short notice.

Mike didn't want the Air Force to fight the fair fight, rather he wanted to dominate the fight. The plain fact was the Air Force was pushing the technological frontier faster than its main customer the Army was able to accommodate. The Air Force role in both Afghanistan (Operation Enduring Freedom, OEF) and Iraq (Operation Iraqi Freedom, OIF) remained but had lessened. The Air Force had been shifting its focus to the use of unmanned aerial vehicles (UAVs).

Looked at in a larger context, the ICBM was simply an unmanned extension of the Air Force long-range bomber. In fact, the Air Force referred to early versions of the Atlas ballistic missile as its pilotless bomber program. The next evolution was drones, which were simply unmanned versions of spy and reconnaissance planes. Drones were quickly becoming unmanned versions of fighter-bomber aircraft in their ability to deliver ordnance.

While the Air Force was fighting a very technological war, the Army was fighting a brutal, blunt-force war. As the Air Force pushed a technology toward the Army, it oftentimes received a knee-jerk no or another specious argument. When the initial response later became a yes, the Air Force would be behind schedule. The experience with UAVs was a perfect example. In fact, an ongoing argument existed between the Air Force and Army concerning what altitude each would command.

In the 2005 budget, the last one Mike worked before rising to SECAF, the Air Force had asked for a significant increase in funding for the unmanned vehicle program. The Army lobbied successfully against the increase, largely because of its own efforts with similar systems, so the Air Force lost the majority of the funding request. Step forward a year, and the Air Force and Army were fighting between themselves as to who would control the assets over the battlefield, with particular application to unmanned vehicles.

The Army had its own version of UAVs such as the Shadow and other tactical instruments that were smaller devices. The Air Force had the larger machines such as the Predator and Global Hawk. The services were arguing over altitude. Mike felt the Air Force should control the battlefield assets above a pre-agreed altitude; below the standard, the Army would have total control. The Army, on the other hand, felt it should have control of all assets including helicopters, spotter planes, and drones in the air space above the battlefield.

Mike supported a compromise of establishing an independent UAV post that would have responsibility for determining appropriate altitude levels. In select cases, the Army might only need roof-top control, whereas in others it might need air space up to 13,000 feet and higher for operations. An independent UAV executive could broker these decisions depending on battlefield conditions. This idea took form and bubbled up to the deputy secretary of defense with a measure of interservice support but when the proposal was ready for signature, the Army had a change of heart and lobbied to kill the concept. The Army didn't want its hands tied in the middle of an Army-directed war. The compromise died.

When Defense Secretary Rumsfeld left in 2007 and was replaced by Robert M. Gates, the Army and Air Force were still battling the UAV issues. As the new leadership reviewed budgets, it found that the Air Force had not appropriated enough for UAVs. Not realizing the Air Force had had its UAV budget request cut, the new secretary told them to ratchet up the allocation. Fair or not, surely in the back of Secretary Gates' mind was the notion that the Air Force was caught standing still on an important issue instead of taking the lead. Besides the fact that not enough UAVs were in service, no one had enough personnel to fly them.

While Wynne and Moseley could take a measure of satisfaction in that their ideas for UAVs were gaining traction and their argument for control of the airspace was taking root, they understood complaining about the false image of the Air Force dragging its heels would not accomplish anything. The old saying, "the second liar never has a chance," applied. The sum and substance was that the Army-directed wars in Afghanistan and Iraq may not have utilized Air Force capability as much as it might have, so Wynne and Moseley worked to change that.

Another facet of the problem was that the Air Force often operated from distant commands, far from its customer. For example, the Air Force ran its Taliban hunting operations from Creech, Nevada, about 40 miles northwest of Las Vegas. So the Army often did not view the Air Force in its larger responsive form and only saw it in small battles where it was called for air support and it either arrived on the scene in timely fashion or not. At times, the Army and the media didn't give the Air Force much credit for even being a part of the fight. So another of Mike Wynne's missions was articulating a coherent story of why the Air Force played a crucial role in the tactical fight. He was the front man for the Air Force.

DURING THE WYNNE-MOSELEY LEADERSHIP, the Air Force released its 2006 Vision Document in February. "Lasting Heritage… Limitless Horizons: A Warfighter's Vision" really dated back to the previous December when the Air Force first verbalized a new mission. This policy statement replaced the 1997 version, "Vision 2020," and clearly stated the "Heritage to Horizon" perspective of a modern Air Force. Cyberspace was unmistakably identified in the statement where Secretary Wynne offered, "I see the mission of the Air Force as: Deliver sovereign options for the defense of the United States of America and its global interests – to fly and fight in Air, Space, and Cyberspace".[153] This report was published under the auspices of the Secretary of Defense Donald Rumsfeld.

Wynne and Moseley changed the Air Force, the military, and the defense community when they put cyberspace in the Air Force mission. The Air Force always was a high-impact, high-visibility service. It was widely respected as being the dominant force when put into use. When Mike put cyberspace into the mission, right next to air and space as part of the Air Force warfighters' domain, it was no accident. He felt it was important to use the word cyberspace. The term had been used before, but Mike put it in a military context.[154]

Articulating cyberspace was a major challenge for the beltway, and it made a big splash. Everyone soon flocked to the term and the concept. America thought it was a good idea too, but now countless corners in Washington caught the "not invented here" virus. Many thought the Air Force was trying to take ownership of cyberspace, and they fought the possibility. Wynne and Moseley had grabbed the stage and leapt out ahead of everyone else. While they probably harbored thoughts that someone might say "nice job in bringing the issue out into the open" or "how can I help," they really received nothing but grief for the idea. Just the same, it galvanized the beltway.

"Sovereign options" and "cyberspace" were lofty notions. Quite possibly, conceptualizing cyberspace as an Air Force issue was a bit parochial as its application had implications across the board for the government. But that meant Secretary Wynne and Chief of Staff General Moseley were a bit ahead of their time, not wrong. After enunciating the cyberspace focus of the Air Force, Secretary Wynne and General Moseley pushed it forward in November 2006 by establishing a provisional cyber command, designated as the Eighth Air Force out of Barksdale Air Force Base in Louisiana. One month later, Robert Gates replaced Donald Rumsfeld as secretary of defense.

Pretty quickly, the other military departments lobbied the new secretary of defense against the Air Force taking the lead, posturing that cyberspace was a universal issue. The result of this interservice rivalry would have each service working on its own version. But the Navy's main interest remained protecting its impressive but vulnerable surface fleet, especially the aircraft carriers. The Army's focus remained the land battle, the close fight. Meanwhile, the Air Force continued to have a focus that was a bit more strategic, and many would agree that it still leads in cyberspace. Wynne and Moseley's vision of cyberspace forced the services to take up its call.

MIKE WYNNE INVESTED much of his time advocating for important programs, such as a new long-range bomber, an air dominance escort, and a second engine for the F-35 joint-strike fighter. The higher-level question was whether the country was to have a strategic air force. Secretary Gates often seemed to favor missiles at the expense of manned aircraft, but replacements for the ageless B-52 Stratofortress and the aging B-1 Lancer were needed. Air dominance was required to clear the skies for the high value assets of intelligence, surveillance, and reconnaissance being developed to film and command the battlefield; the F-22 Raptor had no peer in that category. With the joint-strike fighter expected to sell in the thousands of units, reliability and cost control came with an alternative engine.

As THE HIGHEST CIVILIAN OFFICIAL in the military department of the Air Force, much of Mike's time was spent in public appearances, dedications, memorials, and other official duties around the globe. His availability for these events always provided a welcome diversion from Washington. Mike's visits would take him to Al Udeid Air Base outside Doha, Qatar; to Kirkuk, Balad, and Ali Air Bases inside Iraq; and Bagram Air Base near Kabul, Afghanistan. Other journeys included travel to Kadena Air Base on the island of Okinawa, and Ramstein-Landstuhl and Spangdahlem Air Bases in Germany. His outings to the installations stateside brought him through practically every state in the union, including Alaska and Hawaii.

In May 2006 Mike officiated at the retirement of the last Lockheed C-141 Starlifter that had ferried Vietnam prisoners of war (POWs) out of Hanoi in February 1973—the "Hanoi Taxi." The occasion was a Vietnam POW reunion held in Fairborn, Ohio

Secretary of the Air Force Michael Wynne visits airmen at Kunsan Air Base in South Korea (above) and Yokota Air Base in Japan (below) in March 2006. In the Kunsan photo, the WP tail code on the fighter in the background signifies the Wolf Pack of the 8th Tactical Fighter Wing, which transferred to Kunsan from Ubon Thailand in 1974 after nine years of service in Vietnam. *Source:* United States Air Force photos (above) by Senior Airman Joshua DeMotts released at www.af.mil/shared/media/photodb/photos/060322-F-0000D-001.jpg and (below) by Yasuo Osakabe released at www.af.mil/shared/media/photodb/photos/060324-F-0938O-104.jpg.

and memorial flights were hosted by nearby Wright-Patterson Air Force Base personnel. The assembled former-POWs were given the opportunity to have a last ride in the C-141, which most of them did, wheelchair bound or not. Mike Wynne was on the first of three flights, accompanied by Medal of Honor recipient, Colonel George "Bud" Day, U.S. Air Force, Retired.

Left to right: Chief Master Sergeant Rodney McKinley, Secretary of the Air Force Michael Wynne, Chief of Staff General Michael Moseley, and Secretary of Defense Donald Rumsfeld meet prior to the dedication ceremony of the Air Force memorial in October 2006. *Source:* Department of Defense photo by Staff Sgt. D. Myles Cullen (reference 061014-F-0193C-002).

Mike had the privilege, along with his partners Chief of Staff General Michael Moseley and Chief Master Sergeant Rodney McKinley, of officiating when the 270-foot-tall stainless steel spires of the Air Force Memorial in Arlington, Virginia, were dedicated in October 2006. He also had the distinction of being SECAF during the 60th anniversary of the founding of the Air Force. This occurred on September 18, 2007, and was celebrated around the world. Mike's ceremonial activities included a few that were even closer to his heart.

HE CHANGED THE SLANT on one Air Force tradition. Instead of simply commemorating hardware such as aircraft and consecrating them as memorials, he altered it so the tributes also honored Air

Force personnel. During his time as SECAF, Mike proudly dedicated a memorial to his brother's August 1966 flight. This remembrance took the form of an F-4C Phantom II placed on static display at Gate 2 of the Arnold Engineering Development Center at Arnold Air Force Base, located in the approximate center of the triangle formed by Nashville and Chattanooga, Tennessee and Huntsville, Alabama. The families of both airmen, Larry Golberg and Patrick Wynne, attended the dedication on November 27, 2007.

Mike also made it a point to increase and improve communications with Air Force personnel. He wrote monthly letters to airmen across the globe to keep them up to date on what was happening in their service. Barb Wynne had the opportunity to address the airmen in one of the bulletins. While staff had insisted only the SECAF address formal messages to the airmen, Mike's Christmas 2006 correspondence consisted of 29 words from him, bracketing a two-page dispatch from Barb that offered thanks and appreciation to airman and their families around the world. Collectively, these letters acted as a morale booster, making sure everyone knew how important they were to the overall effort.

MIKE ELECTRIFIED THE AIR FORCE with his personal brand of leadership, presence, and message. Few before him began their association with such commitment and enthusiasm. His theme was leadership rather than management, and this carried high military value.

Mike did not become a leader on the day he rose to secretary of the Air Force. Leadership was a skill he had learned and honed on his way there. Having been in the Pentagon for 4 years and having held successively more demanding corporate positions for 20 years prior to that, Mike had had a long time to prepare for his secretariat. While he was open to suggestions and discussion, he knew where he wanted to take the Air Force. He was after all a trained military officer with the habit of command. He was not a bureaucrat who issued directives down the line but rather one who was first in command and out in the trenches. Mike could speak both fluent Army since he was a graduate of West Point and fluent

Secretary of the Air Force Michael Wynne presents Tech. Sgt. Travis Crosby with the Silver Star for gallantry in action while deployed in Operation Iraqi Freedom. *Source:* United States Air Force photo by Dave Davenport. Released at www. af.mil/shared/media/photodb/photos/060626-F-9841Z-001a.jpg.

Air Force as a former Air Force officer. This spoke to his credibility.

Mike's command presence was revealed through his travel pace and schedule. As secretary of the Air Force, he spent anywhere from one-third to one-half of his time out of the Defense Department and in the field. His presence was felt worldwide. Mike's travel pace was unrelenting. Unlike others who are more comfortable working only at the staff level, Mike established his presence down to the troop level. He would speak just as easily with airmen at a maintenance shed on any Air Force base as he would with troops deployed in harm's way in Afghanistan or with Predator pilots working in the States. This was his time with the airmen of his service.

By his message and policies, Mike brought his values right out into the field; Air Force personnel would continue to be warfighters, would be the dominant force in any fight, and would make smart and intelligent use of technology. These powers, which had been earned by Americans in previous generations of war, would be placed in the hands of the president who could choose when and where to use them. Mike Wynne was clear in his priorities. By consistently giving this simple message, he changed the Air Force.

MIKE ALSO HAD OCCASION to extend the thread from his past at the Military Academy. Service academies were a shared experience that lived on. In the ensuing years, many mini-reunions were held. Hundreds of graduates came back, and a number of widows even kept their ties. The academy experience forged a formidable bond among young men at an impressionable stage in life, a bond found among individuals who had participated in and persevered through something bigger than themselves. As their independent lives unfolded, their connections joined and rejoined.

When Norm Gunderson, one of Mike's West Point classmates, was hospitalized and near his end, he left instructions for no visitors, which Wynne promptly ignored in paying his respects. In the course of a reflective moment during the visit, Norm said of all the people who would ignore the instruction, Mike would have been tops on his list. For the funeral procession of classmate J.T. Unger of electrical switch fame, Mike arranged for an official escort, a car with mars lights, for the interment at Arlington National Cemetery. These experiences took place decades after graduation. But not every memory was a sad one.

West Point classmate Frank Hartline's daughter, Carey, became an F-15 fighter pilot, call sign "Mamba." She took her air combat maneuvering instruction from Mike's brother-in-law, Al Guarino, at Tyndall Air Force Base and sometime later flew Secretary Wynne through the range in Alaska in his only high-performance flight as SECAF. Also on a cheerful note, Mike reunited with another classmate, Jack Wheeler, who came to work on his staff in the Office of Secretary of the Air Force. At every opportunity, Mike supported the grand mission of the five service academies, ever mindful of the important role they played in the defense of America through the education and training of commissioned officers.

Secretary of the Air Force Michael Wynne (left) and Air Force Chief of Staff General Michael Moseley (right) welcome Secretary of Defense Robert Gates to Peterson Air Force Base in Colorado on May 29, 2007. Secretary Gates was in town to deliver the commencement address at the Air Force Academy graduation. *Source:* Department of Defense photo by Cherie A. Thurlby (reference 070529-D-7203T-023).

IN THE FINAL ANALYSIS, Mike Wynne was accused of spending too much time planning for the next war. This was a bit disconcerting because Department of Defense people were usually accused of planning the last war all over again. Rather than focusing on the next war, some quarters believed the leadership of the Air Force should have been concentrating on the current war. That was a significant point of departure.

Whether framed as future wars versus current wars or strategic projection versus tactical engagement, the fact was that Mike Wynne and Robert Gates were not like-minded. Mike's forceful personality and presence in the Pentagon, in front of an ever-widening and accepting audience, was becoming a problem. It was starting to appear as if two secretaries of defense existed. The dichotomy might have been too much at odds for repair. Mike was asked to step down from his secretariat.

Sometimes serendipity is repeated, and sometimes the messenger is recognized. Mike was out in Colorado Springs at the Air Force Academy. Deputy Secretary Gordon England and his wife, Dottie, flew out to meet him. In a brief encounter, England told Mike that he was being asked to step down as secretary of the Air Force. To some it would appear that by bringing his wife, the deputy secretary made this just another routine stop on one of his jaunts around the country. This did not reflect the grace one might have hoped for at this level of government.

It just wasn't a polished, professional dissolution of the Air Force civilian leadership. Staffers knew that England was flying out of Washington that day on a trip. Later they heard on the newscasts that England had fired Mike Wynne. Few in the office believed it; they thought it was just the media getting another story wrong. They never thought they would hear about it first on television. Mike's brother, Pete, even called the Pentagon and Mike's secretary, Caroline, told him she thought it was just a mistake. But it wasn't. The firing caught many people by surprise. Not very classy but the intended consequence was the same. Mike was being pressured to retire and Gordon England probably volunteered for the mission.

As Secretary Gates cast about for personnel concerns, Mike's obstinacy concerning the F-22 Raptor probably made him an easy target that stubbornly projected on Gates' heads-up display. If anyone knew Mike Wynne and could offer an opinion on him, it was Gordon England since they had a 30-year relationship. As deputy, England undoubtedly counseled Secretary Gates, and likely offered the opinion that Mike Wynne was a man of strong principle. If one didn't appreciate Mike's position, one would have to live with it or move him out. But personnel issues were rarely as simple as they appeared on the surface, and this one might have been a case where an issue spiraled out of control for England.

Whether Gordon England had it in for Mike Wynne or just started a ball rolling that he couldn't stop remains a question mark. Early in 2008, Mike had squabbled with Gordon over the F-22

Raptor and would not back down on the matter. This was an issue of particular importance to Mike and his Air Force. Deputy England, acting on behalf of Secretary Gates, was pushing to kill the F-22 program, and Mike Wynne was doing what he could to thwart that effort. After the two had their disagreement, much of the support Mike had previously enjoyed in the department was withdrawn. Since Mike wouldn't play ball, they froze him out of the game.

Mike was too vocal and too outspoken in front of the administration on the F-22 issue. He didn't know his place. After the falling out, any little problem with the Air Force department would end up shoved in Mike's face. For example, as SECAF, Mike did not have a deputy for awhile, even though the position carried one. But his leadership decided to hold that position ransom, rather unspoken punishment for his stand on the F-22. Mike Wynne wasn't rowing in the same direction anymore, and it was coming to a head.

When Mike was informed that he was on the outs, it was late in the president's last term. It would have been easy for the department to wait for a change in administration or even just three months or so for the budget work to be completed. But Mike was not sitting on his hands. He was in Congress collecting votes to keep the F-22 Raptor production lines open and was getting close to beating the opposition. He was also unrepentant, which is why department leadership couldn't wait for a change in the presidency. They had to move Mike out of the way. They needed him on the sidelines.

MIKE WYNNE HAD GONE ON RECORD, opposing the secretary of defense, on December 20, 2007. The Defense Department had submitted to the Office of Management and Budget a financial plan for the Air Force for fiscal year 2009. Having worked to accommodate a variety of positions, Mike had asked his Defense leadership for only two special considerations. When both were rejected and not provided for in the final submittal, he refused to "take possession of the budget."[155] Mike would not accede to what he believed was flawed policy.

Mike reached his limit when it came to closing the F-22 production line and not allowing a reallocation of funds for the

Long Range Strike, the replacement for the 20 aging Northrop Grumman B-2 Spirit long-range penetrating stealth bombers. With Mike refusing to support the Air Force budget as submitted, Secretary Gates faced a challenge. He could not allow an individual service department to move forward with an unfunded list of priorities, yet the secretary knew full well that he could not muzzle Air Force leadership who would be asked by members of Congress for opinions on the budget.

Secretary Gates did not fire Mike Wynne for his December 20, 2007, letter. That would have been a message to all concerned that speaking truth to power was not tolerated. But as indications of how Congress was leaning on the 2009 budget emerged, it was obvious that the Air Force was going to do very well on its issues. Gates had to do something, but he had to be a bit circumspect with his response.

HAD MIKE WYNNE BEEN on the same wavelength with Secretary Gates, he would have made a better ally than adversary. Mike had been around long enough that he had gained a measure of gravitas with Congress. He had become a player, but Mike's relationship with Robert Gates was different from that with Donald Rumsfeld.

Secretary Rumsfeld, who was a bit of an intimidating personage, always made the effort to gather his senior people together from time to time. Rumsfeld was more socially conscious and more of a team builder. Rumsfeld and his wife, Joyce, threw an annual Christmas party without fail. In addition, twice a year when the combatant commanders were in Washington, their wives would join together with the service secretary wives and the Rumsfelds would sponsor the group at a Defense Senior Leaders Conference spouse luncheon.

Robert Gates followed a different path. He had come to government service through the Central Intelligence Agency. While recruited by the agency during graduate school in the 1960s, Gates found himself in an Air Force uniform for two years, serving as a second lieutenant in the Strategic Air Command. But intelligence was his vocation, where he served for 26 years with a career culminating as the director. After a period out of government, during which he became president of Texas A&M University, Gates returned to Washington in 2006 as secretary of defense.

Unlike Rumsfeld, Secretary Gates was more a man of all work and did not invest much of himself in the social scene in Washington. He did little if any entertaining of his service secretaries and deputies. Secretary Gates' wife, Becky, pretty much remained at their previous home in College Station, Texas, and only occasionally ventured up to the Washington area. The fact was Mike Wynne was not very close with Secretary Gates. But there was more to this story.

CHAPTER EIGHTEEN

Service Summons Sacrifice

ON THURSDAY, JUNE 5, 2008, Secretary of Defense Robert Gates asked for and received the resignations of Air Force Chief of Staff General T. Michael Moseley and Air Force Secretary Michael Wynne, the number one uniformed and civilian Air Force leaders. General Moseley, the 18th Air Force chief of staff, retired in a ceremony held at Bolling Air Force Base in Washington on July 11, concluding 37 years of service to his country. Mike Wynne, the 21st secretary of the Air Force, had his retirement ceremony on June 20, 2008 at the Air Force Memorial in Washington.

The party line was that the forced resignations were due to a "lack of effective leadership oversight" in the handling of the nation's nuclear mission. As one might expect, the truth is always more involved than the sound bite. The espoused reason, while of sufficient gravitas, oversimplified the situation. The "triggers to Taiwan" and "nukes across America" incidents belied the motivation behind the removal of Moseley and Wynne from office.[156]

The triggers to Taiwan episode was a shipment of MK-12 forward-section assemblies in place of helicopter batteries. The significance was that these assemblies were used as part of a trigger mechanism for a specific nuclear weapon in the U.S. arsenal, one delivered on a Minuteman ballistic missile. The cargo was from Hill Air Force Base in Utah to the government of Taiwan. In March 2005, eight months before Mike Wynne became secretary of the Air Force, the fuze assemblies had been shipped from Warren Air Force Base in Wyoming and stored incorrectly at Hill, setting the stage for the mix-up. The August 2006 errant consignment from Hill contained four electrical fuzes in cone-shaped containers. While in its unadorned simplicity the delivery was an inventory problem, no excuse could be made for missile detonators being sent in place of helicopter batteries. The fact that it took more than a year to figure out the mistake simply compounded the folly. In the final analysis, the shipment contained no nuclear materials, the detonators could not be used to trigger other weapons, and American citizens were not in jeopardy.

The nukes across America shipment of six cruise missiles tipped with nuclear warheads was unquestionably a fundamental breach of nuclear handling and security measures. Raytheon AGM-129 advanced (stealth) cruise missiles were being ferried to Louisiana for decommissioning, part of a U.S. program of arms control treaty compliance. Scores of AGM-129 cruise missiles had been ferried from Minot Air Force Base in North Dakota to Barksdale Air Force Base in Louisiana, a dozen at a time on twin pylons mounted under the wings of B-52 Stratofortresses. The missiles were mounted six to a pylon, with dummy training warheads. On the date in question, instead of training warheads one pylon carrying six cruise missiles had been left with nuclear, albeit inactive, components installed. Negligent as this three-hour flight on August 30, 2007, was, these nuclear warheads were unarmed, incapable of being armed, and had not left the control of U.S. Air Force personnel or facilities. But this was not a minor lapse.

Two disturbing aspects emerged, the potential discharge of radioactive substances and the possible theft of the weapons. Had the B-52 crashed or somehow dropped the cruise missiles, the resulting accident could have released a cloud of toxic substances that would have posed an inhalation and contamination hazard. No risk of a nuclear detonation existed, but the high explosives in the warhead could have explosively dispersed weapon-grade plutonium into the atmosphere, the essence of a "dirty bomb."[157] Another concern was the remote possibility of someone stealing the weapons, either at an accident site or when in Air Force custody, facilitated by the fact that the Air Force didn't even know the nuclear weapons were missing for 36 hours. These scenarios were highly unlikely, but that wasn't the point. No matter how improbable, for a brief time a window of weakness was open.

The shipment of nuclear cruise missiles across the United States prompted Air Force leadership to scrutinize lapses in policy and procedure that led up to the incorrect handling of nuclear materials. A series of remedies were instituted, as was a strong measure of discipline throughout the ranks. Seventy airmen were disciplined. Of those, more than 60 airmen lost their certification for nuclear duty, as did the 5th Bomb Wing at Minot Air Force Base, and four colonels were relieved of their commands.[158] When news of the Taiwan incident appeared in March 2008, the second embarrassment for the Air Force, Secretary Gates reached his limit and stepped in.

Secretary Gates felt the Air Force was dragging its feet on addressing these troubling issues. The secretary commenced his own special investigation of the Air Force handling of sensitive nuclear components. Admiral Kirkland Donald, the head of naval nuclear propulsion, was given the task of directing the special review. Once in receipt of Admiral Donald's assessment, Secretary Gates had his opening to drive out the Air Force leadership that quite frankly had been a thorn in his side on any number of issues.

The two Air Force embarrassments were perfect notes on which Secretary Gates could dump the leadership because they involved "nuclear," and no one really wanted to talk in detail about anything "nuclear." The Taiwan incident ruffled U.S. China relations. The transcontinental trip of cruise missiles may have been interpreted as saber-rattling to North Korea and Iran. Who knows? Quite possibly, the details in the Donald Report would have been such a humiliation for the Air Force that the leadership decided to quietly shoulder the blame entirely in order to retain a measure of respect for their beloved service branch. It is difficult to determine since the version of the Donald report that was made public was extensively redacted.[159]

The fact was a slow deterioration had occurred in America's focus on its nuclear mission. This did not begin with Moseley and Wynne. It began more than a dozen years earlier when the Cold War ceased having relevance. In September 1991 President George H. W. Bush initiated an arms-reduction program with the stand-down of America's strategic bombers from nuclear alert. All of a sudden, the nuclear mission began to fade. A few even date the weakening to the 1980s, when Air Force leadership concluded a subtle transition from a bomber-general culture to a fighter-general culture. The salient point is that the loss of focus on the nuclear mission dates back at least to the early 1990s, but it did not explode into headlines until the mistakes of the mid-2000s.

While the public sacking of both military and civilian leaders in a single service branch at the same time was unique, it certainly wasn't Secretary Gates first foray into house cleaning. Secretary Gates had been routing out all things even remotely associated with Donald Rumsfeld and his team since he replaced the former secretary of defense in December 2006. Secretary Gates' rise to the larger stage of the Defense Department was accompanied by the massacre of enough top level careers to compare with Michael Corleone's resolution of family business in *The Godfather*.

Army Secretary Francis Harvey was forced into resigning in March 2007, after the deplorable conditions at Walter Reed Army Medical Center were exposed. Secretary Gates did not recommend the chairman of the Joint Chiefs of Staff, Marine General Peter Pace, for a second term. This resulted in General Pace's retirement after only two years as chairman, the shortest serving chair in four decades. The deputy chairman of the Joint Chiefs of Staff, Admiral Edmund Giambastiani, followed General Pace's lead and took retirement, after the same two years. The head of U.S. Central Command, Admiral William Fallon, also retired in 2008, rather spontaneously and some say with Secretary Gates encouragement.

So the Wynne and Moseley dismissals were not news. Nor were they solely due to the Taiwanese or cross-country shipments. The relationship between the Air Force leadership and the Department of Defense had been on shaky ground for months, and the Air Force missteps masked much of the back story. Mike Wynne was hired to do a job in November 2005 by Donald Rumsfeld and 13 months later was inherited by Robert Gates. The fact is many reasons led to the forced retirement of Mike Wynne.

Bob Gates' Department of Defense and Mike Wynne's Air Force diverged on a number of fronts. Besides Secretary Gates' desire to distance himself from everything Rumsfeld, first and foremost, the two men differed on the overall strategy for the service. In addition, a number of decisions made and actions taken by Mike Wynne as service secretary were probably perceived as slights by the Department of Defense. No matter how one views the situation, a number of complaints against the Air Force garnered the sympathy of Secretary Gates. These included a promotion for Terryl Schwalier, a position on cyberspace, an apparent change of heart on joint-basing, and a comment about peer competitors.

❧

Strategy Departure

Men and women blessed with long careers accumulate "baggage" as they make friends and accrue enemies through the years. Service to one's country is no different. Few run the gauntlet of public service for any length of time, operating at the highest levels of government and politics, and come out without at least a bit of baggage. Mike Wynne undoubtedly began public service in Washington as many others. At first, he wanted to do no harm in all that he did. After a few years of service, his do no harm evolved into do some good. The final transformation was to have an agenda of one's own, and Mike had designs for the Air Force. While in concert with Rumsfeld, his plans were in competition with Gates.

After years working with Congress, both in business and in government, Mike was popular, vocal, and persuasive on the Hill with things he wanted to accomplish for the Air Force. He knew exactly which aisles to walk and what offices to visit when he wanted to promote something. The fact that a new secretary of defense had been named did not change Mike Wynne's mission. He was not beholding to Bob Gates. He was subordinate but not submissive. Over time, this independence came off as being a bit of a "lone ranger" or as others might phrase it, "doing your own thing." Secretary Gates wanted more attention paid to the current wars going on in Iraq and Afghanistan, the insurgent wars. Air Force leadership was more focused on its strategic vision, the future wars. This divergence was no more neatly exemplified than by the poles-apart positions on Lockheed Martin F-22 Raptor fighter aircraft purchases.

The F-22 Raptor advanced tactical fighter was the Air Force replacement for its aging F-15 Eagle. With roots dating back to 1981, the F-22 reached production in 2001 and 183 had been ordered. The Air Force requirement was for 381 aircraft but funding stymied further orders. In lieu of more orders for the $140 million Raptor, Defense had been shifting funds to the $80 million F-35 Lightning II, a product of the Joint Strike Fighter program.

The F-35, with development dating back to the 1980s, was demonstrated in 2000 and had its first flight in 2006. It was intended to replace the F-16 Fighting Falcon and F/A-18 Hornet. An advanced tactical fighter in its own right, the F-35 was second only to the F-22 in performance. To maintain its role as guardian of air superiority, the Air Force continued to push for more funding of the F-22 program. The Raptor was not the deciding factor in relations between the Defense Department and the Air Force service branch, it was just emblematic.

The justification for the F-22 was that it carried overwhelming authority just sitting in the American arsenal. As the current world bullies, North Korea and Iran, shake world opinion and fears, they provide the best case for the Air Force F-22 Raptor. Each time a rogue nation threatened, the simple existence of the F-22 sitting on the end of a runway somewhere in the world would give them pause to reconsider their options. The political value of the F-22 was significant. High-altitude missiles guaranteed the ability to respond and defend, but the F-22 appended the capability to mount an offense. The global reach provided by the F-22 and its ability to deliver ordnance anywhere in the world at any time made many sit up and take notice.

The United States achieved such reach only by being far in advance of everybody else on the technology curve, which was what the F-22 brought to the table. This was the part of Secretary Wynne's consistent message that envisioned the Air Force dominating any fight it joined. With his industrial experience, Mike was acutely aware of how long it took to position new equipment on the flight line and ready for airmen. He was incessant in pushing for a realistic approach to planning for new weapons. The Air Force possessed the edge with the F-22, and Mike fought to maintain the advantage.

The F-35 was a compromise, designed and built for eight different nations and three different services. In cutting F-22 production, the Defense Department trimmed deterrence and played to China's strength, a huge standing army. Chinese strategists wanted to see the United States cut its air-dominance fleet because China could compete with occupation forces not technology. For America, it was the ability to strike, not to defend, that provided deterrence.

Following Secretary Gates' lead, Defense was cutting back on F-22 purchases and increasing troop recruitments; this was the essence of taking down strategic deterrence and building up invasion and occupation forces. With its budget threatened, Air Force leadership responded by approaching congressional supporters with regard to particular programs. If the Air Force could not increase its F-22 fleet, it wanted to at least keep the production lines open. Defense leadership wanted the lines closed.

Mike felt the planned Defense Department cuts were inconsistent. The fact was that most American military tactics were centered on the U.S. Air Force gaining air superiority. The F-22 Raptor guaranteed this posture. Shutting down the production lines bet everything on the F-35. In the end, Air Force leadership pushing ahead with internal agendas was at odds with the Pentagon's plans and procedures. It was starting to seem as if the secretary of defense had to compete in his own house.

Schwalier

Another point of divergence between Mike Wynne, as secretary of the Air Force, and Robert Gates, as secretary of defense, revolved around a terrorist bombing that happened in Saudi Arabia almost a decade before either of these men rose to their positions. While the facts became shaded with political, media, civilian, and military overtones in the ensuing years, it proved to be another speed bump in Mike Wynne's relationship with his boss.

Khobar Towers was a building complex in Dhahran used to house servicemen from the U.S. Air Force's 4404th Wing (Provisional). The Air Force presence was in continuing defense and support in the Middle East after the Gulf War of 1990–91. The 4404th was the Air Force unit responsible for enforcing the no-fly zone established in southern Iraq after Operation Desert Storm. Hundreds of servicemen and civilians were housed in the Khobar Towers complex. Air Force Brigadier General Terryl Schwalier was assigned commander of the 4404th in July 1995.

Terryl Schwalier, a 1969 graduate of the Air Force Academy, had had a long and distinguished career in the service of his nation. A command pilot with more than 3,400 hours flying time, he had seat time in the F-4 Phantom II, F-16 Fighting Falcon and F-111 Aardvark. In 1995 Brigadier General Schwalier had been selected for promotion to major general. The Senate approved his promotion on March 15, 1996. In line with official procedure, the Air Force set January 1, 1997, as his official promotion date. Sandwiched between these dates, terrorists set off a huge truck bomb next to the Khobar Towers housing complex on June 25, 1996.

Schwalier, as commander of the 4404th Wing, had instituted what he felt were reasonable and appropriate precautions at Khobar Towers. This included roof top guards and concrete perimeter barricades around the 30-building complex. When the truck bomb convoy failed to gain entry at the main entrance, it drove around to an adjacent parking lot, where it could move within 70 feet of one building, and detonated the bomb. The resulting blast killed 19 servicemen and injured hundreds.

In the ensuing tempest, one position held that Schwalier's foresight prevented more bloodshed while the opposite view held that he did not institute enough precautions to protect his men. Schwalier's promotion to major general was summarily canceled by President Clinton's secretary of defense, William S. Cohen. Schwalier, his career shattered, retired soon after. Was Schwalier unfairly made a scapegoat or fairly held accountable?

During the next decade, review boards were impaneled and legal opinions sought, the sum and substance of which was inconclusive or at least at odds. One position held up the October 1983 bombing of U.S. Marines in Beirut as the benchmark, where neither Navy Captain Morgan France nor Marine Colonel Timothy Geraghty were held responsible.[160] The contrasting view used the October 2000 bombing of the U.S. Navy destroyer USS *Cole* (DDG-67) in the Yemeni port of Aden as the appropriate yardstick, where Commander Kirk Lippold was forever after denied promotion to captain. Schwalier felt he was being measured against the wrong standard, especially since no one had ever been "held accountable" for 9/11. In the end, the U.S. Air Force felt it had the legal authority to pin that second star on Schwalier and the Pentagon felt it had the legal authority to deny the promotion.

On December 20, 2007, the Air Force Board for Correction of Military Records ruled that the denial of Schwalier's second star in 1997 was improper and ordered his promotion reinstated. As secretary of the Air Force, Mike soon found this order on his desk. He sought counsel from the Air Force attorneys who advised him that the Board was congressionally mandated and had powers of its own. They advised Mike that he played no role in the proceedings, unless he interjected himself in the deliberations. Mike chose to not intervene and to allow the ruling to stand, thus not thwarting Schwalier's promotion. This ruffled feathers throughout the Pentagon.

Secretary of Defense Gates felt that it was not Mike's decision to make or allow and that it was beyond the Air Force's legal authority to push through the promotion. Gates felt it was a Department of Defense decision. In March 2008, Mike Wynne was ordered to rescind the promotion. While the issue has not come up again, it was another example of Mike Wynne and Robert Gates being at odds on an issue. In the vernacular, Wynne was getting off the ranch again.

CYBERSPACE

Being at odds with Secretary Robert Gates was becoming a habit that sometimes rose from Mike Wynne being too vocal and articulate on issues. Operating the Air Force at the van of the services could foment problems for the Defense Department. Sometimes it resembled a wagon train traversing the plains, where Air Force leadership of Wynne and Moseley were so far out front on a number of issues that those bringing up the rear felt vulnerable. An example was the concept of cyberspace.

While Mike Wynne certainly didn't invent the concept, he and his service partner, General Mike Moseley, helped bring it to the forefront of Air Force planning when they established a provisional Cyber Command at Barksdale Air Force Base in Louisiana in 2006. They were early in the process. In fact, it was during the Pearl Harbor anniversary in 2005 when the Air Force leadership first added cyberspace to the mission with the words, "…to fly and fight in Air, Space, and Cyberspace." They wanted to begin controlling and taking responsibility for the tremendous flow of information throughout the service. When Secretary Rumsfeld was replaced by Secretary Gates, the Air Force kept moving full-speed ahead, but the provisional command was not allowed to become permanent.

To an extent, Wynne and Moseley's press for a cyber command, essentially the stage for the cyberspace discussion, was viewed as a power grab, and the secretary of defense couldn't have his subordinates grabbing the podium. It placed Secretary Gates in a reactive posture, rather than a creative one. But cyberspace was already in the Air Force mission and he really couldn't ask them to take it out, even though the intelligence community largely considered it a go at their turf.

The new defense secretary, with more than 20 years experience in the intelligence community, embraced the initiative but moved up implementation under his purview. Secretary Gates augured for a multiservice, cross-cabinet form of a cyber command. This was his solution to the upheaval on the beltway regarding cyberspace. It would be a two-step process.

On May 12, 2008, Deputy Secretary Gordon England issued a

memorandum which effectively defined cyberspace for the Defense Department. The practical effect of the note was to announce for all to hear that the Defense Department did not believe any single department should have authority over cyberspace.[161] This was the wagon master pulling hard on the team of horses to slow them up in their lather to cross the frontier. The objective bore fruit when the president announced his intention to create a cyber czar. In the final analysis, Wynne and Moseley were more than three years ahead of their time.   .

While it was a bit of kismet that England was in the role of talking head, the real absurdity was that Wynne and Moseley could not have agreed any more strongly with the notion that the conversation belonged in a larger frame of reference. It was their pushing that launched the issue to a grander stage. Air Force leadership gave it the boot in the butt it needed, since most everyone else was just conceptualizing cyberspace. A report prepared by the National Defense University, an institution funded by the Department of Defense, drew attention to the same dichotomy. The bona fides of the Air Force was obvious, as it was putting men, materials, and money in a new command. The report noted that "…it appears that the Air Force is not only 'talking' about cyberspace, it is 'walking' as well."[162]

Of course, focusing on the frontier in space was somewhat of a genetic predisposition for Mike Wynne. His father had a similar predilection with the U.S. missile program at both Cape Canaveral and General Electric. Ed Wynne, tagged a "space pioneer" in his 1997 obituary, might have even had a hand in helping select landing sites on the moon for the Apollo Program.[163] Weapons developers at their core, both were concerned with the possibilities in space.

Joint-basing

In moving from AT&L to secretary of the Air Force, Mike changed perspectives. While he still worked in the Pentagon, he was champion for a more discrete constituency, the men and women of the Air Force military department. As time progressed, he found that a few of the projects on which he worked earlier were changing as they reached the implementation stage. This was exemplified by joint-basing.

When joint-basing was originally studied through AT&L, the salient point was to have the administration of facilities that were in fence-line proximity centered in one service. But as joint-basing came up for realization, it looked as if bases were simply being transferred to other services. That was not the original intent, as the separate cultures were supposed to be preserved.

Mike saw the questions surrounding traditions and customs unanswered, and he began having reservations and making inquiries. His exploits slowed everything down and engendered disputes in the department. Absent support from the Pentagon, Mike pressed on with his vision and appealed to select members of Congress about the issue. When the May 2008 Supplemental Spending Bill was approved, it included provisions that effectively held up the execution of joint-basing until the culture questions were resolved.

While Mike's lobbying endeavors may have played a part in delaying implementation, his actions were viewed as more than an apparent change of heart. It was another case where Mike looked as if he was not on the team, and undoubtedly represented another silent issue widening the breach between Air Force leadership and the Defense Department.

Peer Competitors

Another perceived slight probably occurred in a conversation involving Mike Wynne and General Moseley in Secretary Gates' office. The secretary of defense was making a point in the course of a conversation—quite a big point—about peer competitors. This traced back to the dichotomy presented by the discussion of current wars and future wars.

Secretary Gates felt that America would not be fighting peer competitors in the future but would be facing peer weaponry. Given that train of thought, the secretary continued and concluded that he believed the country should be preparing to fight peer weaponry and not unnamed futuristic war weaponry that might never materialize or be a threat. This was a reasonable thought since America had spent 40 years preparing for a war that never came. Secretary Gates was simply driving home his focus on insurgent wars, rather than the Air Force's strategic vision of future wars. The conversation had been another subtle spat between Secretary Gates and the Air Force leadership of Wynne and Moseley.

But with that peer competitor comment, Mike warmed to the issue. He had experience on this subject that transcended "I feel" or "I believe." Responding off the cuff and probably to his own detriment, Mike shot back that he did not consider Vietnam to be a peer competitor, but the Air Force still lost more than 1,000 aircraft and the Wynne family lost their first-born son. The conversation slammed to a stop. Sometimes one's convictions come across identical to a slap in the face. Mike could tell that he and Chief of Staff General Moseley had crossed an unseen line. The conversation stalled and wrapped up a short while later.

As Wynne and Moseley left the secretary of defense's office, Mike turned to his Air Force partner and put forward, "I think you and I are history. I don't know when or how, but I think our number is up." The old axiom of a person having an intuitive feeling when they are going to be dismissed held true. When you work at a high level long enough and are in touch with the undercurrent of affairs, down deep you know when the proverbial ax is coming. It is not a total surprise.

❦

So why exactly was the Air Force leadership forced into retirement? Were they dismissed because of the two Air Force administrative errors, sending detonator assemblies to Taiwan and shipping nuclear-tipped cruise missiles across the midsection of the country? The Navy had been selected to explore the issues and write a report on the Air Force's handling of its nuclear mission. So the Navy went through the mistakes of the Air Force, fortunate that they could overlook nuclear shortcomings everywhere else.[164]

Admiral Kirkland Donald, who was in charge of looking into the errors, was a 1975 graduate of the Naval Academy with a distinguished career. He was appointed director of the Naval Nuclear Propulsion Program on November 5, 2004. In March 2008, Secretary Gates gave Admiral Donald the task of investigating the nuclear mishaps in the Air Force. After the report was issued, the leadership of the Air Force was ousted.

While Admiral Donald undoubtedly gave a fair assessment, he was under enormous pressure. When Donald was asked to lead the investigation into the Air Force nuclear troubles, it was a Hobson's choice because it came at a time when the Navy was trying to smooth over problems with its own nuclear responsibilities.

In October 2007, 11 Navy personnel aboard the SSN-767 *Hampton*, a *Los Angeles*–class nuclear submarine, were disciplined for fraudulent documentation and reports concerning the submarine's nuclear reactor safety inspection records. The implicated seamen did not perform required inspections and then falsified the records to cover up that mistake. In May 2008 the Navy's aircraft carrier USS *George Washington* (CVN-73), equipped with a pair of nuclear reactors for propulsion, suffered a massive fire while at sea that could have scuttled the vessel. The Navy later reported that the fire was preventable and repairs across eight decks and 80 compartments would exceed $70 million. In both cases, Secretary Gates reviewed inquiries. It was in this roiling atmosphere that Admiral Kirkland Donald undertook the study of Air Force nuclear blunders.[165]

The Donald Report was completed promptly and sent to Secretary Gates in May 2008. Shortly after Secretary Gates received the account, Wynne and Moseley were mustered out. Wynne and Donald handled their bit parts in Secretary Gates' play with class and without enmity. It was a compliment to both men. But the shipments were not the substance of the sacking. In truth, it was becoming impossible for Secretary Gates to run the Defense Department with Mike Wynne in the Pentagon.

THE TRIGGER ASSEMBLIES sent to Taiwan was an incident that began with a warehouse mistake, when parts were shipped from Warren Air Force Base to Hill Air Force Base. This took place months before Mike rose to secretary of the Air Force. The subsequent consignment from Hill to Taiwan, which happened two months after he took office, was simply a continuation of the first error. Confusing the issue was the fact that the international movement was not even an Air Force mistake, it was a Defense Logistics Agency shipment.

The cross-country move of nuclear warheads happened on Mike's watch, but was an ordnance inventory mistake, not a lack of senior leadership. Service secretaries do not personally sign off on each shipment of cruise missiles, but there are those who do and they were disciplined. For General Moseley's part, he was not even in the chain of command. The chief of staff's duties were to advise the president and secretary of defense, not run day-to-day operations.

The substantive reason was that Mike Wynne was too independent of his leadership in the Pentagon. He was a bit comparable to the Navy's Admiral Hyman G. Rickover, not in style but in substance. When Mike couldn't achieve what he felt was required by working through the Pentagon Department of Defense channels, he went over its head directly to Congress, where he was beginning to build a bit of a personal following. Mike was in good company. Air Force General Curtis LeMay had been accused of doing the same thing in clashes with his secretary of defense, Robert McNamara.

Mike Wynne was a powerful personality with a major message. His ideas and presence were not lost on Congress and those in national security. As Wynne and Gates thrust and parried over issues, staff members undoubtedly began to choose sides. The clear implication was that a number of people were beginning to display more deference to Mike.

Someone had to reel Mike back in to the fold or, absent that, install an associate more accommodating to the secretary of defense. With intractable disparity between the secretary's insurgent wars and the Air Force's technology wars, Secretary Gates wanted Mike on the sidelines. If he couldn't control him, at least he could curb him. Robert Gates and Michael Wynne knew the real reason for the dismissal, and both were gentlemanly enough to just let it drop. This is the orderly transfer of power in America.

Secretary Gates had lost control of the Air Force department leadership and had to wrest it back. Taken in this light, the dismissal was just business for Secretary Gates; it wasn't personal. He had to put his mark on the agency and establish his authority. While many would view this almost a patronage issue, the fact is principals usually prefer to name their own associates. It happens in business, politics, and government.

Was the secretary of defense wrong in forcing out the Air Force leadership? In point of fact, no wrong was committed. Secretary Gates had the authority and the mandate to change leadership, which he was doing throughout the Department of Defense. Donald Rumsfeld had had an eye towards the possibility of future wars and a focus on business executives in leadership. Secretary Gates reversed both courses.[166]

Secretary Gates' general impression was that the Air Force was already strong, too strong for what the nation required. The thought was that the United States could lower defense expenditures and development in select quarters where it was decidedly far ahead and redirect those funds to the current wars. The hope and prayer was that, even with this reapplication, America would remain on the leading edge of technology, albeit with narrowed dominance. This was the core disagreement between Air Force leadership and the secretary of defense.

In direct contravention with Secretary Gates' position, Mike continued to push for a realistic assessment of how long it took to ready new equipment. It had taken years to bring the Air Force to its current position, and he fought any effort to backslide. Mike wanted more F-22s in the air so it would be complete dominance when the Air Force took wing—no fair fights. Mike's forceful presence on these issues bordered on intransigence and made it near impossible for Gates to execute his plans.

Should Mike have been more amenable to change when the new secretary of defense came in? Maybe. Wynne had been on the Hill long enough and had established his advocacy for the Air Force firmly enough so that any sudden course change would have been interpreted as a waffling in allegiance. It was a matter of principle to Mike and a matter of authority for the secretary of defense.

With his subordinate enjoying favor on the Hill, Secretary Gates needed a stratagem for the change and the nuclear gaffes were the answer. So with Secretary Gates pushing, Air Force leadership took responsibility and agreed to part ways. Accountability had an absurd inconsistency, and it happened more often than one would hope, sometimes with nuclear events and sometimes not.

The Navy experienced its share of slippage regarding the nuclear mission with its ships at sea during the same period, yet the senior leadership was left intact. As for the Army, it seemed incongruous that not a single officer—not one with bars, oak leaves, eagles, or stars on their uniform—was disciplined or sanctioned for abuses at Abu Ghraib, yet the entire senior leadership of the Air Force was run off for two events, one that began before they arrived on the scene and the other in which they were not even in the chain of command. Maybe theirs was the real show of accountability and service to one's nation.

As Mike would later encapsulate the distinction, "my boss and I had a difference of philosophy, and when that happens, your boss gets the philosophy and you get the difference." They parted comfortably enough that Secretary Gates attended Mike's retirement ceremony and even spoke a few words at the event. He also honored Mike with the Defense Distinguished Civilian Service Medal for his years of service in the Pentagon. That was the highest civilian decoration the Department of Defense could bestow. To some, the award appeared paradoxical, but Mike did not suffer contradiction.

Mike retired as secretary of the Air Force on Friday, June 20, 2008, just two days after the Government Accounting Office upheld Boeing's protest of the Air Force award of the aerial refueling tanker program to EADS/Northrop Grumman. The Air Force was 0 for 2 on tankers. But then, Mike had a flair for the dramatic and a sense of history. He had arranged it so that he was sworn in as secretary of the Air Force at the Air Force Academy in Colorado Springs and retired from government service in front of Air Force Memorial in Washington. One could not have orchestrated the events in better surroundings. "Cast Your Fate to the Wind" was prophetic for a guy who had guided the Air Force.

❖

WYNNE HAD A WAY WITH PEOPLE, maybe it was the Irish in him. He had cared about his workforce, what they did and what happened in their lives. Mike always extended himself with his team. If one of his Pentagon personnel had a baby, flowers soon followed. He did not miss birthdays without sending cheery greetings, a card and maybe flowers. His close staff generally received a little Christmas present or holiday remembrance from Mike and Barb Wynne. But his attention to his people extended to more than just gifts and knick-knacks.

After the fateful September 11, 2001, it was not just business-as-usual at the Pentagon the next day. Mike had flown back from Edwards Air Force Base overnight and caught a few hours sleep at Dover Air Force Base. In the morning, he jumped on the van that made daily runs between Washington and Dover. One hundred miles later, he reported to work on September 12. He was met by one of his senior staff members, and they immediately took a tour. Not of the damaged area which was on the opposite side of the Pentagon from his office, but of the AT&L offices spread throughout the building. Mike personally visited every AT&L office in the Pentagon to tell his people that he was proud of their service and appreciated their carrying on in troubling times. He had nothing but enormous respect for the civil servants of the Pentagon.

Mike was loved by his staff, and he and Barb attended as many of their life events, such as weddings, as they could. If one of his staff told him so and so needed a pat on the back, the distressed person received the encouragement in quick order and directly from the boss. His confidential secretary, Caroline Wilson, was with him for all his years in the Pentagon, and she experienced his kind demeanor on a regular basis. He was a man who cared about others and who was loved by his staff in return.

As he transitioned to secretary of the Air Force, this part of his life did not change. Caroline's dad had passed away a few years earlier and her mom wasn't able to be up in Washington visiting very often, so Mike made sure his secretary had the time to be with family. On another occasion, when Mike traveled to Alaska on business for the Air Force, he brought back Alaskan salmon for each of his staff. He knew how to build a team.

Caroline, with the call sign "Moat Dragon" in the Office of the Secretary of the Air Force, attended college late in life, working her way through classes at night school and on the weekends at the University of Maryland. She had struggled through her last math class and Mike insisted that staff help make time available so she could finish. Mike counseled her to be sure and walk across the graduation stage, even if she felt a bit uncomfortable as one of the older guard in the group. She had earned the walk, and Mike encouraged her to have that pleasure, in spite of her calendar approaching two score. And finish she did.

She also walked across that stage, head high in knowing she'd earned something of value. Out in the audience, standing in as proud as her parents would have been were Mike and Barb. In fact, Caroline's surrogate parents caused quite a stir at the University of Maryland graduation exercises. As secretary of the Air Force, Mike was a personage of some measure, including having a bodyguard. Having the SECAF attend the graduation turned into a bit of an event. Mike and Barb came early and stayed late, allowing any and all at the graduation to take pictures and receive autographs, which many took the opportunity to do. Caroline could not have been prouder, being made the belle of that graduation ball. This was not the only example, as the Wynnes also attended the law school graduation of one of Mike's security agents as well as many other events. Here was a man who took time with his people.

WHEN MIKE LEFT his office at the Pentagon on June 19, 2008, the scene turned out to be anything but a simple farewell party. When the time to leave arrived, unexpectedly and unplanned, Pentagon employees—Air Force staff and members of the Office of the Secretary of Defense—came out of their offices and into the hallway. They began to clap for Mike as he walked down the passageway. As the round of applause became a river of approbation, other colleagues ventured out to see what the commotion was about. In fact, they lined the corridor from his office in Room 4E878 on the fourth floor all the way down the hall, down two flights of stairs and out on to the second floor, riverside exit of the Pentagon, where a car was waiting to take him away. They clapped and cried. As he left, they saluted.

Mike Wynne's brothers and sisters join him in the office of the Secretary of the Air Force at his retirement in 2008. Left to right: Steve, Cathy, Mike, Maureen, and Peter. *Source:* Wynne Family.

What had Mike taken out of the whole adventure? First and foremost, he had the thanks and respect from thousands of young airmen throughout the world who knew he had fought for them and their Air Force. He had always had the attitude that, if one could help, one should help. The bigger picture for Mike was the impact he was able to have on national affairs. Only in America could someone rise from humble beginnings to the grand stage where they could influence affairs of state, in Mike's case the defense of the most powerful country on earth.

❦

MIKE LEFT THE OFFICE of Secretary of Air Force but has not left the field of battle. Sometimes the win goes to the last man standing. In Washington, if you don't leave town, one tends to rotate in and out of leadership positions, akin to baseball managers. Such as Tony

LaRussa, who started his managing career with the Chicago White Sox, moved to the Oakland Athletics and now manages the St. Louis Cardinals. While Mike was out of the Pentagon, he certainly was not out of the picture. Since June 2008, the transition team for the administration of President Barack Obama has asked Wynne to come in and interview with incoming service secretaries, sharing his experience to help them gain a faster start.

With his strong and forceful personality, Mike remains an activist for the Air Force and its airmen. Since departing the Pentagon, he continues to advocate his past agenda of strategic projection rather than tactical engagement forces. His views are shared by many in Washington and have been branded by others as the "Wynne Doctrine." Mike has become something of a folk hero in Washington, and all the while has remained true to form.

British statesman John Morley, in writing *On Compromise* in 1874, said, "You have not converted a man because you have silenced him." So it will be with much of Mike Wynne's powerful message while he was secretary of the Air Force. During his secretariat he spoke frequently to any and all who might assemble. His message was clear and compelling and consistent.

The presence and leadership practiced by Mike Wynne, experienced by the generation of enlisted men and young officers he led, will be more fully realized as those servicemen and women rise to become the next generation's senior enlisted airmen and general officers. Wynne's forceful ideas will resurface—it is an inevitable consequence of vision. Thoughts and theories magnify with time. His initiatives will be more fully appreciated by future administrations and Congresses. Gates, England, Wynne and Moseley will move on. The ideas will outlast them.

For the F-22 weapon system, a centerpiece of strategic projection, this undoubtedly will be a period of bridging. The current administration has determined to not place orders for additional Raptor aircraft. With provisions already in force to prevent the destruction of tooling devoted to F-22 fabrication, it becomes a matter of waiting for a more favorable administration to resume the production line in the future. For Mike's part, he will persist in

A forum held in 2010 at the Pentagon with a number of former Air Force secretaries joining the current leadership. Left to right: Hans Mark, 13th secretary; Jim Roche, 20th; Mike Wynne, 21st; Mike Donley, 22nd and current; Tom Reed, 11th; and Wit Peters, 19th. Twenty-two men have served as the permanent secretary of the Air Force. Many had prior military background but none was a rated pilot. *Source:* Department of Defense photo courtesy of Wynne Family.

the promotion of the F-22 and what it heralds for the defense of the United States. He will continue to proffer the logic and language that will be picked up by others.

After more than 40 years in the service of his country, Mike Wynne cast his fate to the wind and started on the next adventure in his life.

Chapter Nineteen

Closing the Circle

LEAVING WASHINGTON WAS NOT AN OPTION for the Wynnes. Mike and Barb were settled, at least settled on the nation's capital. They took a little time off and began the rest of their lives. They did not view the opportunity as one to travel and vacation. After all, they had seen the world with the Air Force. Barb settled into her quilting, and Mike foraged for small business consulting opportunities. He had always been an idea man, and he wanted to continue. The situation was lining up to be precisely what Barb would dub: Mike's second failed attempt at retirement.

Mike was contacted about board openings with a few companies but only a few. Because of his strident positions on challenging and highly visible issues, he was considered too hot for many of the major corporate boards that would usually seek executives with his experience in business and government. He probably would remain untouchable until the leadership of the Defense Department changed. Unable to sit still, he returned to consulting with start-up, high-tech small business operations. He was in the offices of one such firm when he received the call.

Mike excused himself from the meeting to take the call, "Hello, is this Mike Wynne?" an unknown voice asked.

"Yes, what can I do for you?"

"Is this the Mike Wynne who was secretary of the Air Force?" the caller continued.

Mike momentarily considered hanging up, that it might be someone selling something who had obtained his number somehow, but he decided to stay for one last round.

"My name is Roger Schreiber."

Far from fully invested in the conversation, "What is it exactly that I can do for you."

"I don't know if I have the right Michael Wynne, but did you have a brother named Patrick Edward Wynne?"

Receiving a "Yes," Schreiber finished his introduction, "You may want to sit down. I have something that belonged to your brother Patrick."

With that call, out of the blue, the Wynne family would find out more about Pat's last hours, not everything but so much more than they had ever heard. Their imagination would still have to fill in gaps but far fewer gaps than before.

"Sit down because I have a story to tell."

Pat had not been alone.

❦

THE RED RIVER DELTA, covering almost 6,000 square miles of rich alluvial bottomland, spread out around the capital city of Hanoi in the fashion of a spider web, just as it had for a millennium. Far off to the west of Hanoi was Dien Bien Phu, a remote valley where the French and Viet Minh battled until France was shaken from her colonial dreams. East of Hanoi was Haiphong harbor, and bordering that port city was Ha Long Bay with its weather-fashioned limestone islands. Proceeding northeast up the coast one passed through a series of marshy lagoons, centuries-old plains of rice, and secluded fishing villages. To the north of Hanoi, following the same Highway 1 that snaked the whole length of the country, the geography was a panorama of woodland, karst, and rice paddies. This territory slowly transformed, the farther north one went, into the highlands building toward China, narrow valleys twisting among the low lying mountains. Highway 1 ceased its north northeast trek at Lang Son, just a few miles shy of the Chinese border, where Pat's F-4C Phantom II came to ground.

As he lay on the ground and recovered from the ejection, Pat probably triple-timed through the emergency and survival procedures that had been drilled into him in training. Release the harness, dispose of the parachute, find your bearings, and begin to reconnoiter the area. The beginnings of hide and evade. Or not. He was probably injured enough that he would be lucky to slip off his unwieldy PCU-3 torso harness. Unwieldy but life saving. But what went through his mind as his pulse and respiration returned to some semblance of normal after the trauma of ejection?

It was arguable whether his circumstance was his choice. Pat had always pushed himself. Maybe that was the curse of the firstborn son. He put himself in challenging situations. He liked to explore the edges of life, to see what he could accomplish, whether it was football and debate in high school or turning down scholarships from world-class universities to attend the Air Force Academy. Then it was pilot training, where only the finest succeeded. Pat was but 24 years old. It was not his choice to leave life so early in the game, but he might be forced to do just that.

For Pat Wynne and Larry Golberg, the time between taking fire from the antiaircraft artillery and ejecting from the crippled fighter was just a matter of minutes. After getting hit, they began losing flight controls—one afterburner was out and they had lost the RAM air turbine, the backup system for hydraulics. They were steering with rudders only. The two pilots fought for altitude. Unable to hold a higher angle of attack, it became a distressing endgame for Ozark 3. They were losing control of their F-4's energy state. Soon it would not be their decision. After calling in a last location, the ejection sequence was started.

The canopy bolts exploded open and cleared. In an instant, Pat hurtled at 80 feet per second up the rails on the back of the Martin-Baker Mk. H-5AF ejection seat.[167] Near the end of the catapult stroke, he entered the airstream and the drogue gun fired, its chute slithering out on exit. He shot up and out, and the rush of wind found the drogue chute, stabilizing the seat before separation as the seat belt and leg restraints released. The main chute deployed seconds later. In a race to earth that appeared but a lapse of moments, he slammed into the ground, still alive but grievously injured.

Pat was separated from his pilot, as he settled to the ground. It was questionable whether he saw any of his buddies flying overhead in search and rescue. Undoubtedly, they were in the area or on their way. He may even have seen the telltale smoky trail of the J79-GE-15 turbojet engines that powered the Phantom IIs or heard the exhaust from their efforts. As its last gasp at obeying the commands of its air crew, Pat's mount, F-4 serial 63-7560, had rocketed him out of the cockpit. Though he had called in a final location, he knew he dropped out of the sky only close to that. Even descending at a high sink rate, the aircraft covered much additional ground as the ejection sequence fired and he drifted back down to mother earth. He could be miles in any direction from his last call. He had to wait and see. He thought he was alone.

NORTH VIETNAM DURING THE WAR in Southeast Asia was not particularly bountiful, unless one lived in the bordering area of southern China, from which Vietnam seemed to be the land of plenty. Many Chinese peasant families drifted south across the border into North Vietnam during the war in search of work and sustenance. While the peasants farmed the land with hand tools, the American war effort filled the skies with jet aircraft. Each month the heavens seemed crowded with more planes, often amplified with Russian-designed MiG jets responding from air bases in China. In July 1966 the American effort notched up once again.

Rolling Thunder was the American air campaign designed to punish the North Vietnamese rather than defeat them, which might provoke a response from China or Russia. With Rolling Thunder 51, in an average 30-day month, more than 325 aircraft would take to the air each day and blanket the northern regions of Vietnam. It was a busy time in contested areas. On August 8, 1966, as Patrick settled to the ground, he was not alone. At least one family farming the land had noticed the crash of his F-4C.

The leader of this Chinese household was drawn by the fire in the distance and went to investigate the crash site. On the way, he came across Pat, injured but alive. With nothing to offer but one man's hope of alleviating the suffering of another, these two men, both strangers in a foreign land whose language neither spoke, connected with each other. The Chinese family took Pat to its village and tried to minister to his wounds. Absent aggressive medical intervention, life drained from Pat's face as he succumbed to his injuries. Unable to do any more for the downed American pilot, the Chinese family, who had but meager necessities themselves, kept Pat's few belongings. In time, the military drove the Chinese occupants from North Vietnam back across the border into southern China.

❦

MILLIONS OF AMERICA'S YOUTH shared the experience of Southeast Asia. Pat Wynne, an officer and a gentleman soaring on high in North Vietnam for the U.S. Air Force, was one. Herbert J. Schaffner, a young soldier with a Ranger tab on his uniform, serving in the U.S. Army in South Vietnam, was another. Kentucky-bred just across the Ohio River from Cincinnati, Herb hailed from the town of Cold Spring. He served with honor and distinction in Vietnam and, with just enough luck, returned safely to his native soil in Campbell County, Kentucky. Once home, Herbert J. settled down and in the years that followed was blessed with a wonderful family. His son, Herbert G, was born and raised in Kentucky during this period.

Herbert G. eventually followed in his father's footsteps in a number of ways, including military service. He served in the Army during the 1991 Persian Gulf War. Also akin to his father, Herbert G. returned to the Kentucky area after his service. He attended Kentucky College and then Southern Ohio College in Cincinnati, studying information technology and business. After developing an information technology consulting company, H&S Systems, in the tri-state area between 1994 and 2006, Herbert G. took a position in the IT department of Consortium Companies in neighboring Erlanger, Kentucky, in April 2006.

The towns of Cold Spring and Erlanger straddle the Licking River, which drains much of the territory of northeastern Kentucky into the Mississippi watershed via the mighty Ohio River. Cold Spring was approximately a mile east of the Licking River, whose mouth sat opposite Cincinnati on the Ohio. Erlanger was but a few miles farther but on the west side of the Licking River

In 2005 Consortium Companies had begun a joint venture in southern China, in Guangzhou, Guangdong Province. Two years later in August 2007, Herbert G. was transferred to the China office as its IT director. Guangzhou, the capital city of the province, was situated on the southeast coast in China, topping the Pearl River Delta roughly 75 miles north of Hong Kong. Guangzhou was the traditional Chinese name for the ancient city of Canton. Guangzhou was roughly 500 miles from Hanoi in North Vietnam and 400 miles from the location of Pat's downed aircraft.

Herbert G. settled in to life in China with the Consortium venture and eventually became acquainted with a young Chinese girl in the office. The young woman was one of the first of her family to make the transition from the farmlands to the city. Herbert G. and the young lady married a few months later in early 2008. Soon after, the newlyweds were attending a family gathering south of the city. While at the event, one of the new bride's uncles sought them out. He had a story to tell.

He shared with them that he had been a youngster during the Vietnam War. He was about 10 years old when his family was in North Vietnam trying to eke out a living from the land. His father had come across an American airman who had crash landed and after being unable to save his life had come into possession of the airman's ring. His father kept the ring and approximately 15 years later passed it on to him.

From time to time, the uncle tried to locate the rightful heir but even with the assistance of a translator and a journey to the U.S. Consulate in Guangzhou, he was unable to help the ring find its way back home. The ring held the promise of value for a poor farming family in southern China, but it was a promise without a path. Unsure of what to do with the ring, something inside beckoned him to preserve it. He had had the ring for 25 years by the time he met his niece's new husband, the young American Herbert G. Schaffner.

On seeing the article, Herbert G. was able to discern that it was a college ring from the 1963 graduating class of the Air Force Academy. He could not quite make out the name inscribed inside 40 years earlier, but he promised his wife's uncle he would try and repatriate the memento. On the next occasion communicating with his firm's headquarters back in Kentucky, he mentioned the object to Roger Schreiber, one of Consortium Companies' executives, who offered to help and said, "Send it in, and I will find out what I can about it."

"I'll do that, but please take special care of it. It is a treasured object in my wife's family. They have had it for 40 years."

A few days later, arriving in a singularly American FedEx box, the ring made its appearance back in the United States, 42 years after leaving for Southeast Asia. Once cleaned up, it was identified in short order. No 21st century technology was needed to perform a sophisticated DNA match of the ring to the owner—Pat Wynne's name was inscribed within. It was a quick study for Schreiber to connect Pat to Mike Wynne and complete the circle. While

Pat Wynne's Air Force Academy ring as it arrived back from Southeast Asia. *Source:* Roger Schreiber.

the Wynnes and Schaffners fought in different areas of Vietnam, functioned in different services, and resided in different regions of America, these two families had been destined to bridge the distance between their separate segments of the circle. Herbert J.

and Herbert G. Schaffner had become slivers of the circle.[168]

❦

HERBERT G. ASKED his Vietnam-veteran father if he had an interest in being a part of the ceremony delivering the ring back to the Wynne family. While his father had the interest, he did not have the vigor. He retained thoughts and feelings from the war years that he could not shake. He was one of those servicemen with wounds that could not be seen and would not heal. On October 22, 2008, it was Roger Schreiber, the chief financial officer of the company, who had the honor of returning the ring to Mike Wynne, who accepted it on behalf of the entire family. On the occasion, Herbert G. was in China and his father was in Kentucky. Vietnam still resonated.

Fresh out of service as secretary of the Air Force where he had fought battles that others may not have undertaken due to the personal sacrifice required, Mike felt as if his brother Pat had "reached out across the decades and said job well-done." Receiving something back from a war zone was such a rare occurrence, this was his brother speaking directly to him.

WHERE ELSE BUT IN AMERICA could ordinary young people, of any race, color, or creed have the opportunity to reach the highest levels of service, where they could influence and inspire others, and be a part of making the world a better place? In the Wynne family, it was a trio of first and second generation Irish boys who made a difference. The Wynnes had faith in the system and had been open to work wherever their abilities helped. All three had been called upon to work in the defense of their country. One of them was still at it. This was one family's experience in the circle of service to our nation.

Epilogue

MIKE'S FIRST VISIT to the Vietnam Veterans Memorial in Washington was difficult. It had taken about three years before he felt he could control his emotions enough to visit the monument. The names of several of his West Point classmates were on that commemorative and even more troubling was his older brother's. When Pat Wynne was shot down over North Vietnam on August 8, 1966, he became the first American casualty with the surname Wynne. Pat would not be alone.

By the time the Vietnam War ended in 1973 and Saigon fell two years later, there were more Wynnes. The Vietnam memorial, the Wall, listed more than 58,000 casualties of that war. Since the listing was in chronological rather than alphabetical order, it was difficult to determine how many of a particular surname were inscribed, but five Wynnes were on that wall.

Situated in West Potomac Park just north of the Reflecting Pool, the wall is within sight of the Lincoln Memorial. With the Korean Memorial to its south, these two war remembrances form bookends for the west end of the Reflecting Pool. The Vietnam Veterans Memorial is in the shape of the top two legs of a triangle and memorializes each casualty.

Organized across 140 panels, the Wall begins with panel 1E and extends to 70E, where the memorial takes a 45 degree turn and

continues from 70W counting back down to 1W. Pat Wynne, a
casualty so early in the war, is listed on panel 9E, line 119. The other
Wynnes, two Army soldiers and two Marines, are listed on panels
15E, 25E, 12W and 13W. All five Wynnes—Pat, Larry, Jerry, John and
Tom—were in their 20s and Patrick at 24 years old was the senior
representative of the group.[169] As some of the most gallant men
our nation would ever bring forth, each was one more fragment
of the circle of service.

❧

MIKE KNEW EXACTLY how he wanted to conclude the journey of
his brother's ring back to America. He began by donating Pat's 1963
class ring to the Air Force Academy Association of Graduates in
the summer of 2010, and it made arrangements for displaying the
keepsake. Now Mike could see in his mind's eye, in precise detail
all the way down to the road trip, how he would arrive at the
exhibition of Pat's memento. It was unfinished business for Patrick,
and Mike knew in his heart and his head how it should be brought
to an end. He envisioned each step of the finale.

MIKE HAD MADE the trek a number of times, probably dozens. The
first was 47 years earlier, when his older brother was married in
Pauline Chapel. Mike had made the same journey as an instructor,
returning to the academy from various temporary duty stations.
More recently, he had traveled to Colorado Springs as a member
of the Air Force Academy Endowment Foundation Board, where
his efforts on behalf of the cadets helped underwrite programs
unfunded by restrained academy budgets. But this time was
different.

Mike traveled commercial and flew in through Denver's
International Airport, located on the northeast side of Denver
proper. He had a 75-mile commute to the Air Force Academy. When
he was secretary of the Air Force, he could easily reach the academy
by flying through Peterson Air Force Base, a joint facility with the
Colorado Springs Municipal Airport. But he was a civilian now.

As favored customers of the local rent-a-car operation, Mike and

Barb quickly gathered up their transportation and were on their way to the academy. They speculated about how Pat and Nancy probably traveled this same route when they were courting. The beauty of the countryside never failed to take their breath away. From Fort Collins to Pueblo, with Denver anchoring the middle, the Front Range of the Colorado Rockies was majestic. As they drove south on Interstate 225 and then 25, landforms with names such as Cherokee Mountain, Dawson Butte, and Monkey Face passed by their right shoulder. Millennia in the making, these were the substance of geomorphology.

The ride south from Denver paralleled much of the original route of the Denver & Rio Grande Railroad, along 120 miles of track between Denver and Pueblo laid out 140 years earlier when the Front Range was the frontier. After the academy was opened, the railroad ran weekend specials for years from Denver to accommodate the crowds attending football games. But the entire region around Colorado Springs had built up with military installations during and since World War II.

Before the Air Force Academy, Fort Carson Army base arrived and took up a large percentage of the Front Range territory between Colorado Springs and Pueblo. Following the academy, the North American Air Defense Command (NORAD) located its Cheyenne Mountain Complex outside Colorado Springs. These military installations, which stood in marked contrast to the recreational areas of Pike's Peak and the Garden of the Gods, were the largest employers in the vicinity. As Mike and Barb's car approached Cathedral Rock, marking the northern point of the Air Force Academy property, their thoughts continued to drift.

The Air Force Academy was located on more than 17,000 acres of high, flat plain at the foot of the Rocky Mountains. Ten miles to its south was Colorado Springs; looking east, the whole of the Great Plains opened to adventure. Viewed north to south along the mountains, the academy property was a section of land roughly seven miles long by four miles wide with its own zip code, 80840. Banked into the east side of the Rockies, the climate provided relatively mild winters and dry seasons.

Taking Interstate 25 down from Denver, they left the road at exit 156B, North Gate Boulevard, and drove west a short distance, crossing both Monument Creek and the old Rio Grande tracks, to the academy entrance. They zigzagged the car through and around the concrete barricades that served as protective barriers, showed their identification at the gate, and at least this time drove right in as the security forces personnel did not inspect the car. They continued west to Stadium Boulevard, turned left at the corner where a Boeing B-52D Stratofortress mounted on concrete stanchions was on display, and headed south toward Parade Loop. Taking Parade Loop west brought them to the Academy Cemetery, a green splotch of holy ground on the right-hand side of the road surrounded by lightly wooded areas.

Having cleared the visit beforehand, Mike and Barb stopped briefly at the cemetery to have a private moment and pay their respects to Pat. The cemetery was situated on barely undulating land with but a handful of trees spread throughout, arranged in an apparently random fashion. Practically all the cemetery markers were flush with the ground, making everyone equal in death even though rank had been singularly important in life. More than a thousand souls were posted to this special garrison.

During the identification of his remains in 1977, it was surmised that Pat had ejected from his aircraft. Pat's case had remained in that posture for almost 30 years. The possibility of his surviving an ejection, rather than having died in a crash, was supported by the claims of Chinese family members who helped an injured airman near the Chinese border on August 8 in 1966. Pat's death was determined to be 1974, when he was declared legally dead after seven years. The military identification command dated his death as of the date his remains were returned, 1977, since no other definitive date was established. But how long Patrick actually lived is only conjecture. It was somewhere between 1966 and 1977. His burial marker on the academy grounds fixed it as August 8, 1966.

Here in the Air Force Academy Cemetery, Pat rested among other Air Force notables such as Carl Spaatz, a founding father of the service and its first chief of staff; Curtis LeMay, the driving force behind the Strategic Air Command and the fifth chief of staff; and Robin Olds, a fighter pilot cum brigadier general who took command of the 8th Tactical Fighter Wing in Vietnam just weeks after Pat was downed. Spaatz and Olds were West Pointers, LeMay a product of Ohio State University. All were important to the Air Force.

Mike and Barb had come to Colorado to participate in a brief ceremony dedicating the display of Pat's ring in the Air Force Academy's Association of Graduates exhibit memorializing the Class of 1963. It was be a tribute to Patrick and his generation of airmen, and a lasting challenge for future Air Force cadets. Pat had lived his military career according to the Air Force measure—service, integrity and excellence. His service and his ring would be a model for all.

When the Consortium Company, located outside Cincinnati, returned Pat's ring, they hadn't just popped it in an envelope and mailed it to Mike in Washington. Senior officials had insisted on personally handing it to the recently retired secretary of the Air Force. The company had shown respect for the item.

The ring was mounted in a foam backing and placed in a six-sided, silver-colored metal presentation case. The lid of the case was engraved with the stylized wings of the official Air Force symbol and Patrick Wynne's name. The case was then enclosed in a purple velvet sleeve. This was exactly how it was delivered to the Association of Graduates, along with a photograph of Pat from his academy days.

With a history of just over half a century, recording the feats of Air Force Academy graduates was a work in progress. Since most academy graduates were still alive and active, no concerted effort had been made to provide commemoratives for each graduating class. As it turned out, the Class of 1963 was pretty active back at its alma mater with a heritage display.

Through the Association of Graduates, the Class of 1963 had already established a tontine display in Arnold Hall. While generally used with respect to insurance or finance matters, a tontine was a situation where the members of a group shared in a certain benefit. As members passed away, their benefit was spread among the remaining participants. The tontine period generally ran until only one living associate remained, at which time the benefits of the group, presumably bragging rights at being the last living member of the Class of 1963, belonged wholly to him.

With the Association of Graduates, the Class of 1963 had set up a glass display case in Arnold Hall, the de facto student union of the cadets. The thin mahogany-colored cabinet was roughly five feet across and eight feet high. It contained a small silver cup for each member of the Class of 1963 plus the single honorary graduate. As a graduate passed away, that event was marked by having his cup inverted. This ritual was to continue, marking the passing of the entire class.

The tontine display in Arnold Hall holds 500 sterling silver cups, one each for the 499 graduates of the Class of 1963 and one for the sole honorary graduate—John F. Kennedy. *Source:* United States Air Force Academy photo by Ryan Davis. http://www.usafaclasshistories.org/1963-heritage-cups.php?y=1963. © 2010 Ryan Davis Photography. Reprinted with permission.

The Class of 1963 was the only one to establish such a display to date. It was in this cabinet, overlooking the ballroom in Arnold Hall, that Pat's ring had a central place of honor alongside the tontine display managed by the Association of Graduates and members of the class. The circle was made whole, as it was in the very same Arnold Hall almost 50 years earlier that Pat waltzed his way through a giant replica of the class ring at the June 1962 Ring Dance.

Now the name Wynne would be across the campus in multiple locations. Pat was in the academy cemetery and in the Arnold Hall tontine display of the Class of 1963, and Mike was already in one of the research laboratories. The Ground Operations section of the Space Systems Research Center had been re-dedicated as the Wynne Space Professional Center for Excellence, in honor of Mike's loyalty and perseverance as secretary of the Air Force. These two sons, descended from a military colonel who was every bit a pioneer in the United States Air Force himself, now were a permanent part of the history and lore of the service. And the circle was closed.

Notes and Citations

Chapter One: The Many Shades of Service

1 Interestingly enough, toward the end of Schillereff's Air Force career, the service contacted him about that waiver. With the Tet Offensive jarring everyone to the realities of Vietnam, the Air Force began a push for pilots, which soon reached Schillereff. His original request for a waiver of his color blindness so that he could attend pilot training was now thought more acceptable and he was offered the chance. But too much wind had fluttered under Ron's wings and he declined the opportunity, leaving the Air Force shortly after.

2 The Tonkin Gulf Resolution (Public Law 88-408, 88th Congress, August 7, 1964) was based on reports that United States ships operating in international waters had been attacked on August 2 and 4 by Soviet-built torpedo boats operated by the North Vietnamese. Well after the resolution passed, the second attack was proven false. Even the United States Navy repudiates the episode. See *Summary of the Tonkin Gulf Crisis of August, 1964* by Edward J. Marolda of the Naval Historical Center found at www.history.navy.mil/faqs/faq120-1.htm.

3 Morrocco, *Thunder from Above*, 64; Van Staaveren, *Gradual Failure*, 153–7.

4 This debate continues. The commander in chief, Pacific in 1965—Admiral U.S. Grant Sharp—strongly voiced his opinion that the United States could win the war in short order if the restrictions on bombing in the north were lifted. His article in *Reader's Digest* in May 1969, laid out his position. Mark Clodfelter, a professor at the U.S. Air Force Academy, wrote in 1989 on *The Limits of Air Power*, outlining an opposing view.

5 Johnny Unitas and Brooks Robinson both made it to their respective halls of fame and had their numbers, 19 and 5, retired.

6 Wherry and Capehart were Department of Defense family housing projects constructed in a number of states. The Wherry Project, named after Nebraska Senator Ken Wherry who introduced the legislation, entailed private companies building and leasing homes on government property. This program began in late-1949 and produced more than 84,000 housing units. The replacement for the Wherry program was the Capehart project, named after sponsor Indiana Senator Homer Capehart. The Capehart project started in 1955 and produced more than 115,000 housing units (Baldwin, *Four Housing Privatization Programs*).

7 Brown, *The Nongraded High School*.

Chapter Two: Ed Wynne's Army Air Corps

8 The 1920 United States Census shows Ed's father, Patrick Edward Wynne (born New York City, March 22, 1894), as a conductor with the New York Railways Company, a streetcar line. It shows Ed's mother, Mary Cunningham Wynne (born County Galway, Mayo, Ireland April 4, 1898), an operator doing factory work (HeritageQuest.com). Foreign-born Mary, who immigrated to the United States in 1911, was shown as a naturalized citizen in the 1920 census. Patrick Edward's 1942 draft registration card lists his occupation as a bus driver on the 86th Street Crosstown working for the New York City Omnibus Corporation (Ancestrylibrary.com). New York City Omnibus was the bus subsidiary of that same New York Railways Company. So Patrick Edward was employed with the same company throughout the changeover from streetcars to buses.

9 Ancestrylibrary.com.

10 New York was one of the cities to recognize that not all of the brightest lights came from the ranks of privilege. Many academically gifted students were buried in the masses of first and second generation immigrants. To uncover and develop these quality students, New York City early on created three high schools with the sole mission of concentrated and advanced instruction in mathematics and the sciences. Stuyvesant (1904), Brooklyn Technical (1922), and Bronx Science (1938) were the originals. Stuyvesant began as a trade school for boys but switched to a science curriculum with a merit-based entrance system in 1919. Starting with the 1934–35 school year, Stuyvesant and Brooklyn Technical instituted a uniform entrance examination from which future students would be selected. In time, all three schools had to fight off claims of elitism, cultural bias in the examinations, and even an attack by advocates of affirmative action (Mac Donald, *How Gotham's Elite...*). Of the 80,000 to 100,000 eighth grade students in New York City in a given year, about 20,000 take the entrance exam for the approximately 2,500 seats available at these schools.

11 Stuyvesant High School claims among its graduates four Nobel prizewinners, actors Jimmy Cagney '17 and Tim Robbins '76, jazz musician Thelonious Monk '35, businessman and cofounder of Home Depot Arthur Blank '60, and two of the most senior people in the administration of the 44th President of the United States—United States Attorney General Eric H. Holder '69 and Chief Campaign Strategist and Senior Advisor David Axelrod '72 (shsaa.org and ourstrongband.org).

12 A few months after the Eighth Avenue subway began service south to Chambers Street in lower Manhattan, the Cranberry Street Tunnel under the East River opened and brought the line to its final destination in Brooklyn Heights (Crowell; Feinman). Today the Eighth Avenue subway is called the Washington Heights, Eighth Avenue, and Church Street line.

13 Congressman John J. Boylan represented the Fifteenth District for as many years (1923 to 1938) when he died in office. That seat today is held by Congressman Charles B. Rangel who was elected to the Ninety-second Congress in 1971, defeating Adam Clayton Powell in the primary. He has been reelected to each succeeding Congress and has held the seat in the Fifteenth District, reached through a redistricting, since 1993 (Congressional Directory).

14 Paulick, et al., *1940 Howitzer*, 274.

15 Henney, "Record Throng...," *Washington Post*, June 10, 1940.

16 For good histories of the Air Force, see *A Concise History of the U.S. Air Force* by Stephen L. McFarland (Virginia, 1997) and *Beyond the Wild Blue: A History of the United States Air Force, 1947-1997* by Walter J. Boyne (New York, 1997). The former was written by a university professor in conjunction with the Air Force History and Museums Program and is less inclined to delve into the politics surrounding the establishment of an independent service. The latter, written by a career Air Force pilot, has no such reservations. Both books provide background material and illustrate the evolution of the Air Force during its first 50 years.

17 Patent number 37,771 issued to Charles Perley of New York on February 24, 1863.

18 Miller, "The Founding of the Air Force Academy," 3.

19 Boyne, *Beyond the Wild Blue*, 9.

20 Navy personnel had an anonymous letter floated in April 1949 claiming corruption in Air Force contract awards. Chairman Carl Vinson's House Armed Services Committee found the charges baseless in the fall of 1949. For good histories of this dispute, see *The Revolt of the Admirals* by Andrew L. Lewis (Virginia, 1998) and *Arms and Men* by Walter Millis (New York, 1956).

21 "Beatrice Hickey...," *Washington Post*, June 13, 1940.

22 Chilkoot Barracks/Fort Seward outside Haines represented the U.S. Army presence in 1940, until World War II spawned the construction of a number of posts and air fields. Scores of facilities were constructed in Alaska, including Army Air Force and Navy stations. Most of these were closed or converted to civilian and commercial airports when the services reduced after the war (Brooks, "Military Airfields in WW2"). The two primary Air Force facilities that rose above the realignment are Eielson and Elmendorf. Part of Ladd Field, which dates to the early 1940s, evolved into Eielson Air Force Base, on the outskirts of Fairbanks. Elmendorf Field, the air facilities of Fort Richardson adjacent to Anchorage, dates to 1940. When the Army moved to new facilities after World War II, the Air Force renamed the entire garrison Elmendorf Air Force Base.

23 Lethbridge, *The History of Cape Canaveral*.

24 Missile ranges in the Continental U.S. would come together in two locations,

the western range at Vandenberg Air Force Base, roughly 160 miles northwest of Los Angeles, and the eastern range at Cape Canaveral in Florida. The western range, situated on roughly 100,000 acres of remote land with the Santa Ynez Mountains nudging it into the Pacific, was used for polar orbit launches, which could be accomplished without flying over land. The eastern range was used for equatorial orbit launches, dispatched eastward and taking advantage of the earth's rotation while still overflying little in the way of landscape. Vandenberg was established nine years after Cape Canaveral.

25 United States Military Academy, "Annual Report of the Superintendent—1957," 73.

26 Neufeld, "The End of the Army Space Program," 737.

27 Barbree, *Live from Cape Canaveral*, 12.

28 Patrick Air Force Base began as the Banana River Naval Air Station on the Atlantic coast of Florida in the late-1930s. With the development of rockets during World War II, the military had begun looking at sites for a test range and it eventually settled on the Banana River Naval Air Station. The plan was to use the station for support, to connect launching facilities at nearby Cape Canaveral, and to position tracking stations down through the Bahamas. By the end of 1950, this came to pass. The Navy transferred its Banana River facility to the Air Force, and the British government agreed to allow the United States to fly missiles near the Bahamas, as well as establish tracking stations there. In quick order, the Air Station was renamed Patrick Air Force Base and the test range relabeled the Air Force Missile Test Center (Patrick AFB, "US Air Force Bases").

29 In later years, as launch objectives became more complex, the demands placed on tracking and data acquisition followed suit. Different networks were established for different projects, and although some overlap existed, three distinct tracking networks came into being. Discrete networks were established for unmanned satellite orbits, for manned space flight such as that for Project Mercury, and for voyages into deep space such as those to the moon in the Apollo Program. Over time, three dozen land-based tracking stations would be used for the various projects, as would additional water-based tracking ships and instrumented aircraft stations (Van Nimmen, *NASA Historical Data Book*, 521, 548).

30 Ryba, "First 100 U.S. Human Space Flights."

Chapter Three: Pat Wynne's Air Force

31 In the 18-year period from 1922 to 1939, the United States Military Academy was hard pressed to supply officers for the Air Service. West Point graduated an average of 272 second lieutenants each year. On average, 72 of the 272 were assigned to the Air Corps, yet only 38 would continue on and graduate from

advanced flying school (Miller, "The Founding of the Air Force Academy," 114, Note 28). After World War II, an enlarged West Point planned to assign 40 percent of its graduates to the Air Corps. Even with Reserve Officer Training Corps programs and civilian schools added, these numbers were not high enough to satisfy postwar Air Force demands. Thus, pressure for a separate Air Force academy increased.

32 Miller, "The Founding of the Air Force Academy," 432.

33 The Supreme Court had a squad of four, boy pages. Chuck Bush became the "Court's first Negro page boy" ("The Supreme Court…," *Time*, August 2, 1954).

34 Wynne, "Graduate School…;" Fullerton, *1963 Polaris*.

35 In preparation for this comprehensive changeover in aircraft and schooling, the Air Force phased out the single-engine propeller-driven Beechcraft T-34 Mentor trainer and cancelled instruction classes 62-D, 62-E and 62-F. The newly formed Undergraduate Pilot Training program was consolidated at eight bases: Craig, Laredo, Laughlin, Moody, Reese, Vance, Webb, and Williams (Mitchell, *Air Force Officers*, 218–19).

36 The way the training wing was structured, new classes of approximately 40 students started every six weeks as older classes graduated. The 40 student-pilots would be divided between the two training flights. At any particular time, eight active classes were under the wing commander, such as classes A through H. Class 65-A would be at the end of its 55-weeks of training when class 65-H was beginning. While the earlier classes 65-ABCD would be in the basic training section (T-38 aircraft), the newest classes 65-EFGH would be in the primary training section (T-37 aircraft). Each squadron section of 80 men was further subdivided into about four flights of student-pilots (Fryer Interview).

37 Ashcroft, *We Wanted Wings*, 70.

38 The military is famous for the variety of insignia and patches its members wear. The Air Force was no different back in the 1960s, with patches of every

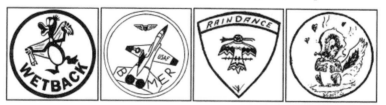

description. Each new class at Williams Air Force Base chose a design for the two phases of training. For Pat Wynne and the 3525th Pilot Training Squadron of class 65-G, primary training was as a member of Wetback flight, stylized much as one would expect Sylvester the Cat to appear drying off at the beach. Pat's basic training was in Boomer flight, a line drawing of the T-38 Talon rocketing off to the horizon. The 3526th Squadron had Raindance and Schatzi flights, the former showing an Indian Thunderbird symbol and the latter sporting a Pepé Le Pew character, complete with malodorous scent lines (Young et al., *Class Book 65-G*).

39 The Student Pilot Time Certificate detailed Pat Wynne's actual time in the cockpit. During the primary phase (T-37), he spent 103½ hours accompanied by the instructor and 21½ solo. Almost 31 of the hours with the instructor had Pat outfitted with a hood. This simulated flying on instruments, as if under severe weather conditions. The primary phase included very little time flying in night conditions. In the basic phase of training, Pat flew 120 hours in the T-38, 91¼ with the instructor. More than 32 of the instructor hours were hooded, and this phase included more than six hours of night flying. In total, Pat had 245 hours of actual cockpit time. These cockpit hours came after he had 45 hours instrument training and 11¾ hours operating flight controls in the flight simulator (Schultis, "Student Pilot Time Certificate").

40 The 8th Tactical Fighter Wing, tagged the "Wolf Pack" by Colonel Robin Olds who had replaced Joe Wilson, earned a measure of notoriety in January 1967 with Operation Bolo, where it shot down four MiG-21s in a single aerial action. Thirty days later, on February 1, 1967, Bob Hope's USO Christmas Show, his annual tour of the Southeast Asian military bases, began with a stop at Ubon Royal Thailand Air Force Base (RTAFB), home of the 8th Tactical Fighter Wing. Noting the wing's recent success, Hope led off the show with a lethal play-on-words, referring to the 8th as "the world's largest distributor of MiG parts" (Department of Defense, Department of the Air Force, "Bob Hope Christmas Special").

41 The military has an affectation for acronyms. For the air crew that flew the two-seat F-4 Phantom IIs, it began with pilots, ACs and GIBs, and led to PSOs, WSOs, and RIOs. The easy one was the pilot, always in the front seat and commanding the aircraft. When a rated pilot was also in the back seat, the front seat became the AC, aircraft commander. The "guy in back" was universally called the GIB, but different types of GIBs existed. The Air Force valued the Vietnam-era F-4 Phantom II because of its tandem-seat arrangement. In the Air Force version, both seats had full flight controls. The Air Force utilized this capability to train its pilots. Oftentimes, both seats were occupied by pilots, the AC (usually the senior officer) in front and the PSO or pilot systems operator in the back. The luxury of having two, rated pilots on the aircraft allowed the rear-seat pilot to gain experience in the aircraft while he operated the weapon systems. As the war ground on and the need for pilots eclipsed the supply, trained navigators were put in the rear seat as weapon systems operators (WSOs). The WSO's duty was to monitor and utilize the electronic weapon systems on an aircraft, such as missiles and bombs and radar. In the Navy, that position was called a radar intercept officer (RIO).

42 Bunny Talley, assigned to the 433rd Tactical Fighter Squadron, was brought down by a SA-2 Guideline surface-to-air missile on September 10, 1966, 33 days

after Pat Wynne. Talley evaded capture for a day but was finally caught and interned as a prisoner of war. He was repatriated in 1973. Joe Merrick and Bob Clements, also from the 433rd, were brought down by ground fire. Merrick was downed on October 20, 1966, on his second dive on target by automatic weapons fire. Clements, a 1963 West Point graduate, was shot down on January 24, 1969, by 37 mm antiaircraft artillery fire. Merrick and Clements safely ejected and were recovered (Clinton, "Phantoms Lair...," www.8tfw.com/pages/8thhistory1966.htm; .../8thhistory1969.htm).

Chapter Four: Mike Wynne's Winding Way

43 West Point stopped the practice of issuing cullum numbers that indicated General Order of Merit, or class ranking, in 1978. While a number of people feel the change was simply an attempt to be more politically correct, the cullum numbers after 1978 were based on alphabetical order at graduation.

44 The definitive history of the United States Military Academy's Class of 1966 was written by Rick Atkinson, *The Long Gray Line* (Boston, 1989). The book details the academy years and later exploits of many of the graduates, many of whom became war heroes and a number of whom lost their lives in Vietnam.

45 United States Military Academy, "Annual Report of the Superintendent: 1 July 1965-30 June 1966," p. C-3.

46 Ibid.

47 Atkinson, *The Long Gray Line*, 3, 558.

Chapter Five: Teach, Taught, Teaching

48 Freeman, "Abandoned & Little Known Airfields."

49 AFIT/PA, *AFIT History*.

50 Holdeman, et al., "Synthesis of a Suboptimal...."

51 Parkinson, et al., "Sight Line Autopilot: A New Concept in Air Weapons."

52 After his work on the AC-130 gunship, Brad Parkinson would continue research in navigation and control for the Air Force until his retirement in 1978, the culmination of a 22-year military career. One lasting result of Colonel Parkinson's work was his leadership of the joint-service development of global positioning—GPS (Geselowitz, "Oral History: Brad Parkinson").

53 Johnson Space Center, "NASA, Astronaut Biographies... .

Chapter Six: The Family Circle

54 Larry Guarino's life experience qualifies for book-length treatment. As a

New Jersey-born 19-year-old in 1942, he signed up with the Aviation Cadet Program of the Army Air Forces. Earning his wings in less than a year, he flew propeller driven aircraft in World War II, transonic jet aircraft during the Korean War, and went supersonic during the Vietnam War. He ejected from his F-105 Thunderchief fighter-bomber on his 50th mission, over North Vietnam, on June 14, 1965, and remained a prisoner of war until repatriated in 1973. He was the oldest rated pilot to be captured and for a time was the senior ranking officer at one of the prison camps. He was awarded the Air Force Cross for extraordinary heroism and retired from the Air Force as a colonel.

55 81 TRW, *A Brief History of Keesler AFB...*, 16.

56 Selective Service System, "History & Records."

57 The First Cavalry Division had been converted into an airmobile unit in 1965 with the assimilation of the 11th Air Assault Division resources. In July 1965 the new First Cavalry Division (Airmobile), with a complement of more than 400 helicopters, was ordered to Vietnam. The division arrived in-country in August and September, 1965. The majority of the First Cavalry Division stood down and returned to the States in April 1971 under the Phase VI Redeployment. The final elements were withdrawn in June 1972. The Paris Peace Accords ceasefire was signed in January 1973.

58 "Tall Comanche," 13 April 1971.

59 Ryba, "Kennedy Space Center."

60 Stout et al., "United States Government Awards Lockheed...," press release dated June 6, 2008.

Chapter Seven: Transition to Entrepreneur

61 "Cast Your Fate to the Wind" was written and recorded by Vince Guaraldi in 1962. It won the Grammy Award for Best Original Jazz Composition in 1963 (http://grammy.com/). The Sounds Orchestral cover of this tune in 1965 brought it even greater fame.

62 Lorenzini, et al., "A Root Locus Analysis... ."

Chapter Eight: Final Flight - 21°33'N, 106°46'E

63 RTAFB airfields at Ubon and Udorn were standard bases for the U.S. Air Force. Both had been improved so they could handle jet aircraft, and they stood on a par with the air bases in South Vietnam, such as those at Cam Ranh Bay, Chu Lai, Da Nang, Phan Rang and Phu Cat. Each of these had runways made from permanent materials, usually concrete, and lengths exceeding 9,000 feet (*Indochina Airfields*).

64 The 8th Tactical Fighter Wing began conversion from the F-105 Thunderchief to the F-4C Phantom II in November 1964, receiving deliveries from the McDonnell Aircraft plant in St. Louis, Missouri. By February 1965, the 8th Tactical Fighter Wing had outfitted four tactical fighter squadrons, the 68th, 431st, 433rd, and 497th. In September 1965, the 433rd and the 497th squadrons began the transfer of assets to Ubon RTAFB. The headquarters flags came from Naha Air Base in Okinawa, Japan, and the operational units from George Air Force Base in California. Effective December 6, 1965, the 8th Tactical Fighter Wing was officially assigned to Ubon RTAFB with these two squadrons (O'Sullivan, "Kunsan Air Base").

The Triple Nickel, the 555th Tactical Fighter Squadron, was activated in early 1964 and attached to the 12th Tactical Fighter Wing, completing the wing transition from three to four squadrons. As the 555th completed an air defense rotation at Naha Air Base, it was supposed to deploy to Cam Ranh Bay with the 12th Tactical Fighter Wing. Instead, it was diverted. The 555th first had temporary duty with the 51st Fighter-Interceptor Wing at Naha Air Base and then forward deployed on February 24, 1966, to Udorn RTAFB. It subsequently transferred to the 8th Tactical Fighter Wing at Ubon RTAFB (12th TFW, "12th Tactical Fighter Wing History").

65 Thompson, *To Hanoi and Back*, 308-309.

66 Ibid., 313.

67 Correll, "The Vietnam War Almanac," 52; APC Maxwell AFB, "Air and Space Power Course, Excursions."

68 Van Staaveren, *USAF Plans and Operations*, 35.

69 Hopkins, Unpublished E-mails to John Hallgren.

70 Records of the 8th Tactical Fighter Wing list F-4C 63-7560 as coming from Holloman Air Force Base in July, while most of the wing's assets had already transferred in-country to Phan Rang Air Base in March (Clinton, "Phantoms Lair...," www.8tfw.com/pages/8thhistory1966.htm; 366th Fighter Group, "366th Fighter Group," http://366fightergroupassoc.org/History-RVN.htm).

71 Earlier in the year, Captain Lawrence H. Golberg and First Lieutenant Gerald D. Hardgrave teamed up to register a MiG kill in air-to-air combat. They brought down a MiG-17 with an AIM-9 Sidewinder missile on April 30, 1966. This was the fifth MiG tally in Vietnam for the 555th Tactical Fighter Squadron, giving the squadron the ACE status that came with at least five aerial victories (Clinton, "Phantoms Lair...," www.8tfw.com; Van Staaveren, *Gradual Failure*, 274). The Triple Nickel would go on to score more air-to-air MiG kills than any other U.S. Air Force unit during Vietnam (Thompson, *To Hanoi and Back,* 275). The 8th Tactical Fighter Wing was credited with a total of 39 (rounded up from 38.5) aerial victories (Futrell, *Aces & Aerial Victories*, 154). The 555th accounted for 19 of those.

72 Personal call signs were a construct of the 1970s and later. Neither Pat's wife, Nancy, nor Pat's pilot training partner, Mac Armstrong, remember individual call signs in the early 1960s period. It is quite possible that the call signs used to identify various flights of aircraft became so prevalent and popular in Vietnam that the custom resulted in the creation of personal call signs.

73 Of the eight officers in Ozark Flight on that August 8, 1966, mission, four were graduates of the Air Force Academy. Clifton, Smyth and Salzarulo were members of the Class of 1964, while Pat Wynne was from the Class of 1963.

74 U.S. Department of Defense. "Ozark Flight August 8, 1966 Mission Report."

75 *Indochina Administrative Divisions*, and *Indochina and Thailand* maps.

76 Van Staaveren, *USAF Plans and Operations*, 38.

77 Thompson, *To Hanoi and Back*, 310.

78 See Robertson, *555 Fighter Squadron*. The term ACE dates back to World War I and refers to a pilot downing at least five enemy aircraft in aerial combat. The United States Air Force was credited with shooting down 137 aircraft during the Vietnam War. One pilot and two weapon systems officers were scored as ACES. The lone pilot, Steve Ritchie, was assigned to the 555th Tactical Fighter Squadron and became the first Air Force ACE of the Vietnam War. On four of his five aerial victories, he had Chuck DeBellevue as his weapon systems officer. DeBellevue also became an ACE, gaining his fifth and sixth credits on missions with pilot John Madden. The third Air Force ACE of the Vietnam War, flying as a weapon systems officer with four different pilots, was Jeff Feinstein, who flew with the 13th Tactical Fighter Squadron (Haulman, "USAF Aerial Victory Credits On-Line"). Both weapon systems officers, DeBellevue and Feinstein, returned to pilot training after Vietnam and earned their wings—their pilot rating. Feinstein and Ritchie were graduates of the Air Force Academy.

Chapter Nine: The Business of Weapons Development

79 Military-industrial complex was a term of art first used by President Dwight D. Eisenhower in his farewell address on January 17, 1961. He warned "…we must guard against the acquisition of unwarranted influence…by the military-industrial complex" (Eisenhower, "Farewell Address").

80 With the air war experience in Vietnam, aircraft design in the 1960s began the shift from heavier, missile-oriented delivery systems to lighter, air-superiority aircraft. One competitor for the title was the comparatively lighter McDonnell Douglas twin-engine F-15 Eagle, which had an empty-weight of 28,600 pounds in the F-15C version (Jane, *Jane's All the World's Aircraft*, 1985–86, 451). This compared to the F-4E Phantom IIs 30,328 pounds (Ibid, 1980–81, 381). Some

From above: An F-4 Phantom II from the 1960s (Air Force file photo—reference 020903-0-9999b-027), an F-15 Strike Eagle (Air Force photo by Staff Sgt. Joshua Garcia—reference 100825-F-9919G-518), and an F-16 Fighting Falcon (Air Force photo by Senior Airman Christopher Boitz—reference 090417-F-6044B-122). *Source:* United States Air Force Web site, www.af.mil/photos/index.asp.

factions believed even lighter would be better. A group of Air Force pilots, led by John Boyd, in company with a number of defense experts augured for a truly lightweight fighter. Boyd, a pilot with experience in air-to-air combat, believed weight was the crucial element and advocated a doctrine of energy-maneuverability. Energy-maneuverability posited that agility was more important than speed, and being able to manage energy-maneuverability would be decisive. Boyd's self-styled "fighter mafia" helped push for the design, which resulted in the General Dynamics single-engine F-16 Fighting Falcon, with an empty weight of 16,794 pounds in the F-16C version (Ibid, 1985–86, 410).

81 Ralph's Rules: "The information provided to the customer has to make sense within his frame of reference and the information available to him, not necessarily in the seller's perspective. Very much as in other interdependent discussions, success depends on evaluating something that seems right to the customer and what he thinks the seller is thinking. Of course, once important information comes into the customer's hands, he is bound to look for confirmation. You must think out what inquiries will be made (not what inquiries you will make) and give him the answer to those inquiries, so as to satisfy him. In other words, you must remember that a customer does not think and react as a seller does, and you must put yourself into his mind."

82 France was one of the founding members of the North Atlantic Treaty Organization (NATO) but withdrew by 1966 when Charles De Gaulle felt the United States dominated the alliance. In 2009, 43 years later, France rejoined NATO. Sweden has always had a neutral posture. It never has been a member nation, even though it has a history of cooperation with other nations seeking peace.

Chapter Ten: Unfinished Business

83 Aiipowmia, "Histories: US Army CILHI."

84 Correll, "The Vietnam War Almanac," 45.

85 Association of Graduates, "USAFA Graduate Memorial Wall."

86 Newman, "A General Salutes by Quitting," *U.S. News & World Report*, August 11, 1997.

87 Mulson, "Pop Singer's Performance at AFA Hits Home."

88 United States Air Force Academy, *Register of Graduates... .*

Chapter Twelve: Chariots of Iron

89 The acknowledged father of the M-1 Abrams tank was Dr. Philip Lett. A mechanical engineer by training, he was educated at Auburn University and then

served two years in the United States Army. While working on his terminal degree in mechanical engineering at the University of Michigan in Ann Arbor, he began working with Chrysler Corporation. A specialist in all types of armored vehicles, he rose to vice president and assistant to the general manager of Chrysler's tank works (Donaldson, "Guide to the Philip W. Lett Collection, RG 740").

90 Jasper, Indiana–born B. Edward Ewing was a rising star in the General Dynamics firmament. He had come over in 1978 at age 33 from International Harvester where he had made a name for himself in the truck division. At General Dynamics, he was part of the acquisition team that engineered the takeover of Chrysler's tank works. Ewing ended up being involved in the tank and F-16 programs, with responsibility for a number of plants. Ed Ewing and Mike Wynne worked together in Michigan with the tank program. Ewing left General Dynamics as part of the deal that transferred the Fort Worth F-16 program to Lockheed in 1993. In 1997 Ewing left Lockheed to join a partnership involved with turnarounds and restructurings.

91 George Psihas was a 1950 graduate of the United States Military Academy. One of George's teachers in Ordnance at West Point was Mike's father, Ed Wynne.

92 Manufacturing know-how went all the way to knowing where the welds were placed. Human engineering included placement and protection of the crew members. When a foreign country received a contract to domestically produce a version of the M-1, it acquired this expertise.

93 Besides its manufacturing problems and cost overruns with the SSN-688 submarines, General Dynamics had experienced a flurry of other bad press in the early 1980s. These included revelations about kickbacks, claims by union workers of unsafe factory conditions and unfair bargaining, and the appearance of design flaws in early models of the M-1 tank. Add in lawsuits by laid-off employees, and investigations by the Justice Department and five different congressional committees, and it became obvious General Dynamics had an image problem. The company was wallowing in the news. See, for example: Curley, "On the Defensive," *Wall Street Journal*, May 18, 1984; Kurtz, "Defense Contract Woes," *Washington Post*, February 12, 1984; and Williams, "Bungling the Military Buildup," *New York Times*, January 27, 1985.

94 Conahan, *Operation Desert Storm...*, 2-3.

95 Henderson, "Aircraft-Style Avionics... ."

96 Corporate finance in the 1980s was often a frenzy of deal-making, driven primarily by leveraged buyouts that required rising stock prices. This set the stage for abuse. Ivan F. Boesky and others were accused of profiting from trading the stock of FMC, a supplier of armored vehicles to the Marine Corps, with information unavailable to other investors (Cox, "Insider Trading," 2). The bad press might have played a part in the Marine Corps looking at its options.

97 EFV.USMC.mil., "EFV Program Highlights by Acquisition Phase."

98 Company lore had passed down hearsay from a trip of senior executives to Taiwan a few years earlier. The General Dynamics executives heard from their Taiwanese counterparts that this Mike Wynne fellow was hard to work with. Wynne demanded too much in negotiations. The Taiwanese could not know that they probably were giving Mike their highest recommendation as far as General Dynamics senior leadership would view it.

Chapter Thirteen: Rockets and Russians

99 Boyne, *Beyond the Wild Blue*, 112.

100 It was atop an Atlas D missile that astronaut John Glenn rode to fame and fortune aboard Gemini 6, call sign "Friendship 7," on February 20, 1962, as the United States' first man to orbit the earth.

101 Arianespace and the European Space Agency were Western Europe's answer to the polarization of rocket science to Russia in the east and America in the west.

102 Gawdiak, *Astronautics and Aeronautics*, 55.

103 Ibid., 239.

104 Ibid., 347.

105 The Atlas-Centaur I program initiated launches in 1990 before Mike Wynne arrived at Space Systems and continued after he left the scene. In total, the Atlas-Centaur I was launched 11 times. Three were failures, all during Mike's watch. The Atlas-Centaur II versions began launching during his tenure at Space Systems and continued after he departed. The Atlas-Centaur II program (II, IIA, and IIAS) recorded a perfect 63 for 63 success rate (Wade, "Encyclopedia Astronautica").

106 Once the idea of purchasing Russian engines became public, pressure would mount to build the rocket motors in the United States. With a collapsing Soviet Union, Americans would not want to prop up a faltering industry in Russia. For their part, the Russians would not want to give their technology to the Americans, always fearing for their security. But it made sense: it fast-tracked the Americans years down the development path and kept the Russian production lines in operation. Both countries had to learn to trust each other.

107 For an excellent review of the defense industry, see *The US Defense Industrial Base: Past, Present and Future* by Barry D. Watts (Washington, D.C., 2008). In time, the industry would go from two dozen to but a handful of major defense contractors.

108 U.S. Securities and Exchange Commission. *Form 10-K for 1993. General Dynamics*, 5, 23–4.

109 Ibid. *Form 10-K for 1997. General Dynamics*, 28.

110 Mintz, "Launching a Drive for Federal Help," *Washington Post*, January 12, 1994, F1.

111 U.S. Congress. House. *International Competition...*, 38, 173.

112 The purchase of GE Aerospace, which made satellites, by Martin Marietta, operator of launch systems, conflicted everyone. Norm Augustine wanted his satellite division free to use the most cost-effective delivery systems but not to the detriment of his other division, the launch guys in Denver. On one of Augustine's trips to San Diego while acquiring the Atlas-Centaur system, Mike Wynne had occasion to lobby with the chief executive. Martin Marietta was paying more than $200 million for the delivery system and needed to earn that back. Mike asked Augustine to give him three years to effect the consolidation and realize the savings before opening up GE satellite launches to unfettered competition. For the most part, that is exactly what happened.

113 Mathews, "Defense Firms' Merger Plan Hailed," *Washington Post*, August 31, 1994.

114 Concept validation began in 1995, followed by predevelopment contracts in 1996. The RD-180 was tested at the Marshall Space Flight Center in 1998. In 2000 an Atlas-Centaur IIIA, also called an Atlas-Centaur IIAR, rocketed into the atmosphere on top of a RD-180 powered first-stage. The Atlas-Centaur IIIA, the first true two-stage Atlas, evolved into the Atlas V program, which continued to utilize the Russian engine in the first stage.

115 U.S. Department of Justice, "Two Former Boeing... ." The Air Force would later penalize Boeing for its misdeeds by transferring seven of Boeing's launch contracts to Lockheed Martin (see Ray, Justin).

116 James Ling was an early devotee of the conglomerate structure in business organizations. Using his Dallas-based electrical contracting firm, Ling Electric, he fashioned LTV by 1962 through takeovers of Temco Aircraft and Chance Vought Aircraft. Conglomerates in general and LTV in particular were successful during the 1960s. LTV's acquisition of Jones & Laughlin Steel in 1969 would prove to be one too many and its undoing. Vought Aeronautics, and Vought Missiles and Space continue as divisions of Northrop Grumman and Lockheed Martin, respectively.

Chapter Fourteen: Big Business, Small Business

117 Alliant Techsystems was a company created in 1990 by a Honeywell spinoff. In that period of corporate restructuring, many companies would spin off subsidiaries to shareholders as a defensive maneuver. Since Wall Street accorded conglomerates a lower multiple, penalizing stock price, companies often generated increased shareholder value by splitting off divisions. For whatever reasons, Honeywell decided to spin off its defense business, resulting in the

creation of Alliant Techsystems. In fleshing out its independent business plan, Alliant Techsystems acquired Hercules Aerospace in 1995. For its fiscal year ending March 31, 1996, Alliant Techsystems sales exceeded $1 billion for the first time.

118 U.S. Securities and Exchange Commission. *Form 10-KSB for 2000. The IXATA Group*, 1, 10, 23.

Chapter Fifteen: Launching Government Service

119 Scarborough, "Rumsfeld's 'Defense Inc.' Reasserts Civilian Control," *Washington Times*, January 6, 2005, A1.

120 Federal Election Commission records for the Republican National Committee for the year 2000 listed receipts of $190 million and disbursements of $171 million (http://images.nictusa.com/cgi-bin/fecimg/?21036830011). Mike Wynne's contributions totaled $10,250 during the period (ibid., Report page 3231 of 3763).

121 See *A History of the Committee on Science and Technology*, 120-7. (http://science.house.gov/sites/republicans.science.house.gov/files/documents/Committee_History_50years.pdf).

122 According to Federal Election Commission records Mike Wynne contributed $750 to the Leahy for U.S. Senator Committee on May 20, 1998 (http://query.nictusa.com/cgi-bin/com_ind/C00068353/U-Z/) and the same amount to the Feinstein for Senate campaign on August 5, 1999 (http://query.nictusa.com/cgi-bin/can_ind/S0CA00199/2/W/).

123 U.S. Congress. Senate. Committee on Armed Services, *Nominations.... .*107th Congress, 1st Session, 935–1030.

Chapter Sixteen: A&T, E-mails, and Appointments

124 Delos Cosgrove graduated Williams College in 1962 and received his medical training at the University of Virginia. As a young physician Dr. Cosgrove served in the United States Air Force in Vietnam and was decorated with the Bronze Star. Dr. Gillinov received his doctor of medicine in 1988.

125 Bush, "A Period of Consequences."

126 U.S. Congress. Senate. Committee on Armed Services, *The Crusader Artillery System*. 107th Congress, 2d Session, 41–2.

127 Butler, "Wynne 'Throws the Book' at Services over Joint UCAV Office Issue."

128 "...not expressed any urgency..." (Lepore, *Military Aircraft*, 7). "...a weakening economy..." The chairman of the Council of Economic Advisors

under President Clinton noted in remarks in 2002 that "…the economy was slipping into recession even before Bush took office…" (Stiglitz, "The Roaring Nineties," 77). The NASDAQ peaked at 5,048 on March 10, 2000 and sank 45 percent by the time President Bush took office. The National Bureau of Economic Research, of which Ben Bernanke was a Business Cycle Dating Committee member, eventually fixed the span of the recession from March to November 2001 (NBER, "US Business Cycle…"). In any view, the economic engine in 2001 was sputtering, and the White House wanted to reenergize the economy.

129 Curtin, *Military Aircraft*, 3.

130 U.S. Department of Defense. *Department of Defense and Emergency Supplemental Appropriations…*, 2284–85.

131 Mike Wynne had a bit of history with Druyun, from his time running Space Systems for Martin Marietta in Denver in the mid-1990s. He was ill at ease with the way she handled herself and generally avoided Druyun on her visits to Waterton Canyon. Mike's associates cautioned that he not be so obvious in his disdain for her.

132 Between 1993 and 2002, the four secretaries of defense were Les Aspin, William Perry, William Cohen, and Donald Rumsfeld. The four Air Force chiefs of staff were Merrill McPeak, Ronald Fogleman, Michael Ryan, and John Jumper. The three secretaries of the Air Force were Sheila Widnall, Whitten Peters, and James Roche. The four assistant secretaries of the Air Force for acquisition, to whom Darleen Druyun reported, were Clark Fiester, Arthur Money, Lawrence Delaney, and Marvin Sambur.

133 U.S. Department of Defense. Office of the Inspector General. "Management Accountability…," iv.

134 Ibid, "decision memorandum" 20, "tacitly" 34.

135 Ibid., iv.

136 In time, the Air Force was allowed to reopen the aerial refueling tanker proposal. Wanting true competition for the tankers, the Senate insisted on a bidding process to prevent a sole-source contract. This was easier said than done because few companies had the wherewithal to produce a refueling tanker of the size envisioned. The airliner market in 2005 was different from that in 1985.

The commercial airline market had gone through a significant restructuring. What began as rivalry among Lockheed's L-1011, McDonnell Douglas' DC-10, and Boeing's 747 evolved into just one player in the 1980s, the Boeing Company. Overconfident and arrogant, Boeing was positioned for downfall in its own classical tragedy. The company had allowed a new competitor to gain a foothold in the market, a young, risk-taking enterprise that used government subsidies to gain the time needed to carve out its niche.

Airbus traced its lineage back to the Anglo-French development of the Concorde SST in the 1960s. While only 20 SSTs ever flew in scheduled service, the design and manufacturing know-how generated by the first supersonic transport proved decisive. Airbus, which became the aircraft manufacturing division of EADS (European Aeronautic Defense and Space), started as a consortium owned by France, Germany, Great Britain, and Spain. Active management of the company settled into the hands of France and Germany. Success with its A-300 series of commercial airliners led to development of other uses, such as refueling tankers.

With the original Boeing deal disqualified and canceled, the Air Force started over again, this time with Mike Wynne as SECAF. Two serious bids emerged. One led by Boeing, the inventor of the refueling tanker "flying boom," and the other by a partnership of EADS (Airbus) and Northrop Grumman, trying to bid their way into a contract that had never before been open to competition. Boeing structured its bid on the B-767 airframe. The Airbus consortium based its bid on the A-330 airframe. The EADS–Northrop Grumman proposal was chosen by the Air Force, but the award was ill fated.

While EADS–Northrop committed to having at least 50 percent of the tankers content "Made in America," pressure remained for "Buy American." Even though an assembly plant would be built in the United States and thousands of jobs created, many felt the award would place a critical program in the hands of foreigners. Boeing protested the award, and in 2008 based on what many would posture as technicalities, the Government Accounting Office tossed out the award and urged the Air Force to reopen the project for competitive bids. This second failed attempt at acquiring refueling tankers cast the process as ridiculous.

The Pentagon would rework its request for proposal yet another time, some say to more closely align the military prerequisite with the Boeing product, and call for a new round of bids. Feeling the process Sisyphean and simply a charade to crown Boeing, Northrop Grumman withdrew from contention and left EADS on its own. The fact that a representative from Boeing's home state of Washington was succeeding to the chair of the House Appropriations subcommittee on Defense may also have weighed on the decision. It was expected that Boeing would be the supplier if it could best any EADS proposal, albeit a sole-source one, just as the Senate feared.

On February 24, 2011, the Pentagon awarded Boeing a contract for 179 tankers valued at more than $30 billion (www.defense.gov/releases/release.aspx?releaseid=14292). While the award may experience political opposition and is subject to appeal, quite possibly the third time is the charm. New tankers are not expected to appear on the ramp for six years, and even though the arrangement is a fixed-price contract it is probably fair to expect pricing issues to surface. The Pentagon steadfastly refused to consider a split-award.

137 U.S. Department of Defense. Office of the Inspector General. "Management Accountability...," 124–34. Secretary Roche asking help in pressuring Mike Wynne was also noted by Senator McCain at U.S. Congress. Senate. Committee on Armed Services, *Department of Defense Authorization...* . 108th Congress, 2d Session, 54.

138 U.S. Congress. Senate. Committee on Armed Services, *Nominations...* . 108th Congress, 1st Session, 473–545. "two paragraph prepared statement," 484.

139 Ibid., 481–86 and 494–95.

140 Ibid., 484.

141 U.S. Department of Defense. "Base Closure and Realignment Report," E-1, E-5, E-65.

142 The Navy ended up being the lead at four joint bases, while giving up control at four others. The Army became lead at two joint bases, while relinquishing control at five. The Air Force became lead at six joint bases and turned over support at five others (Joint Base Oversight, "Joint Base Pearl Harbor-Hickam," 4).

143 The Pentagon issued its recommendations on May 13, 2005. The commission held site visits and hearings, most of which were carried live on C-SPAN. The commission forwarded a final list to the president on September 8, 2005.

144 U.S. Congress. Senate. Committee on Armed Services, *Department of Defense Authorization...* . 108th Congress, 2d Session, 53.

145 *Congressional Record*, S11536–S11542.

146 At the end of the then-current session of Congress, all pending nominations died, one of which was Mike Wynne's. The Washington rumor mill, quoted through unnamed senior defense officials, senate aides and the like, predicted that his nomination would not be advanced a second time (Scarborough, "Pentagon Likely, to Drop...," *Washington Times*, January 6, 2005, A10).

147 "Pentagon Official...," *Defense Daily*, March 29, 2005.

148 Hoque et al., *CRS Report for Congress: Recess Appointments...*, i.

149 Ibid., 13.

150 Lok, "Big Spenders," 67.

151 U.S. Congress. Senate. Committee on Armed Services, *Department of Defense Authorization...* . 109th Congress, 1st Session, 656.

Chapter Seventeen: Nudging Serendipity

152 Pat Wynne's old Triple Nickel, the 555th Tactical Fighter Squadron, played a role in the Yugoslav Wars. Stationed at Aviano Air Base in Italy with the 31st Fighter Wing in 1994, the 555th flew in both the War in Bosnia and Herzegovina, recording hundreds of sorties in enforcing the no-fly zone, as well as the Kosovo

War, flying more than 1,000 sorties.

153 Wynne, "Lasting Heritage...," 2.

154 The term cyberspace, an allusion to the massing of computer networks, was coined in the early 1980s by science fiction writer William Gibson. He wrote about computer networks and hackers in his 1982 short story "Burning Chrome" and in his 1984 novel *Neuromancer*.

155 Wynne, "Objections to the Budget Submitted for the Air Force for Fiscal Year 2009," 1.

Chapter Eighteen: Service Summons Sacrifice

156 "lack of effective leadership oversight" (Gates, "Remarks to Airmen").

157 As a matter of policy, the Department of Defense neither acknowledges nor denies the location or movement of nuclear components. As a corollary, it is difficult to find information on what the worst-case scenario might have been in a release of weapon-grade plutonium into the atmosphere. Professor Theodore Liolios of the Hellenic Arms Control Center fashioned an approximation of the inhalation and ground contamination hazards that might have resulted had the nuclear cruise missile incident become an accident. Conducted at the Center for International and Security Studies at the University of Maryland, his report estimated a release would "increase the individual cancer risk by (at least) an amount of 5%-20%" within one kilometer of the discharge, and in the surrounding five kilometers "decontamination operational costs would be of the order of $75 million." Roughly $8 million per day would be required for evacuation expenses.

158 Alderson, "US Punishes 70 for Warhead Blunder," *Sunday Telegraph (LONDON)*, October 21, 2007. Two months after Wynne and Moseley left office, new leadership in the Air Force took administrative action against six generals and nine colonels in connection with the Admiral Donald Report. The administrative actions were letters of reprimand, admonishment, or counseling (Secretary of the Air Force Public Affairs, "Air Force Takes Action...," October 2008).

159 Admiral Kirkland H. Donald, *Report of the Investigation into the Facts and Circumstances Surrounding the Accountability for, and Shipment of, Sensitive Military Components to Taiwan.* N00N/08-0051, May 22, 2008. A copy of the report is available in the electronic reading room of the Office of the Secretary of Defense and the Joint Staff at: www.dod.mil/pubs/foi/operation_and_plans/ NuclearChemicalBiologicalMatters/08-F-1244_ADM_Donald_Rpt_sanitized_v3 .pdf.

160 The Marine contingent in Beirut, inasmuch as it was an amphibious operation,

had a blended command. Navy Captain Morgan France was Amphibious Task Force commander and Marine Colonel Timothy Geraghty was Marine Amphibious Unit commander. France was the senior commander, while Geraghty was the on-site commander. Both reported to the commander, Sixth Fleet. The House Committee on Armed Services Investigation Subcommittee report of December 19, 1983, in the executive summary determined the bombing had "…a series of circumstances beyond the control of these commanders…" (Long, *Report of the DoD Commission…*, 7).

161 Castelli, "Defense Department Adopts New Definition for 'Cyberspace.'"

162 Kuehl, "From Cyberspace to Cyberpower."

163 Sangalang, "Space Pioneer… ."

164 The investigation of accountability regarding the Air Force shipments to the government of Taiwan was commissioned on March 25, 2008, and tasked to Admiral Kirkland Donald. On June 12, 2008, exactly one week after dismissing the Air Force leadership, the secretary of defense appointed James Schlesinger to conduct an overall assessment of the Department of Defense stewardship of its nuclear mission. In phase II of the Task Force on DOD Nuclear Weapons Management report, issued December 18, 2008, the executive summary states, "…the Task Force found that the lack of interest in and attention to the nuclear mission and nuclear deterrence … go well beyond the Air Force. This lack of interest and attention have been widespread throughout DoD and contributed to the decline of attention in the Air Force. …" (Schlesinger, *Report of the Secretary of Defense Task Force…*, iii).

165 After the Donald Report was issued, the Navy continued to have problems with its nuclear mission. On August 1, 2008, six weeks after Wynne left office, the Navy reported that its SSN-713 *Houston*, a *Los Angeles*–class submarine with an acting credit in *The Hunt for Red October*, was found to be leaking radioactive water while on patrol. While the leak released "negligible" radioactivity, it was later revealed that the problem had existed for two years (Yamaguchi, "US Tells Japan…," Associated Press Worldstream). In all cases, the senior leadership of the Navy was not held accountable for the nuclear failures.

166 Secretary Gates' selections for permanent service secretaries illustrated his predilection for politicians. He chose Ray Mabus, former governor of Mississippi and ambassador to Saudi Arabia, for secretary of the Navy. His two preferences for secretary of the Army were both congressmen. Pete Geren was an aide to U.S. Senator Lloyd Bentsen and served four terms in Congress; John McHugh was state senator from New York and an eight-term U.S. Congressman. For secretary of the Air Force, he chose Michael Donley, basically a career civil servant with experience working with the Senate Armed Services Committee, National Security Council, and Department of the Air Force. He also worked with a defense contractor heavily involved with Pentagon work.

Chapter Nineteen: Closing the Circle

167 Early production models of the McDonnell Aircraft F-4C Phantom II were equipped with the Martin-Baker Mk. H-5 ejection seat. In September 1965 the Navy began upgrading the ejection seats on their F-4Cs to the Mk. H-7 designation (Martin-Baker, *The History and Development...*, 33). The primary differences were the change from an 80-feet per second to a more spine-friendly 60-feet per second catapult and the addition of an underseat rocket pack, which gave it zero-zero capability. Upgrades to the F-4s in the Air Force's 8th Tactical Fighter Wing inventory did not begin until January 1968 (Clinton, "Phantoms Lair...," www.8tfw.com/pages/8thhistory1968.htm). Pat Wynne's ejection on August 8, 1966, dates his aircraft as not having been upgraded to the newer seat.

168 Schaffner, Herbert G. *The Ring of a Fallen Soldier.*

Epilogue

169 4/9 Infantry Manchu (Vietnam) Association, "The Vietnam Veterans Memorial, The Wall-USA."

BIBLIOGRAPHY

12th TFW Association. "12th Tactical Fighter Wing History." 2006. 12th TFW Association. http://www.12tfw.org/history.htm (accessed October 2, 2009).

366th Fighter Group Association. "366th Fighter Group Association—History-Vietnam." 1995–2010. 366th Fighter Group Association. http://366fightergroupassoc.org/History-RVN.htm (accessed June 29, 2010).

4/9 Infantry Manchu (Vietnam) Association. "The Vietnam Veterans Memorial, The Wall-USA." 1996–2006. 4/9 Infantry Manchu (Vietnam) Association. http://thewall-usa.com/ (accessed September 28, 2010).

81 TRW History Office and U.S. Air Force. *A Brief History of Keesler AFB and the 81st Training Wing.* Mississippi: Keesler Air Force Base, 2007. http://www .keesler.af.mil/shared/media/document/AFD-080226-025.pdf (accessed May 24, 2009; site now discontinued).

AFIT/PA. *AFIT History.* Ohio: Air Force Institute of Technology, 2008. http:// www.afit.edu/about.cfm?a=history (accessed August 23, 2009).

aiipowmia. "Histories: US Army CILHI." AII POW-MIA InterNetwork. http:// www.aiipowmia.net/histories/histcilhi.html (accessed August 22, 2009).

"Air Force Scraps Plans for Cyber Command in Favor of New Nuclear Organization." *Defense Daily,* October 10, 2008. http://www.lexisnexis.com .ezproxy.dom.edu/us/lnacademic/ (accessed May 23, 2010).

Alderson, Andrew, and Tim Shipman. "US Punishes 70 for Warhead Blunder." *Sunday Telegraph (LONDON),* October 21, 2007, sec. NEWS, 16. http://www .lexisnexis.com.ezproxy.dom.edu/us/lnacademic/ (accessed November 19, 2008).

Alexander, Charles P., Christopher Redman and John E. Yang. "General Dynamics Under Fire." *Time,* April 8, 1985. http://www.time.com/time/magazine/ article/0,9171,965505,00.html (accessed April 5, 2010).

Ancestrylibrary.com. "World War I Draft Registration Cards, 1917-1918; U.S. World War II Draft Registration Cards, 1942." Ancestry.com Library Edition. http://search.ancestrylibrary.com (accessed January 29, 2009).

APC Maxwell AFB. "Air & Space Power Course." United States Air Force, May 1, 2008. http://www.apc.maxwell.af.mil/main.htm (accessed February 8, 2009).

Ashcroft, Bruce, et al. *We Wanted Wings: A History of the Aviation Cadet Program.* Randolph Air Force Base, Tx.: HQ, AETC, Office of History and Research, 2005.

Association of Graduates. "USAFA Graduate Memorial Wall." 2008. Friends of The Air Force Academy Library. http://memwall.usafalibrary.com/person .asp?action=list (accessed August 22, 2009).

Atkinson, Rick. *The Long Gray Line.* Boston: Houghton Mifflin, 1989.

Baldwin, William C. *Four Housing Privatization Programs: A History of the Wherry, Capehart, Section 801 and Section 802 Family Housing Programs in the Army.* Alexandria, Va.: U.S. Army Corps of Engineers, Office of History, October 1996. http://www.acq.osd.mil/housing/docs/four.htm (accessed July 6, 2009).

Barbree, Jay. *Live from Cape Canaveral: Covering the Space Race, from Sputnik to Today.* 1st ed. New York: Smithsonian Books/Collins, 2007.

"Beatrice Hickey Becomes Bride of Lieut. Arnold: Son of Army Air Corps Chief Married in New York Hotel." *Washington Post (1877-1954)*, June 13, 1940, 14. http://www.proquest.com.ezproxy.dom.edu/ (accessed January 23, 2009).

Bessette, Cathy. "Oral History Interview: An Illinois Vietnam Veteran Recounts His Experience in the War." Unpublished Term Paper. Joliet, Illinois: May, 1999.

Bessette, Philip. Unpublished Letters Sent Home from Vietnam. 1971.

Biddle, Wayne. *Barons of the Sky.* New York: Simon & Schuster, 1991.

Booth, William D., et al., ed. *1966 Howitzer.* Dallas, Tx.: Taylor Publishing, 1966.

Boyne, Walter J. *Beyond the Wild Blue: A History of the United States Air Force, 1947-1997.* 1st ed. New York: St. Martin's Press, 1997.

Brooks, David W. "Military Airfields in WW2, 1941-1945." 2009. http://www .airfieldsdatabase.com/WW2/WW2.htm (accessed June 17, 2009).

Brown, B. Frank. *The Nongraded High School.* Englewood Cliffs, N.J.: Prentice-Hall, 1963. Available at: http://catalog.hathitrust.org/api/volumes/oclc/190105 .html (accessed May 4, 2010).

Bush, George W. "A Period of Consequences." Speech by President on September 23, 1999 at The Citadel, South Carolina. http://www.citadel.edu/pao/addresses/ pres_bush.html (accessed May 11, 2010).

Butler, Amy. "Wynne 'Throws the Book' at Services Over Joint UCAV Office Issue." *Inside the Air Force*, April 18, 2003. http://www.lexisnexis.com.ezproxy .dom.edu/us/lnacademic/ (accessed July 31, 2010).

Byrne, John A. *The Whiz Kids: The Founding Fathers of American Business—and the Legacy they Left Us.* 1st ed. New York: Doubleday, 1993.

Carhart, Tom. "Interview with Michael W. Wynne '66, Acting Undersecretary of Defense for Acquisition, Technology and Logistics." *Assembly* LXII.3 (2005): 34.

Castelli, Christopher J. "Defense Department Adopts New Definition for 'Cyberspace.'" *Inside the Air Force,* May 23, 2008. http://www.lexisnexis.com .ezproxy.dom.edu/us/lnacademic/ (accessed July 16, 2010).

Cima, Ronald J., Library of Congress, and Federal Research Division. *Vietnam: A Country Study.* 1st ed. Washington, DC: Federal Research Division, 1989. http://purl.access.gpo.gov/GPO/LPS40664 (accessed February 12, 2009).

Clinton, Robert F. "Phantom's Lair, Home of the 8th TFW's Famous 'Wolf Pack.'" 1995–2009. http://www.8tfw.com/pages/index2.htm (accessed October 2009).

Clodfelter, Mark. *The Limits of Air Power: The American Bombing of North Vietnam.* New York; London: Free Press; Collier Macmillan, 1989.

Conahan, Frank C. and United States General Accounting Office. *Operation Desert Storm Early Performance Assessment of Bradley and Abrams: Report to the Chairman, Subcommittee on Regulation, Business Opportunities, and Energy, Committee on Small Business, House of Representatives (GAO/NSAID-92-94).* Washington, DC: GAO, January 1992. http://archive.gao.gov/d31t10/145879.pdf (accessed May 15, 2011).

Congressional Directory. "Biographical Directory of the United States Congress." United States Congress. http://bioguide.congress.gov/biosearch/biosearch.asp (accessed January 23, 2009).

Congressional Record. 108th Cong., 2d sess. 2004: Vol. 150, No. 134. http://frwebgate.access.gpo.gov/cgi-bin/getpage.cgi?dbname=2004_record&page=S11515&position=all (accessed April 4, 2010).

Correll, John T. "The Vietnam War Almanac." *Air Force Magazine* 87.9 (2004): 42. http://www.airforce-magazine.com/MagazineArchive/Magazine%20Documents/2004/September%202004/0904vietnam.pdf (accessed February 8, 2009).

Cox, Charles C. "Insider Trading—the Market's Albatross." Abstract of remarks to the Center for the Study of Banking and Financial Markets, University of Washington, Seattle, by the Commissioner of the U.S. Securities and Exchange Commission. http://edgar.sec.gov/news/speech/1987/022087cox.pdf (accessed December 22, 2009).

Crowell, Paul. "Gay Midnight Crowd Rides First Trains in Subway." *New York*

Times, September 10, 1932, 1. Archived at: http://nycsubway.org/articles/nytimes-1932-indopen.html (accessed January 22, 2009).

Curley, John. "On the Defensive: Business is just Fine at General Dynamics, Yet Troubles Abound --- an Ex-Officer's Indictment, Probes and Angry Union Beset Defense Contractor --- F-16s and the Peanut Farm." *Wall Street Journal*, May 18, 1984, 1. http://www.proquest.umi.com.ezproxy.dom.edu/ (accessed November 29, 2010).

Curtin, Neal P. *Military Aircraft: Observations on DOD's Aerial Refueling Aircraft Acquisition Options (GAO-04-169R)*. Washington, DC: GAO, October 14, 2003. http://www.gao.gov/new.items/d04169r.pdf (accessed February 21, 2010).

Department of Defense. Department of the Air Force. "Bob Hope Christmas Special, 02/01/1967." Posted Online by Public.Resource.Org on YouTube. http://www.youtube.com/watch?v=SzOsLRT7d5c&feature=related (accessed April 29, 2010). Also archived at: http://www.archive.org/details/gov.archives.arc.64135.

Dodd, Jan, Mark Lewis, and Ron Emmons. *Vietnam*. 4th ed. New York; London: Rough Guides, 2003.

Donaldson, Anthony. "Guide to the Philip W. Lett Collection, RG 740." Auburn University Special Collections and Archives 2002. http://www.lib.auburn.edu/archive/find-aid/740.htm (accessed December 22, 2009).

EFV.USMC.mil. "EFV Program Highlights by Acquisition Phase." 2009. U.S. Marine Corps. http://www.efv.usmc.mil/ (accessed May 8, 2010).

Eisenhower, Dwight D. "Farewell Address." Radio and Television Address by President on January 17, 1961 from Washington, DC. Available at: http://millercenter.org/scripps/archive/speeches/detail/3361 (accessed May 10, 2010).

Federal Election Commission. "Campaign Finance Reports and Data." Federal Election Commission. http://www.fec.gov/disclosure.shtml (accessed May 9, 2011).

Feinman, Mark S. "History of the Independent Subway." New York City Subway Resources. http://www.nycsubway.org/articles/historyindependentsubway.html (accessed January 20, 2009).

Flight Helmet LLC. "Ejection Seat Torso Harnesses & Fittings." 2003. CSA Corporation. http://www.flighthelmet.com/info/koch.htm (accessed May 3, 2010).

Freeman, Paul. "Abandoned & Little Known Airfields: Southwestern Ohio." 2007. Paul Freeman. http://www.airfields-freeman.com/OH/Airfields_OH_SW.htm (accessed August 23, 2009).

Fryer, Thomas. "Pat Wynne Reflections 1959–1966." Unpublished Personal Papers. November, 2009.

Fullerton, A. W., et al., ed. *1963 Polaris*. Vol. #5. Marceline, Mo.: Walsworth Publishing, 1963.

Futrell, Robert Frank, et al. *Aces & Aerial Victories: The United States Air Force in Southeast Asia, 1965-1973*. Maxwell Air Force Base, Al.; Washington, DC: Albert F. Simpson Historical Research Center, Air University; GPO, 1976. http://www.airforcehistory.hq.af.mil/Publications/fulltext/aces_aerial_victories.pdf (accessed October 2009).

Gates, Robert M. "Remarks to Airmen." Comments by Secretary of Defense on June 9, 2008 at Langley Air Force Base, Virginia. Available at: http://www.defense.gov/speeches/speech.aspx?speechid=1256 (accessed May 26, 2011).

Gawdiak, Ihor, and Charles Shetler. *Astronautics and Aeronautics, 1991-1995: A Chronology*. Washington, DC: National Aeronautics & Space Administration, Office of Policy and Plans, NASA History Division, 2000. http://history.nasa.gov/AAchronologies/1991-1995.pdf (accessed December 30, 2009).

Geselowitz, Michael and Brad Parkinson. "Oral History: Brad Parkinson." 1999. IEEE History Center. http://www.ieeeghn.org/wiki/index.php/Oral-History:Brad_Parkinson (accessed June 2, 2010).

Griffin, Charles J. G. "New Light on Eisenhower's Farewell Address." *Presidential Studies Quarterly* XXII.3 (1992): 469-80.

Guarino, Larry. *A POW's Story: 2801 Days in Hanoi*. 1st ed. New York: Ivy Books, 1990.

Gunzinger, Mark Alan, and Center for Strategic and Budgetary Assessments. "Sustaining America's strategic advantage in long-range strike." 2010. Center for Strategic and Budgetary Assessments. http://www.csbaonline.org/4Publications/PubLibrary/R.20100914.Sustaining_America/R.20100914.Sustaining_America.pdf (accessed November 4, 2010).

Hallgren, John F. "Ozark Flight." Unpublished Personal Papers. January, 2000. Revised April, 2005.

Hallion, Richard P. *Control of the Air: The Enduring Requirement*. Washington, DC: Air Force Historical Studies Office, September 1999. http://www.airforcehistory.hq.af.mil/Publications/fulltext/control_of_air.htm (accessed February 2, 2009).

Hartung, William D. "Eisenhower's Warning: The Military-Industrial Complex Forty Years Later." *World Policy Journal* 18.1 (2001): 39-44. http://www.lexisnexis.com.ezproxy.dom.edu/us/lnacademic/ (accessed May 3, 2010).

Haulman, Daniel. "USAF Aerial Victory Credits On-Line." 2000. Air Force Historical Research Agency. http://www.afhra.af.mil/factsheets/factsheet .asp?id=11421 (accessed September 14, 2009).

Henderson, Breck W. "Aircraft-Style Avionics Add Punch to U. S. Army's Next-Generation Tank." *Aviation Week & Space Technology*, January 7, 1991, 45. http:// www.lexisnexis.com.ezproxy.dom.edu/us/lnacademic/ (accessed July 29, 2010).

Henney, Elizabeth. "Record Throng Sees West Point Graduates Parade, Get Honors." *Washington Post (1877-1954)*, June 10, 1940. http://www.proquest .com.ezproxy.dom.edu/ (accessed 2009).

HeritageQuest.com. "1920 United States Federal Census Records." ProQuest. http://persi.heritagequestonline.com (accessed January 28, 2009).

Hogue, Henry B. and Maureen Bearden. *CRS Report for Congress: Recess Appointments made by President George W. Bush, January 20, 2001-October 31, 2008. (RL33310).* Washington, DC: Congressional Research Service, November 3, 2008. http://fas.org/sgp/crs/misc/RL33310.pdf (accessed April 5, 2010).

Holdeman, Richard E., Michael W. Wynne, and Air Force Inst. of Tech.—Wright-Patterson AFB OH School of Engineering. "Synthesis of a Suboptimal Guidance Law to Minimize the Terminal Error of an Entry Vehicle." (GGC/ EE/70-10). Master's Thesis, Air Force Institute of Technology, 1970. http:// www.dtic.mil/ (accessed December 17, 2008).

Hopkins, Robert S. Unpublished E-mails to John Hallgren. [2006?].

Indochina Administrative Divisions. Washington, DC: Office of Basic and Geographic Intelligence, U.S. Central Intelligence Agency, 1970. Map. http:// www.lib.utexas.edu/maps/indochina_atlas/txu-oclc-1092889-78343-8-70.jpg (accessed February 11, 2009).

Indochina Airfields. Washington, DC: Office of Basic and Geographic Intelligence, U.S. Central Intelligence Agency, 1970. Map. http://www.lib.utexas.edu/maps/ indochina_atlas/txu-oclc-1092889-78335-8-70.jpg (accessed February 11, 2009).

Indochina and Thailand 1:250,000. Washington, DC: Army Map Service, Corps of Engineers, 1957. Map. http://www.lib.utexas.edu/maps/ams/indochina_and_thai land/txu-oclc-6535632-nf48-12.jpg (accessed February 12, 2009).

Isserman, Maurice. *The Vietnam War.* New York: Facts on File, 1992.

Jane, Fred T. *Jane's All the World's Aircraft.* New York: McGraw-Hill, 1981 and 1986.

Johnson Space Center, NASA. "NASA, Astronaut Biographies, Former Astronauts, Biographical Data." Johnson Space Center, NASA. http://www.jsc.nasa.gov/ Bios/astrobio_former.html (accessed August 13, 2009).

Joint Base Oversight Working Group. "Joint Base Pearl Harbor-Hickam." March 2008 presentation. http://afceahi.org/briefs/2008/jun(u).ppt (accessed March 11, 2010).

Kelley, Tim and Dave Brann. "Alaska Lost Ski Areas Project." ALSAP. http://www.alsap.org/Chilkoot/Chilkoot.htm (accessed June 21, 2009).

Kuehl, Dan. "From Cyberspace to Cyberpower: Defining the Problem." Paper by Dan Kuehl presented to Information Resources Management College/National Defense University. http://www.carlisle.army.mil/DIME/documents/Cyber%20Chapter%20Kuehl%20Final.doc (accessed July 1, 2010).

Kurtz, Howard, and Michael Isikoff. "Defense Contract Woes; General Dynamics Under Fire; Contracts Virtually Assure High Profits into the 1990s." *Washington Post*, February 12, 1984. http://www.lexisnexis.com.ezproxy.dom.edu/us/lnacademic/ (accessed November 29, 2010).

Lepore, Brian J. *Military Aircraft: DOD Needs to Determine its Aerial Refueling Aircraft Requirements (GAO-04-349)*. Washington, DC: GAO, June, 2004. http://www.gao.gov/new.items/d04349.pdf (accessed February 21, 2010).

Lethbridge, Cliff. *The History of Cape Canaveral Chapter 2: The Missile Range Takes Shape (1949-1958)*. Florida: Spaceline, 2000. http://www.spaceline.org/capehistory/2a.html (accessed August 26, 2009).

Lewis, Andrew L., and Air Command and Staff College Maxwell AFB AL. *The Revolt of the Admirals*. Virginia: Ft. Belvoir Defense Technical Information Center, 1998. http://handle.dtic.mil/100.2/ADA398600 (accessed June 27, 2010).

Liolios, Theodore. "Broken Arrows: Radiological hazards from nuclear warhead accidents (the Minot USAF base nuclear weapons incident)." Paper, Hellenic Arms Control Center, 2008. Available at: http://arxiv.org/abs/0902.3824 (accessed April 29, 2011).

Lok, Corie. "Big Spenders." *Technology Review* 108.5 (2005): 66-71.

Long, Robert L. J., et al. *Report of the DoD Commission on Beirut International Airport Terrorist Act, October 23, 1983*. Department of Defense, December 1983 as transcribed by Peter Clauncey for the HyperWar Foundation: October 2001. http://www.ibiblio.org/hyperwar/AMH/XX/MidEast/Lebanon-1982-1984/DOD-Report/index.html#page2 (accessed June 24, 2009).

Lorenzini, Dino A., Michael W. Wynne, and Frank J. Seiler Research Lab—Air Force Academy CO. "A Root Locus Analysis of a Seismic Isolation Control System." Technical Paper, Frank J. Seiler Research Laboratory, 1974. http://www.dtic.mil/docs/citations/AD0783615 (accessed December 17, 2008).

Mac Donald, Heather. "How Gotham's Elite High Schools Escaped the Leveller's Ax." *City Journal*, Spring 1999. http://www.city-journal.org/html/9_2_how_goth ams_elite.html (accessed January 19, 2009).

Martin-Baker. *The History and Development of Martin-Baker Escape Systems.* Martin-Baker Aircraft Co. http://www.martin-baker.co.uk/getdoc/8c3022 ba-e798-4a97-826c-f8b83e1cb17b/History--26-Development-of-MBA-Mk1-Mk 10.aspx (accessed February 9, 2009).

Mathews, Jay. "Defense Firms' Merger Plan Hailed." *Washington Post*, August 31, 1994. http://www.lexisnexis.com.ezproxy.dom.edu/us/lnacademic/ (accessed January 7, 2010).

McFarland, Stephen L., and Air Force History Support Office—Bolling AFB DC. *A Concise History of the U.S. Air Force.* Virginia: Ft. Belvoir Defense Technical Information Center, 1997. http://handle.dtic.mil/100.2/ADA433274 (accessed December 17, 2008).

Miller, Edward Anthony. "The Founding of the Air Force Academy: An Administrative and Legislative History." Ph.D. diss., University of Denver, 1970.

Millis, Walter. *Arms and Men; a Study in American Military History.* New York: Putnam, 1956.

Mintz, John. "Launching a Drive for Federal Help; U.S. Rocket Firms, Facing Tough Competition from Abroad, Seek R&D Aid." *Washington Post*, January 12, 1994. http://www.lexisnexis.com.ezproxy.dom.edu/us/lnacademic/ (accessed January 7, 2010).

Mitchell, Vance O. *Air Force Officers: Personnel Policy Development 1944-1974.* Washington, DC: Air Force History and Museums Program, 1996.

Morrocco, John, and Boston Publishing Company. *Thunder from Above: Air War, 1941-1968.* Boston, Ma: Boston Pub. Co, 1984.

Mulson, Jennifer. "Pop Singer's Performance at AFA Hits Home." *Gazette. Com*, May 16, 2008. http://www.gazette.com/common/printer/view .php?db=colgazette&id=36411 (accessed June 20, 2010).

NARA—National Records and Archives Administration. "Combat Area Casualties Current File (CACCF)." NARA. http://www.archives.gov (accessed May 24, 2009).

NBER—National Bureau of Economic Research. "US Business Cycle Expansions and Contractions." 2010. NBER. http://www.nber.org/cycles/cyclesmain.html (accessed February 21, 2010).

Neufeld, Michael J. "The End of the Army Space Program: Interservice Rivalry and the Transfer of the Von Braun Group to NASA, 1958-1959." *Journal of*

Military History 69.3 (2005): 737-57. http://www.jstor.org/stable/3397117 (accessed April 20, 2010).

Newman, Richard J. "A General Salutes by Quitting." *U.S. News & World Report*, August 11, 1997, 5. http://www.lexisnexis.com.ezproxy.dom.edu/us/lnacademic/ (accessed January 7, 2010).

Norris, Floyd. "A 'Merger of Equals,' with Martin Marietta the most Equal." *New York Times*, August 31, 1994, sec. Market Place, 6. http://www.lexisnexis.com .ezproxy.dom.edu/us/lnacademic/ (accessed June 29, 2010).

Origins of the US Air Force. Washington, DC: Air Force Historical Studies Office, 2002. http://www.airforcehistory.hq.af.mil/PopTopics/origins.htm (accessed February 2, 2009).

O'Sullivan, Kalani. "Kunsan Air Base: How it was—8th Fighter Wing History (1954-1974)." http://kalaniosullivan/kunsanab/8thfw/howitwasb1a4.html (accessed October 1, 2009; site now discontinued).

ourstrongband.org. "Timeline & Notable Graduates." The Campaign for Stuyvesant. http://ourstrongband.org/history/timeline.html (accessed January 19, 2009).

Parkinson, Bradford W., Michael W. Wynne, and Leonard Richard Kruczynski. "Sight Line Autopilot: A New Concept in Air Weapons." Research Report 73-4, U.S. Air Force Academy, 1973. http://www.dtic.mil/dtic/tr/fulltext/u2/a005402.pdf (accessed December 17, 2008).

Parsch, Andreas. "Directory of U.S. Military Rockets and Missiles." July 9, 2007. http://www.designation-systems.net/dusrm/app1/index.html (accessed June 16, 2009).

Patrick AFB. "US Air Force Bases: Patrick Air Force Base, Florida." http://www .techbastard.com/afb/fl/patrick.php (accessed July 8, 2009).

Paulick, Michael, et al., ed. *1940 Howitzer*. Buffalo, NY: Baker, Jones, Hausauer, 1940.

"Pentagon Official Takes Over Major Air Force Acquisition Programs." *Defense Daily*, March 29, 2005. http://www.lexisnexis.com.ezproxy.dom.edu/us/ lnacademic/ (accessed May 23, 2010).

Principi, Anthony Joseph, United States, and Defense Base Closure and Realignment Commission. *2005 Defense Base Closure and Realignment Commission: Report to the President*. Arlington, Va.: Defense Base Closure and Realignment Commission, 2005. http://www.brac.gov/docs/final/ BRACReportcomplete.pdf (accessed April 6, 2010).

Ray, Justin. "Pentagon Strips 7 Launches from Boeing Delta 4 Rocket." *Spaceflight*

Now, July 24, 2003. http://spaceflightnow.com/news/n0307/24eelv/ (accessed June 8, 2010).

Robertson, Patsy. *555 Fighter Squadron (USAFE)*. Montgomery, Al.: Air Force Historical Research Agency, 2008. http://www.afhra.af.mil/factsheets/factsheet.asp?id=12031 (accessed September 14, 2009).

Ryba, Jeanne Ed. "First 100 U.S. Human Space Flights." 2008. NASA. http://www.nasa.gov/centers/kennedy/news/facts/hundred-toc.html (accessed June 17, 2009).

———. "Kennedy Space Center—Launch Vehicle Archives." 2009. NASA. http://www.nasa.gov/centers/kennedy/launchingrockets/archives/elv_archive-index.html (accessed August 13, 2009).

Sangalang, Jennifer. "Space Pioneer Col. Ed Wynne Dies at 79." *Florida Today*, January 17, 1998.

Scarborough, Rowan. "Pentagon Likely to Drop Weapons Buyer Nominee." *Washington Times*, January 6, 2005, sec. NATION, A10. http://www.lexisnexis.com.ezproxy.dom.edu/us/lnacademic/ (accessed January 14, 2010).

———. "Rumsfeld's 'Defense Inc.' Reasserts Civilian Control." *Washington Times*, April 24, 2001, A1. http://www.lexisnexis.com.ezproxy.dom.edu/us/lnacademic/ (accessed January 25, 2010).

Schaffner, Herbert G. "The Ring of a Fallen Soldier: Patrick Edward Wynne." Unpublished Personal Papers. 2008.

Schlesinger, James, et al. *Report of the Secretary of Defense Task Force on DoD Nuclear Weapons Management*. Washington, DC: Department of Defense, December 2008. http://www.defenselink.mil/pubs/pdfs/PhaseIIReportFinal.pdf (accessed June 26, 2009).

Schultis, Joseph E., John C. Burris and U.S. Air Force. "Student Pilot Time Certificate." Unpublished 3525th Pilot Training Wing Papers. Mesa, Az.: Williams Air Force Base, 1965.

Seaver, William J., et al., ed., ed. *1952 Howitzer*. Buffalo, NY: Baker, Jones, Hausauer & Savage, 1952.

Secretary of the Air Force Public Affairs. "Air Force Takes Action Against Officers for Donald Report Deficiencies." *Air Force Print News Today*, October 2008. http://www.whiteman.af.mil/news/story_print.asp?id=123117655 (accessed November 30, 2008).

Selective Service System. "History & Records—The Vietnam Lotteries." 2009. Selective Service System. http://www.sss.gov/lotter1.htm (accessed December 24, 2009).

Sharp, U. S. Grant. *We could have Won in Vietnam Long Ago*. Pleasantville, NY: Reader's Digest Association, 1969.

shsaa.org. "SHS History." Stuyvesant High School Alumni Association. http://shsaa.org/ (accessed January 19, 2009).

Smith, R. J. "Roche Cited for 2 Ethics Violations; Inspector General Says Former Air Force Secretary Misused His Office." *Washington Post*, February 10, 2005, A21. http://www.lexisnexis.com.ezproxy.dom.edu/us/lnacademic/ (accessed February 20, 2010).

Stanton, Shelby L. *Vietnam Order of Battle*. New York: Exeter Books, 1986.

Stiglitz, Joseph, and Anya Schiffrin. "The Roaring Nineties." *Atlantic Monthly* 290.3 (2002): 75-89. http://web.ebscohost.com.ezproxy.dom.edu/ (accessed February 20, 2010). Stout, Joe and Laurie Quincy. "United States Government Awards Lockheed Martin Contract to Begin Production of Advanced F-16 Aircraft for Morocco." Lockheed Martin (Press Release June 6, 2008). http://www.lockheedmartin.com/news/press_releases/2008/060608ae_f16morocco.html (accessed June 18, 2009).

"The Supreme Court: Implementing a Decision." *Time*, August 2, 1954. http://www.time.com/time/magazine/article/0,9171,890971,00.html (accessed June 20, 2010).

"Tall Comanche—Company C, 2nd Battalion, 5th Cavalry, 1st Cavalry Division (Airmobile): Vietnam 1965-1972." 2006. Tallcomanche.org. http://www.tallcomanche.org (accessed May 15, 2009).

Thompson, Wayne. *To Hanoi and Back: The United States Air Force and North Vietnam, 1966-1973*. Washington, DC: Smithsonian Institution Press, 2000. http://handle.dtic.mil/100.2/ADA439924 (accessed February 13, 2009.

Timmerman, Kenneth R. "Khobar Towers Shame—Ten Years After." *FrontPageMagazine.com*, June 23, 2006, 1. http://www.frontpagemag.com/readArticle.aspx?ARTID=3867 (accessed August 31, 2009).

Tirpak, John A. "Tanker Twilight Zone." *Air Force Magazine* (February 2004): 46. http://www.lexisnexis.com.ezproxy.dom.edu/us/lnacademic/ (accessed February 20, 2010).

Tyler, Patrick. *Running Critical: The Silent War, Rickover, and General Dynamics*. 1st ed. New York: Harper & Row, 1986.

United States Air Force Academy and Association of Graduates. *Register of Graduates of the United States Air Force Academy*. Colorado Springs, Co.: Association of Graduates, USAFA, 1984, 2002, 2008.

United States Military Academy and Association of Graduates. *Register of Graduates and Former Cadets of the United States Military Academy*. West Point, NY: Association of Graduates, USMA, 2008.

United States Military Academy. "Annual Report of the Superintendent—United States Military Academy." 1957, 1966. United States Military Academy. http://digital-library.usma.edu/collections/books/superep/index.asp (accessed July 24, 2010).

U.S. Congress. House. Committee on Science, Space and Technology. *International Competition in Launch Services: Hearing before the Subcommittee on Space of the House Committee on Science, Space, and Technology (Serial 103-22)*. 103rd Cong., 1st sess., May 19, 1993, 36. (Testimony of Michael W. Wynne). Washington, DC: GPO, 1993.

U.S. Congress. Senate. Committee on Armed Services. *The Crusader Artillery System: Hearing before the Committee on Armed Services*. 107th Cong., 2d sess., May 16, 2002. Washington, DC: GPO, 2003.

———. *Department of Defense Authorization for Appropriations for Fiscal Year 2005: Hearings before the Committee on Armed Services, United States Senate, 108th Cong., 2d sess., on S. 2400, to Authorize Appropriations for Fiscal Year 2005 for Military Activities of the Department of Defense, for Military Construction, and for Defense Activities of the Department of Energy, to Prescribe Personnel Strengths for such Fiscal Year for the Armed Forces, and for Other Purposes*. Washington, DC: GPO, 2005.

———. *Department of Defense Authorization for Appropriations for Fiscal Year 2006: Hearings before the Committee on Armed Services, United States Senate, 109th Cong., 1st sess., on S. 1042, to Authorize Appropriations for Fiscal Year 2006 for Military Activities of the Department of Defense, for Military Construction, and for Defense Activities of the Department of Energy, to Prescribe Personnel Strengths for such Fiscal Year for the Armed Forces, and for Other Purposes*. Washington, DC: GPO, 2006.

———. *Nominations before the Senate Armed Services Committee: Hearings before the Committee on Armed Services, United States Senate, 107th Cong., 1st sess., on Nominations of Donald H. Rumsfeld; Dr. Paul D. Wolfowitz; Dr. Dov S. Zakheim ... January 11, February 27, April 24, 26, May 1, 10, June 5, 7, 22, 27, July 31, August 1, September 13, 25, October 11, 23, November 8, December 4, 2001*. Washington, DC: GPO, 2002.

———. *Nominations before the Senate Armed Services Committee: Hearings before the Committee on Armed Services, United States Senate, 108th Cong., 1st sess., on Nominations of Paul McHale; Christopher Ryan Henry; Stephen A. Cambone; John Paul Woodley, Jr.; Linton F. Brooks; Lt. Gen. John P. Abizaid,*

USA; Thomas W. O'Connell; Paul M. Longsworth; Gen. Richard B. Myers, USAF; Gen. Peter Pace, USMC; Gen. Peter J. Schoomaker (Ret.), USA; Ltg. Bryan D. Brown, USA; Gordon R. England; and Michael W. Wynne, January 30, February 27, June 25, July 10, 24, 29, September 23, November 18, 2003. Washington, DC: GPO, 2005.

———. *Nominations before the Senate Armed Services Committee: Hearings before the Committee on Armed Services, United States Senate, 109th Cong., 1st sess., on Nominations of John Paul Woodley, Jr.; Buddie J. Penn; Adm. William J. Fallon, USN; Hon. Anthony J. Principi; Hon. Gordon R. England; Adm. Michael G. Mullen, USN; Kenneth J. Krieg; Lt. Gen. Michael V. Hayden, USAF; Gen. Peter Pace, USMC; Adm. Edmund P. Giambastiani, Jr., USN; Gen. T. Michael Moseley, USAF; Ambassador Eric S. Edelman; Daniel R. Stanley; James A. Rispoli; Lt. Gen. Norton A. Schwartz, USAF; Ronald M. Sega; Philip Jackson Bell; John G. Grimes; Keith E. Eastin; William C. Anderson; Hon. Michael W. Wynne; Dr. Donald C. Winter; Hon. John J. Young, Jr.; J. Dorrance Smith; Delores M. Etter; Gen. Burwell B. Bell III, USA; and Lt. Gen. Lance L. Smith, USAF, February 15, 17, March 15, April 19, 21, June 29, July 28, October 6, 25, 27, 2005.* Washington, DC: GPO, 2007.

U.S. Department of Defense. Office of the Inspector General. "Management Accountability Review of the Boeing KC-767A Tanker Program." 2005. Inspector General, Department of Defense. http://www.dodig.mil/fo/foia/tanker.htm (accessed March 4, 2010).

U.S. Department of Defense. "Base Closure and Realignment Report." Vol. 1, Part 1 of 2. 2005. Base Closure and Realignment Commission, Department of Defense. http://www.brac.gov/DocBrowse2005.aspx (accessed March 2, 2010).

———. *Department of Defense and Emergency Supplemental Appropriations for Recovery from and Response to Terrorist Attacks on the United States Act, 2002.* Washington, DC: GPO, 2002. http://purl.access.gpo.gov/GPO/LPS18923 (accessed February 21, 2010).

———. "Ozark Flight August 8, 1966 Mission Report." Declassified May 29, 1974. Department of Defense.

U.S. Department of Justice. "Two Former Boeing Managers Charged in Plot to Steal Trade Secrets from Lockheed Martin." United States Attorney, Central District of California (Press Release). June 25, 2003. http://www.justice.gov/criminal/cybercrime/branchCharge.htm (accessed June 8, 2010).

U.S. Securities and Exchange Commission. *Form 10-K for the Fiscal Year Ended 31 December 1993. General Dynamics Corporation.* Edgar Online. http://yahoo.brand.edgar-online.com/DisplayFilingInfo.aspx?Type=HTML&FilingID=1039306 (accessed January 4, 2010).

————. *Form 10-K for the Fiscal Year Ended 31 December 1997. General Dynamics Corporation.* Edgar Online. http://google.brand.edgar-online.com/ DisplayFilingInfo.aspx?Type=HTML&FilingID=928936 (accessed January 6, 2010).

————. *Form 10-KSB for the Fiscal Year Ended 31 December 1998. SecurFone America, Inc.* Edgar Online. http://yahoo.brand.edgar-online.com/ DisplayFilingInfo.aspx?Type=HTML&FilingID=565361 (accessed January 17, 2010).

————. *Form-10-KSB for the Fiscal Year Ended 31 December 2000. The IXATA Group, Inc.* Edgar Online. http://yahoo.brand.edgar-online.com/ displayfilinginfo.aspx?FilingID=1024194-1403-282644&type=sect&TabIndex =2&companyid=6585&ppu=%252fdefault.aspx%253fcompanyid%253d6585 (accessed January 17, 2010).

Van Nimmen, Jane, et al. *NASA Historical Data Book.* Vol. II. Washington, DC: GPO, 1988. http://purl.access.gpo.gov/GPO/LPS49327 (accessed July 9, 2009).

Van Staaveren, Jacob. *Gradual Failure: The Air War Over North Vietnam, 1965-1966.* Washington, DC: Air Force History and Museums Program, 2002. http:// www.genealogycenter.info/military/images/gradualfailure/GradualFailure .pdf (accessed August 13, 2009).

————. *USAF Plans and Operations: The Air Campaign Against North Vietnam, 1966.* Washington, DC: USAF Historical Division Liaison Office, 1968. http:// www.afhra.af.mil/shared/media/document/AFD-090430-086.pdf (accessed June 24, 2009).

Wade, Mark. "Encyclopedia Astronautica." 2009. Mark Wade. http://www.astro nautix.com/lvs/atlas.htm (accessed January 4, 2010).

Watts, Barry D., and Center for Strategic and Budgetary Assessments. *The US Defense Industrial Base: Past, Present and Future.* Washington, DC: Center for Strategic and Budgetary Assessments, 2008. http://www.csbaonline .org/4Publications/PubLibrary/R.20081015._The_US_Defense_In/R.20081015 ._The_US_Defense_In.pdf (accessed May 10, 2010).

Wayne, Leslie. "Air Force at Unease in the Capital." *New York Times*, December 16, 2004, C1. http://www.lexisnexis.com.ezproxy.dom.edu/us/lnacademic/ (accessed February 20, 2010).

Williams, Winston. "Bungling the Military Buildup." *New York Times*, January 27, 1985, 1. http://www.lexisnexis.com.ezproxy.dom.edu/us/lnacademic/ (accessed November 29, 2010).

Wynne, Michael W. "Objections to the Budget Submitted for the Air Force for Fiscal Year 2009." Unpublished Memorandum. Department of Defense, Washington, DC: December 20, 2007.

Wynne, Michael W., et al. "Lasting heritage—limitless horizons: a warfighter's vision." United States Air Force, 2006. http://www.af.mil/shared/media/document/AFD-060228-054.pdf (accessed May 29, 2009).

Wynne, Lt. Patrick E. "Graduate School as an Initial Assignment: Report from Georgetown." *The Talon*, October 1963. Colorado Springs, Co: Air Force Academy, 1963.

Wynne, Peter A. "Wynne Family History." Unpublished Family Papers. August, 1997.

Yamaguchi, Mari. "US Tells Japan Sub Leaked Radiation Over 2 Years." Associated Press Worldstream, August 7, 2008. http://www.lexisnexis.com.ezproxy.dom.edu/us/lnacademic/ (accessed September 28, 2010).

Young, Bob, et al. *Class Book 65-G*. Mesa, Az.: Williams Air Force Base, 1965.

Acknowledgments

✦ ✦ ✦

THIS VOLUME CERTAINLY OWES much of its existence to the extended Wynne family. Mike's siblings—Maureen (Wynne) Guarino, Cathy (Wynne) Bessette, Stephen Wynne, and Peter Wynne—each readily submitted to the intrusions of a zealous interviewer. They were generous with their time and talent, sharing personal stories and family history. Maureen and Cathy also turned out to be the keepers of much of the past in articles and e-mails. The Wynne family in-laws also were most generous with their time, especially Al Guarino and Phil Bessette.

Mike's life partner of 45 years, Barbara, was a wonderful source of stories and remembrances. One could not find a more supportive mate. She and Mike have come a long way since a Christmas social at Patrick Air Force Base in December 1964. With four daughters, four sons-in-law, and more than a dozen grandchildren, their journey continues.

Appreciation is extended to a number of readers who worked through early versions of this manuscript. They don't put themselves through the process for money or fame, but for the love of writing and books. This story was always a good one, but their comments and suggestions moved it closer to Mark Twain's "a good story, well told." A tip of the hat to readers Patricia Lee and Timothy Matson. Thanks also to Ellen SooHoo who took on the editing. She helped make sure the text stayed clear and consistent the CMS way.

Praise is extended to Don Kroitzsh of Five Corners Press in Plymouth, Vermont. Don helped fine tune the photographs so they come to life in the story. A salute also goes out to Ryan Davis who was generous in allowing his photo of the tontine display at the Air Force Academy to be reprinted. Dick Swanson, a Time-Life photographer at Ubon RTAFB in 1966, tried his best to locate some old photos from Pat's time at Ubon. While our search was not successful, he was very supportive of the project.

Thanks go to a number of people at the United States Air Force Academy: Paul Martin—curator of collections, Janet Edwards—mortuary officer, and Mary Elizabeth Ruwell—academy archivist and chief of special collections in the library, for supplying historical information and photographs. Tom Kroboth of the Association of Graduates at the Air Force Academy was helpful in filling in many details regarding graduates of the academy from the 1960s. Murlea Vance also gets an assist, as does the staff at Cadet Wing Media. Kent Laudeman, vice dean for administration and interim librarian at the United States Military Academy at West Point, New York, receives a round of applause. He was helpful in settling a few research questions for this biography. Suzanne Christoff, the associate director for special collections and archives, gets a big thank you for helping supply photographs related to the Wynne family experience on the Hudson River. Casey Madrick, the archives technician, gets the assist. The Air Force Academy and the Military Academy played a major role in the Wynne family history, in general, and Mike Wynne's life, in particular.

Gratitude is also due Caroline Wilson, Mike's personal confidential secretary from his Pentagon days. Caroline started with Mike one week after he arrived in 2001 and stayed with him through it all, including his service as secretary of the Air Force. If Mike had two women in his life during his government service, it was Barb at home and Caroline at work. Every man should be so lucky.

Besides his family, standing in for Patrick were Tom Fryer, John NePage, Bill Koelm, and Lieutenant General (ret.) Malcolm Armstrong who were generous with their time in working to recall details of events from 1964–66. Don Dodgen was another from Pat's past who helped with details. Of note was Pat's wife, Nancy. She was kind enough to go back in time and relive parts of their life from the 1960s. For her, it had to be as if living in two worlds, recalling the 1960s while living in the present. She was generous with her emotions.

Roger Schreiber and Herb Schaffner, both from Consortium Companies in Kentucky, were wonderfully effusive with information surrounding important life events. They are simply good people. Ron Schillereff and the late Jack Wheeler, the former a graduate of the Air Force Academy and the latter a graduate of the Military Academy, both had links back to the 1960s with Mike and both remained a part of his life for decades. They were giving of their time and talent in sharing stories from the past and present, helping bridge the fifty years between then and now.

Of singular note, of course, was Mike's willingness to sit for a number of interviews during 2009–11. While everyone likes to talk about themselves to an extent, having an interviewer badger you about details and dates for a seemingly endless procession of events, many that you hate to admit you cannot recall in all the glorious detail, takes a measure of discipline. Mike approached the task with his usual mix of restraint and preparation.

On a personal note, love and appreciation goes out to Jane, Eliot, and Claire. They could not have been more supportive, and without their love nothing is quite worth the effort.

INDEX

❧ ❧ ❧

Page numbers in italics refer to photo captions.

ABOUT THE AUTHOR

RICHARD BESSETTE is an amateur historian and author of three previous nonfiction books. He is currently a graduate student in the Public History program at Loyola University Chicago.

ABOUT THE TYPE

The text is set in Minion Pro typeface designed by Robert Slimbach. Titling is in Myriad Pro fashioned by Slimback and Carol Twombly. Captions are set in Georgia typeface constructed by Matthew Carter. Section separators noted with Kingthings Flourishes designed by Kevin King.